Joining the Revolution
in Theology

Joining the Revolution in Theology

The College Theology Society, 1954–2004

Sandra Yocum Mize

A Sheed & Ward Book

ROWMAN & LITTLEFIELD PUBLISHERS, INC.
Lanham • Boulder • New York • Toronto • Plymouth, UK

A SHEED & WARD BOOK

ROWMAN & LITTLEFIELD PUBLISHERS, INC.

Published in the United States of America
by Rowman & Littlefield Publishers, Inc.
A wholly owned subsidary of The Rowman & Littlefield Publishing Group, Inc.
4501 Forbes Boulevard, Suite 200, Lanham, Maryland 20706
www.rowmanlittlefield.com

Estover Road, Plymouth PL6 7PY, United Kingdom

British Library Cataloguing in Publication Information Available

Library of Congress Cataloging-in-Publication Data

Mize, Sandra Yocum.
  Joining the revolution in theology : the College Theology Society, 1954-2004 / Sandra
Yocum Mize.
     p. cm.
  Includes bibliographical references and index.
  ISBN-13: 978-0-7425-3195-6 (cloth : alk. paper)
  ISBN-10: 0-7425-3195-3 (cloth : alk. paper)
 1. College Theology Society. 2. Catholic Church—Doctrines—History—20th century.
3. Catholic Church—Education. 4. Catholic universities and colleges. I. Title.
  BX922.M59 2007
  230'.206073—dc22
                                    2006027422

Printed in the United States of America

∞™ The paper used in this publication meets the minimum requirements of
American National Standard for Information Sciences—Permanence of Paper
for Printed Library Materials, ANSI/NISO Z39.48-1992.

In gratitude to my family, Bryan, Matt, Chris, and Vi
and to my theology teachers, Tom Boyd, Joe Ross, and Patrick Carey.

Contents

List of Abbreviations

AAR	American Academy of Religion
AAUP	American Association of University Professors
ACCU	Association of Catholic Colleges and Universities
ACLS	American Council of Learned Societies
ACTHUS	Academy of Catholic Hispanic Theologians of the United States
ACUA	Archives of Catholic University of America
ATLA	American Theological Library Association
ATLAS	American Theological Library Association Serials Project
CBA	Catholic Biblical Association
CCD	Confraternity of Christian Doctrine
CCMA	Catholic Campus Ministry Association
CCSR	Coordinating Committee for the Study of Religion
CDF	Congregation for the Doctrine of the Faith
CLSA	Canon Law Society of America
CSR	Council on the Study of Religion
CSSR	Council of Societies for the Study of Religion
CTS	College Theology Society
CTSA	Catholic Theological Society of America
CUA	Catholic University of America
EcE	*Ex corde Ecclesiae*
IFCU	International Federation of Catholic Universities
JAAR	Journal of the American Academy of Religion
JBL	Journal of Biblical Literature
JCCLSS	Joint Committee of Catholic Learned Societies and Scholars
NABI	National Association of Biblical Instructors
NABPR	National Association of Baptist Professors of Religion

NCCB	National Conference of Catholic Bishops
NCD	National Catechetical Directory
NCDD	National Conference of Diocesan Directors of Religious Education
NCEA	National Catholic Educational Association
NCRPE	National Council on Religion in Public Education
SBL	Society of Biblical Literature
SCCTSD	Society of Catholic College Teachers of Sacred Doctrine
SRHE	Society for Research into Higher Education
SSHE	State System of Higher Education
SSSR	Society for the Scientific Study of Religion
TAK	Theta Alpha Kappa: National Honor Society for Religious Studies/Theology
TOIL	Teaching Opportunities Information Listing
UPA	Usability Professionals' Association
USCCB	Unites States Conference of Catholic Bishops

Acknowledgments

$\mathcal{I}$ have many people to thank in the writing of this history. First to the College Theology Society for having confidence in my abilities. Second, I offer my thanks to Timothy Meagher and John Shepherd as well as the entire staff at the Archives of the Catholic University of America (ACUA), who offered me hospitality and guidance in reviewing the archives. I also thank all of those who sent me additional materials that have not made their way into the archives. Third, I extend my gratitude to Ross Miller for his encouragement when I most needed it, and to Sheed and Ward for their willingness to publish a history of the College Theology Society—a history of a revolution in theology.

Several people have read portions of this history and given sage advice that has improved the final product. These readers are Una Cadegan, Patrick Carey, William Collinge, Dennis Doyle, William Portier, Anthony B. Smith, Terrence Tilley, and William V. Trollinger Jr. Terrence Tilley, William Collinge, William Portier, and Patrick Carey endured reading a draft in its entirety. I also need to thank the graduate students who assisted me. They are Michael Lombardo, Timothy Dillon, Daniel E. Martin, and Damian Costello who ferreted out sources and double-checked footnotes. Damian Costello and Justin Menno also read the text in its entirety and assisted with the index.

Another thank you goes to those cheery young people who made me feel ever so welcome as I sat at that little table in the hallway of a well-known purveyor of fine and very strong coffee with my computer plugged into the shop's outlet. This book would have suffered far more delays without their hospitality accompanied by generous doses of caffeine.

I offer special thanks to Christopher Mize, Matthew Mize, and Bryan Mize for their assistance at the bitter end of this project. You may have noticed a pattern: The first two are sons, and the third is their father, my husband. They double-checked more footnotes than one should ever have to check in a lifetime. Matthew did enough for two lifetimes. In addition, they generally put up with my craziness and crankiness.

I thank all of those mentioned for helping me avoid egregious errors even as I take full responsibility for any mistakes that remain.

Finally, let me again thank Christopher, Matthew, and Bryan and my mother, Violet Yocum, for their loving support and encouragement in bringing this project to completion. I do love you all!

Introduction

$\mathscr{M}$y principal task in writing this history is to provide a coherent narrative that reflects something of the life of the College Theology Society (CTS) from 1954 to 2004. I write this description advisedly since my intended audience is not only the Society's members, but anyone interested in how Catholic theology as an academic discipline has developed in the last half of the twentieth century. In 1959, 231 Catholic colleges and universities had members in the CTS. The vast majority came from one of the 241 U.S. institutions. While no exact statistics exist, a 1999 CTS membership directory indicates a similar demographic. With the exception of at most five institutions, all of the 230 Catholic colleges and universities had CTS members on their faculty. In presenting fifty years of CTS's engagement with college theology, this book traces the diverse theological currents that traversed the ever-changing landscapes of U.S. Catholicism and American higher education. These currents ran through not only the CTS annual meetings but also presumably entered many undergraduate classrooms at Catholic colleges and universities.

This book's even-numbered chapters provide a synthetic, thematic account of the theological discussions that occurred in each of the Society's five decades of existence and provide a chronologically ordered account that is suggestive of wider theological debates as they developed in the last half of the twentieth century. One can trace in those chapters the eclipse of neo-scholasticism with theologies reflecting influences as varied as historical-critical biblical studies, Christian existentialism, transcendental Thomism, Marxist social analysis, second-wave feminism, interdisciplinary studies, social sciences, historical consciousness, literary theory, critical theory, cultural studies—to name only the more obvious.

1

The odd-numbered chapters tell the story of the Society itself, and, in telling that story, trace the gradual development of an academic discipline, "theology" or "religious studies," housed not in seminaries but in U.S. Catholic colleges and universities. Society members gradually became not only teachers of college theology but also the producers of what they taught. Lay men and women, along with the ordained and religious, identified themselves as theologians and scholars of religion. This new self-understanding affected their perceptions of their relationship to church and academy and found expression in everything from Society publications to formal resolutions offered at conventions to membership qualifications. Even the structure of the Society's annual meetings changed in light of the new scholarly role claimed by the college theology teacher. All of these factors tell us a great deal about the academic persona of "theologian" as he and she emerged in the twentieth-century Catholic community in the U.S. as participants in America's burgeoning knowledge industry.

Tracing these intellectual and professional developments through the Society's evolution demonstrate that "theology" was subject to the same influences that affected every academic discipline in the university—a heightened sense of professionalism equated with producing cutting-edge scholarship within an increasingly delineated discipline. The CTS, like every other professional academic society, supported its members, "theologians" who sought to meet the academic standards prized throughout the university community. Like colleagues in other disciplines, theologians valued critical thinking, historical consciousness, and openness to the changing contours of contemporary culture. By the mid-1980s, theologians, like so many other academics, began to explore the permeable boundaries between "theology" and other academic disciplines. Earlier attempts at demarcating "theology" gave way to the varied approaches to theological and religious studies so evident in the final four chapters of this book.[1]

I am not the first person to write a historical account of the College Theology Society. Rosemary Rodgers, O.P., wrote *A History of the College Theology Society*. Published in 1983 by the College Theology Society, its principal task was to cover the Society's first twenty-five years. Rodgers's history is organized chronologically with chapters on the Society's pre-history, origins, first decade, research and publications of the 1970s, and a brief look at the 1980s. The author's own familiarity with the persons involved and the events described informs the account in ways that I am unable to replicate. My book's first six chapters cover most of what appears in Rodgers's history though with greater detail, especially in reviewing the annual volumes. I appreciate the way in which Rodgers placed so much detail in so few pages and

I am grateful that her work corrected my erroneous assumptions about the Society's history.

I have little doubt that Rosemary Rodgers would commiserate with me in admitting to one of the greatest challenges in producing a history of the College Theology Society—the dizzying array of resources available. One major source for this text is the Society's annual volume; it provides a unique, amazing resource—fifty years of theological conversation in a period of rapid change in theological and religious studies. These volumes taken together contribute to our understanding of the how, when, and what of the changes previously mentioned. One has an opportunity to examine essays of leading figures from Raymond Brown to Elisabeth Schüssler Fiorenza, Avery Dulles to Rosemary Radford Ruether, Bernard Lonergan to David Tracy, Charles Curran to Stanley Hauerwas. One also has an opportunity, at least as significant, to hear from those whose names may be unfamiliar but whose works help us to understand how theological currents flowed into and shaped the wider Catholic landscape, principally from the vantage point of those who taught undergraduate theology. The volumes themselves began as one hundred pages of proceedings, peaked at close to four hundred pages, and then leveled off to an average of two hundred and fifty pages per volume.

I also chose to review all the materials contained in the archival collection at Catholic University of America, plus all materials given to me by former officers or board members. These materials include minutes of board meetings; correspondence between the leadership and members, church officials, and officers in other learned societies; as well as Society-initiated reports and other official statements. I will not try to quantify those sources. Suffice to say that I had plenty of material to use and had to omit a few thousand details.

Other potential sources that I did not utilize to any extent are articles from *Horizons*, the Society's journal, and oral history drawn from members. I am fully aware that both would serve to enhance my understanding of the Society's history, but time constraints combined with the vast quantities of the previously described sources made the omission necessary. Practical factors notwithstanding, I had other reasons for not utilizing these sources. The Society's founding of and continuing support for *Horizons* is of critical importance, but the articles themselves do not serve the same purposes as those contained in the annual volumes. My decision to limit reliance on oral history arises from the fact that potential interviewees abound with little clear criteria at this juncture for selecting one member over another. I did have an open discussion at the 2002 annual convention (St. John's University, Jamaica, New York), where those who selected the session shared memories of CTS. I have also consulted with Gerard Sloyan, one of the Society's founding members, about the Society's origins.

The potential for such extensive use of oral history leads me to consider another oddity of this history. In explaining to my students what I do as a historian, I usually quip, "I study dead people." Well, as already noted, the vast majority of the people featured in this history are very much alive as this work goes into publication. Given the fluidity of memory, its dependence on a person's location, and the complexity of the last fifty years in the United States, in the Catholic Church, and in the field of theology, readers who lived during these years may remember events differently than appear here or have different perspectives and insights. I would beg a modicum of forbearance in that I depend on the written sources to give an accurate account. The sources' rendering of an event may not provide the account exactly as certain readers remember.

I have wondered whether what follows can in any meaningful way be called a "history." As I write this introduction, the final annual volume treated appeared less than a year ago; some decisions made in 2004 have yet to go into effect. The closer one comes to the present in writing a history, the more difficult it becomes to gain perspective. When I imagine myself "gaining perspective," I conjure the image of standing at some distance to view the whole picture and how that picture fits into its wider setting. Standing at a distance is difficult to do with events so closely linked to the present. Of course, being a dutiful postmodern, I recognize that no one escapes the particularity of one's social location. My proximity to this history is not only a matter of chronology but also a matter of participation. I have been an active member of the College Theology Society since 1986. Yet, my membership did not function as a substitute for the written sources. The story that follows extends far beyond any single member and even beyond the Society itself.

What follows is the story of a revolution in theological studies in every aspect from who produces theology to what is produced, from who teaches to who learns, and from where theological studies take place to what is actually taught in the undergraduate college classrooms. Telling the history of the College Theology Society, a professional society with a national constituency, provides an opportunity to tell the story of theological studies as it has developed in the last half of the twentieth century in the United States. Though the story treats issues unique to Catholic theology, it bears much in common with wider movements in theology, religious studies, and other academic disciplines transformed in the dramatically altered world of twentieth-century American higher education.

Let me now offer an explanation of the principle that guided my writing and the narrative's basic organization—a kind of reader's guide if you will. I take my cue from another historian, Patricia Byrne, C.S.J., who has described her history of a religious community as a biography of a living entity, an organism, whose distinctive life is analogous to that of an individual. I have found that description apropos in so far as the College Theology Society has a unique personality, distinct from other learned societies. To convey this personality has proven difficult. It is most apparent in those descriptions of annual meetings as hospitable, engaging, and scholarly or those debates about membership in which the board inevitably finds a way to include those who have some kind or any kind of commitment to teaching college theology. In presenting the development of the Society's personality, I have tried to allow the reader to learn of the Society through members—their discussions, their actions, the essays they selected for their annual volumes. In other words, I have tried, though not always succeeded, to avoid interjecting myself into the narrative. My evaluative comments remain minimal and attempt to reflect the wider debates of the period.

The narrative is organized into ten chapters, with two chapters dedicated to each of the five decades. The odd-numbered chapters feature sections that organize material thematically to convey the multiple currents of change over time in the Society. So the chapters on the Society's institutional structures and activities include discussion of membership, internal organization, annual meetings, publications, and interactions with external constituencies, particularly the U.S. episcopacy and other learned societies whose members engage in scholarship related to religious and theological studies.

The even-numbered chapters also feature themes rather than essay-by-essay renditions of the annual volumes. My choice of the thematic approach is my attempt to convey the conversational quality of the meetings in which many of these essays received their first public hearing as convention papers. The conversations, of course, extend beyond any given year and are a part of various streams of theological discourse within the Society and reflect those in the wider academy and church. One will discover a multitude of streams including the influences of Rahner's and Lonergan's thought; developments in biblical studies; questions concerning interpretation and hermeneutics; the importance of historical-theological studies; questions surrounding pluralism, interreligious, and intercultural dialogues; the emergence of multiple forms of liberation theology; the pervasive influence of feminist consciousness-raising; issues concerning the church—its teaching authority and its relationship with the world; and the role of the theologian as teacher, as academic, and as participant in the life of the church. The point is that to examine the annual volumes from 1955 to 2004 is to examine the vast array of changes over time in the work of theologians as scholars and teachers.

My decision to use the decade as a means of periodization has no completely satisfactory explanation. Any one who delves into historical work is aware of the problematic. One year bleeds into the next with few clearly de-marcated ruptures with the past. The division by decade does, however, reflect certain historical markers—some external, others internal to the Society. The years from 1953 to 1964 obviously do not constitute a "decade" but include the events that precipitated the Society's founding as the Society of Catholic College Teachers of Sacred Doctrine through the initial reception of the Sec-ond Vatican Council. The period from 1965 to 1974 begins with the end of the council and provides an account of the surge of activity that followed. The Society changes its name to College Theology Society and begins to rethink its relationship to church and academy.

In the third decade, from 1975 to 1984, the changing circumstances in church and academy intensify. The Society's officers wrestle with the CTS's identity even as the annual volumes represent an extended reflection on the-ology's identity as an academic discipline, in search of the right methods and aware of its hermeneutical limitations. The decade from 1985 to 1994 opens with worries about the Society's solvency and about theologians' survival in light of the second attempt to remove Charles Curran from teaching theol-ogy at Catholic University of America. This time his bid to remain failed. The decade closes with increased focus on *mandatum*. The volumes feature in-creasing engagement with questions of teaching authority and with the status of other religions and cultures relative to Christianity's exclusivist claims. The years from 1995 to 2004 continue the focus on *mandatum* as well as on the Society's ability to pass on its own traditions. The annual volumes provide a kind of recapitulation of the last forty years of theological work in highlight-ing the various trends in current theological studies. In a more summary fash-ion, the first decade treats the founding; the second, responses to the Coun-cil; the third, reconnoitering of the Society's organization and purpose as well as theology's fundamental understanding of its task; the fourth, explorations of theology's boundaries relative to church and world; the fifth, recapitulating and preserving the CTS's traditions even as theology begins to reflect the concerns and interests of a new generation, born well after 1965, with none of those memories that have driven the previous generations.

I have not tried to smooth over the ruptures, fractures, or inconsistencies in the narrative.[2] These are a part of the Society's history as much as the flu-idity of continuous development. Such inconsistencies reflect the fragmenta-tion of the period from 1954 to 2004—a fragmentation not limited to theol-ogy or even the church. I have tried to show some of the sources for the fragmentation even as I recognize that often in the fragments was a desire for deeper unity. What drives the narrative is my assumption that even monu-mental change occurs gradually, but not smoothly over time, noticed in the details of the Society's ongoing existence over fifty years.

NOTES

1. The history of the College Theology Society exemplifies developments addressed in Philip Gleason, *Contending with Modernity: Catholic Higher Education in the Twentieth Century* (Oxford: Oxford University Press, 1995) that covers the first decade of the Society's founding. The later period is treated in Alice Gallin, *Negotiating Identity: Catholic Higher Education Since 1960* (Notre Dame, IN: University of Notre Dame Press, 2000). Two studies that follow the development of the study of religion as an academic discipline from very different perspectives are Walter H. Capps, *Religious Studies: The Making of a Discipline* (Minneapolis: Fortress Press, 1995) and D. H. Hart, *The University Gets Religion: Religious Studies in American Higher Education* (Baltimore: Johns Hopkins University Press, 1999). A potentially fascinating study for comparison is Peter Novick, *That Noble Dream: The "Objectivity Question" and the American Historical Profession* (Cambridge: University of Cambridge Press, 1988).

2. Spelling errors and other minor editing errors in quotes have been corrected to avoid the intrusive use of "sic." Emphases in quotes are in the original.

A Society of Their Own (1953–1964)

FROM RESOLUTION TO CONSTITUTION

As a result of the stimulating and profitable exchange of ideas concerning the common objectives, the diversified procedures, and multiple problems of the departments of Theology in our undergraduate colleges, we are convinced of the need for the formation of some national organization of college teachers of Theology comparable in academic dignity and high intellectual standards to those proposed and maintained in organizations which seek to further the advancement of other disciplines on the same level of instruction.[1]

This statement announced the first official act initiating the College Theology Society's founding. On 18 June 1953, in the midst of a workshop on theology and the social sciences at Catholic University of America, Sister M. Rose Eileen Masterman, C.S.C., a religion professor at Dunbarton College, responded to her colleagues' encouragement with a resolution to found a professional society for those teaching theology to undergraduates. Originally bearing the ponderous name the "Society of Catholic College Teachers of Sacred Doctrine," the organization has created a space in which, for fifty plus years, those deeply committed to teaching theology to undergraduates and to the scholarship that such a commitment inspires have had opportunities to discuss with and learn from one another.

Defining the qualifications for membership in a society of Catholic college theology teachers proved a complex task, especially in the Society's early years. In the original resolution, Sister M. Rose Eileen specified restricting active membership to "those members of the clergy and religious orders, both male and female, and of the laity, who have fulfilled the requirements for

9

higher degrees in the Sacred Sciences or in the Philosophy of Religion or their equivalent" and who actually teach in the subject matter.[2] These specifications, on the one hand, cast a wide net for eligible members. On the other hand, requiring an advanced degree excluded many actually teaching college religion in 1953. Back then, Catholic colleges and universities often relied upon members of the sponsoring religious communities, regardless of their academic preparation, to teach theology or religion courses, often part-time, in addition to other teaching or administrative duties. Whether teaching experience was enough of a qualification remained a point of repeated debate. In the series of meetings that led to a ratified constitution, participants concluded "that qualifications for membership should be liberal rather than strict," because to do otherwise "would tend to defeat the purpose of this proposed organization." The group made subject matter taught, rather than degree held, the determinative factor for membership. This decision provided more opportunities for "the development of effective teachers of Theology on the college level." Another stated objective of the nascent Society acknowledged "that degrees in religious education or in Theology are very helpful, . . . [but] not necessary to achieve this objective or to be a member of [the] society." The final decision reflected the organizers' acceptance of the actual situation among many who taught college religion or theology in the 1950s.[3]

Sister M. Rose Eileen's resolution had specified organizing the society through "a committee of competent, interested teachers of Theology representing the diverse systems of thought in scientific Theology." Key to understanding what she intended are the adjectives "diverse" and "scientific." To embrace the "scientific" aligned the association with the scholastic approach outlined in the *Summa*'s first article where Aquinas defended theology as a "science" in the Aristotelian sense, i.e., a systematic exposition of doctrines based upon first principles. The adjective had a broader meaning, connoting an intellectual more than a formative emphasis. "Diverse" indicates that this society also sought varied perspectives in approach and emphasis shaping contemporary college theology. The organizing committee, as described, implied a professional influence to ensure the society's role as "a potent means of improving the teaching" of theology. A further goal was to enhance "the esteem and respect for the department of Theology among the secularistically minded educators," especially those responsible for accreditation.

The resolution's final sentence makes clear that more than professional benefits were at stake.

> The weight of authority in the professional aspects of teaching Theology gradually acquired and developed through a College Theology Teachers' organization of high academic achievement and objective might be a com-

pelling factor in solving the many professional problems created in a society that is overwhelmingly neglectful of the role of Theology, not only in achieving academic integration, but in the only essentially ultimate integration, namely, that of the whole man in the Mystical Body of Christ on his way to the Beatific Vision.[4]

To evoke the "Mystical Body of Christ" locates this society at its founding squarely within a network of movements like liturgical renewal, Catholic and social action, and the lay apostolate that were transforming not only theological studies but also many other dimensions of that broad expanse called "Catholic culture." The organic dimensions of the "Body" inspired many to reimagine the laity's role in bringing Christ's life that they experienced through the church into that "society that is overwhelmingly neglectful of the role of Theology." Out of this reimagining emerged a growing recognition that the laity required a solid theological education to fulfill their ecclesiastical charge of restoring all things to Christ.

After passing the resolution unanimously, the group discussed specific implementation strategies from informing friends and colleagues to seeking episcopal support. People identified to consult included Father Joseph Fenton, instrumental in the founding of the Catholic Theological Society of America (CTSA) and Father Cyril Meyer, head of the National Catholic Educational Association (NCEA), the college and university division. Consultation meant only that. The founders had little desire to join an existing group. The workshop participants did determine, however, that NCEA's 1954 national meeting provided a convenient venue for informing potential members of a new national society for Catholic college theology teachers.[5]

Theology and religion faculty from the Washington, D.C., area came to a follow-up meeting on 11 October 1953. The result was a letter, dated 16 October 1953, under Father John Harvey's name, inviting all college teachers of religion/theology in the Northeast, i.e., from New York, Pennsylvania, New Jersey, Maryland, and Washington, D.C., to attend a meeting at LaSalle College, Philadelphia, 8 December 1953. The letter made the agenda clear—the founding of a "national organization" comparable to other professional societies in the academy. "[I]n view of the multiple problems of the departments of Theology in our undergraduate colleges, not to mention the intellectual ferment which has arisen in recent years in regard to scientific methods of presenting Theology to the laity, an organization of college teachers of Religion is an acute need."[6] In a preparatory meeting for December, the group reaffirmed the primary focus was serving teachers directly and students and administrators only indirectly. Possible members were limited to those actively engaged in teaching theology. The fledgling society's commitment was

reflected in Father Gerard Sloyan's suggestion of the society's name: "The Society of College Teachers of Sacred Doctrine." With a clarified purpose, Father John Harvey and Sister M. Rose Eileen wrote a draft of the Society's
constitution. Minutes of a 15 November meeting name the societies whose
constitutions served as guides, including the Catholic Biblical Association,
Catholic Theological Society of America, and the Association of Teachers of
Mathematics. Father Sloyan's suggestion for the Society's name appears in the
first article of the constitution with the addition of a single word, "Catholic."
The full name adopted was the "Society of Catholic College Teachers of Sacred Doctrine" (SCCTSD). The constitution's first article also named the Society's patron—Mary Immaculate, Seat of Wisdom.[7]

Forty-four teachers from twenty-six colleges and universities came to
LaSalle on December 8 to affirm the need for a society with an ultimate objective of "assist[ing] teachers in imparting to college students adequate religious instruction well integrated with the rest of the curriculum."[8] They did
debate whether the group ought to claim the discipline of theology as its own.
"The term 'Sacred doctrine' was acknowledged to be a compromise label, am-
ply justified, its proponents noted, in light of St. Thomas's consistent use of it
in his treatment of 'theology.'"[9] Father Sloyan recollects that acceptance of the
term "resulted directly from the discussion of the polyvalent nature of the
term *sacra doctrina* found in the early articles of Aquinas' *Summa Theolo-
giae.*"[10] "Theology" remained too closely associated with manual-based seminary training, and the other option, "religion," raised questions of academic
credibility.

The constitution's gradual formulation culminated at Fordham University, on 22 February 1954, when representatives of forty-seven East Coast colleges ratified a constitution for the Society of Catholic College Teachers of
Sacred Doctrine. A few participants proposed a last-minute amendment to
change the name to the Society of Catholic College Teachers of Theology.
The motion was narrowly defeated 46 to 43. Unanimously passed was making Mary Immaculate, Seat of Wisdom patroness of the Society. In the meeting's minutes and in a press release announcing the Society's formation, Sr.
M. Rose Eileen received recognition as the person who originated the idea.[11]

The last-minute attempt to insert theology in the Society's name and, in
a different way, the recognition of a woman, Sr. M. Rose Eileen, as the Society's founder reveal the growing ferment in theological education during the
1950s. The SCCTSD's first president, Reverend Eugene Burke, C.S.P., speculated on how the Society "may shape the forces of Catholicism in the generations that succeed us. It is Catholic and corporate in its aims and functions."[12] To participate in shaping these Catholic forces required a payment of
a mere $5 for full membership and $3 for associates. Burke called upon those

involved in teaching sacred doctrine "to reflect that you, as administrators and as teachers of Sacred Doctrine for whom the Society was planned, possess a tremendous power for the future of Catholicism in America. That potential has not lain dormant; it has been actuated. The Society of Catholic College Teachers of Sacred Doctrine was established in order to contribute to that actuation."[13] This organization of undergraduate teachers of theology specified membership qualifications that had nothing to do with official ecclesiastical status. The Society's primary purpose was to reflect collectively on teaching the sacred science to nonspecialists. To found such a society with this stated purpose was a significant moment in the transformation of theological studies from a seminary-defined to a university-defined academic discipline.

THINK NATIONALLY, ACT REGIONALLY

Important to actuating the members' potential on a broad basis was the founders' decision to balance "a national organization with regional groupings that will take into account the particular problems of the various regions." Implementation demonstrated a firm commitment to gaining the widest participation possible including those members unable to attend the national convention. To ensure an accurate reflection of local concerns, regional leaders were to include "priests, brothers and sisters so that all engaged in teaching Sacred Doctrine may have adequate representation on the committee."[14] The Society's national leaders also anticipated "a reciprocity of effort whereby the national meetings will contribute to the national group, and the national group in view of its wider potential of experience and information will contribute to the regional meetings." The first constitution established a "Current Problems Committee" for "crystallizing and directing the discussion of both the regional and national groupings" and thus ensuring a more coherent discussion on various aspects of teaching sacred doctrine within the Society.[15]

The Northeast established the first eight regions at the 1954 NCEA national convention, and meetings soon followed. On 8 May 1954, almost a year prior to the Society's first national meeting, the New York Metropolitan area held its first meeting at Manhattan College. Thirty-two attended—fifteen priests, five Christian brothers, and twelve sisters.[16] Father John F. Dwyer, S.J., of Fordham generated a lively exchange about the Le Moyne plan, recently adopted at his institution.[17] By December 1954, seventeen regions had been established across the country including Chicago, New Orleans, and San Francisco.

The Society's leadership maintained great hope in the impact that regional activities could have on advancing the work of the national organization well into the 1980s. To reiterate that each region, determined geographically, was to coordinate its efforts with the national organization, an undated "Directives for Regional Chairmen" made very clear that membership was in the national society, not regions, though nonmembers could participate even as speakers when appropriate. An extensive and detailed instruction outlined policies and procedures including reiteration of representative membership on the executive committee. One of the meetings was to address the topics annually "designated by the national Current Problems Committee and approved by the Board of Directors" as well as other "pertinent problems" that can serve "as fruitful sources of topics and discussions for the national efforts of the Society." The directives state clearly that every regional chairman must "obtain *episcopal approbation*" in writing for each meeting convened and "*no meeting should be held without such approbation.*" Regional files must preserve these documents as well as submitting all meeting records to the executive secretary for insertion in the Society's newsletter, *Magister*, as well as for an annual report.[18]

Evidently some local ordinaries took note of SCCTSD regional meetings. Rev. Sebastian Carlson, O.P., had informed his local ordinary of a regional meeting in Chicago in December 1954. Samuel Cardinal Stritch, archbishop of Chicago, in a letter dated a year later, praised the Society's commitment to improving college teaching of theology for the sake of the "educated Catholic layman" who now requires more than "a small catechism knowledge of his religion." Stritch suggested instructing lay faculty, especially those in the social sciences and literature, to facilitate "integrat[ing] the whole faculty in the teaching of religion." With integration of theology across the curriculum, Catholic colleges can then be prepared to counter "the breakdown and bankruptcy of the old liberalism" and respond to "a certain unexpressed craving on the part of many for a better knowledge and understanding of religion." Stritch's response indicates just how widespread the great expectations of "college theology" were.[19]

At a meeting on 18 December 1954, at St. Paul's Rectory, New York City, the national board of directors confirmed broad-based interest in the SCCTSD before such expressions of episcopal enthusiasm. Membership had already increased to 217 plus seven associate members, with 127, or a little over half, of the 241 Catholic colleges represented, and regions now numbered seventeen, each with at least a few members. The leadership planned to distribute a questionnaire through the regions. "Collecting objective data concerning the present status of the theology curricula in our colleges" served the Society's major objective—the improvement of college theology.[20]

A NATIONAL SOCIETY IN PRACTICE AS WELL AS IN THEORY

The board attended to the many details of the first national gathering at a December meeting and another in February. A seemingly insignificant decision, agreeing to common meals as part of the first program, contributed to a collegial atmosphere providing opportunities for informal exchange among clergy, sisters, brothers, and eventually laity. In a letter to members, Sister M. Rose Eileen explained "that this service [meals] would not only be more convenient, but afford an admirable opportunity for conversation and informal discussion with the members from the various regions which is an important function of our national meeting."[21] Even today, sharing common meals remains a distinctive part of the national meeting where chance encounters with colleagues still create "an admirable opportunity for conversation." The very first meeting also featured a book display, in this case from "Newman's Book Shop and the Bruce Publishing Company." The early presence of publishers highlights the wide-ranging effects the shift in theological education had as Catholic publishers sought to offer the latest in textbooks and other resources for college theology. The Society's own publication ventures help define its first fifty years of existence.

Reviewing the minutes of the February preparatory meetings makes clear that no detail was too insignificant for consideration. As secretary, Sr. M. Rose Eileen provided National Catholic Welfare Conference news service with a national press release and sent similar announcements to twenty-five Catholic newspapers and magazines. The February minutes also recorded a discussion about paper stock for the program which was "to be a pastel shade, preferably blue in honor of Our Lady, Patroness of the Society, if procurable at reasonable price. If blue is used for the stock, a contrasting shade of blue ink might be appropriately chosen for the type."[22] A pastel blue cover of the program did announce in blue ink type the "First Annual Meeting of the Society of Catholic College Teachers of Sacred Doctrine," Trinity College, Washington, D.C., 11 to 13 April 1955, "Under the Patronage of His Excellency, The Most Reverend Patrick A. O'Boyle, D.D. Archbishop of Washington." The program's cover speaks volumes about the interesting mix that informed the Society's corporate persona. It offers a touch of Catholic devotionalism, acknowledgment of dependence on episcopal authority, and recognition of new actors in church and academy, Catholic College Teachers of Sacred Doctrine—all before opening to the list of presentations. The theological content of these and other presentations are discussed in the next chapter.

The 143 who attended the first national meeting heard expansive encouragement from the Society's first president, Reverend Eugene M. Burke,

C.S.P. He praised the dedicated board members, especially Sister M. Rose Eileen, who drew "energy and vitality from the ideal which gave it [the Society] birth"—an "educational vision" informed by "the content and motivations of Christian revelation." Burke emphasized the communal nature of the venture requiring "the joint labor of a large body of Catholic teachers who are personally conscious that each of them is a coadjutor of God's redemptive purpose." In defining the Society's purpose, Burke made clear that the SCCTSD had no aspirations to provide official accreditation of programs and reinforced the Society's founders' hope for producing organic "standards that are the result of mutual experience and discussion and take their authority from their common acceptance by the members as inescapable necessities of sound and effective teaching in our common field." Burke's exhortation authorized every member, whether lay or religious, ordained or not, to engage in the discussion—another portent of change among Catholic theologians.[23]

Coordinating the business of a national society proved difficult given the limited financial resources, vast geographical distances, and an already overworked membership, often teaching theology or religion in addition to full-time teaching in another discipline plus administrative duties and community obligations. After three presidents each served a one-year term, the Society amended its constitution in 1958 to increase the length of office terms for board members and officers to two years, with the past president serving as a ninth board member. The other eight were to be elected by fours in alternating years. The change was to provide more continuity in leadership.[24] Until 1980, men served as president; one was a brother, another was a layman, and the remainder were priests, at least at the time of their presidency. The vice president and secretary were frequently women religious. In fact, Sister M. Rose Eileen, acting as national secretary, proved to be a key source of continuity in leadership for the fledgling organization. Besides passing the constitutional amendment, the 1958 national business meeting passed a resolution giving special thanks "to Sister Rose Eileen, C.S.C., of Dunbarton, of whom it is impossible to begin to mention the infinity of things she has done from the very beginning for the Society. Sister is more than a pioneer or charter member. She can only justly and aptly be described as the mother of the Society."[25] She remained the Society's secretary for another three years.

Over the next few years, the Society regularized its organizational structure and developed a rhythm of meeting practices. During the first two decades of the Society's existence, the annual meetings took advantage of Catholic colleges' Easter break and also coordinated their dates and place to meet just prior to and geographically near the NCEA's national meeting. This link points to the Society's members' self-understanding of their roles as educators distinct from scholars.[26] Unlike the present-day practice of meeting on college campuses, the Society met in a major urban hotel until 1974, with the exception of the first two annual meetings. Organizing a meeting of priests, sisters, and brothers in the first decade had its own peculiar challenges like arranging altars for private masses or securing permission from a chancery office for sisters to "reside in the hotel during the convention and to attend evening sessions."[27] To facilitate organizing private masses in 1958, the secretary sent a postcard that did double duty. It asked all members to indicate courses taught: "Dogma, Morals, Sacred Scripture, Fundamental Theology, Liturgy." Priests could then on that same card, fill in the blank of a very polite request. "Kindly arrange for me to offer Holy Mass on Monday, April 7th, at _____ a.m."[28] An update announced final arrangements for "priest delegates to offer the Holy Sacrifice of the Mass . . . in the hotel, in the Governor Room." Common practice also required separate arrangements for "Sisters and Brothers to co-offer the Holy Sacrifice." The president, Brother Alban of Mary, F.S.C., agreed to explore the availability of "a Missa Cantata or a Missa Recitata which would be attended by all the delegates."[29] The routine quality of certain practices, uninterrupted even when a national meeting disrupts every other aspect of one's daily schedule, provides perspective on the concern for and confidence in the formative dimensions of Catholic practices from liturgy to religious life that members exhibited in the early years of the Society's discussions of college theology.

Attending to such details did not distract the national leadership from the Society's main reason for existence—improving the teaching of college theology. The first annual meeting provided three presentations on distinct approaches to teaching theology and a series of discussions on teacher preparation over two days, Tuesday and Wednesday, April 12 and 13. All who attended had an opportunity to hear every presentation since none occurred simultaneously. This pattern remained for two more annual meetings. "The 1958 Philadelphia convention will always be remembered for the inauguration of the work group sessions."[30] The meeting organizers assigned the groups to provide a "diversity of colleges and Sacred Doctrine courses taught, thereby providing opportunity for wider exchange of experience and viewpoint."[31] The fifteen groups of approximately twelve participants received five suggested topics and approximately an hour and fifteen minutes to produce a report. The orchestrated interaction had the desired effect of making "the individual engagement in general debate more intimate than had been previously the case." In the May 1958 *Magister*, the new president, Brother Alban of Mary, F.S.C., reported favorably on the "strong evidence of the 'vox populi'" in the work groups. He endorsed "greater emphasis on the expression of the grass-roots views of the membership" and wanted to establish the practice as "the policy of future national meetings."[32] The 1959 meeting added another opportunity for discussion in "special interest sessions" focused on "practical teaching problems and techniques in the various branches of sacred doctrine."[33] These new configurations confirmed the leadership's sincere desire to maximize participation among its members. In fact, a 1959–1960 SCCTSD planning file contains a brochure entitled "Modern Meeting Planner" reprinted from "SALES MEETINGS," 4 January 1957. It outlines a five-step planning process that asks a sequential set of questions concerning desired accomplishments, kind of meeting, necessity of subgroups, presentation methods, and audience involvement. It features a series of silhouette drawings that demonstrate different meeting configurations from convention to clinic to seminar and a variety of groupings including general session, plenary, work groups, special interest groups, application groups, and off-the-record.[34] It appears that the Society borrowed techniques of modern communication used in the corporate world to organize its meetings.

Publication became another venue for providing resources to members for improving college theology. Only one month after the first annual meeting, the board determined that publishing the annual meeting proceedings directly aligned with its primary purpose.[35] At the 12 November 1955 board of directors meeting at Dunbarton, the Current Problems Committee reported that the Chandler Printing Company agreed to print a thousand copies at $7.35 per page. Mailing five hundred copies cost $40, according to the Baltimore Post Office.[36] Advanced preparations were made to obtain the second national convention's papers to facilitate their quick publication as the *Proceedings*.[37] The *Proceedings* gradually changed to an annual volume, a collection of essays selected in light of the convention's theme, occasionally featuring articles not delivered at the national meeting and rarely publishing every paper delivered.

In the November meeting of 1956, the board approved the quarterly newsletter, *Magister*, to inform members about national trends in college theology.[38] Like so much of the Society's efforts, this work-intensive project depended upon dedicated volunteers drawing upon very limited financial resources to further the exchange among college teachers of sacred doctrine. Typed on standard paper and stapled in the corner, the newsletter was informative and conversational in tone, especially in surveying current books useful in teaching college theology. Father David Bowman, S.J., discussed the publication of the first two issues of *Magister*. "We have conceived of it as a written 'bull-session' or meeting of the SCCTSD, wherein all members share the experience and spirit of our Society; this should supply much-needed solidarity, especially for those who cannot attend regional or national meetings." Bowman estimated that it took approximately 100 hours to put together the first issue and mentioned Sister M. Rose Eileen's extensive time commitment to the project. Evidently, the product was valuable enough to generate requests for subscriptions. Bowman suggested a dollar per year for nonmembers.[39] Though radically different from the College Theology Society–sponsored scholarly journal, *Horizons*, *Magister* established the precedent for the Society's publishing a periodical.

By 1958, only four years after its founding, the SCCTSD could boast 505 members representing all but thirty of the Catholic colleges. The secretary also reported frequent "unsolicited requests . . . concerning its objectives and history." The *Proceedings* garnered the Society national and international attention. The *Catholic Periodical Index* agreed to index the annual *Proceedings*, and *Sursum Corda* (Australian Franciscan) and *Homiletic and Pastoral Review* requested copies of the annual publication to review. The board even discussed securing the "services of a well established department of public relations in some college in New York. . . . to effect adequate coverage" of the 1959 convention.[40] An increasing number of topics came to the board's attention including additional revisions of the constitution, incorporating the Society to avoid "possible legal complications," securing college credits for sacred doctrine courses, composing a freshman placement test, establishing a senior theology medal, and founding an honor society. Each project had its own complexities. The seemingly straightforward task of establishing course credit varied from state to state so that in Texas, for example, all religion courses had to appear under the heading, "Bible." With the exception of incorporation, all the topics concerned raising college theology's academic profile in the wider Catholic and academic world.

The challenges notwithstanding, the SCCTSD marked its fifth anniversary with a letter of recognition, dated 24 March 1959, from Cardinal Pizzardo, "Prefect of the Sacred Congregation of Seminaries and Universities." Addressed to Brother Alban, the Society's president, the letter praised the Society on the occasion of its fifth national meeting. The letter noted the Society's membership, representing 231 Catholic colleges, including some in Canada, Bolivia, Australia, Italy, and Belgium. The cardinal also mentioned *Proceedings* and *Magister* for their "sharing of facts and experiences proper to [the Society's] exalted end, . . . the knowledge of God." The Society's fostering of intellectual formation, especially "Religious engaged in the Apostolate of the Church," appears as critical, "for if we do not know God, we cannot love Him." Such efforts in the intellectual realm produced profound effects. "Knowledge leads to love, and love yearns for more knowledge. On this ascending staircase where as teachers you lead the way for your pupils, you will reach God."[41] Pizzardo's final comment is reminiscent of the closing line of Sister Rose Eileen's resolution acknowledging "the role of Theology, . . . in the only essentially ultimate integration, namely, that of the whole man in the

Mystical Body of Christ on his way to the Beatific Vision." Such elevated views of college theology situated the teacher in an ambiguous position of power, able to form the theological perspectives of youth without requiring any official authority to do so—an ambiguity that only increased over the next forty-five years.

Sister M. Rose Eileen, C.S.C., found much to celebrate at the fifth annual convention, including a total membership of 558. "From those of us who have intimately witnessed the progress of the past six years of effort there is an ardent act of loving thanksgiving to God for the prudent and experienced leadership to which Divine Providence has entrusted the destinies of the Society during the formative period. From the few audacious pioneers [five] to a membership of 558 within a span of six years is evidence under the blessing of God of a rather remarkable progress."[42] The four hundred members of two years prior was thought to be the maximum possible, but of course membership continued to increase. In 1964, at the tenth anniversary, Sister M. Rose Eileen provided a detailed report on the Society's membership and the number of degrees. The Society membership consisted of 542 priests with 118 holding S.T.D.s and 53 Ph.D.s; 310 sisters with 36 holding Ph.D.s. in theology; 52 brothers with 2 S.T.D.s and no Ph.D.s; 21 laymen with 9 S.T.D.s and 3 Ph.D.s; and 7 laywomen with 3 Ph.D.s. The grand total of 932 more than doubled the maximum of four hundred.[43]

Another sign of the Society's vitality was an increase in committee activity. Amidst the plans for the 1961 national meeting, the board established several new committees named for specific duties: Nominations, Resolutions, Book Display, Publicity, Credentials, Registration, and Hospitality committees for priests, brothers and sisters (no mention of laity). The publicity committee met with some success in issuing press releases from the "National Headquarters" of the SCCTSD.[44] A bold *Boston Pilot* headline declared "Teachers Convention Stresses Communism and Christian Unity." A small headline added "Christian Instruction of Youth Seen Key to Victory over Reds." The headline reflected a major theme in Cardinal Cushing's speech at dinner, but little of the Society's carefully crafted press release that had emphasized Christian unity. The newspaper did report that five hundred attended "under the spiritual patronage of 'Mary Immaculate, Seat of Wisdom' guided by the theme, 'the Perfection of Charity.'"[45]

Increased national initiatives did not escape criticism from the rank-and-file members. The "Report of the Louisville Region to the seventh national convention" expressed frustration over the amount of "control" the national leadership was attempting to exercise. A "good society" requires "greater autonomy" for the regions.[46] Evidently their complaint hit a sensitive nerve. The "Suggestions for Regional Activity 1961–1962" offered a rather pointed

introductory paragraph. "It goes without saying that the following suggestions from the national office are suggestions. Regional planning groups are,
obviously, quite free to initiate programs and activities, . . ."[47] Evidence suggests that most regions in this period combined local and national interests.

COMING OF AGE

The Society also sought to assert some influence in international ecclesiastical matters. Two active members, Dominican priests James Egan and Leo
Arnoult, from Saint Mary's Graduate School of Theology, had fashioned a
modest "Petition Regarding the Legislation of the Church on the Prohibition
of Books" to discuss at the 1961 convention business meeting. Issues around
censorship and restrictions on reading proved a challenging topic since en-
forcing them gave credence to those who dismissed Catholic academic credibility, especially in theology. In 1959, John Harvey had presented "an approach that shows the reasonable nature of censorship." He had urged
teachers of sacred doctrine to make clear that "students capable of scholarship" should have relative ease of access to "all the works which bear upon the
object of his research." Harvey had provided a relatively complex view of the
"correct moral judgment" involving "the dignity of the artist, the value of his
work, and the serious nature of the study of his work." The key moral issue
remained, however, the effect on the "viewer." To assist in forming prudential
judgment, Harvey offered an extended analysis of aesthetics with an emphasis on "the formal object of serious study," particularly useful given U.S. college students' "almost obsessional curiosity about sexual matters." He used an
America article, "Teaching 'Dirty' Books in College," by Father Edward Romogosa, to illustrate this approach. Romogosa evidently gauged each student's "intellectual and moral index of maturity" by focusing "on the literary
aspect of the writing" rather than the moral. "As a part of the maturing
process, the teacher then finds an occasion to discuss the Christian critical approach to literature, so as to impart to his students an 'ascetic as well as an es-
thetic distance from which to view the world of their reading.'" Harvey's reflections have the ring of confidence in teacher and student rather than a
defensive or even paternal attitude. His gradualist approach reflected wider
trends among Catholic educators—trends that would accelerate in the next
five years.[48]

   The 1961 petition, intended for the Vatican Council's consideration, had
been the result of a resolution process initiated sometime after the 1959 convention though there is no evidence to suggest that Harvey's presentation

inspired the resolution. In an undated and unsolicited memorandum, James Egan, O.P., proposed a "preliminary exploration" of the effects of the Index of Prohibited Books on "scholars and educated priests, religious and laymen, with emphasis on the conditions in America." John XXIII's commitment to revising the *Codex Iuris Canonici* created an opening "to initiate discussions that will be both calm and frank concerning the question of Prohibited Books by groups whose fidelity to the legislation of the Church is well-known."[49] Egan had hoped to include contributions from the Catholic Theological Society of America, Canon Law Society of America, and the American Catholic Philosophical Association. There is no evidence that this collaboration occurred.

The SCCTSD's initiative concerning the index highlights again the unique situation of the college theology teacher. M. C. Wheeler, R.S.C.J., wrote to Father Arnoult at length about the process that an instructor with a doctorate must undertake to gain permission to read each prohibited book or to use the text in a class. Each student had to be listed for each book. Wheeler questioned the logic of the practice. "In an age where the Church is doing all she can to push Catholic laymen and women into positions of leadership it can be very hard to train them solidly with the present set-up."[50] A "special interest session" at the 1960 convention included speeches from Father Gerard Sloyan, Catholic University of America, and Father Arnoult, substituting for a gravely ill James Egan. Sloyan argued vigorously "that the legislation should be repealed immediately as a part of the pastoral concern of the Church." Given the proliferation of media disseminating ideas contrary to Catholic teaching, "attempts to control reading constitute . . . a danger to the life of the Church." In dramatic fashion, Sloyan called upon his listeners to "face the bitter truth that every man-jack of us in this room was irreparably maimed in his education in its early stages." The Society ought to petition the Holy See "humbly and respectfully" to identify "types of books that might be easily harmful to faith and morals" as an assistance in "forming a conscience but not as binding on the conscience." Father Arnoult's presentation focused on "what revisions of law and policy we might reasonably hope and respectfully request will be effected by the one supreme law-making authority in the Church." The petition presented at the 1961 business meeting contained the basic elements of Arnoult's proposal.[51]

Maintaining an irenic tone, the 1961 petition opened with recognition of "the unquestioned duty and right of the Church" to prohibit reading "pernicious books of any sort." Then, appealing to *Humani Generis* with its call for study of modern intellectual currents including those contrary to Catholic philosophical and theological positions, the petition noted that the restrictions found in canon 1399 make such efforts very difficult for all Catholics "engaged professionally in intellectual pursuits." Suggested changes included refining the definitions of books prohibited and permitting those with advanced degrees in sacred science and literature to read materials relevant to their field. To facilitate gaining permission, the resolution argued for allowing bishops and ultimately university presidents the power to grant the permission "with the understanding that the natural law forbids any reading that is a proximate occasion of ruin to faith and morals and that there are obviously no dispensations here for any reason."[52]

A debate ensued at the business meeting with Father Sloyan voicing strong opposition on the grounds that it effected little change. "Catholic Theological Faculties of the world would hopefully present much better petitions to Rome and Rome should not think that the present petition is the sense of a group as important as ours." With no one defending the petition, Father Egan, a principal author, "wanted nothing more to do with the decision." Given the sharp divisions and the importance of the matter, the decision was brought to the entire membership through *Magister* and a letter from Bernard Cooke, S.J., president. Ironically, *Magister's* editor, James Egan, O.P., had to instruct the members to reread the 1960 *Proceedings* on the Index and to vote on either support of Sloyan's position or on the 1961 petition.[53] A resolution appeared in the 1964 *Proceedings* calling for "the next session of the Council" to look "to reform thoroughly that section of Canon Law dealing with prohibited books and the Roman Index" to allow "Catholic scholars" an ability to engage in "more meaningful dialogue with the contemporary world."[54]

John XXIII's call for an ecumenical council sparked more than the petition. The Society took additional initiatives in 1962 that reflected the building momentum of change in college theology. *Magister* described the Society at the 1962 annual meeting "as it were, coming of age." The national convention had "crowded sessions" that helped to affirm "the interior quality of maturity."[55] The board orchestrated adjustments in membership and national leadership. The Admissions Committee secured the elimination of associate membership by a 3 to 1 vote at the 1962 business meeting. According to the committee, the amendment aligned with the Society's title and purpose but changed no current member's status. One can surmise that the change reflected a more well-defined role for college theology teachers.[56] In refining national leadership roles, *Proceedings* and *Magister* editors remained appointed members of the board but their lack of voting privileges was made explicit. *Magister's* editor was limited to a two-year renewable term. Bylaw amendments allowed for flexible meeting agendas to respond to "circumstances."

These organizational changes aligned with other shifts in members' increasing activity in theological studies per se. The national officers agreed to a "careful study" of the viability of "directed groups to meet under competent leadership in specific areas of theology." Reverend Richard W. Rousseau, S.J., appears to have originated the idea in a "spirit of healthy reevaluation of procedures" as the group approached its tenth anniversary. He suggested a "workshop" to promote engagement with "the latest Theological ideas" in the context of "purposeful meetings and discussions, [with] professors from all over the country, teaching and specializing in one or two Theological areas." Rousseau implied the current pattern, with formal presentations and discussions of pedagogy, produced frustration among members granted no time to "talk shop" with others in their field.[57] Still another troublesome omission is apparent in a recommendation "that Sisters be invited more frequently to present papers, to conduct panel discussions, and generally to be more vocal in the work of the Society."[58] National leaders also sought an editorial board for *Magister* with "designated responsibilities in particular areas of theology" such as "Scripture," "moral-ascetical," and "sacramental-liturgical."[59] The newly elected president, Urban Voll, O.P., introduced yet another topic whose significance only increased over the next four decades, though perspectives have changed dramatically. According to Voll, "the Bishops have a right to ask what we are doing that contributes to their work." Sister M. Rose Eileen agreed and hoped, for the Society's sake, that "we could get a Bishop to tell us this."[60] These seemingly minor adjustments and passing comments reflect the gradual changes in understanding theology as an academic discipline and the SCCTSD's members' roles not only as teachers but as theologians in the academy and in the church. They also suggest some of the fault lines in increasing specialization, women's participation, and the relationship to ecclesiastical authorities.

Other indicators that the SCCTSD had "come of age" are in correspondence with other professional organizations. The Catholic Biblical Association (CBA) made an "official request" for "an 'observer exchange.'" Upon Bernard Cooke's recommendation, Manning M. Pattillo, from the Danforth Foundation, wrote the Society's secretary, Sister Julie, seeking copies of the *Proceedings*, as part of "a comprehensive assessment of church colleges and universities in the United States."[61] Fordham Jesuit John M. Culkin requested the Society's members serve as a resource for a "two year television course on college theology" produced through the Catholic Television Cooperative. The plan as outlined was to produce around "160 half-hour programs" enlisting "the finest talent in the country."[62] The March 1962 *Magister*, in announcing the project, acknowledged "the immediacy, continuity, and visual potential of television." No evidence exists that the plan ever came to fruition.[63]

RETROSPECTIVES ON THE SOCIETY'S FUTURE: 1964

Nineteen sixty-four, of course, marked an important milestone for the Society as it prepared to celebrate its tenth national meeting. The impending tenth anniversary sparked new initiatives like a brochure whose cover featured in bold print—"Society of Catholic College Teachers of Sacred Doctrine What is it?" The answer came directly from the newly amended constitution already discussed. A short-lived "Newsletter for Regional Officers" appeared in February 1964. Its introductory comments made the regions a part of deep and broad movements affecting every aspect of life in the church and society. The regions were the source of "the future movement of the Society" emerging "from a real pooling of ideas flowing from the broad base of the general membership up through the regional Planning Committees to the Board of Directors."[64]

The tenth national convention opened in the midst of the great stir from the Second Vatican Council with some documents, most notably on the liturgy, already promulgated and others greatly anticipated. Yet, the better portion of the meeting's presentations provided retrospectives on the Society's ten years of existence and prospectives for its immediate future. Like the first convention, it took place in Washington, D.C., though at the Statler Hilton Hotel rather than Trinity College. Acting as the Society's secretary, Sister Julie promised in her letter of invitation "exclusive use of general sessions" to "encourage all of us present to concentrate in a spirit of reappraisal and redirection on topics closely linked to the goals of our Society." Some new directions were evident in her description. Rather than arranging for private masses, Sister Julie offered an opportunity "to experience together the Holy Mass, the sacrament of unity" on the first morning of the convention. The convention organizers arranged for the hotel to place twenty round tables in its Federal Room. Such arrangements "may encourage us to carry over that union and make it incarnate there through the informal discussion of the program topics." Suggested preparation for the convention was a review of "constitutional goals" and the annual *Proceedings*. Urban Voll's presidential address focused on the "Sacred Teacher." Before turning his attention to his topic, Voll mused over the Society's lengthy and tautological name—"the Catholic College Teachers of [the] Sacred [act of] Teaching." In a footnote, he suggested a shortened version, the "Sacred Doctrine Society"—with the deliciously ironic abbreviation, SDS.[65] The mind reels at missed opportunities.

The tenth convention appeared in a *Washington Post* story with the headline "Catholic Teachers Ask Revised Index." The opening line described how the "organization of Catholic college teachers overwhelmingly passed a resolution yesterday aimed at drastically revising or completely abolishing the centuries-old Roman Catholic 'Index of Prohibited Books.'" The *Post* also reported the Society's vote to send letters "urging [U.S. bishops] to 'support the sections of the proposed schemata on religious liberty and Jews.'" Another resolution "appealed to members of the society to 'use every opportunity to support the civil rights of all persons, especially the American Negro in his current struggle for equality.'" The *Post* even gave election results, with Rev. Raymond Parr succeeding Urban Voll as president and Sister Julie and Brother Stephen being re-elected as secretary and treasurer respectively. The newspaper's readers also learned that "the society has 918 members, including 80 from Italy, 46 from Canada, four from France, and three from the Philippines."[66] Of course, these resolutions were not the only topics of discussion of the previous decade. It is time to consider "the stimulating and profitable exchange of ideas concerning the common objectives, the diversified procedures, and multiple problems of the departments of Theology in our undergraduate colleges" that the Society of Catholic College Teachers of Sacred Doctrine had facilitated.

NOTES

1. "Sixth Session," Thursday, June 18, 1953, in "Workshop on Theology and the Social Sciences in Catholic College Programs: Notes on proceedings compiled by Reverend Gerald Van Ackeren, S.J.," Catholic University of America, June 1953, "Secretary's Data Notebook 1953–1956" Binder, Box 2, College Theology Society [CTS] Collection, Archives of Catholic University of America [ACUA].

2. "Sixth Session" for all quoted.

3. A planning meeting was held 15 November 1953, Dunbarton College of the Holy Cross, quotes taken from "Meeting of College Teachers of Religion, La Salle College, December 8, 1953," "Secretary's Data 1953–1956" Binder, Box 2, CTS Collection, ACUA.

4. "Sixth Session."

5. "Sixth Session."

6. Dunbarton College of the Holy Cross, "Secretary's Data 1953–1956" Binder, Box 2, CTS Collection, ACUA.

7. All materials are in "Secretary's Data 1953–1956" Binder, Box 2, CTS Collection, ACUA.

8. Quoted in Cyril Vollert, S.J., "The Origin, Development, and Purpose of the Society of Catholic College Teachers of Sacred Doctrine," *Bulletin: National Catholic Educational Association* LI, no. 1 (August, 1954); *Report of the Proceedings and Addresses—Fifty-first Annual Meeting* (Chicago, Illinois, April 19–22, 1954), 250.

9. "Report of the Panel Discussion of Theology," NCEA College Regional Meeting, Marymount College, Tarrytown, New York, February 20, 1954 [Report submitted by Sister M. Rose Eileen, C.S.C., Dunbarton], "Secretary's Data 1953–1956" Binder, Box 2, CTS Collection, ACUA.

10. Gerard S. Sloyan, "Religious Studies in Roman Catholic Colleges and Universities"* in *Speaking of Religious Education* (New York: Herder and Herder, 1968), 94. *First published by

the Department of Higher Education, National Council of Churches, in *The Study of Religion in College and University* (New York 1967), 24–31.

11. "Minutes of the Constitutional Meeting of the Society of College Teachers of Sacred Doctrine," Fordham University, New York, February 22, 1954, "Secretary's Data 1953–1956" Binder, Box 2, CTS Collection, ACUA.

12. "Minutes of the Constitutional Meeting," Rosemary Rodgers's account describes Eugene Burke as "a dynamic leader capable of rallying wide support" who helped to establish the Society. She also mentions Roy Deferrari as a "prime mover of the Society." He was a classicist and dean of the College of Arts and Sciences at Catholic University of America. Rodgers refers to a letter that appointed Deferrari as representative of CUA at the Fordham constitutional meeting. Evidence of Deferrari's longterm influence is scant in the archives. Burke's influence extends beyond SCCTSD given his active leadership in the Catholic Theological Society of America, including serving as their president. His involvement in both suggests that early tensions between SCCTSD and CTSA are not as pronounced as later accounts suggest. Rosemary Rodgers, O.P., *A History of the College Theology Society* (Villanova, PA: College Theology Society, 1983), 8–9.

13. "The Origin, Development, and Purpose of the Society of Catholic College Teachers of Sacred Doctrine," "Secretary's Data 1953–1956" Binder, Box 2, CTS Collection, ACUA.

14. "Recommendations for the Organization of Regional Meetings" included in the account of the "Meeting of the Society of Catholic College Teachers of Sacred Doctrine," "National Convention of the NCEA," Lower Tower Room, Conrad Hilton Hotel, Chicago, Illinois, 3:00 p.m., April 20, 1954, "Secretary's Data 1953–1956" Binder, Box 2, CTS Collection, ACUA.

15. Cyril Vollert, S.J., "The Origin, Development, and Purpose of the Society of Catholic College Teachers of Sacred Doctrine," *Bulletin: National Catholic Educational Association*, 254.

16. "Minutes of the first meeting of the New York Region of the Society of College Teachers of Sacred Doctrine," Manhattan College, New York, May 8, 1954, "Regional Reports" File, Box 5, CTS Collection, ACUA.

17. The Le Moyne plan is discussed in the second chapter.

18. Italicized portion underlined in the original. All quoted texts in the history with emphasis are as found in the original. In "Secretary's Data 1956–1958" Binder, Box 2, CTS Collection, ACUA.

19. Samuel Cardinal Stritch to Father Sebastian Carlson, O.P., January 12, 1956, "Secretary's Data 1953–1956" Binder, Box 2, CTS Collection, ACUA.

20. "Minutes of the Board of Directors," St. Paul's Rectory, New York, NY, December 18, 1955 [1954], "Secretary's Data 1953–1956" Binder, Box 2, CTS Collection, ACUA.

21. Sister M. Rose Eileen, C.S.C., to "Member," January 13, 1955, "Secretary's Data 1953–1956" Binder, Box 2, CTS Collection, ACUA

22. "Minutes of the Meeting of the Officers of the Society of Catholic College Teachers of Sacred Doctrine," Dunbarton College of Holy Cross, Washington, DC, February 17, 1955, "Secretary's Data 1953–1956" Binder, Box 2, CTS Collection, ACUA.

23. "Address of Welcome, First National Meeting of the Society," in *Proceedings of the First Annual Convention of the Society of Catholic College Teachers of Sacred Doctrine*, ed. Urban Voll, O.P., (Washington, DC: Dunbarton College of the Holy Cross, 1956), 5–7.

24. "Proposed Amendment to Present Provisional Constitution of the Society [undated but with 1958 materials], "Secretary's Data 1956–1958" Binder, Box 2, CTS Collection, ACUA.

25. "Business Meeting and Reports; E. Report of the Committee on Resolutions," in *Proceedings: Fourth Annual Meeting of the Society of Catholic College Teachers of Sacred Doctrine*, (Philadelphia, Pennsylvania, April 7–8, 1958), (Weston, Massachusetts: Regis College, reprint 1964), 125.

26. "Board of Directors' Meeting, Secretary Report," Dunbarton College of Holy Cross, Washington, DC, November 12, 1955, "Secretary's Data 1953–1956" Binder, Box 2, CTS Collection, ACUA.

27. "Society of Catholic College Teachers of Sacred Doctrine, Minutes of the Board of Directors Meeting," Saint Mary's College Notre Dame, Indiana, November 8, 1958, "Secretary's Data April 1958–April 1959" Binder, Box 2, CTS Collection, ACUA.

28. Postcard accompanied letter, Sister M. Rose Eileen, C.S.C., to "Fellow Member," January 15, 1958, "Secretary's Data 1956–1958" Binder, Box 2, CTS Collection, ACUA.

29. Minutes of the Board of Directors Meeting," Saint Mary's College Notre Dame, Indiana, November 8, 1958.

30. "Work Group Sessions," Summary by Editor [Brother C. Luke, F.S.C.] in *Proceedings: Fourth Annual Meeting*, 35.

31. "Fourth National Meeting, Society of Catholic College Teachers of Sacred Doctrine," Penn Sherwood Hotel, Philadelphia, April 7–8, 1958. The Work Sessions, April 7, 1958, at 1:30 p.m., "Secretary's Data 1956–1958" Binder, Box 2, CTS Collection, ACUA.

32. President's Letter, *Magister: Bulletin of the Society of Catholic College Teachers of Sacred Doctrine*, edited at West Baden College, West Baden Springs, Indiana, vol. II, no. 3. (May 1958); 1. University of Notre Dame Archives, Box 1, Folder 8, *Magister*, SCCTSD Bulletin, 1957–1965.

33. "Special Interest Sessions" [summary Brother C. Luke, F.S.C.] in *Proceedings of the Fifth Annual Convention of the Society of Catholic College Teachers of Sacred Doctrine, March 30–31, 1959, New York, NY*, (Society of Catholic College Teachers of Sacred Doctrine, 1959, reprint Weston, MA: Regis College, 1964), 103.

34. "Modern Meeting Planner Brochure" including "Guide to Styles, Groups, Methods" by Hugh Gyllenhaal, "Secretary's Data April 1959–1960" Binder, Box 2, CTS Collection, ACUA.

35. Meeting of the Washington Area Officers of the SCCTSD, Dunbarton College of Holy Cross, Washington, DC, May 11, 1955, "Secretary's Data 1953–1956" Binder, Box 2, CTS Collection, ACUA.

36. "Board of Directors Meeting, Secretary's Report," November 12, 1955, "Secretary's Data 1953–1956" Binder, Box 2, CTS Collection, ACUA.

37. "Meeting of the Washington Officers of the Society of Catholic College Teachers of Sacred Doctrine," Dunbarton College of the Holy Cross, Washington, DC, February 25, 1956, "Secretary's Data 1953–1956" Binder, Box 2, CTS Collection, ACUA.

38. Board of Directors Meeting, Society of Catholic College Teachers of Sacred Doctrine, Dunbarton College of the Holy Cross, Washington, DC, November 3, 1956, "Secretary's Data 1956–1958" Binder, Box 2, CTS Collection, ACUA.

39. "Report of the Committee on Sacred Doctrine Studies" Fr. David Bowman, S.J, "Secretary's Data 1956–1958" Binder, Box 2, CTS Collection, ACUA.

40. "Society of Catholic College Teachers of Sacred Doctrine, Minutes of the Board of Directors Meeting," Saint Mary's College Notre Dame, Indiana, November 8, 1958, "Secretary's Data April 1958–April 1959" Binder, Box 2, CTS Collection, ACUA.

41. G. Cardinal Pizzardo *Sacra Congregatio de Seminariis et de Studiorum Universitatibus*. Rome, to Brother Alban, F.S.C., president of the Society of Catholic College Teachers of Sacred Doctrine, March 24, 1959, "Hierarchy" File, Box 5, CTS Collection, ACUA.

42. Sister M. Rose Eileen, C.S.C. [secretary, St. Mary's College], "Business Meeting and Reports: A Report of the National Secretary," in *Proceedings: Fifth Annual Meeting*, 130.

43. Unfortunately, no record exists of the source of the degrees. One can assume that the women's doctorates in theology were primarily from Saint Mary's Graduate School and Catholic University of America. Sister M. Rose Eileen, C.S.C., "Academic Preparation of Col-

lege Teachers of Sacred Doctrine, 1953–1964" in *Proceedings: Society of Catholic College Teachers of Sacred Doctrine* (Tenth Annual Convention, Washington, DC, March 30–31, 1964, Weston, MA: Regis College, 1964), 85.

44. The first is untitled, the second is "Society of Catholic College Teachers of Sacred Doctrine Have Chosen the Concept of the Church as the Subject of Its Seventh National Convention to be Held in Boston," and the third is "Society of Catholic College Teachers of Sacred Doctrine to Hold Seventh National Convention in Boston," "Secretary's Data April 1961–April 1962" Binder, Box 2, CTS Collection, ACUA.

45. Boston, April 8, 1961, "Clippings" File, Box 5, CTS Collection, ACUA.

46. Submitted by William J. Cole, S.M., associate professor of theology [University of Dayton], chairman of the Louisville region, April 3, 1961, "Regional Reports—DC, Maryland" File, Box 5, CTS Collection, ACUA.

47. "Society of Catholic College Teachers of Sacred Doctrine, Suggestions for Regional Activity 1961–1962," "Secretary's Data 1961–1962" Binder, Box 2, CTS Collection, ACUA.

48. Reverend John F. Harvey, O.S.F.S., S.T.D., "Censorship and Moral Evaluation in the Catholic College" in *Proceedings: Fifth Annual Meeting*, 51, 53, 54, 63, 97, 100. See Una A. Cadegan's discussions of shifting Catholic perspectives on censorship relative to literature and film in "Guardians of Democracy or Cultural Storm Troopers? American Catholics and the Control of Popular Media, 1934–1966," *The Catholic Historical Review* LXXVII, no. 2 (April 2001): 25, 82.

49. "Submitted to the National Board of SCCTSD," by James M. Egan, O.P, "Secretary's Data April 1959–April 1961" Binder, Box 2, CTS Collection, ACUA.

50. M. C. Wheeler, R.S.C.J., Newton College of the Sacred Heart, Newton, Massachusetts to Fr. Arnoult, April 27, 1960, "Committee on Prohibited Books" File, Box 5, CTS Collection, ACUA.

51. "Special Interest Sessions: The Problem of Prohibited Books and the American Intellectual," summary by Reverend Leo A. Arnoult, O.P., Reverend Thomas Heath, O.P., and Sister M. Rose Eileen Masterman, C.S.C., in *Proceedings: Sixth Annual Meeting of the Society of Catholic College Teachers of Sacred Doctrine* (Chicago, Illinois: April 18–19, 1960; Weston, MA: Regis College, reprint 1964), 84, 86, 87, 89.

52. "A Petition Regarding the Legislation of the Church on the Prohibition of Books," attached to a letter from Bernard Cooke, S.J., president, to "member of Society," Ca., May 1960 in nonarchived materials.

53. "Society of Catholic College Teachers of Sacred Doctrine, Office of the President," "Secretary's Data April 1961–April 1962" File, Box 2, CTS Collection, ACUA.

54. "Report of the Committee on Resolutions" in *Proceedings* (Tenth Annual Convention), 145.

55. *Magister: Bulletin of the Society of Catholic College Teachers of Sacred Doctrine* (May 1962), 1.

56. "Statement from Committee on Admissions, submitted on floor of convention" [on Rev. Leon D. Kennedy, Madonna College, Livonia, Michigan letterhead, no date] in "Admissions" File, Box 5, CTS Collection, ACUA

57. "Memorandum to the National Board," in "Secretary's Data April 1962–1964" Binder, Box 2, CTS Collection, ACUA.

58. "Addenda: Recommendations Received at the Meeting of Regional Chairmen and Secretaries with the Board of Directors," Statler-Hilton Hotel, Detroit, Michigan, Tuesday, April 24, 1962, "Secretary's Data April 1961–April 1962" File, Box 2, CTS Collection, ACUA.

59. Society of Catholic College Teachers of Sacred Doctrine "Minutes of Meetings of the Board of Directors," Statler-Hilton Hotel, Detroit, Michigan, April 22–24, 1962, "Secretary's

Data April 1961–April 1962" Binder, Box 2, CTS Collection, ACUA. Whether these several changes come in the aftermath of the index debacle is never mentioned.

60. Society of Catholic College Teachers of Sacred Doctrine, "Meeting of Officers," Cardinal Cushing College, Brookline, Massachusetts, June 18–19, 1962, "Secretary's Data April 1962–1964" Binder, Box 2, CTS Collection, ACUA.

61. Manning M. Pattillo, Saint Louis to Sister Julie, October 22, 1962, and Sister Julie, C.S.J., to Manning M. Pattillo, November 7, 1962, "Danforth" File, Box 5, CTS Collection, ACUA.

62. "Memorandum, from National Catholic Educational Association to the Society of Catholic College Teachers of Sacred Doctrine, re: *Production of a two year television course on college theology*," from Reverend John M. Culkin, S.J., Fordham University [no date], "NCEA" File, Box 5, CTS Collection, ACUA.

63. "Sharing of Teaching Resources in Sacred Doctrine through Television and its Offshoots, presented at the Saint Louis Regional Meeting of the Society, December 1961," Reverend R. C. Williams, S.J., Creighton University, in *Magister: Bulletin of the Society of Catholic College Teachers of Sacred Doctrine* (March 1962), 5 and 6.

64. "Society of Catholic College Teachers of Sacred Doctrine Newsletter for Regional Officers," Number 1, February 1964, "Secretary's Data April 1962–1964" Binder, Box 2, CTS Collection, ACUA.

65. Sister Julie, C.S.J., national secretary to "Fellow Member," Regis College, Weston, Massachusetts, January 1964, "Secretary's Data April 1962–1964" Binder, Box 2, CTS Collection, ACUA.

66. "Catholic Teachers Ask Revised Index," by Caspar Nannes, the *Washington Post*, April 1, 1964, "Clipping" File, Box 5, CTS Collection, ACUA.

· 2 ·

College Theology as Academic Discipline (1923–1964)

RELIGION OR THEOLOGY: FROM J. M. COOPER TO J. C. MURRAY

Theology had a relatively marginal status as an academic discipline in most undergraduate curricula at Catholic colleges and universities in the mid-twentieth century. So the founding of a professional society of teachers in that discipline took imagination, foresight, and more than a modicum of courage. Catholic educators had debated the effectiveness of various approaches to teaching college theology for at least the past three decades. In 1923, John Montgomery Cooper published a four-article series on teaching "religion" rather than "theology" to undergraduates.[1] Cooper identified "theology" with seminary education that relied on a derivative form of Thomist scholasticism further distilled into a manual format. Cooper argued not only against adopting the scholastic approach to undergraduate education but also against assuming seminary-educated men could translate their theological knowledge into an effective high school or even college course. His alternative, detailed in the four-volume *Religion Outlines for Colleges*, relies upon an inductive method to draw students into considering how to live as fully committed Catholics. Under Cooper's leadership, Catholic University of America shaped not only a distinctive undergraduate religion program but also a graduate program that admitted all academically qualified applicants—men and women whether lay, religious, or ordained. According to the National Catholic Educational Association (NCEA), in surveys of religion programs in the 1940s and 1950s, approximately 50% of Catholic colleges surveyed used one or more volumes of the *Outlines*.[2]

31

John Montgomery Cooper turned his attention away from teaching "religion" toward the emerging field of anthropology, founded Catholic University of America's department in that social scientific study of culture, and became noted in that field, even serving as president of the American Anthropological Association in 1940. Cooper's successor in the Religion Department was Father William Russell, a diocesan priest from Dubuque, Iowa. Using Cooper's methods as his starting point, Russell championed what he called the Christocentric method, an adaptation of the kerygmatic approach identified with Josef Jungmann. Russell's successor, Gerard Sloyan, a priest from the diocese of Trenton, sought to revitalize the program's intellectual quality by integrating contemporary explorations in scripture, liturgy, and sacraments into theological studies. Sloyan, as already noted, had significant influence in the founding and development of the SCCTSD.

John Courtney Murray provided the next major contribution to the theology/religion debate in a two-part *Theological Studies* article, "Towards a Theology for the Layman," considering first the "problem of finality" and second, "the problem of pedagogy." In terms of finality, the priest, in Murray's estimation, received a professional degree in theology to uphold magisterial teaching within the ecclesial context. The layperson, on the other hand, carries out an apostolate located in "the lay zone, the frontier between the temporal and the spiritual, with a view to gaining not this soul or that (this remains its ultimate finality), but a whole milieu, the whole profane milieu, civil society." An appropriate "theology for the laity" must provide "intelligence of faith, especially in relation to human life and the common good of mankind" to ensure the laity's full cooperation with the hierarchy in "the renewal and reconstruction of the whole of modern social life." Effective pedagogy must integrate three existing movements—intellectual, liturgical, and social—already influencing a "theology for the laity."[3] Murray's articles served as a frequent reference point in debates throughout the 1950s about theological education for college students.

PREPARING COLLEGE THEOLOGY TEACHERS

Another obstacle for college theology lay in the scarcity of well-trained and effective college teachers. Women and laymen had few options for study other than Catholic University. In 1939, Saint Bonaventure started a summer master's program that permitted women, lay and religious, to receive master's degrees. Father Plassman, O.F.M., is credited with founding the program. His inspiration came from an unnamed sister who, at the NCEA annual meeting, expressed her frustration over exclusion from the study of theology. Plassman returned to Saint Bonaventure and fashioned a course of study using the seminary curriculum as his guide. In his own account of the school's founding, he noted its specific "purpose is not to train Theologians . . . but teachers of Religion" who "acquire a fair understanding of Religion as a science, which is Theology." He made clear that "we theologians do not want the Sisters to learn more than we know ourselves." His comments indicate clear distinctions between theologian and religion teacher even in a college setting—a distinction also assumed among the Society's founding members.[4]

In 1944, five years after Saint Bonaventure founded its program, Saint Mary's College officially opened a year-round graduate program which admitted qualified women, both lay and religious. The college's president, Sister Madeleva Wolff, C.S.C., founded the Graduate School of Sacred Theology. Sister Madeleva drew upon historical highlights of women's theological exploits to situate the school in the Catholic tradition. In a brief article in the Saint Mary's publication, the *Courier*, she featured the women who, with Jerome, translated scripture producing the Vulgate: Catherine of Siena who persuaded the pope to return to Rome, and Teresa of Avila who reformed the Carmelite order. Her conclusion revealed as much about her expectations in the present circumstances as her perspectives on the past. "Two lay women [including Eustochium] gave us our Bible. One lay woman saved Rome for the Church. One cloistered nun reformed the spiritual life of her time." She hoped for no less from the women who engaged in study at Saint Mary's. Several women influential in the Society's founding received degrees from Saint Mary's, including Sister Mary Charles Borromeo. Both James Egan and Leo Arnoult taught in the program.

Other Catholic colleges and universities soon added graduate education for high school and college religion teachers. In 1950, La Salle College and the University of Notre Dame introduced master's programs. The next year, Providence College, the Aquinas Institute for Theology and Philosophy, Saint Xavier (Chicago), and Marquette University joined in the endeavor. As discussions began about founding a society for college teachers of theology (1953), four more programs appeared—Catherine Spalding College (Louisville), St. John's (Jamaica, NY), Villanova University, and College of Saint Thomas (St. Paul). The threat to academic quality posed by proliferation given the scarce resources soon became a topic for debate, but proliferation also suggested a growing demand for advanced theological studies.[5]

Of great symbolic significance in the 1950s was the opening of *Regina Mundi*, an "Institute of Higher Studies for Religious," the "Religious" here being women, the site being the Eternal City, Rome. Its founding came about in part due to a request from "the Congress of Superiors General in 1952." A letter, signed by G. B. Montini, announced Pius XII's support of the new institute "in giving the Religious a more complete formation and one better adapted to present needs, and in the deepening of religious culture, particularly for those who have the noble mission of educating youth in faith and practice of Christian life."[6] In "The Inauguration of '*Regina Mundi*,'" as reported by a "Dominican sister," Cardinal Valerio Valeri, prefect of the Sacred Congregation of Religious, placed *Regina Mundi* within a familiar historical narrative. "St. Jerome's cenacle on the Aventine was, we may say today, the first Roman Institute of Sacred Studies for women."[7] *Regina Mundi*'s Roman location validated the right of the laity, especially women, to study theology in ways that no program in the United States could have in the 1950s. It also suggested a certain transnational character to the widening boundaries of theological studies.

EXPERIMENTS IN COLLEGE THEOLOGY

Given the novelty of college theology, both content and preparing teachers became frequent topics of papers and panels throughout the first decade of annual and even regional meetings. The first two New York regional meetings focused upon the Le Moyne plan, a creative and coherent response to Murray's vision of "Theology for the Laity."[8] As Le Moyne College's Father Fernan, S.J., explained, the four-year program taught the New Testament "not through metaphysics but through history and literature." Only four months later, participants in the first national meeting engaged in similar discussions about three distinctive approaches to college theology. Father Gerard Sloyan, Catholic University of America, entitled his approach, "From Christ in the Gospels to Christ in the Church." Thomas Donlan, O.P., of St. Rose Priory, Dubuque, presented a "Thomistic" approach from the "Dominican School of Thought," and John Fernan, S.J., of Le Moyne College described a "Historical, Scriptural Approach."[9]

Father Sloyan's presentation demonstrates that interest in experimental approaches made its appearance from the Society's first meeting. In his curricular schema, undergraduates in their first semester would confront a series of difficult moral questions on relatively familiar topics to gain an understanding of their lack of knowledge. Such an awareness, Sloyan conjectured, would generate a desire for more advanced theological studies. Subsequent semesters would then offer a careful examination of scripture with attentiveness to the person of Christ as well as consideration of the liturgy and sacraments to respond to the now recognized need for a theological outlook. Only one woman, Sister Marie Therese Charles, O.S.U., from New Rochelle appeared on the first meeting's program. Her topic, like that of Brother Celestine Luke, F.S.C., and Father John Harvey, O.S.F.S., was to consider another perplexing issue of the day—"The Content, Method, and Opportunities Presently Available in the United States for the Preparation of College Teachers of Sacred Doctrine."[10]

Both Sloyan and Fernan integrated scripture into the course content rather than using a strictly scholastic approach to give a distinctive shape to their curriculum. The *Proceedings* and other accounts of SCCTSD discussions provide multiple examples of how the renewed interest in scripture studies among Catholics reshaped college theology. In the 1956 meeting's discussion of "finality," Gerald Van Ackeren, S.J., asked whether college theology's "proper end" is "perfection of the intellect, or a perfection of the will, or . . . both powers?" Whether it should focus upon "speculative knowledge . . . of things to be contemplated: [or] practical . . . knowledge of action to be performed." Finally he asked whether "scientific" or "humanistic" better describes the task. "Scientific" refers to a theology based upon an Aristotelean-informed "philosophy, especially metaphysics," exemplified in the *Summa Theologica*. "Humanistic" relies upon "insights and methods of the humanities" utilizing a wide variety of sources from early Church writings to "some modern attempts at biblical theology." Ackeren insisted that whatever approach is chosen, the course must form the intellect as part of an "academic curriculum" rather than an extension of a sodality.[11] His commitment to the intellect reflects the Thomistic framework that shaped the humanistic as well as the metaphysical approach.

Gerald Van Ackeren's identification of a humanistic approach with "biblical theology" is not idiosyncratic. John F. McDonnell, O.P., St. Rose Priory, Dubuque, delivered a paper the next year entirely focused on scriptures' emerging significance in college theology as a text to be read for "its theological meaning, not merely for its literary interest, nor its apologetic questions, nor other subsidiary reasons."[12] Scriptures' importance only continued to grow throughout the late 1950s. By 1961, Gustave Weigel could mention in passing "a humanistic presentation of the revealed message of God" as central to college theology courses in his 1961 address on trends in ecclesiology.[13]

Another implication of this emphasis on a humanistic approach is theology's increased potential for impact across the college curriculum—a role that philosophy had previously played. The third convention offered a focus on integrating theology into the sciences, history, and philosophy, though in each case, the discipline to be integrated with theology maintained a certain autonomy.[14] The next year, in 1958, Edwin G. Kaiser, C.P.S., from St. Joseph's College, Indiana, proposed "social theology," an integration of the social sciences with the sacred science. Theology here "orders the whole of lesser science in relation to the divine truths." Christianity's ability to adapt to different social contexts reinforced its cultural autonomy. Kaiser wrote, "If there is no timeless Christianity, there is also no essentially time-bound or culture-bound Christianity. No cultural form is essentially Catholic, none essentially uncatholic." The changing circumstances of past civilizations should instruct "social scientists who are so readily misled by the religion of material-social betterment, that the Church of the future is not the religion of progress by salvation of man through man, for this is the great sin of modern man."[15] Humanism's limits, at least for Kaiser, remained clear.

This search for integration broadens and intensifies in the midst of the Second Vatican Council. In his 1963 talk, "Christian Existence in the Church and the Contemporary World," Augustin Léonard, O.P., depicted a "new Christian humanism" not limited to "the liberal arts" but including "the total historical experience of men, personal and social, scientific and technical, economic and political." Bearing some resemblance to the religion of progress that Kaiser criticized, this new humanism originated from "the creativity, the beauty and the autonomy of created beings, of their activities, their work and their achievements." Its effects may include "a new spirituality, . . . a new Christian education" that "does not forget the Cross, but endures the passion as a dialectic passage towards a rebirth and a resurrection." Léonard mentioned space exploration specifically as an activity that may foster "a second and mature naïveté, a new faculty for wonder and awe." He acknowledged challenges from the "generalized criticism" inherent in "the modern or postmodern mind" and from "pluralism" militating against "a point of convergence, a common ground, an ecumenical reason of accepting pluralism itself." The Catholic Church has an opportunity to offer itself to the world as that point of convergence, "as a communion of faith and love made tangible in an historical community" that also transcends any particular period or "civilization." The church "is not the property of any human power, but God's property, and therefore without frontiers and truly universal."[16] Léonard's expansive vision of Christianity's engagement with the world foreshadows that in *Gaudium et Spes* and raises tantalizing, though not easily answerable, questions about the SCCTSD members' exploration of the "new theology" with their peers and students prior to the council.

BIBLICAL THEOLOGY GOES TO COLLEGE

"Biblical theology" offered the most compelling alternative, at the time, to scholastic theology and provided an unquestionably traditional, normative source for a new vision of the church in the world. This theologically oriented approach is not equivalent to contemporary biblical studies but did rely upon historical-critical approaches to dislodge scripture passages from their more familiar apologetical use. In 1958, the first year in which general sessions treated theological topics per se, one of three sessions featured a Catholic biblical scholar, David M. Stanley, S.J., discussing "The Divinity of Christ in Hymns of the New Testament." His careful analysis of the Christological hymns in Philippians, I Timothy, and Ephesians introduced SC-CTSD members to moderate applications of form criticism. Assuming his audience's familiarity with biblical criticism, Stanley claimed it "hardly necessary" to note "the superlative value of this most ancient testimony to the divinity of Christ and its effectiveness in presenting his dogma to college students of religion."[17] Father Stanley assumed the historical verity of Gospel accounts of the miraculous.

The value proved less than self-evident to some in the audience who had serious concerns about the approach's deleterious impact on scriptures' use in apologetics. Stanley made "a practical pedagogical point" to counter their objections. Students must learn how using "the gospels apologetically, as mere historical documents" renders them "a pale shadow of what they really are."[18] Others questioned the "pedagogical prudence" of exposing undergraduates to Stanley's biblical material for fear of fostering "doubt on the proof value of traditional texts"; still others expressed surprise in learning that "the apostles did not realize the divinity of Christ during His public life." Some did welcome Stanley's informing them "of recent trends in scriptural scholarship" and providing an opportunity for "facing realistically these inevitable exegetical difficulties" in a "Catholic environment." A few noted how modern biblical criticism highlighted "the need for renewed stress on the magisterium of the Church as the proximate norm of faith." Stanley, however, reiterated that faith is a "complex process" and "not the result of a syllogism: this is true, but that is true, ergo Christ is divine."[19] Scripture, when properly understood, assisted the faith process. Evidently concerns remained. At the Lake Erie regional meeting the following February, discussion on the relevancy of biblical scholarship elicited a tale of alarm. An attendee spoke of an acquaintance "fresh from the Biblical School in Jerusalem—who maintains that the new scriptural views would invalidate St. Thomas' teaching on the knowledge of God!"[20]

Only two years later, SCCTSD hosted three more Catholic biblical scholars representing "the best modern Scriptural scholarship." Bruce Vawter, C.M., provided a lecture on "Genesis and the College Teacher of Sacred Doctrine." John McKenzie, S.J., considered "Messianism and the College Teacher of Sacred Doctrine," and Caroll Stuhlmueller, C.P., gave instruction on "The Use of Old Testament Liturgy in Teaching College Sacred Doctrine." Each utilized moderate, modern methods for interpreting scripture that *Divino afflante Spiritu* not only allowed but encouraged. In his opening remarks, Vawter recollected that considering "the very meaning of Genesis" in such a meeting would have been unthinkable only a generation ago. He believed "a real revolution" had occurred, resulting in our being "much more unsure of ourselves," an attitude Vawter welcomed. He insisted that his historical approach need not scandalize students and identified "a misguided fundamentalism" that divorces "faith and reason" as far more likely to give scandal.[21] In discussing "messianism" from the Old through the New Testament, John McKenzie, S.J., affirmed that the "Gospel narratives [provide] . . . a true representation of that reality which was Jesus Christ," but stated quite bluntly that "the traditional apologetic messianism has no place in a modern course of theology." When asked, McKenzie affirmed reading Bultmann as "my duty" and "my pleasure." He then added, "I do hope that I read him critically." When asked when a "published synthesis of biblical scholars' theories" might appear, McKenzie's response was "never." The threat is "to be frozen by another textbook, another authority," and he noted that "at the moment some of us are fed up with authorities." McKenzie's enthusiasm for "modern biblical studies" as a "moving living thing" meant avoiding a single normative text.[22]

Other biblical scholars focused more explicitly on scripture as a lens through which to view the contemporary life of the church. Carroll Stuhlmueller utilized historical-critical methods to examine "the liturgy of the Old Testament." In his concluding remarks, Stuhlmueller suggested that "frequent references to Old Testament liturgy in college religion courses will impart a prayerful spirit to Biblical studies." Students might connect ancient Israel's faith with their own. "The vocation of being God's Chosen People will retain its glorious ideals, yet at the same time it will be seen as a practical reality"—practical because of the practice of the liturgy.[23] The following year, Barnabas Mary Ahern, C.P., examined "The Concept of the Church in Biblical Thought." He explicitly challenged liberal Protestants like Adolph Harnack and Albert Schweitzer who "treat the Church as a foundling fathered by an ingenious primitive community and laid on the doorstep of an unsuspecting Christ." Ahern then defended scripture, especially the Acts of the Apostles and Pauline corpus, as a source of "the basic elements of the Church's organization, the rationale of its disciplinary activity, and the richly eminent source of its divine life and teaching." When asked whether the expectation of an "imminent Parousia" is "a cause of embarrassment today," Ahern emphasized the "practical value of Paul's teaching" that allowed for imagining a "total renovation not merely of man but of the whole world." Today, this "renovation" translates into "true Christian Humanism" exemplified in international development projects identified as "doing our part to make the world move forward to its glorious apotheosis at the Parousia." Ahern's humanism echoed the thought of Jacques Maritain and Christopher Dawson not to mention certain aspirations of U.S. foreign policy.[24] This eschatological turn also anticipated the soon-to-be ubiquitous appeal to the "Kingdom of God" as defining Christianity's relation to the world.

At the 1962 annual meeting, another biblical scholar, relatively new on the scene, the Sulpician, Father Raymond E. Brown examined "The Eucharist and Baptism in St. John." Even this brief paper displays Brown's signature style with its careful textual analysis in examining two pericopes, his measured use of historical criticism, his knowledge of the secondary literature, and his attention to Catholic theological concerns, in this case, an affirmation of the church's sacramental life. His extensive footnotes confirm Brown's facility with contemporary biblical scholars' debates and exemplifies the academic benefits anticipated by those who argued for abrogating the index of forbidden books. Unlike David Stanley's 1959 presentation, no one apparently voiced alarm over student exposure to historical-critical methods, though the March *Magister* included a warning preceding the bibliography offered in preparation for Brown's talk: "Caution: this bibliography contains a spectrum of views on the sacramentality on John, including extremes [e.g., Bultmann and Cullmann]. Catholics are asterisked."[25]

With R. A. F. MacKenzie's examination of "The Scriptural Foundations of the Christian Life" in 1963, the necessity of integrating scripture studies into college theology seemed to be taken for granted. The critical shift is to the reading of the text in itself, "first, as for instruction." Reading the text "tends to form a habit of thought and judgment which puts God in the center and refers all things to him." MacKenzie considered "the consolation of the Scriptures" as the basis for convincing students to "make the reading of the Scriptures a part of the[ir] religious life."[26]

The emphasis on placing oneself within the biblical narrative as suggested in Stuhlmueller's approach to Old Testament liturgy or Ahern's description of the "true Christian humanism" or MacKenzie's "habit of thought" is carried into historical studies, particularly of the early church. The Jesuit Edward Kilmartin, from Weston College, considered patristic views of the sacraments. He linked the early church's embrace of "sacramental sanctification" as in continuity with scripture where "the economy of salvation is presented as a process of redemption still in progress." The baptized enter "into the history of salvation." Like so many other Catholic theologians in the early 1960s, Kilmartin used history to signify "a dynamic character for the People of God who remain under the sign of the pas encore." The language suggested ongoing change, both personal and communal, that reaches into the present.[27]

HISTORICAL STUDIES; LITURGICAL MOVEMENTS

Walter J. Burghardt, S.J., at the tenth annual meeting, goes to the heart of the matter in posing the question: "The Fathers of the Church: Obsolete or Relevant?" Though his affirmation of the Fathers' relevance probably came as no surprise, what is interesting is introducing the either/or choice at all. Burghardt identified five areas in which early church writings prove useful. They are "history, liturgy, Scripture, homiletics, and ecumenism." He found above all "the advantage of patristic theology is its warmth and its vitality; and it is warm and vital because of its method and its objective. Its method? The word of God. Its objective? The salvation of men." To study "the Fathers," Burghardt suggested, is to provide a significant contribution to the question "'Where do you come from?'" To provide even a partial answer to that question allows further reflection on developments in Christian understanding of God's word and our salvation.[28]

Burghardt's list confirmed the importance of scripture and history in the reshaping of college theology and rightly mentioned others of great significance: liturgy and ecumenism. The liturgical movement was well established in the United States at the time of SCCTSD's founding. As already noted, the Society's own liturgical practices reflected the gradual changes that culminated in the Second Vatican Council's Constitution on Sacred Liturgy. Mass attendance played such a significant role in Catholic lives during this period that one can easily comprehend why these changes garnered so much attention. At an Upper New York regional meeting, 19 October 1958, discussion about liturgy indicated uncertainty about the longevity of liturgical reforms. Participants speculated whether Pius XII's passing would mark the demise of "developments in the Liturgical Movement." Most thought such a possibility doubtful given how well established certain changes were. They pointed to recent transitions in "mandatory" Holy Week celebration, Easter Vigil in particular, in which compliance "no longer exists as a problem." Evidently enforcement effected success. "Little by little, Rome is solving our problems by making obligatory for the whole Church what up until now has not been put upon this level of decree." Several anecdotes at this regional meeting celebrated the laity's acceptance of the Dialogue Mass, now a regular feature in some parishes and college chapels since the practice of attendees responding in Latin along with the altar boys no longer required permission.[29]

Liturgy is frequently identified as critical to students' theological formation. Arnold Tkacik, O.S.B., from Saint John's in Collegeville, where the U.S. liturgical movement originated, considered the "Practical Liturgical Formation as the Complement to Sacramental Theology" at the 1962 convention. He described liturgical participation as theological instruction's "corresponding experience to its members as a people of God." Introducing themes usually associated with the later 1960s, Tkacik explained how "rebellion is necessary for growth" and how communal singing can "crystallize purpose and conviction. Such songs have a mystique of their own." Liturgy's power of "formation" is located in "creating the consciousness of a community with a historical destiny and a commitment to that destiny in the shaping and transforming of history." The Christian's destiny is "the Kingdom of God [which] is constantly being shaped out of the City of Man." Liturgy plays a critical role in "preserv[ing] the vital stream of life by which this is accomplished."[30]

Another Benedictine, Sister Mary Anthony Wagner, from the College of Saint Benedict's, St. Joseph, Minnesota, extended liturgy's influence into theological work itself. Her 1963 talk has historical significance within the Society. It was the first major theological presentation delivered by a woman at the national meeting, though women had previously provided substantive contributions to panels or in small special interest sessions. Her focus, the "Christian Life in the Mystery of the Church," drew from Pius XII's encyclicals on the Mystical Body and liturgy as well as the recently promulgated conciliar document. Drawing from Thomistic theology as well as contemporary ecclesiology and sacramental theology, she outlined the integration of a "theological treatment of the Liturgy" into the study of theology as key to "a more positive moral theology." She challenged her peers to create a "living Summa Theologica, such as the great and inimitable St. Thomas did for his day."[31]

In 1964, two other presentations focused on the way in which liturgy, especially the Eucharist, ought to inform college theology or any form of religious education. Bernard Cooke emphasized the interrelationship between scripture and sacrament especially in the Eucharist. In this sacramental action, students may come to "have this experience" of Christian faith, "'an encounter with Christ.'" What was critical to this project was providing students some guidance in scripture studies. "Only Scripture is an explanation profound enough and yet simple enough to feed their minds and their faith and their charity for the remainder of their Christian life." The vitality of this sacramental encounter must be communicated to the students without sacrificing the intellectual.[32] Gerard Sloyan specifically focused on "The Constitution on the Sacred Liturgy and Prayer-Life in the College." Sloyan argued for the definitive quality of "liturgy, chiefly the eucharistic action." It serves as "the *fons* and *culmen* of all the Church's activity, so the common prayer of a college is the test of whether her existence is justified precisely as Christian, precisely as Catholic, since so many things that go on in a Catholic college could be as well done elsewhere."[33] Liturgical practice informs not only individual students, but the entire campus community, setting it apart from other institutions of higher learning.

The focus on scripture, history, and liturgy together with a new awareness of ecumenism led to a reconsideration of "church." The annual meeting under Bernard Cooke's presidency had as its focus ecclesiology within a context of ecumenical dialogue. Gustave Weigel, S.J., reviewed the "Present Status of Catholic Ecclesiology." General consensus at the time was to view "the Church as essentially and primarily a mystical entity wherein the believer truly but analogously shares in the human nature of the existing God Man, Jesus Christ, risen from the dead." Reminiscent of McKenzie's and Vawter's aversion to normative textbooks in biblical studies, Weigel cautioned that the current situation demands that "each ecclesiologist must construct his own version of ecclesiology. He cannot rely on a textbook tradition," and he left no doubt that ecclesiology is being transformed.[34] The Society's members also welcomed two especially notable guests, John Meyendorff, who described the "Contemporary Orthodox Concept of the Church," and Lutheran Walter Leibrecht, who provided a Protestant's perspective.[35] The special interests sessions allowed for continued dialogue with Meyendorff and Leibrecht.[36]

DOCTRINAL DEVELOPMENT AND MAGISTERIAL AUTHORITY

The unsettled state of theology even prior to the council led some to look to the magisterium for guidance and stability. John Hardon, S.J., specifically addressed the relationship between "The Church's Magisterium and College Fundamental Theology." He began with a startling item of data. Between 1878 and 1957, 160 encyclicals had been promulgated—approximately one every six months. Hardon then considered the "*implications of the Church's living magisterium.*" The increased "emphasis on the authority of papal encyclicals and the Church's right to spell out the applications of the natural law" arose from a "new insight" about "Christian tradition." It is "identified more and more with the Church's magisterium and less exclusively as the genetic source, along with Scripture, of the deposit of faith." The magisterium serves as "perpetual interpreter of that faith in every age to the end of time. . . . [as] the vital function of the living organism." Hardon identified this particular use of the teaching office as a new expression of its power.[37] In discussing the role of the magisterium at a 1959 Lake Erie regional meeting two years after Hardon's presentation, Father Peterson laid out a string of consequences that began with the denial of the church's teaching authority and led inexorably to the denial of God's existence and then our own.[38] Later that same year, affirmation of magisterial teaching at the national meeting also elicited a cautionary remark "that with all this stress on authority, it was necessary also to encourage individual thinking." A clarification noted that "individual thinking" was not equivalent to "unguided speculation."[39]

If Hardon is correct and the magisterium is a *"living,"* organic reality, then it becomes the primary agent of doctrinal development. Catholic University's Edmond D. Benard opened his remarks on "The Development of Doctrine: A Basic Framework" with mention of the "present Holy Father" and his recently announced plans for a council. Benard granted the magisterium "the dominant and what we have called the constitutive role in doctrinal development." Theologians serve in the "role of the contributory elements" especially in confirming the doctrine's appearance in the sources.[40] In the work group sessions immediately following, "several members admitted that they had never realized the extensive implications for the teaching of college theology in the problem of the development of Catholic doctrine." One group even considered and then rejected the possibility of "doctrinal regression." Echoing concerns related to scriptures, several wondered "whether the problem of doctrinal development should be taught in the college theology course, and if so, when and how." The summary noted "that, like theologians, its members would be seeking the answers to these difficulties for a long time to come in the pursuit of their teaching vocation."[41] This clear distinction here between the theology teacher and the theologian meant at this juncture that the college teacher's role as theologian remained inchoate.

The college theology teacher was certainly not "seeking the answers to these difficulties" in an isolated ecclesial context. The changing nature of higher education itself had its impact on college theology. One has only to consider the increase in those attending college, veterans of World War II, and the children of a growing Catholic middle class. College played a key role in the education of a professional class who embraced the postwar drive to consensus as "America" became more clearly defined against the Soviet threat. In response to the changing circumstances, the third president, Father Thomas Donlan, O.P., presented several contemporary "heresies" threatening the integrity of teaching sacred doctrine whose "entire history" has been "a heroic struggle against compromise." Pelagianism, defined as "an over-reliance upon techniques and material instrumentalities," highlights a commodification of higher education. This trend is evident in "decreasing emphasis upon the liberal arts and the humanities . . . [and] proliferation of courses that produce graduates who are over-trained and under-educated. Prospective students are offered brochures that ape the products of Madison Avenue." To resist compromise, in this case, demands that sacred doctrine remain "an intrinsic element in the education we offer."[42] This concern in 1957 stands in contrast to those discussed in Catholic University professor Robert

Hovda's paper entitled "Pastoral Assessment of the College Product" delivered only five years later at the District of Columbia–Baltimore 1962 regional gathering. The "product" here is a "new Christian" meaning "wholly committed and authentically lay" in its secular dimension. "The kerygma of good news and contemporary human needs must be presented, and the student must be shown how to harmonize religious and secular currents in establishing the Kingdom of God here and now."[43] Harmonizing the religious and secular seems a far cry from the "heroic struggle against compromise."

SACRED DOCTRINE FOR ATOMIC-AGE STUDENTS

Brother Alban used the occasion of the Society's fifth anniversary to reflect explicitly on the state of Catholic higher education and its impact on college theology as an academic discipline. Looking to the relatively recent past, he recalled the "sad anomaly" of Catholic institutions treating the "Queen of the Sciences" as "the ragged orphan of the academic household" with departments of theology the last to be organized formally. The SCCTSD effected significant change by pressing "the theology departments of virtually every Catholic college in the nation" into discussions about their curriculum content and faculty preparation. Turning to the present, Brother Alban invoked the "appearance of Sputnik in the heavens" which startled Americans into realizing "that some notable deficiencies were chargeable to our educational system." Catholic institutions especially "labor under the reputation for academic mediocrity." Citing a *Newsweek* article, "Catholic Soul Searching," the Christian brother recounted the article's main point—"that you and I earn our keep by running a kind of glorified high school home-room program wherein our main function is to preside over the recitation of answers from a blown-up edition of the catechism." Brother Alban countered that college theology is now "a serious and scientific discipline, comparable in its intellectual excellence with its sister departments." In light of recent progress and continued commitment to excellence in theological education, Brother Alban concluded in "a spirit of high optimism born of Christian hope that the Lord will be ever near to second our endeavors in the spread of his Kingdom on Earth."[44]

By way of contrast, Brother C. Luke Salm, F.S.C., provided a sobering look at "The Status of Theology in the College" at the tenth national meeting. He described his presentation as a "collective examen." He rehearsed some familiar challenges including theology's enduring lack of academic status. Certain regions still refused to grant credit to theology courses; administrators refused to hire well-trained faculty; colleagues viewed with suspicion theology faculty who were not broadly trained. The glimmer of hope was the increase in lay teachers who committed themselves to college theology, but their possession of doctorates remained unusual.

The other challenge, according to Salm, was the contemporary students who "resist the element of authority that theology must use." He suggested permitting student questions, listening, and replying "with some genuine questions of our own instead of trying to rephrase their questions so as to leap in right away with a pre-fabricated answer." For an effective "dialogue" between teacher and student, "questions on both sides must be real." He also suggested offering "courses in comparative religion and non-Catholic thought." The ultimate goal is recognizable—"to bring this transitional generation of American college students to commitment in Christ." Yet, his final comment, a prayer really, suggested such a goal to be elusive. "May God grant above all that our mission in the Church be truly a way of bringing His salvation to the world and the world of our crazy mixed-up collegians back to Him."[45]

Brother Luke Salm was hardly the first to raise questions and offer suggestions about the college theology teacher's impact on the student. As early as 1956, some considered inciting students to be critical not only of secular affairs but also of ecclesial ones. The second annual meeting featured a panel discussion concerning student formation. Father Lancelot G. Atsch, O.S.B., from St. John's in Collegeville, Minnesota, offered caricatures of ineffective teaching types: "the 'blackboard happy' teacher" who values orderly presentations; "the 'moralizer'" who fails to treat students as adults; and "the 'authoritarian'" who makes simple appeals to authority. The preferred alternative, "the 'stimulator,'" conveys "great respect for the student made in God's image and endowed by nature and grace with the powers of knowing and loving." This teacher becomes "like Christ on the road to Emmaus" with the students who respond to questions and reveal "what goes on in their minds." With this knowledge, the teacher can "begin to thaw out the store of abstract doctrine." Atsch intended to form students who are "prudently disturbed about the right things such as the enforced role of silent spectator at community worship." Students learn "indignation at the prevailing low conditions of religious and liturgical art . . . [and] tolerance for modern attempts at its reform. Indignation can be a far nobler virtue than complaisance."[46] Such formation might feed more than prudential dissatisfaction. Three years later, the working group session included discussions of conflicts between pastors and informed laity. Pastors expect laity to organize bingo or participate in the sodality or the youth organization. "The laymen are given roles only begrudgingly, often temporary, and far below what they were trained to perform and expect." Clergy treat enthused laity "as interfering" and seldom allow them to teach.[47]

The educated layperson, in this case, attends to intraecclesial reforms rather than external "secular" transformation.

Serving on the same panel as Father Atsch, Sister Mary Charles Borromeo insisted upon theology's content and pedagogy overcoming any "dichotomy which secularistic attitudes set up between religious truths and daily practice." In contrast to a more cautious approach, Sister Mary Charles sought a blurring of boundaries between students and teachers since all "are human beings, members of Christ now in 1956." They share a common project, "working toward a full Christian humanism in their own lives and in the gradual development and adaptations in their school." Only the teacher who "works vitally with students' needs in the area of real life, as, for instance through contact with liturgical and apostolic activities" can effect this interchange.[48] In a sense, the secular has entered the world of the religious, and those distinct spheres of influence for religious and laity merge in Sister Mary Charles Borromeo's description.

Francis M. Keating, S.J., from St. Peter's College in Jersey City, also speaking at that convention emphasized a different and more familiar Catholic view of the secular in 1956. In examining college theology in light of the "finality of the Layman," he insisted that the secularism the laity faces is "an organized paganism" or, more disturbingly, "a new system of salvation, setting its own goals for man, using its own means to reach its end, inevitably shaping man's destiny"—a view shared by many Catholic officials from the period. The laity had an organized alternative, "Catholic Action," which was "the modern Church's social and cultural program for mankind." This papal-generated initiative, with Pius XII as its most recent champion, permits the "Catholic layman" to participate "in the universal redemptive work of Christ the Priest" based upon "the inner configuration and power of the sacramental characters of baptism and confirmation." Borrowing from the applied sciences, Keating described "reading of Scripture, liturgical participation, initiation into contemplative prayer, essays in apostolic aid activities, e.g., programs of witness and enterprises of effective sympathy for human beings in misery" as "laboratory sessions."[49] The layman's "finality" remains in the practical— "the *economy*, i.e., the redemptive plan in which Christ is central, . . . [rather] than the *theology*, i.e. the knowledge of God in Himself." The creation of such curriculum "must haunt 'the midnight meditation and the noon repose' of the college teacher of sacred doctrine. But while it is haunting, it is also our glory. The world will not be brought to Christ without our Christian layman. Our Christian layman will not be formed for his role without the shaping influence of sacred doctrine."[50] He could have easily continued the logic to a focus on the teacher's necessary role in the layperson's learning sacred doctrine.

Brother Alban's 1960 presidential address revisited the standard account of a theology of the laity. Tapping into deep Roman Catholic sensibilities, Brother Alban used "pontifex," as an appropriate designation for "the educated Catholic layman, for he, rather than the professional theologian, can function as the bridge builder between the Church and the secular world." His access "in the apostolate of higher education" is greater than that of "the hierarchy, the parish priest or the religious." John XXIII's call for a "General Council" with an anticipated focus on Christian unity made the need for an educated laity that much greater. Brother Alban then launched into criticism of courses that lack academic rigor as well as those that possess little appeal to undergraduates. He placed "sacred doctrine courses" in an "open market" where other courses "have a much higher selling index" because they are directly related to "livelihood." Even a sacred doctrine "course must yet be adopted to the temper of the fast-changing world which is our atomic age, its concepts must be native to the climate of thinking that marks modern man, they must be couched in language with which he is at home and at ease." Its ultimate goal, however, remains "the habitus of theology" so that students "learn to think consistently and constantly about all being, of the transcendent God and of His creatures, in terms of a few master principles that have been formed into a well-knit integral system" and that can be applied in a multitude of situations. Such an integration requires "a worthy, meaningful use of Holy Scripture" utilizing "the best modern Scriptural scholarship." Alban challenged his audience to propel college theology into "first-class intellectual citizenship in the academic community" as well as into "the outlook and the real-life needs of the flesh-and-blood students." The results, "a genuine theology for the layman. . . . would be nothing short of revolutionary in American Catholic education."[51] Brother Alban's talk received coverage in the *Chicago Sun-Times*, 19 April 1960. The article highlighted the laity's emerging importance as "the bridge builder between the church and the secular world" and noted the "blame" laid on Catholic colleges for not making "the same intellectual demands in theology courses."[52]

Two years later, Bernard Cooke, S.J., in his presidential address, challenged his audience to bring their students to the point where "they can think in biblical categories and words about all major points of Christian revelation" as a way to "automatically be conditioning our students for ecumenical discussion." Finally, he called his fellow teachers to "understanding the Church as an historically developing reality," and to lead students toward a commitment to "Sacramental living." He concluded with a note of confidence in the Society's ability to make "an important effort towards educating Catholics who will witness with mature faith in a twentieth-century world, Catholics whose understanding and love will hasten the desired day of Christian union."[53] Cooke's assessment assured that the Society's work had only just begun.

MAKERS OF SOULS?

Many topics that preoccupied the Society in its first decade, from the vantage point of present perspective, may appear alternatively quaint, naive, or amusing—a world apart from the academic study of theology now located in Catholic colleges and universities. From another vantage point, that of historical retrospective, these early years provide evidence of strands of thinking that anticipated the vast changes that would occur in theology—who is teaching theology, what is being taught in theology, and why it is being taught. In retrospect, the Society's meetings became occasions for the undercurrents of change to surface. If questions and concerns swirled around new approaches to teaching, similar uncertainties attached to the college teacher of sacred doctrine.

Given expectations of students engaged in college theology, their teachers had to have comparable responsibilities. In the very first presidential address to the Society, Eugene Burke, C.S.P., conveyed "to its members a vital conviction of the sacred dignity and eternal importance of being ministers of the word of God in the classrooms." Such ministry demands "an ideal of true Catholic professional competence" which he later called "Christian craftsmanship"—teaching as practical wisdom. Yet, teaching theology requires more, it is "not just a profession but a rich and central and abiding Catholic vocation." One is called to be "not only a living channel whereby our Christian heritage is transmitted but a fashioner and maker of souls." This vocation requires an "enthusiasm that springs from conviction, is controlled by intelligence, marked by competence, blessed by patience and never loses sight of the fact that as Dante writes, 'the blessedness of this life consists in the proper exercise of man's power.'"[54] Burke certainly left little doubt about the theology teacher's potential influence on students' formation in faith.

Those who returned for the 1956 annual meeting at Notre Dame heard His Excellency, Bishop Pursley speak in terms as lofty as Burke's. He commended those before him, whom he assumed shared a "common faith," for their "dedication to a task which is, by its nature, a direct participation in the essential work of the Church, which cannot be fulfilled by the ordinary talents of ordinary teachers of ordinary curricular branches of learning." It is more than "merely a professional career but a vocation, a mission, a sacred office."[55] The language here suggests a quasi-official teaching role within the church. One can only speculate whether Pursley's language would have been more circumspect if the majority of Catholic college teachers of sacred doctrine before him had not been priests. Though in fairness to Pursley, he had supported women's theological education at Saint Mary's Graduate School of Sacred Theology operating in his diocese.

The Society's second president, John J. Fernan, S.J., reiterated Burke's and Pursley's points about "the uniqueness of this vocation and the enthusiasm it should engender." To be effective in the God-given task of providing students a "deepened, systematical, theological grasp of his faith," the teacher must not only study theology but "must continually study the living minds of his students, constantly searching for the right psychological approach, the right degree of treatment, the right words, the right examples, the right questions to open up the minds of this particular group of students and fill them with that degree of light which they are capable of receiving." So, for Fernan, "the enthusiasm of the teacher is not just an enthusiasm for the subject matter but a zealous enthusiasm for the student." This enthusiasm has little to do with projecting a charismatic personality. The enthusiasm John Fernan had in mind is "an inexhaustible capacity for plodding through homework assignments, correcting stupid mistakes, patiently explaining and re-explaining the obvious, in the face of one's own itch to get to the real depths of the problem." Fernan connected this "inexhaustible capacity" with that of Jesus "looking full into the face of His Father every time He taught the Apostles" or to St. Paul's labor pains for his gentile converts. "This 'being in labor' with our students in order to form the mind of Christ in them is the enthusiasm that our vocation demands."[56] Such lofty expectations remain attached to teaching theology long after the neo-scholastic confidence had dissipated.

The third president, Thomas Donlan, O.P., called upon "great and saintly theologians" to be "a source of strength in this struggle" against compromise. Donlan found in St. Thomas a clear delineation of what it means to be a teacher. "To teach someone is simply to lead him to knowledge." It is a "cooperative art like medicine . . . not an operative art like sculpture." Knowledge is "the indispensable qualification for teaching." The teacher, even of theology has neither the same power nor the same pastoral obligation of a bishop, who must display "eminent charity." Teaching requires those practices that improve and refine the art. "The credentials of our knowledge can be constantly validated by study; the art of communicating can be polished by self-criticism and intelligent practice; the patience and humor needed for the daily grind can be cultivated through charity; and merit can be gained through the mercy of instructing the ignorant."[57] Teaching becomes a practice in virtue, even a spiritual work of mercy.[58]

Subsequent debates, discussions, and arguments among members of the College Theology Society reflect many of the issues found in the addresses of the first three presidents and the bishop, all of whom consider the "Catholic college teacher of sacred doctrine." These issues include the theologian's relationship to the church and the academy, his or her responsibility to the student, the theologian's understanding of her or his own work as a profession and as a vocation, the theologian's determination of course content, and the relationship between theological studies and faith formation. At the celebration of the tenth convention, the president, Urban Voll, O.P., suggested that the teacher's role "may be something more than preachers, our real dignity lies rather in our participation in the Church's ministry of the word." This ministry received support in a Society that "has remained a free forum for all shades of Catholic opinion." The "practice of the teaching art is a work of mercy" directed to our students who happen to be "twentieth century American Catholics." Teaching must reflect "intelligent transposition to our actual situation, rather than slavish imitation missing the mark." Voll acknowledged the magnitude of the challenge and appealed to reliance on "Christian hope."[59]

In the mid-1950s, a major concern was making theology a credible academic discipline in college. These early addresses fluctuate between phrases associated with religious vocation and magisterial authority and the language found in that ubiquitous twentieth century movement, professionalization.[60] To note this fluctuation is not intended as a negative comment; rather it is intended to highlight the complex identity of those in the discipline of theology as it has developed beginning in the twentieth century. To win the appellation "professional" usually requires specialized training in the specific area in which one wishes to be known as competent. Competency is usually associated with educational credentials which then allow one to be hired for specific positions. As already noted, many of those assigned to teaching college theology had little specialized training in that field. Yet, by 1954, many Catholic college teachers no longer presumed that the vowed religious could teach theology by virtue of their religious formation. Like any other academic discipline, theology or sacred doctrine required a graduate degree. At the same time, the Society's founding members presumed that graduate training was not enough. Teaching theology was qualitatively different from teaching in any other discipline because theology touched at least indirectly on the student's faith in God and a commitment to the church as mediator of that faith. Effective teaching as Burke suggested ought to produce not only "right thinking" but also "right actions." Fernan called his colleagues even more boldly "to form the mind of Christ" in the students." And Donlan insisted on "docility to the Church and the truth." College theology thus had more than the usual share of competing demands on it as an academic discipline situated in an institution of higher education as a bridge between the academic and ecclesial.

The Society expended a lot of time and energy in trying to establish standards for the preparation of college theology teachers. An undated report,

"Training Brothers and Sisters to be Teachers of Theology on the College Level," demonstrates how rapidly the field of college theology was expanding.[61] A major question was whether curriculum-specific training, i.e., the "philosophical" or the "humanistic" adequately prepares teachers to answer "specialized questions" from "seminars and study clubs." Rather than specialization, the report opted for a comprehensive "core curriculum" including "fundamental theology, dogmatic theology, moral, pastoral and ascetical theology, Sacred Scripture, Liturgy, Catholic Action or the Modern Apostolate of the Layman." Supplemental courses cover the spectrum from "Modern Church history" to "the Papal Social Encyclicals and the entire social program of the Church" as well as the "marvelous modern advances in archaeology." Absent was the course on "apologetics" as well as "historical theology." The former became a course of the past, the latter one for the future. The report also affirmed the "modern moral-pastoral theologian" with "aware[ness] of an increasing dependence upon a first hand knowledge of such sciences as psychology, sociology, economics." "Languages" and other "related subjects" from music to missiology receive mention in ten additional items listed. The ambitious course of studies, though never realized in practice, demonstrates the unique challenge of teaching college theology where general theological knowledge appeared to have few disciplinary boundaries. A separate report, "Problems of Priest-Teachers of Sacred Doctrine at the College Level," echoed the criticism of John Montgomery Cooper three decades earlier. The scholastic approach of the "best seminary education" provides little preparation for teaching undergraduates.[62] In other words, priests teaching college theology need an instruction comparable to that outlined for everyone else teaching in the field.

Given that the Society had a founding mother, Sister Mary Rose Eileen Masterman, C.S.C., members assumed women's participation in teaching college theology. A 1959 discussion about the "mind of the church" in canon 490, for example, noted that in many cases "dispositions concerning religious even when expressed in the masculine gender apply equally to religious women.'" One could easily observe "that the faculty of theology is no longer the province and privilege of priests and monks alone." Women religious have increasingly important roles in "christianizing society in the U.S. and elsewhere." Brothers have taken on similar roles "in religious training of youth."[63] Some even suggested women's particular suitability to college theology as it was developing. Robert S. Pelton, C.S.C., compared women religious to Mary Magdalene, who "hasten to bear the good news of the risen Christ." Catechesis, now "often person-centered and intuitive, rather than rationally argumentative," suits women and makes sisters more effective in communicating to youth "the existentialism of salvation-action." Of course such an assessment of women's nonrational tendencies, even if intended as a compliment, endangered their participation as college teachers began to be "theologians" rather than "catechists."[64]

Richard Cardinal Cushing offered his own reflections on Catholic college teachers of sacred doctrine in a dinner address at the 1961 annual meeting in Boston. He opened with the image of the *alter Christus* who is "any Christian, who follows Christ, who reproduces Christ as far as is humanly possible." Cushing recognized the priest as Christ only in so far as he, like every other Christian, acts Christlike. To act as Christ requires college theology teachers to forego "standing at a lectern or sitting at a desk and presenting thesis after thesis from a book." What Cushing wanted conveyed is that "theology is something alive; it is living in the professor, it is part of his nature, degree or no degree in the subject." Cushing imagined the "ideal teacher . . . walk[ing] up and down the aisles of the classroom without a note, and giv[ing] his students what is part of his life, what is in his blood, not what is in a book." Such teaching would produce a well-formed laity.

Cushing then offered a remarkable description of laity who are no longer "on the outside looking in. . . . the laity of the future must be identified with and prepared for their responsibilities to the Catholic Church." To convince the laity that "they are that Church, just as much as any one of us" requires "bypass[ing] all the old bad traditions of the past." Educated laity must understand "that they are welcome into the scaffolding, into the structure of the Church, to go forth and teach, not as volunteers, but as paid workers." Cushing had Latin America in mind where "a well trained lay apostolate coming from our institutions of higher learning" could match the "zeal of the Protestants." To facilitate this work, Cushing argued for making a "place in the Church structure as we know it for the lay teacher. Why cannot we have lay deacons, lay deaconesses who can function for the welfare of souls in every possible way save through the purely sacerdotal functions?" He ended on a note of great hope calling upon teachers of sacred doctrine to provide such qualified workers.[65]

FROM RESTORATION TO TRANSLATION

John XXIII, of course, made clear his desire for the laity's full participation in the life of the church. The previously mentioned 1962 presidential address of Bernard Cooke gave just due to that year's impending major event, at least for those teaching sacred doctrine. Cooke could hardly have known how accurately he had judged his own historical moment when he declared, "With the opening of the second Vatican Council in October we will witness one of the key events of our twentieth century." He identified "two tasks at least" in John XXIII's statements—"that of working seriously toward the reunion of Christians, and that of bringing the expression of the Church's life more closely into contact with our contemporary world."

The remainder of Cooke's presidential address seems equally prescient in its articulation of themes that will preoccupy most Catholic theologians in their writing and in teaching for at least the next two decades. Citing Genesis, Cooke called his audience to affirm "the world is good, and that man is good"; he then drew the conclusion "that man is meant to master his world, to bring it under subjection." Such a conclusion reflected an American confidence in progress through development coupled with a conviction in the transformative power of God's grace. Addressing them as teachers, Cooke called upon the Society's members to "prepare our students to see the reality of this [Christ's] redemption operative in the men and structures of our day." Their preparation must ensure their ability to seize "the breath-taking opportunities of our times"; so they can "build a world worthy of man who is a son of God." Their task is to "translate the vision of faith into society and culture." In the single word "translate," Cooke indicated a shift in understanding the layperson's engagement in the world. The laity no longer were called to "restore all things to Christ," but to "translate the vision" to make it intelligible to the world as it was found. Cooke's vision contained elements contrary to those found in Cardinal Cushing's description of a lay apostolate.

Cooke expanded on translating, identifying specific "symbolisms of our contemporary world" that the "Church must validate and complement." "The modern city" symbol of human achievement is contrasted with the "suburbs." "Man" escapes the city's "rush and competition" for the "suburbs," that compilation of wealth and creature comforts and distractions that promises "happiness." The search for human freedom finds expression in the "politically free society" as well as the more ambiguous "machine." His final example is "the beautiful woman: a symbol that is so ambiguous in our society, a symbol of promised love and happiness, yet often a symbol of deep human betrayal." These and many more reveal "deep human hopes and longings" that cannot be eliminated, but may find the promise of fulfillment through the church as "the Sacrament of our day," just as it will lead the way in responding to the growing desire for "true unity of mankind."[66]

A sacramentally inspired theology had its champions among the neo-Thomists as well. James Egan presented "Contemporary Approach to Sacramental Grace," with special attention to "the question of the presence of the mysteries of Christ in the sacramental reality of the Church and the immediacy of his action." Despite his reservations about certain contemporary sacramental theology including Edward Schillebeeckx's, Egan's Thomism did offer imaginative space. Invoking the image associating God with "Light," "inaccessible," or "blinding," he then described the sacraments as a "prism" that "bathes the faithful in myriad colors and shades of color, for the manifestation of the glory of God's light and to prepare them to shine like the sun in the Kingdom of the Father." He continued with a reflection of the sacraments' ripple effects in light of God's creative power—first lavished on the individual, "each child, each member, each citizen, each stone, must be carefully fashioned," then shared in "the mystic body, the people of God, the temple" making them "common goods," and thus "diviner goods, giving greater glory to God." A people so formed "must look outward to the world, to all those who imperfectly, or not at all, are children, members, citizens, stones." This latter animated "a vast mission to proclaim the good news to all men." Egan then considered each of the seven sacraments in light of this framework.

He made specific suggestions for modifying practice including adolescent reception of confirmation and a more self-consciously communal rather than private reception of Eucharist to signify "the unity of the Mystical Body." He invoked "the incineration of six million children of the Old Israel and the ashes of Hiroshima and Nagasaki" along with the "threat of a deluge of nuclear destruction" to highlight the extent to which "we, the people of God, need the sacrament grace of penance." Egan expressed a hope that John XXIII would call upon "every Catholic to receive the sacrament of penance before the opening of the Council." The special purpose would be the confession of "any guilt, however hidden, that he and all the members of the Church for the last thousand years have had in bringing about and continuing the great schisms in the Church." He ended invoking "the words of the liturgy, 'Oh God, who renewest the world by thy ineffable sacraments. . . .'" Egan's scholastic framework hardly diminished his sense of the mysterious and communal quality of the sacramental life and allowed him to relate that sense to his immediate surroundings.[67]

SPERABAMUS!

"Hope" appeared to be the watchword for the Society in 1962 and 1963. The October 1962 *Magister* opened with references to "a year of hope . . . of egregious hope, of absurd optimism." Such is the effect of John XXIII whose "infectious enthusiasm" ought to impact "teachers of Sacred Doctrine" and their students. In a radio address, "The Holy Father explicitly witnesses to his own conviction that for the first time in history an ecumenical council of the

Church will truly represent the entire inhabited world."[68] The 1963 *Proceedings* opened with the exclamation, *Sperabamus!* "We were hoping!" as Urban Voll's opening line of "Easter Monday—Liturgical Homily." The challenges of teaching remain. Voll described, "our disappointments—colds and stomach trouble, mountainous piles of exams in place of hair shirts and disciplines." To teach is "a great act of faith." Rather than "saints and doctors sitting at our feet receiving the Word with joy and keeping it, we often find stony ground, brambles and birds of the air." Voll found his hope at the end of the road to Emmaus—in the Eucharist. "Here we truly recognize Jesus risen, living and present. Once this is achieved, Jesus disappears. Our crosses do not always disappear with Him, but we find a new courage to bear them."[69]

Voll's presidential address, "The Present State of Christian Moral Teaching" focused not on hope but on "the problem of labels." He reflected on "an age of crisis and change" where "tradition is old; the future is vital, youthful, new." Labels reiterate this view with distinctions made between "conservatives and liberals, the right and the left, and even the closed door and the open mouth." Voll provided other labels. He described "the new Pharisee: static, oblivious of the ambient culture, living in a ghetto." His opponent, "the Sadducee is avid for novelty, eagerly accepting the latest, not because it is always better, but because it is exciting." This uncritical embrace of the novel "courts disaster—the shipwreck of the faith." Voll's alternative is not the "middle-of-the-road policy," given the contemporary challenge to moral teaching. "Our students seem to encounter not only Jehovah's Witness armed with bible on the front porch, but inside, at the cocktail party, the cultivated sophisticate armed with Fletcher's Morals and Medicine." After citing Pius XII's condemnation of situation ethics, John XXIII's call for better Christian education in *Pacem in terris*, and Garry Wills quoting John Henry Newman in the *National Review*, Voll admitted that no clear solution emerges. "But the study and teaching of the image of God in action, like other parts of theology, require hard work." The Dominican ended with praise for Thomas Aquinas's brilliance in moral theology but finds more relevant that though we may not share his genius, we do share in the Divine help that gave Aquinas the confidence to begin his great theological work.[70]

Among the special interest sessions on "Christian Life in Contemporary Society" are the comments of Mother Emmanuel McIver, O.S.U., celebrating the council's initiating "great and much-hoped for changes." The church no longer exists in "passive irrelevance" but its activities in "renewal and reform has captured the imaginations of Christians everywhere." Key to this "capture" is "the universality made possible by television, radio, and the press." The council provided much to report as "ideas that for years had been frowned upon and met with suspicion broke through with astounding force" thanks to theologians like "Fathers Congar, Chenu, Danielou, du Lubac, and Karl Rahner." Such changes are required in an era when "Man sees himself as incarnate freedom in an open universe with the creative task of humanizing it." Human freedom is historically conditioned but not entirely determined since humans "can make history." McIver urged college teachers to "have something to say about the hunger in the world, about such questions as the racial problem, the armaments race, and the emancipation of women." She suggested following the example of "our Holy Father himself, so fully human, so humble, so loving and wise." John XXIII demonstrated in his life the possibilities of a contemporary Christian's relationship to the world.[71]

Eugene M. Burke, the Society's first president, had accepted an invitation to speak at the tenth anniversary celebration on the future of Catholic college theology. He advocated bringing the "vision" into "a principle of action" which requires "a living idea," "a public idea," and "a social reality." Secularization, now evident in "the urbanization of society," demanded of the church a change in attitude toward the world. Because the secular exists in "independence of ecclesiastical and religious authority," Christian impact "will largely depend on personal choices, personal commitments, personal witness to values, personal communication of Christian values." Burke insisted on full engagement with the world through "theological reflection" based upon recent "biblical theology and the kerygma" as well as "historical knowledge" with an ecumenical sensitivity.

He concluded with a focus on "the primacy of the teacher. If, as I believe, all teaching is a priesthood of influence then this is pre-eminently so for the teacher of theology." What is required is "the kind of personal influence that flows from a teacher who personally believes in the primacy of the teacher." He or she provides "the living reality that encompasses the teaching of revealed truth and its explanation." No text should come between the teacher and student communicating with each other. Burke's final paragraph repeated with surprisingly few modifications the conclusion of his presidential address ten years earlier.

The changes made, though subtle, point toward the transformation that would occur in the next decade. Teaching remained a "vocation" but an "extraordinary" one rather than "Catholic." The teacher is a "shaper" rather than "maker of souls." Omitted is our "mark[ing] the lives of men and women in terms of their eternal destiny." Instead, the teacher has the "power to make men and women for better or worse." The teacher imparts "vitality and persuasion" rather than "life and force to our teaching." But all of teaching still "must rest on an enthusiasm that springs from conviction, is controlled by intelligence, marked by competence, blessed by patience and never loses sight of the fact that in Dante's words: 'the blessedness of this life consists in the proper exercise of man's power.'"[72] Enthusiasm abounded as plans were already underway for the 1965 convention, with the promising theme, "Freedom and Responsibility"—a theme that reflected the Society's quest for relevance in a new era, beginning with its new name, the College Theology Society.

NOTES

1. "The Moral Content of the Advanced Religion Course," The *Catholic Educational Review* 21 (January 1923): 1–13; "The Apologetic Content of the Advanced Religion Course," The *Catholic Educational Review* 21 (April 1923): 207–213; "Historical Content of Advanced Religion Course," The *Catholic Educational Review* 21 (1923): 154–160; "The Ascetic Content of the Advanced Religion Course," The *Catholic Educational Review* 21 (1923): 349–356.

2. See for example "Report of the Committee on Educational Problems and Research: College Teaching of Religion" in National Catholic Educational Association Report, Kansas City, Missouri, 37 (1940). William F. Cunningham, C.S.C.; Sister Clare, O.S.B.; Sister M. Evangela, B.V.M.; Julius W. Haun; Anselm M. Keefe, O.Praem.; Arthur M. Murphy; Walter C. Tredtin, S.M.; and Edward A. Fitzpatrick, chairman, comprised the committee.

3. John Courtney Murray, S.J., "Towards a Theology for the Layman: The Problem of Its Finality." *Theological Studies* (1944): 43–75; John Courtney Murray, S.J., "Towards a Theology for the Layman: The Pedagogical Problem," *Theological Studies* 5 (1944): 340–376. Quotes are from 372 and 375.

4. All of the quotes in this discussion of Father Plassmann's account are taken from his paper entitled "Theology for Nuns," found in Plassmann's file in Saint Bonaventure University Archives.

5. This data is based upon information reported at the 1964 SCCTSD national convention. See Sister M. Rose Eileen, C.S.C., "Academic Preparation of College Teachers of Sacred Doctrine, 1953–1964," in *Proceedings: Society of Catholic College Teachers of Sacred Doctrine* (Tenth Annual Convention, Washington, DC, March 30–31, 1964; Weston, MA: Regis College, 1964):56–57.

6. Letter from the Holy Father on the occasion of the opening of "Regina Mundi" [signed by G. B. Montini, prosecretary to His Eminence, Cardinal Valerio Valeri, prefect of the S.C. of Religious, Rome] (October 16, 1954) in *Regina Mundi Bulletin* 1 (1954), "Secretary's Data 1953–1956" Binder, Box 2, CTS Collection, ACUA.

7. Eustochium appears in a variant form as Eustacia. "Speech of Rev. P. Dezza, S.J., President of the Institute" in *Regina Mundi Bulletin* 1 (1954): 3–4, "Secretary's Data 1953–1956" Binder, Box 2, CTS Collection. ACUA.

8. "Minutes of Second Meeting of New York Region of SCCTSD," December 4, 1954, "Regional Reports—New York" File, Box 5, CTS Collection, ACUA.

9. "Minutes of the Board of Directors," St. Paul's Rectory, New York, NY, December 18, 1955 [1954], "Secretary's Data 1953–1956" Binder, Box 2, CTS Collection. ACUA.

10. "Minutes of the Officers' Meeting," Dunbarton College of Holy Cross, Washington, DC, 1955, "Secretary's Data 1953–1956" Binder, Box 2, CTS Collection, ACUA. The talk appeared in *Proceedings* (1955) as "The Problem of Training Teachers of Theology at the College Level" with Mother Marie Therese, O.S.U., giving the first address, Brother Celestine Luke

detailing "The Problem As It Concerns the Religious Teaching Brother," and Father Harvey, discussing "The Problem As It Concerns the Priest-Professor."

11. Gerald Van Ackeren, S.J., (St. Mary's College, Kansas), "The Finality of the College Course in Sacred Doctrine in the Light of the Finality of Theology," in *Proceedings: Second Annual Meeting of the Society of Catholic College Teachers of Sacred Doctrine* (April 2–3 1956; University of Notre Dame, vol. 2., Weston, MA: Regis College, reprint 1964), 12 [questions], 14–15, and 18–19, 21 passim.

12. John F. McDonnell, "Sacred Scripture Relevant to the College Course in Sacred Doctrine," in *Proceedings: Third Annual Meeting of the Society of Catholic College Teachers of Sacred Doctrine* (Cleveland, Ohio, April 22–23, 1957; Weston, MA: Regis College, reprint 1964), 76–77 and 81.

13. "Present Status of Catholic Ecclesiology," in *Proceedings of the Society of Catholic College Teachers of Sacred Doctrine: Seventh Annual Convention* (Boston, Massachusetts, April 3–4, 1961; Brookline, MA: Cardinal Cushing College, 1961), 30.

14. "D. Digest of the Discussion," in *Proceedings: Third Annual Meeting*, 24–57, 52.

15. Edwin G. Kaiser, C.PP.S. [Saint Joseph's College, Indiana], "Theology and the Social Sciences," in *Proceedings: Fourth Annual Meeting of the Society of Catholic College Teachers of Sacred Doctrine* (Philadelphia, Pennsylvania, April 7–8, 1958; Weston, MA: Regis College, reprint 1964), 70, 76, 77.

16. Reverend Augustin Léonard, O.P., "Christian Existence in the Church and the Contemporary World," in *Proceedings: Society of Catholic College Teachers of Sacred Doctrine, Ninth Annual Convention* (Chicago, Illinois, April 15–16, 1963), 21, 29, 31, 32, 34, 35.

17. David Michael Stanley, S.J. [Jesuit Seminary, Toronto], "The Divinity of Christ in Hymns of the New Testament," in *Proceedings: Fourth Annual Meeting*, 29.

18. "Discussion," in *Proceedings: Fourth Annual Meeting*, 32.

19. Brother C. Luke, F.S.C. [summary],"Working Groups: A Further Discussion of Father Stanley's Paper," in *Proceedings: Fourth Annual Meeting*, 36–39 passim.

20. "Minutes," Lake Erie Region, D'Youville College, February 28, 1959, "Regional Reports—Lake Erie" Box 5, CTS Collection, ACUA.

21. Reverend Bruce Vawter, C.M., S.S.D., "Genesis and the College Teacher of Sacred Doctrine," in *Proceedings: Sixth Annual Meeting of the Society of Catholic College Teachers of Sacred Doctrine* (Chicago, Illinois, April 18–19, 1960; Weston, MA: Regis College, reprint 1964), 31.

22. Reverend John McKenzie, S.J., S.T.D., "Messianism and the College Teacher of Sacred Doctrine," in *Proceedings: Sixth Annual Meeting*, 38, 52, 58, 59.

23. Reverend Carroll Stuhlmueller, C.P., S.T.L., S.S.L., "The Use of Old Testament Liturgy in Teaching College Sacred Doctrine," in *Proceedings: Sixth Annual Meeting*, 82.

24. Reverend Barnabas Mary Ahern, C.P., S.S.D., "The Concept of the Church in Biblical Thought," in *Proceedings: Seventh Annual Convention*, 32, 34, 58, 59. Ahern served as a *peritus* at Vatican II.

25. Raymond E. Brown, "The Eucharist and Baptism in St. John," in *Proceedings: Society of Catholic College Teachers of Sacred Doctrine, Eighth Annual Convention* (Detroit, Michigan, April 23–24, 1962; Weston, MA: Regis College, 1962), 14–33; *Magister: Bulletin of the Society of Catholic College Teachers of Sacred Doctrine* (March 1962): 4.

26. *Proceedings: Ninth Annual Convention*, 39–44 passim.

27. "Patristic Views of Sacramental Sanctity," in *Proceedings: Eighth Annual Convention*, 81, 80.

28. Reverend Walter J. Burghardt, S.J., "The Fathers of the Church: Obsolete or Relevant," in *Proceedings: Tenth Annual Convention, 1964*, 18, 29, 34.

29. Minutes, October 18, 1958, "Regional Reports—Lake Erie" File, Box 5, CTS Collection, ACUA, 2–5.

30. In *Proceedings: Eighth Annual Convention*, 172, 173, 174, 175.

31. Sister Mary Anthony, O.S.B., "Christian Life in the Mystery of the Church," in *Proceedings: Ninth Annual Convention*, 54, 77. See Keith F. Pecklers, *The Unread Vision: The Litugical Movement in the United States of America, 1926–1955* (Collegeville, MN: Liturgical Press, 1998).

32. Reverend Bernard J. Cooke, S.J., "Word of God: Scripture and Sacrament," in *Proceedings: Tenth Annual Convention, 1964*, 122–132 passim.

33. Reverend Gerard Sloyan, "The Constitution on the Sacred Liturgy and Prayer-Life in the College," in *Proceedings: Tenth Annual Convention, 1964*, 110.

34. Gustave Weigel, S.J., "Present Status of Catholic Ecclesiology," in *Proceedings: Seventh Annual Convention*, 29.

35. Reverend John Meyendorff, D.D., "Contemporary Orthodox Concept of the Church," and Reverend William Leibrecht, Th.D., "Contemporary Protestant Concept of the Church," in *Proceedings: Seventh Annual Convention*, 62–101.

36. "Special Interest Session: Orthodox and Protestant Concepts of Church Relation to College Sacred Doctrine Courses," summary by Mother M. C. Wheeler, R.S.C.J. [Newton College of the Sacred Heart]; chairman: Reverend David Bowman, S.J., S.T.D.; discussants: Reverend John Meyendorff, Th.D., and Reverend William Leibrecht, Th.D., in *Proceedings: Seventh Annual Convention*, 102–116.

37. John A. Hardon, S.J. [West Baden College, Indiana], "The Church's Magisterium and College Fundamental Theology," in *Proceedings: Third Annual Meeting*, 74–75.

38. "Minutes," Lake Erie Region, D'Youville College, February 28, 1959, "Regional Reports—Lake Erie" File, Box 5, CTS Collection, ACUA.

39. Brother C. Luke, F.S.C. [summary], "Working Group Sessions: B. Emphasis on the Magisterium in the College Course," in *Proceedings: Fifth Annual Meeting*, 36.

40. Edmond D. Benard, "The Development of Doctrine: A Basic Framework," in *Proceedings: Fifth Annual Meeting*, 27.

41. Brother C. Luke, F.S.C. [summary], "Working Group Sessions: A. Further Discussion of Father Benard's Paper," in *Proceedings: Fifth Annual Meeting*, 31, 33, 34, 35.

42. Thomas C. Donlan, S.J. [St. Rose Priory, Dubuque], "Presidential Address," in *Proceedings: Third Annual Meeting*, 114, 115.

43. "Society of Catholic College Teachers of Sacred Doctrine, District of Columbia–Maryland Region," Mount Saint Agnes College, Baltimore, Maryland, December 2, 1961; "Society of Catholic College Teachers of Sacred Doctrine, District of Columbia–Maryland Region," Immaculata College, Washington, DC, April 7, 1962, "Regional Reports—DC Maryland" File, Box 5, CTS Collection, ACUA.

44. Brother Alban of Mary, F.S.C. [Manhattan College], "Presidential Address," in *Proceedings: Fifth Annual Meeting*, 7–13 passim.

45. Brother C. Luke Salm, F.S.C., "The Status of Theology in the College," in *Proceedings: Tenth Annual Convention, 1964*, 38–50 passim, longer quotes from 46, 49, 50.

46. "C. Discussion by Father Atsch," "Panel Discussion: The Responsibility of the Sacred Doctrine Teacher Precisely as Such for the Catholic Formation of the Student," in *Proceedings: Second Annual Meeting*, 56–61 passim.

47. Brother C. Luke, F.S.C. [summary], "Working Group Sessions: C. Preparation for the Apostolate in the Theology Course," in *Proceedings: Fifth Annual Meeting*, 39–40.

48. "D. Discussion by Sister Charles Borromeo," "Panel Discussion: The Responsibility of the Sacred Doctrine Teacher Precisely as Such for the Catholic Formation of the Student," in *Proceedings: Second Annual Meeting*, 64–65.

49. Francis M. Keating, S.J., "The Finality of the College Course in Sacred Doctrine in the Light of the Finality of the Layman," in *Proceedings: Second Annual Meeting*, 25, 27, 38.

50. Francis M. Keating, S.J., "The Finality of the College Course," 36–37.

51. Brother Alban of Mary, F.S.C., Ph.D., "Presidential Address," in *Proceedings: Sixth Annual Meeting*, 8, 15–18.

52. "Theologian Says Catholics Need Faith Training," in *Chicago Sun-Times* (April 19, 1960).

53. Bernard J. Cooke, S.J. [Marquette University], "Presidential Address," in *Proceedings: Eighth Annual Convention*, 12, 13.

54. Reverend Eugene M. Burke, C.S.P., "Address of Welcome," in *Proceedings of the First Annual Convention of the Society of Catholic College Teachers of Sacred Doctrine, April 11–13, 1955,* (Trinity College, Washington, D.C.), ed. Reverend Urban Voll, O.P., (Washington, DC: Published by the Society at Dunbarton College of Holy Cross, 1956), 5–9 passim.

55. "Address of Welcome by his Excellency, Bishop Pursley," in *Proceedings: Second Annual Meeting*, 5–6.

56. John J. Fernan, S.J. [Le Moyne College, Syracuse], "Presidential Address," in *Proceedings: Second Annual Meeting*, 98–102 passim, 104.

57. Thomas C. Donlan, O.P., [St. Rose Priory, Dubuque], "Presidential Address," in *Proceedings: Third Annual Meeting*, 118.

58. Thomas C. Donlan, O.P. [St. Rose Priory, Dubuque], "Presidential Address," in *Proceedings: Fourth Annual Meeting*, 8–11 passim.

59. Reverend Urban Voll, O.P., "Presidential Address," in *Proceedings: Tenth Annual Convention, 1964*, 8–16 passim.

60. See Philip Gleason, *Contending with Modernity: Catholic Higher Education in the Twentieth Century* (NY: Oxford University Press, 1995), for extensive discussion of the impact of professionalization on Catholic higher education evident in teacher certification and institutional accreditation.

61. A cover letter from "The Committee on Current Problems—Spring Meeting" indicates that the committee met on March 24 and April 14 with no year noted. An attached note at the end listing subcommittees for "Sacred Doctrine Studies" has a date of 1963. The report itself had dates no later than 1956 and makes no mention of the Second Vatican Council. Found in "Committee on Sacred Doctrine Teacher Training" File, Box 5, CTS Collection, ACUA.

62. "Problem of Priest-Teachers of Sacred Doctrine at the College Level" in "Committee on Sacred Doctrine—Teacher Training" File, Box 5, CTS Collection, ACUA.

63. Sister M. Consilia, O.P. [recorder, Mount St. Mary College], "Symposium: Sacred Doctrine for Student Sisters; B. The Mind of the Church: Sister Celeste," in *Proceedings: Fifth Annual Meeting*, 120.

64. "Summary of Special Interest Session: A. Contemporary Theological Developments in Relation to the Intellectual Formation of Sisters: General Introduction," in *Proceedings: Eighth Annual Convention*, 115.

65. "Summary of the Address of his Eminence, Richard Cardinal Cushing at the Meeting of the Society of Catholic College Teachers of Sacred Doctrine, April 3–4, 1961," in *Proceedings: Seventh Annual Convention*, 7, 11, 12.

66. Bernard Cooke, "Presidential Address," in *Proceedings: Eighth Annual Convention*, 7–10 passim.

67. James Egan, O.P., "A Contemporary Approach to Sacramental Grace," in *Proceedings: Eighth Annual Convention*, 95, 98, 102, 103, 104–105, 107.

68. *Magister: Bulletin of the Society of Catholic College Teachers of Sacred Doctrine* (October 1962): 1, 3.

69. Reverend Urban Voll, O.P., "Easter Monday-Liturgical Homily," in *Proceedings: Society of Catholic College Teachers of Sacred Doctrine, Ninth Annual Convention* (Chicago, Illinois, April 15–16, 1963), 7–9 passim.

70. Reverend Urban Voll, O.P., "Presidential Address," in *Proceedings: Ninth Annual Convention*, 14–15, 18–20.

71. Mother Mary Emmanuel McIver, O.S.U., "A. Panel Discussion: Christian Life in Contemporary Society," in *Proceedings: Ninth Annual Convention*, 78, 80–81, 83, 85.

72. Reverend Eugene M. Burke, C.S.P., "College Theology Looks to the Future," in *Proceedings: Tenth Annual Convention, 1964*, 88, 89, 90, 94, 100, 102–104. Cf. Eugene M. Burke, C.S.P., "Presidential Address," in *Proceedings: First Annual Meeting*, 9.

• 3 •

The CTS (1965–1974)

The second decade of the society began as the Second Vatican Council closed with all of its promise and peril. Changes in the content and context of college theology were occurring at an accelerated pace. Certainly the documents promulgated at the Vatican Council provided a dizzying array of theological pronouncements that went to the heart of the Catholic Church's life in its understanding of God's revelation and its expression of that in liturgy, in its communal identity as "People of God," and in its relationship to other Christians, to other religious peoples, and to all peoples in the world. Implementation of conciliar documents occurred as U.S. Catholic colleges and universities were being transformed in the rapidly changing environment of higher education and the charged contexts of the wider society. The social changes here are those repeated mantralike in most accounts of the 1960s— baby boomers coming of age, colleges inundated, young people speaking their minds, protests against Vietnam, urban center meltdown, ever expanding mass media, and the exploding knowledge industry. Movements of liberation followed one after another: first civil rights, then farm workers, the women's movement, gay rights, and people with disabilities, to name only a few. And if that turmoil proved insufficient, the sexual revolution ensured the transformation of social relations at their most basic level. For Catholics in the United States, these changes formed a tightly interconnected network that impacted not only their personal relationships but their relationship to the church as a moral authority. Many named this experience an identity crisis and eventually a crisis of faith.

A NEW NAME, A CHANGING IDENTITY

The Society of Catholic College Teachers of Sacred Doctrine had its own musings about transforming its identity to better reflect its constituency and the changing academic field of religion and theology. The first and most obvious change was its name. At the twelfth annual convention in Denver, the board meeting included an intense discussion concerning changing the society's name. The debate centered around who might belong to a Society of Catholic College Teachers of Sacred Doctrine. Only Catholic teachers? Only those who taught "Sacred Doctrine"? Only those at Catholic institutions? Cathleen Going, a professor at a lay institute in Canada, offered her resignation apparently out of an unwillingness to remain a member "under false pretenses." She was assured that "the term 'Catholic' does not modify 'college' but 'teachers.'" Going then wondered, "whether, without being un-Catholic teaching, what she was doing in a secular university could justifiably be called 'Sacred Doctrine.'" Further discussions recollected "the intended breadth of the term 'Sacred Doctrine' going back to the founding meetings." Her "resignation was unanimously rejected," and her valuable contributions, especially her unique perspectives as a laywoman, affirmed.[1] The cessation of the immediate crisis did not resolve the deeper issues.

At the next meeting, only a few months later, the board revisited the controversy surrounding the name change. "In the early history of the organization each word had a relevant and full meaning. 'Catholic' originally modified 'college', later 'Catholic' modified 'teachers.' This caused ambiguity which has grown more intense in the Post-Conciliar era." Extensive discussions produced two options: the "Association of College Theology" or the "Society of College Theology." Father Sloyan, the president, named Father Richard Rousseau, Father Gavin Reilly, and Brother Gabriel Moran to a committee that would "prepare the necessary proposition for the regions." After completing the regional consultation, the committee was to produce "the necessary amendment in complete form to the membership at the business meeting." Upon Father Reilly's suggestion, the board decided to present one choice. "The name finally agreed upon was Society of College Theology."[2]

The committee evidently wasted little time and had a resolution prepared for the next convention. Prior to the 1967 convention business meeting, the board discussed the name change. They made only one modification. Following the suggestion of several respondents, they had changed the word order to the "College Theology Society." The only major point of contention was the exclusion of the word "Catholic," but the argument failed to persuade the majority of the board.[3] So, in 1967, those who attended the national convention in Pittsburgh voted to adopt the new name. The "Society for the Catholic College Teachers of Sacred Doctrine" would henceforth be known as the "College Theology Society" or simply as the "CTS." There is some irony of coincidence in the change's timing. Father Sloyan, the current president, had first proposed the name, the "Society for College Teachers of Sacred Doctrine," and other founding members, probably Sister Rose Eileen and Father John Harvey, had inserted "Catholic."

The reason now for the omission of the word "Catholic" had as much to do with including Catholics as it did with making a sincere effort at ecumenism. Catholics were now teaching religion at colleges and universities outside of the Catholic sphere. Whether that was Father Sloyan's earlier reasoning is never mentioned in the extant notes either in these debates or in the earlier ones. Father Sloyan introduced the amendment at the board meeting. "He gave the decision of the board, stating the opinion of the majority for change." He also acknowledged the "minority [who] opposed deletion of the word 'Catholic.'" A report from Brother Gabriel Moran, F.S.C., corroborated Sloyan's assessment. In contrast to the debates surrounding the Society's original name, no one questioned the substitution of "theology" for "sacred doctrine" nor did any raise concern about the absence of "teacher." Father Sloyan called for discussion. About fourteen members expressed opinions pro and con. The discussion lasted for about thirty minutes. Father Sloyan then closed discussion and asked for the vote. Fathers Jude Maher and Leon Kennedy counted the votes. The result was 118 to 57 in favor of adoption of the amendment. The new title "'College Theology Society' will be effective at once." 31 March 1967, four days after the vote, the Society initiated a census "on the academic preparation of its members and of others who are teaching theology or religion on the college-university level." The title on the heading was "College Theology Society."[4] Evidence that the other 80% of the members approved or protested the change does not appear in the extant documents.

Other professional academic organizations also experienced significant change in the 1960s. In 1963, the National Association of Biblical Instructors voted to rename its organization, determining the designation the American Academy of Religion (AAR) best described its purpose. A 1964 brochure indicated that the AAR served all "learned men and women united to advance the study of all aspects of religion" including social scientists and humanities professors though it maintained its ongoing commitment to "its heritage from this Bible-oriented association." Like the Society for College Teachers of Sacred Doctrine, the AAR appealed to the "teacher-scholar." Membership required a payment of $6.50 and included a subscription to the *Journal of Bible and Religion.*[5]

In a letter addressed to SCCTSD national secretary, Sister M. Julie Harkins, C.S.J., dated 31 May 1965, Rev. Robert V. Smith of Colgate University requested the release of members' names and addresses. Smith described the past organization as "largely Protestant" though "never intentionally so." Rather than describing the motive for outreach as "ecumenical" in the way the Society had, he appealed to the common commitments among those advancing "the teaching and study of religion."[6] Sister Julie evidently sought advice concerning Smith's request. In response to a letter from Sister Julie, Carroll Stuhlmueller, C.P., encouraged a positive response. Active membership makes possible "a healthy Catholic influence" within the Academy.[7] The SCCTSD board agreed to the request.

Other more familiar topics gained the board's attention once again in the second half of the 1960s. At the 1967 fall meeting, the report of only eight active regions was deemed "not encouraging." In considering appropriate responses, someone suggested "that the effort should be concentrated on the national impact of the College Theology Society."[8] Gradually the focus did migrate to the national level even though an increase in regional activity occurred, and a few regions continued to meet through 2004. The most active regions always had the advantage of a concentration of institutions with strong programs in theology or religious studies in relatively small geographic areas. Even with an increase in the number of active regions, their contribution to the Society's national activities declined significantly in the ten-year period ending in 1974. What remained were individual regions such as those in Washington-Baltimore, Eastern Pennsylvania, and Louisville-Cincinnati that offered local CTS members regular opportunities to select topics of immediate interest, share works in progress, or discuss recent publications in a smaller group composed of nearby colleagues.

The other familiar debate concerned qualifications for membership. The re-emergence of the debate reflects, at least in part, the changing demographics of the profession. The Society had even established a short-lived "Personnel Placement Service" in July 1965. This service, with its "unsalaried Director," was to put "theologians in search of teaching positions into contact with the Catholic colleges and universities in which they are needed, and of providing such institutions with adequate information concerning available personnel." A modest fee of $5 secured this service to members and Catholic institutions.[9] The need for such a service suggests the availability of more academically prepared college teachers which invited a rethinking of Society's membership qualifications to include "at least an M.A. or its equivalent, and actual teaching on the college level." Questions about membership, identity, and viability remained concerns for the next several years, but the leadership displayed a consistent commitment to honoring the Society's focus upon serving the actual teachers of college theology and religious studies.[10]

To make the Society's new title official required amending the constitution; so in 1967, the board proposed that and several other amendments. The additional changes, at first glance, appear minor but actually reflect major shifts gradually taking effect in Catholic theology in the wider disciplinary context of emerging "religious studies." The final document contains the following changes. The name of the society is "The College Theology Society, Incorporated" and remains "under the patronage of Mary, Seat of Wisdom" with a "corporate seal" bearing the "motto: *'Ad perfectionem caritatis.'*" The "Purposes" in "Article II" shift from an "ultimate object" to a "primary objective" and the object—"to maintain the academic discipline of college Sacred Doctrine"—becomes the objective—"to develop the academic discipline of theology." Maintaining a "high professional level" remains unchanged. Secondary purposes shifted adverbially from "proximately" to "specifically." "Sacred Doctrine curricula" changes to "curriculums in religious thought" and rather than examining sacred doctrine as "the principle of integration," the Society intends "to investigate the relation of the study of theology (religion) to other academic disciplines and to determine its proper place in the total college curriculum." "Effective teaching and teachers" remain, and members still "keep abreast of current developments" and "foster communication and exchange . . . through publications . . . national and regional meetings." An eighth purpose highlights working "in an ecumenical spirit." Acknowledging being "Roman Catholic in its foundations," the Society seeks to include in "membership" and "service" "the entire community of scholarship interested in the study of religious thought at the college and university level."

MEMBERS AND THEIR QUALIFICATIONS

The Society's expanding constituency reflected the increase in academically trained teachers. Under Article III, "Membership" the specific descriptors "priests, religious, and Catholic lay men and lay women" were omitted, and now "those who teach theology or religious thought in any college, seminary or university and who hold appropriate graduate degrees in the field" could join. An exception remained for those who had no degree but had taught for a long period. Associate membership reappeared to attract graduate students or permit teachers without graduate degrees to affiliate with the Society. Under "Officers," the vice president received new assignments including "organizing the annual meeting, coordinating the efforts of the program committee, the national officers and board, and the regional officers and chairman of the local committee for the annual meeting." Omitted was the "Committee on Current Problems" given the board's functioning as that committee. Under

"Article IX. Publications," the specific names *"Proceedings"* and *"Magister"* were eliminated while maintaining the board's oversight of an annual proceedings publication and a quarterly newsletter.[11]

In trying to better understand the membership, the board also sent out a questionnaire in April 1967 to the now 1,236 members concerning their professional status, and 870 responded, including 100 nonmembers. The responses provide a snapshot of those teaching college theology, primarily at Catholic institutions, in 1967. Of those who responded, 31% were women, and 69% were men; the median age was forty-two. The number of laity was relatively small with 484 priests (116 secular, 367 regular), 249 sisters, 49 brothers, and only 66 laymen and 19 laywomen (8.6% of the membership, the only percentage noted). Two Protestant ministers and one rabbi also returned surveys. Surprising was the small number who held membership in more than one society: 107 also belonged to Catholic Theological Society of America (CTSA), 107 to the Religious Education Association (REA), 77 to the Catholic Bible Association (CBA), and only 20 to the AAR. The education of those who responded included 136 with an S.T.D., 78 with a Ph.D. in religious studies, and 551 with an M.A. in religious studies. Of the 78 who had Ph.D.s, 27 came from Saint Mary's College. The highest number of master's degrees from a single school were sixty from Catholic University of America. Of those who responded to the survey, 103 had no advanced degree. Ten percent without advanced degrees is significant and makes more understandable the continued discussions of membership qualifications.

The high percentage of ordained and other vowed religious also makes clear that the CTS had many more demographic changes to come.[12] In a memo, dated 10 March 1971, passed from Sister Maura Campbell to Sister Vera Chester through Sister M. Gertrude Anne, C.S.C., Sister Maura's directions suggested that these demographics had changed very little in four years. In Sister Maura's *Suggestions for Registration*, she provided the following schema.

1. Two girls for Clergy registration (those who have returned cards.) These girls can have the cards in three boxes . . . (A-G), (H-O), (P-Z) for easier handling of cards.
2. Then two girls for non-clerical delegates who have sent in cards. Arrange cards as follows: Box for Sisters (A-M), Box for Sisters (N-Z), Box for Brothers and lay men and women (A-Z).
3. If box for Brothers is placed between them, they can easily locate the names from this box.[13]

The fact that the information was passed from one sister to another through a third sister also suggests the legacy of Sister Rose Eileen continued in terms of organizing the Society's work. It brings to mind Dorothy Day's quip attributed to Peter Maurin: "man proposes, woman disposes."

The desire among leadership to broaden the membership base is evident in a brochure distributed circa 1968. The Society's eclectic character appeared as its distinctive attraction. The brochure answered the question: "How Does Membership Differ from that in Other Societies?" The response pointed to other "professional societies which have as their members a preponderance of seminary professors, ethicians, students of the Bible, Protestant-oriented academics, and scientific students of religion" and acknowledged that "their concerns and those of the College Theology Society are not mutually exclusive." It then described the Society's distinctive raison d'être that combines pedagogical and scholarly concerns "at the college level" in theology or "religious thought." "It does not have a pedagogical concern in preference to a scholarly concern or vice versa for the simple reason that it considers professionalism in this field to consist of a close conjunction of the two." The brochure assured that its origins in "Roman Catholic academic circles" did not abrogate a genuine commitment to ecumenism. The Society welcomed any who share in "its chief goal" of improving "college courses in religious thought." Members can benefit "singly, but even more improve their lot corporately by acting as a potent force to ameliorate situations which are out of their hands as individuals and as members of departments."[14]

THE SOCIETY AS PUBLISHER

The Society has one major publication that displays its academic endeavors. For the first eleven years, it bore the title, "*Proceedings of . . .* ," and the convention number. Beginning in 1966, the publication appeared with a distinctive cover and under a specific title, capturing the annual meeting's single, central theme, an organizing principle firmly established in the mid-1960s. At the board meeting in 1972, the editor suggested and the board accepted that the publication is more accurately designated as the "annual volume" rather than "proceedings" to better reflect the practice of including essays and other materials in addition to selected convention papers.[15]

The annual volume as it evolves, like the Society it represents, does not fit neatly into any particular category. Even with clear themes, a volume might include entries that vary wildly in content and in quality from each other. Some provide a preview of a soon-to-be influential theologian or a summary of an already-known and respected scholar. Others leave one wondering whatever happened to the person who produced such a fine essay. Some remain as engaging and insightful as when first published. Others impress as odd, mistaken, amusing, or simply as ephemera. These volumes are, of course, a treasure trove for anyone interested in the fifty years of theology done primarily among Catholics in a U.S. context in the last half of the twentieth century. By any standards, the period from 1954 though 2004 is utterly amazing in the scope of changes and developments.

The Society's ongoing commitment to publishing the volume deserves special commendation given the challenges in securing reliable publishers. After suggesting the designation, "annual volume," George Devine, as editor of the 1972 edition (1971 convention), had to announce a delay in its publication due to the large number of convention papers and the financial constraints due to speaker expenses at the 1971 convention. Securing publishers for the annual volume proved to be an ongoing struggle with several changes in publishers occurring over the years. In 1973, George Devine had to report difficulties for the 1972 convention volume. Alba House had misgivings about publishing "without prior ecclesiastical approbation." In anticipation of changing publishers after the Los Angeles volume, Devine contacted "Ave Maria Press, Pflaum, XXIII Publications, Paulist Press and Fortress."[16] Crossroads published the 1973 and 1974 meeting volumes. Despite the challenges of publishing, Rodger Van Allen suggested, at the same meeting in which Devine reported delays, examining "the feasibility of a scholarly journal as a means of service to the membership."[17]

A Society-sponsored journal represents distinctive, ongoing proof of the CTS's academic credibility that the newsletter had not provided. Certainly, *Magister* and its successors, *Sacred Doctrine Notes* and *College Theology Notes*, promoted academic development among its members with their book reviews, topical bibliographies, and, of course, news of interest to college theology teachers. The Society also had a short-lived collaborative relationship (1969–1971) with the *Journal of Ecumenical Studies* as its "official journal."[18] The April 1973 board meeting decision to publish a semiannual journal, eventually named *Horizons*, sent a different message to the CTS membership. They were not only the teachers of theological and religious scholarship assisted by a newsletter's book reviews and bibliographies but the theologians and the scholars of religion producing the articles and reviews for their colleagues' use.

Rodger Van Allen conveyed this message in his affirmative answer to the question: "Should the College Theology Society Publish a Journal?" In a lengthy, undated memo, he outlined his reasons, opening with his initial negative reaction to the idea. One objection related to the financial risks. The other concerned "whether it [the journal] would be a scholarly success." He asked with all frankness, "Are the 1200 CTS members scholarly enough to fill out a journal?" Van Allen acknowledged the many teaching and service duties placed on the faculty who belonged to the Society. On the other hand, an increasing number of this same faculty had areas of specialization and a desire, even pressure, to publish. These individuals needed publishing outlets given the lack of "worthwhile" journals in "Catholic theology and studies" except those appealing to "a rather narrow constituency."

Van Allen then described the CTS's broad-based constituency. It "includes male/female, religious/lay/clerical, in a quite open way." Their varied teaching and scholarly activity, both "interdisciplinary and relevant," made the Society unique among professional societies. CTS members had "more contact hours with students than any other organization. To speak only of the 260 Catholic institutions, one is dealing with 428,853 students who probably average 6+ hours of religious studies or theology. That is some 3 million contact hours." He stressed the importance of "the projected journal" in contributing "more than almost anything else" to improving what happened during those contact hours.[19]

The correspondence leading up to the journal decision indicated that the CTS board was actively seeking additional opportunities to publish. A memo from Thomas McFadden to the Publication Committee considered a CTS monograph series, including the "benefits," such as "the academic prestige of the CTS," and the "difficulties," especially the limited appeal of any one volume sent to all membership. What emerged in the final analysis was that most of the benefits of the monograph series could be met with a journal with an added benefit of allowing more members to publish.[20]

A letter to "Colleague from Publication Committee Office," signed by Thomas M. McFadden, St. Joseph College, indicated that at the "25 April 1973 meeting during the national convention in Philadelphia, the Board of Directors voted to begin a semi-annual journal of the College Theology Society." The first issue was planned for spring of 1974. The 128-page publication was to be financed through membership dues raised to $15. The letter then called for applications for editor positions.[21] A follow-up letter in early May from McFadden, as chair of the CTS Publication Committee, requested applications "for the editorial staff." Formal application for any of the "four editorial categories" required "a letter indicating your qualifications, your vision of what the journal should be, and (in the case of editor in chief) the degree to which your college or university would support your efforts."[22] Bernard Prusak and Rodger Van Allen became the first editors in chief, and the journal's day-to-day operations received support from Villanova University, its 2004 home. The treasurer's report in this same year focused upon the support of the new journal. While soliciting funds from universities and colleges as sponsors ($25 each) and getting money from foundations such as

Lilly was mentioned, the major financial support would come from raising dues, at first the proposed amount was $15 as noted in correspondence with membership, but the figure was amended to $20 and passed unanimously.[23]

Publishing matters grew even more complicated in this period with the advent of new technologies. A report from the Council on the Study of Religion's Committee on Research and Publications discussed technology's impact "on the working habits of scholars," particularly "micropublishing and the microfiche reader" as the catalyst for revolution. The report from the Council on the Study of Religion (CSR) seemed to confirm the microfiche insurgency, a counter to diminishing support from "commercial publishers or the university press." Two major journals, the *Journal of Biblical Literature* and the *Journal of the American Academy of Religion* "will be issued in microfiche this year and free copies given to each institutional subscriber." One option being examined was the "purchase of microfiche reader for $100 for CSR members." Whether they also looked into good deals on eight-track players was not mentioned. Another technology creating concern was "the copying machine" combined with "the copy center" because photocopying threatened copyright, given the easy availability of "demand publishing." The committee intended to "solicit a carefully prepared statement from a competent person in the American Association of Law Schools which would continue by libraries the doctrine of fair use as it has come to be understood."[24] Amusement over the microfiche "revolution" arises mostly in light of subsequent technologies, especially the personal computer and the Internet, that have revolutionized scholarship in ways unimaginable to those contemplating "demand publishing" in 1973.

THE MAIN EVENT: THE ANNUAL MEETING

Publications provide important and lasting evidence of the Society's scholarly presence, but the major corporate event that defines the CTS remains the annual meeting. Until 1974, with the exception of the 1972 international conference of learned societies of religion, the meetings were held Easter week, even beginning on the evening of Easter Sunday, though rarely, given members' objections. Use of a single organizing theme for each annual meeting became a clearly established practice by 1965. More presentations were offered in simultaneous sessions but usually with one paper per session and plenary sessions with major speakers remaining central. In 1965, with the Second Vatican Council entering its third and final session, theological discussions generated excitement and interest among many Catholics. Convention organizers had even arranged to move Reverend Bernard Häring's session to a larger room to accommodate "local people" who might attend.[25]

An innovation at the 1965 convention, the "Theology Seminar Discussions," made "strictly theological discussions more available at the Convention" with "groups small enough so that all could really discuss and share ideas" in their areas of specialization. The multiple sessions allowed more members "to take a more active part in their own Convention." Seminar topics included "Literary Forms and the Meaning of Scripture," "The Origins of Man," "Infant Baptism," "The Spirit of the New Morality," "Ecclesial Aspects of Faith," "The Presence of Christ in the Liturgy and Sacraments," "Karl Rahner's Ideas on Inspiration in the Bible," "Who Belongs to the Church?" and "Religious Obedience and Holy Disobedience."[26] The seminars, led by men and women—ordained, religious, and lay—evidently attracted significant attendance. Father Sloyan, president of the Society, noted an attempt to keep the number in each seminar below sixty participants.[27]

The desire for widespread active participation that was evident from the beginning remained even after nearly two decades. A "Call for Papers" for the Nineteenth Annual Convention included specific instructions for formal papers, such as a time limit of twenty to twenty-five minutes with presenters providing thirty copies for distribution. Learning work groups offered another interactive option. Instructions suggest that members were limited only by their imagination and willingness to organize. Authors of proposals were to act as coordinators including sending out the list of materials to be discussed. "The working groups might be organized along the lines of the SBL seminars or AAR task forces, or they can follow any format which suits the groups' needs. A group may wish to schedule daily meetings during the convention, or one full-day meeting; it may wish to admit auditors or not. The goals of a working group may be decided upon by the group itself (e.g., production of a position paper, a report of findings, an annotated bibliography, etc.)."[28] An interesting mix of highly organized sessions and open-ended alternatives allowed a variety of members to participate even if it failed to guarantee uniform standards of academic quality.

The twentieth convention marked two important shifts in the CTS's annual meeting. It established the practice of meeting on college campuses and of convening at the end of May or on the first of June. The date was decided by a vote by ninety-six members (less than 10% of total membership). The results were Holy Week, 11 votes; Easter week, 26 votes; 1st week in June (T–Th), 35 votes; and 2nd week of June (T–Th), 24 votes.[29] The twentieth meeting was held at the University of Dayton, May 31, June 1 and 2, 1974, with the theme "Liberation: Freedom and Revolution." While not the first time the meeting was held on a college campus, it was the first of what became common practice for the next thirty years.[30] Still extant in the files is an announcement of a "CTS Social" on Friday and Saturday evenings at the Brass Lantern, Marycrest [dormitory], University of Dayton. Mixed drinks were 60 cents; beer, 30 cents; soft drinks, 20 and 25 cents; and peanuts, pretzels, and chips, no charge. "Pleasant atmosphere, genial companionship, scintillating conversations—An opportunity to renew old acquaintances and develop new ones—A time to share the good things that have happened during the year—A chance to challenge and be challenged—new developments in religious studies new approaches to teaching new courses to offer. An hour or two just to relax—to be yourself and to share yourself with others!!"[31] Whether the Brass Lantern was the site of the first evening social is not the point of its inclusion here. The announcement's casual tone and focus on teaching indicates something of the Society's collegial attitude and professional commitment that continued even at the end of its second decade.

Eucharistic celebrations remained a daily event with the impact of Vatican II's liturgical changes evident. In Saint Louis, the 1965 convention with its theme "Freedom and Responsibility" opened with a "Bible Vigil on Christian Freedom." The first flush of the council's effects appear in descriptions of liturgy. "The Communal Mass on Monday and Tuesday followed by a meal taken together in the same room in which we have worshipped together should stress both the community nature of the liturgy and its teaching force." The convention in its entirety may prove an "experience" of "growth . . . into some more truly appropriate part of the mystery that is Christ." Tuesday morning Mass was to continue as it had in the past, a Mass for the Society's deceased members.[32] The meal, after the "Communal Mass with 'full' participation," received the name, "agape." Some attributed an "increase" in the Society's sense of community to "concelebration of the Eucharist."[33]

Increased liturgical expectations also led to increased criticism. The 1967 minutes of the board meeting reported disappointment "at the minimum liturgy and at the absence of a leader of song, and all agreed that we could have had better celebrations at Mass."[34] The conventions also make clear the local variations in implementation of liturgical changes. In 1965 at Saint Louis, "the local ordinary had requested that priests not celebrate private Masses in the hotel." A 1968 postcard for the San Francisco convention offering three choices for Mass—"concelebrate Monday, Tuesday or private celebration"—suggests that earlier practices remain a part of Catholic life even at an up-to-date professional society of Catholic college theology teachers.[35]

RESOLVING THE SOCIETY'S COMMITMENTS

Another avenue into the CTS membership's professional concerns from 1965 to 1974 is to examine the resolutions offered, debated, passed, and rejected during the annual meetings. The earliest resolutions reflect a Vatican II–generated enthusiasm to embrace the church's call for renewal, and as the decade progressed, resolutions reflected increasing tensions between the CTS's relationship to the church and to the academy. The first resolution of the Society's eleventh year, like its convention theme, struck a balance between "freedom and responsibility." It pronounced an "earnest desire for an increased implementation in the college community of the priesthood of the faithful." Implementing this increase had to follow "the norms enunciated by the II Vatican Council on the Constitution of the Church" to ensure "greater freedom with increased loyalty and responsibility, on the part of the faculty and student body." The remaining resolutions also took their inspiration from the council, including the establishment of "an ecumenical committee" to foster relationships with "colleges from other faiths," an information outlet for locating "competent teachers of Sacred Doctrine" especially to assist "lay people and others outside of the framework of canonical appointments," the organization of regional workshops to assist high school teachers in adjusting to the changing approaches and content in teaching religion, and finally, a resolution "noting that the teaching value of the present liturgy would be greatly enhanced by a further increase of the vernacular."[36]

After the resolutions had been read and the first one re-read, a question arose about the term "priesthood of the faithful." What followed became a long discussion not of proposed resolutions but of missing ones, in particular a submission from the New England region transmitted in a letter to the national secretary, Sister Julie, dated 1 February 1965. Dr. Elizabeth Jane Farians, associate professor of theology at Sacred Heart University, had proposed the following for approval at the spring meeting.

> Resolved that the Society send letters to the bishops of the United States asking that they seek to have the Vatican Council study the status of woman in the church in the light of the biblical teaching that "God made man, male and female, in his own image and likeness", and in the light of woman's position in the modern world.

The resolution also called for a petition to the bishops to ensure that women had "an active part in this study and in the Council, especially in such matters as religious life and the layman in the church." An additional petition would ask the bishops "to reform certain documents of the church, especially the code of canon law, . . . [to] truly reflect the teaching of the church on the dignity of woman as fully a member of the human race and of the people of God."[37] No such resolution was proposed for discussion.

The omission sparked more debate, first concerning the regions' rights to have a voice at the national business meeting, and then to procedural issues with the group concluding that a procedure based on *Robert's Rules of Order* needed to be established. Miss Patricia Ahern volunteered her services in this area. After agreeing on a procedure to establish a procedure, the meeting returned to the resolutions. Dr. Farians' attempt to introduce her resolution failed; the other resolutions passed 43 to 30.[38]

The January 1966 *Sacred Doctrine Notes* included a "Report of the *Ad Hoc* Committee on Procedures at the SCCTSD National Convention." Opening with an affirmation of the "basic freedom" of every member and region "to propose a resolution," the five-page report provided procedural details, specifying that up to 35% or two hours of the business meeting could be devoted to resolutions. Any discussion would follow *Robert's Rules of Order* to protect members' "right to an orderly, relevant and productive meeting." It also suggested the annual appointment of members to a rotating committee on resolutions to help coordinate their generation, submission to membership, and discussion.[39]

At the 1966 national convention in Denver, a resolution was submitted to establish policy and procedure for resolutions. Other resolutions reflected certain tensions beginning to arise in teaching college theology. One proposed a committee to examine the "complicated and pressing problem of academic freedom." Another protested "the silencing and/or disciplining of . . . priests, religious, or lay people . . . speaking out against events their conscience judges to be evil" not as church representatives but as individual Christians. Others dealt with everything from Newman Centers and ecumenical education to conscientious objection and founding a journal. A significantly modified resolution on women in the church appeared. Unlike Farians' focus on the bishops, this resolution focused on the Society establishing a committee to identify ways "to take definite and positive steps to forward the cause of women in the Church."[40] The resolution passed.

The following year in Pittsburgh, seventeen resolutions were proposed and five were accepted at the business meeting. They demonstrate the increase in contentious issues around college theology inclusive of teacher, student, means for studying, and the message in studying. Three concerned availability and content of theological graduate education including a GRE theology exam. Five dealt with various aspects of undergraduate education including substituting electives for required theology courses, determining students' background, and urging administrators to provide "equal status to theology departments and professors" in terms of teaching load, salary, and scholarly support. These appear to have received acknowledgment in a resolution recognizing the "place of Religion as an Academic Discipline." Another, reviewed and passed, sought permission for liturgical experimentation "to render the Liturgy more meaningful to the young people studying in our colleges and universities." College students required special consideration because they constituted "a unique group culturally, sensitive to specific idioms artistically, and intellectually adaptable to further liturgical advancement than the community at large may be." Regulation of reading appeared in two resolution proposals. A combination of the two passed. It called for an end to "prior censorship of books"; the other named the imprimatur as a cause of scholars' doubt of "Catholic freedom of inquiry." The resolution identified "critical review" among scholars as the better regulator of theological deficiencies and requested that the "Canon Law Commission" under the auspices of the U.S. Episcopacy "take steps toward the abolition of previous ecclesiastical censorship of books."[41] Concern over censorship eventually migrated from books to professors.

In Pittsburgh, seventeen "convention rules" were now in place to ensure that the discussion of resolutions proceeded in a fair manner. Only registered members could vote, discussion was regulated including a three-minute time limit with no additional opportunities for speaking, motions had to be submitted in writing, resolutions had to come through the national committee, and a quorum constituted a simple majority of members present.[42] Despite clarification of procedure, the board returned once again to the resolution process to consider in particular those that "come to the floor, which are in no way covered by the constitution." Examples included support of "the A.A.U.P. statement on academic freedom and tenure." Despite "some reservations as to its content and application to the Catholic college milieu," the board "agreed that these resolutions should be brought to the floor, submitted for discussion, and voted on at the business meeting of the members."[43] One controversial resolution had come from the floor, was discussed, and passed. In a letter dated 6 April 1967, Sloyan informed Alexander Zaleski, bishop of Lansing and chair of the "Bishops Commission on Theological Problems," of the controversial resolution. It called for "a thoroughgoing study of clerical celibacy in general and a reconsideration of the present mandatory celibacy" on a theological basis. Zaleski acknowledged receipt of the letter and indicated that he would inform the "President of the Conference of Bishops, who may want to bring it to the attention of its members."[44]

Two equally controversial issues came to the floor in 1968. Both indicate significant changes in Society members' understanding of a Catholic theologian's role and responsibility especially when compared to a 1965 resolution on the "priesthood of the faithful." In that resolution, only three years earlier, explicit mention had been made of abiding by the "norms enunciated by the II Vatican Council." The year of that resolution was the same year of the dismissal of thirty-one faculty at St. John's without due process. The following year the University of Dayton was embroiled in controversy after a faculty member charged another with failure to teach Catholic doctrine and the local ordinary got involved. And in 1967, Charles Curran's appointment at Catholic University had been terminated without due process.[45]

In 1968, discussions of the teaching status of those accused of "heterodoxy" and those identified as "laicized priests" or other former members of religious communities produced policy statements. Laicized priests with "excellent academic qualifications" were welcome as CTS members. The Society recognized laicized priests' "experience, apostolic zeal, and potential intellectual contribution" and "urges a thoroughly Christian attitude" avoiding "pejorative terms as 'derelict' or 'renegade.'" On the issue of heterodoxy, "any accusations or imputations concerning orthodoxy of doctrine taught by a teacher should be referred first to the department chairman for action as he shall determine." If the issue remained unresolved, the person should be judged "by a committee of his peers in the academic community," in a formal process that allowed the accused "to explain evidence prejudicial to his good-standing."[46] Interestingly enough, the resolutions discussed and passed simply affirmed academic freedom without mention of laicized priests or heterodoxy.[47]

The following year, another long list of resolutions appeared for consideration prior to 1 May 1969 even though a letter from the president, Francis J. Buckley, S.J., observed that "no resolutions were submitted to the Committee by individuals or regions." He reminded members that resolutions had not only effected change in the Society but also influenced "policies of college administrators and the National Conference of Catholic Bishops." He cited "resolutions on academic freedom, previous censorship of books, and liturgical experimentation in the colleges."[48] All together, twenty-one resolutions were passed at the 1969 convention, probably generated by the Resolutions Committee.

The variety of topics suggests a growing fragmentation in focus and concern in the college and university, civil society, and even the classroom. Two concerned Catholic higher education. The 1967 Land o' Lakes Statement became the CTS's official position; the 1940 American Association of University Professors (AAUP) statement on "Freedom and Tenure" was noted as applicable to "clerical and religious faculty." Three addressed alternatives to participation in the Vietnam War including affirming Catholic pacifism and "college theology teachers" assisting students with "the moral issues raised by the Vietnam War and draft." Another defended a theology teacher's "right to examine and discuss all aspects of the birth control question." Others were less specific such as support of a general theology requirement since courses were now taught "in such an objective and scientific manner." The range of concerns from military draft to curriculum requirements illustrated the varied roles that the college theology teacher now claimed.

Defending the rights of the college theology teacher returned in several 1969 resolutions. The primary location of college theology teachers was becoming more and more clearly located under the academy's authority rather than the church's. Two resolutions defended laicized priests teaching theology in Catholic colleges; another supported the "academic theologian" in the role of helping "the Christian community" develop "its understanding of doctrine," rather than "merely function[ing] as an advanced catechetical arm." One concerned a specific case: Boston College's possible violation of "the academic freedom of Dr. Mary Daly, a member of the College Theology Society." The resolution permitted an official expression of "concern to the President and Administration of Boston College" with a copy sent to AAUP. Perhaps the most significant resolution in terms of highlighting a changed perspective on theology's work was number seventeen: "Be it resolved that academic competence, not orthodoxy is the proper concern of the Catholic College and University, and that the institution has a responsibility to defend the academic freedom of the theologian in the face of accusations and imputations concerning orthodoxy." This resolution more than any of the others indicates that the College Theology Society had moved itself squarely into the academy even as it continued to seek various working relationships with the U.S. bishops through the National Conference of Catholic Bishops (NCCB).[49]

The major resolutions in 1970 were quite modest by comparison. Two sought to enhance the Society's academic reputation. Both opened with a "whereas clause" quoting from the constitution that "the College Theology Society is 'to develop the academic discipline of theology on a high professional level'" (Constitution, Article II). The first proposed establishing two annual awards: $100 for a book and $50 for an article. The other proposed publishing a bibliography of members' publications in the *Journal for Ecumenical Studies* or another appropriate venue. The former was accepted, the latter was not for fear that the bibliography would appear inadequate. Members' lack of scholarly activity, whether an accurate assessment or not, elicited discussion at several board meetings. The other resolutions focused upon internal Society matters.

A letter from Dr. David Michael Thomas, former chair of the Resolutions Committee, to Dr. James E. Biechler, new chair of the Resolutions Committee, suggested that member-generated resolutions had already reached their peak. "In general, the work is an exercise in frustration, but I was told that in the past our resolutions had some effect so with that hope, I threw myself into the work of compiling resolutions." Only two regions, Eastern Pennsylvania and Washington, D.C., contributed resolutions. "Personally, I should like the CTS to take a more prophetic stance on many issues—it might help to create a stronger sense of national solidarity."[50]

ONE AMONG MANY LEARNED SOCIETIES

Other organizations certainly recognized the CTS as possessing a national voice. The Society received several invitations to join other professional academic societies in various joint meetings. These affiliations illustrate once again the CTS's complex network of allies and constituents that straddled the teacher/scholar as well as the academy/church boundaries. The CTS was among the "Catholic Learned Societies" invited to a "1968 'Summit Conference' on doctrinal freedom in Catholic Schools, announced by College and University Department, NCEA [National Catholic Educational Association]."[51] The stated reason for CTS's participation was "the great good that can come to the Church by a fruitful dialogue between the hierarchy and the academic community" about "doctrinal truth and academic freedom."[52] CTS's growing commitment to the academy did not translate into complete disassociation from the Roman Catholic Church. As will be seen, the Society actively sought working relationships with the NCCB.

The College Theology Society also received an invitation to attend a meeting on 10 and 11 May 1969 in New York City to participate in establishing a Coordinating Committee for the Study of Religion (CCSR). This group constituted a significantly different network of dialogue partners whose common interests only occasionally overlapped with those of ecclesiastical officials. The CTS leadership's willingness to enter into both relationships accurately reflected a certain ambiguity relative to church and academy in a group of predominantly Catholic theologians, who usually taught required courses to primarily Catholic undergraduates at Catholic universities and colleges.

The CCSR envisioned itself as responding to the growing interest over the "past two decades" in studying "religion as a subject of academic inquiry." Given that the field was relatively new and still required determining "appropriate standards and procedures to be employed in the investigation," the CCSR could "facilitate coordination among various scholarly groups and the pooling of resources to help advance the academic study of religion." Among observations attributed to Samuel Z. Klausner and James Burtchaell was CCSR's ability to coordinate joint meetings that provided those rare opportunities for discussions between the humanists and scientists who study religion. Referring to a "common market" among scholars of religion from Catholic, Protestant, and Jewish backgrounds, Robert Funk spoke of the need for a common bulletin to provide information on grants, publications, and academic programs. Claude Welch and Jacob Neusner spoke of other publication ventures.

Robert Michaelson's more general remarks reiterated the distinct perspective and agenda of those trying to establish the "academic study of religion." He compared religious studies to an "underdeveloped country—now more diplomatically referred to as developing or emerging nations." He referred to its "rich cultural heritage" whose value is uncertain in "the modern world" and is fraught with "internal problems" such as "ecclesiastical ties, theology as 'queen', etc." that "tends to leave our field looking quaint, exotic, contentious, or just plain irrelevant." Representatives from the field need to work with "our publics" especially "relevant governmental agencies (where there is still a big job to be done in seeing the scholarly study of religion in an academic rather than a church-state framework), foundations, universities, and professional societies—both national and international." The CCSR, soon known as the Council on the Study of Religion (CSR), could help coordinate such efforts.[53] The CTS officers found the arguments compelling and became one of several learned societies to join CSR.

The Society had a long history of cooperating with "public" education associations. The group sent a representative, Donald H. Wimmer, to the National Council on Religion and Public Education (NCRPE), established in "December 1971 as a coalition of organizations concerned for including religion in public school curriculum." NCRPE sought "ways of studying religion which are educationally appropriate and constitutionally acceptable to a secular program of public education."[54] The existence of such an organization corroborates Michaelson's claims about developments in this field. Only a year after the Society's founding, active SCCTSD member John Hardon, S.J., furnished a report about a "Conference on Religion in Public Education," dated 15 November 1955. This group favored some kind of "religious training" in public schools and had met opposition, according to Hardon, from "sectarian groups," primarily smaller Christian denominations and liberal Jews, "Unbelievers" and "Religious Indifferentists." Hardon's report encouraged Catholics to enter into the fields of public education and work with like-minded Protestants for common goals.[55]

Sixteen years later, the CTS understood their participation as germane to their purpose: "the improvement of collegiate study of religion and theology." Increased understanding of religion in a secular curriculum "can only sharpen awareness of what is desirable (or undesirable) in a religiously oriented program of education." CTS could point to the United States Catholic Conference (USCC) National Center of Religious Education and the Confraternity of Christian Doctrine (CCD) as among "the first national organizations to pay membership dues" as further confirmation of their affiliation.[56] At the 1974 annual convention, Don Wimmer, chairman of the CTS delegation to NCRPE, offered a resolution that passed unanimously. The Society was to "urge departments of theology/religion to recognize the value of and include in their curricular offerings a treatment of the role of teaching about religion in secular programs of education," support efforts for study of religion in secular settings, and remain a member of NCRPE.[57] Wimmer's "study of religion in secular setting" stands in stark contrast to Hardon's "religion training." The shifts reflect not only the CTS's new understanding of its work but developments in the field of religious studies supported through publicly funded education. The efforts of NCRPE, however, had a negligible impact on integrating the study of religion into public education.

The CTS, unlike many of the CSR societies, also initiated efforts for maintaining some of those "ecclesiastical ties" that Michaelson disparaged. Part of the reasoning was no doubt to stave off "internal problems" but also to offer the Society's expertise to the church in a time of tremendous change. The CTS had established a "Committee on Bishops" for the express purpose of fostering good relationships with the NCCB. President Frank Buckley reported to the board in September 1972 that he had stopped in Oklahoma City to see Archbishop John Quinn, chair of the NCCB Committee on Pastoral Research and Practice. Quinn "expressed a desire to work out some form of regular contacts with CTS and put this item on the September agenda of his Committee."[58] How this mutual desire for "good relationships" fit with those resolutions that placed theologians squarely in the academy was not addressed.

THE SOCIETY AS ITS OWN WORST CRITIC

This interaction with such a wide variety of other groups seems to suggest a Society well established and secure in its own existence, but records of internal debates about the Society's continued existence indicate otherwise. As president in 1967, Father Sloyan acknowledged the CTS as perfectly capable of organizing effective annual and regional meetings and publishing a worthwhile newsletter. He insisted "that unless the regions are strong, membership is not worthwhile; unless the regions make the difference, the society will not make the difference." Father Sloyan also voiced a more serious concern—that "professionally" members were "not on a par" with others from the "professorial class." The "slow progress" he attributed to "growing ambiguity between the academic and the pastoral commitment of the profession." He affirmed Christianity's personal significance for students and faculty alike but judged college theology "not nearly as consequential as it should be in academic life." He attributed this failing to the lack of faculty preparation, especially when compared to "other academic professionals."[59]

To justify its continued existence, the CTS frequently highlighted its distinctiveness in serving the slowly emerging profession of college theology. A 1970 letter from James Wieland, president, compared the Society to the CTSA and AAR. He noted a change from early emphasis on Catholic identity "into a more academic and ecumenical one." According to Wieland, the Society possesses the "best features of the other groups . . . in the manner of an Hegelian dialectic."[60] A year later, when the board discussed merging with the CTSA, they remained convinced of the CTS "having broader interests, interdisciplinary concern; relating to the larger community of college administrators, faculty and students. The CTSA's context is seminary education, relations with U.S. bishops, and in research more historical." Merger made little sense to them given that from their perspective, the CTSA would circumscribe rather than expand members' opportunities for academic exchange.[61]

In January 1973, another CTS president, Frank Buckley, S.J., encouraged greater participation especially in regional gatherings and on national committees. He claimed the diminishing publications in the field have made "professional theologians . . . more dependent than ever on personal contacts for intellectual stimulation and growth." Under the heading "Scholarship in the CTS," Buckley observed that CTS's concerns about "professional standards" over the "last decade" fostered "debates . . . on whether and how to specify objectives and methods, on academic freedom and tenure, on interdisciplinary research and teaching." The Society's new journal, *Horizons*, and the newly established publication awards further demonstrated the Society's concern for academic standards. Buckley then encouraged members to publish more. "Keep asking. Keep seeking. Keep knocking on doors!"[62] These words of encouragement have a personal, almost pastoral quality that might lead the reader to wonder to what extent have CTS members remained reticent to publish.

The 1973 board faced more troubling news than Buckley's pep talk suggests. In 1973 an updated list of dues-paying members showed a drop of over a third in membership from 1,152 to 752 with no clear explanation as to the reason for the decline. Not surprisingly, the report generated a lot of discussion among members of the board of directors about promoting the Society. Plans already underway included the bulk mailing of a new brochure to "departments of religion, most of which are not in the Catholic stream." Several board members questioned such a mailing's effectiveness. "The secretary's reply was guardedly optimistic, noting that she was hopeful that by mere exposure through the brochure with its stated purposes, some people might be attracted." Discussion eventually turned to regional chairmen's roles in promoting the Society and the role of the vice president, currently Sister Vera Chester, in activating the regional chairs. Another member, Norm Wagner, pointed to the new journal as key to the Society's future prospects.[63]

The recently prolific Resolution Committee had once again in 1974 received no submissions. The committee attributed the lack of resolutions to the "substantial decrease in . . . dues-paying members"; little interest in committee work; and most critically, "the feeling among members that CTS is a kind of lower class replication of other organizations such as AAR, CTSA, CBA, SSSR [Society for the Scientific Study of Religion], SRHE [Society for Research into Higher Education], etc." They used recent national meeting programs to corroborate "the truth of this observation, for the subjects discussed and the papers presented" replicated those presented elsewhere. They assessed the situation as "not dire" but "critical" and offered a resolution to study the situation with the intended outcome of better defining the Society.[64]

The 1974 board meeting's discussion of a brochure revision reflected similar concerns. In trying to spell out a "precise 'focus' of CTS" three points were made—its "confessional stance," meaning "within the faith, with all that implies, and this qualifies its journal, convention, regional meetings, and studies." It remained Christian but "de facto Catholic," "geared toward undergraduate teaching, with all its ramifications. In this sense, it is in a limited way 'pastoral.'" It embraced a focus on "the *profession* of College Theology Teaching . . . an academic profession, in faith, it has as one of its components, academic research. This research, quite obviously, will for the most part relate to the job of teaching, and hopefully, be relevant to the college setting."[65] Such a discussion brought the Society back to its original focus of improving college theology but within a very changed context in church and academy.

At the annual meeting in Dayton, the board decided to amend the constitution, abolishing the underutilized standing committee on resolutions. This impending change precipitated a discussion of changing the Society's name to better "convey the focus and specific identity of our society as distinct from other organizations." Suggestions included the Association of Professors of Theology (APT), the Society of University Professors of Theology (SUPT), the Association of University Professors of Theology (AUPT), the Society of University and College Professors of Theology (SUCPT), and the Society of Professors of Theology in Universities (SPTU). The first two received the most "votes." General support for the name change was 11 to 2. The common terms in each suggestion were "professor" and "theology" with the new emphasis on the member, i.e., "professor" rather than the discipline, i.e., college theology. The general support went no further, and no name change occurred.[66]

A CTS questionnaire dated August 1974 from "the task force on Membership/Objectives" included suggested topics for investigation including "'salaries' [again] linked to 'slave labor'" of religious, faculty opportunities for women, gaining insight for the future; "greater focus on 'confessional theology'" teaching, the "relationship of society to Roman Catholic Church specif ically" and "merging with AAR." Conjecture on the decrease in membership included the lack of positions, state of profession, poor salaries, and "the departure from priesthood/religious life by former members who exercised a kind of charismatic leadership in the Society, e.g., Bernard Cooke, Maryellen Muckenhirn [Sister Mary Charles Borromeo]." On a more encouraging note someone observed the Society's "potential for developing a living intellectual background for Faith as so many members are associated with Christian institutions." Attention will now turn to that "living intellectual background" found in the volumes during the amazing decade usually identified as "the sixties."

NOTES

1. SCCTSD Minutes of Meetings of the Board of Directors, the Brown Palace Hotel, Denver, Colorado, April 10–12, 1966, "Board Meetings 1965–1967" Binder, Box 4, CTS Collection, ACUA.

2. SCCTSD Minutes of Meetings of the Board of Directors, Alverno College, Milwaukee, Wisconsin, September 30 and October 1, 1966, "Board Meetings 1965–1967" Binder, Box 4, CTS Collection, ACUA.

3. The information on change in word order is found in Rosemary Rodgers, O.P., *A History of the College Theology Society* (Villanova, PA: College Theology Society, 1983), 24. Business Meeting, Thirteenth National Convention, submitted by Maura Campbell, O.P., Penn-Sheraton Hotel, Pittsburgh, Pennsylvania, March 27, 1967, "Board Meetings 1965–1967" Binder, Box 4, CTS Collection, ACUA.

4. From the office of assistant secretary, College Theology Society, "National Meeting 1968" File, Box 1, CTS Collection, ACUA.

5. "American Academy of Religion" brochure, "American Academy of Religion" File, Box 5, CTS Collection, ACUA. An account of the change from NABI to AAR is discussed in D. G. Hart, *The University Gets Religion: Religious Studies in American Higher Education* (Baltimore: Johns Hopkins University Press, 1999), 202. Hart describes NABI as distinct from the Society of Biblical Literature because of the former's focus on teaching. Its transformation into AAR "was an effort to provide teaching and produce scholarship about religion compatible with the public and academic character of the university" (202).

6. Robert V. Smith to Sister M. Julie, C.S.J., May 31, 1965, Colgate University, with a letterhead that includes beside the American Academy of Religion, JOURNAL OF BIBLE AND RELIGION, on the bottom in fine print is noted "Formerly The National Association of Biblical Instructors," "American Academy of Religion" File, Box 5, CTS Collection, ACUA.

7. Father Carroll Stuhlmueller, C.P., to Sister M. Julie, C.S.J., June 12, 1965, Passionist Seminary, Louisville, Kentucky, in "American Academy of Religion" File, Box 5, CTS Collection, ACUA.

8. CTS Minutes of the Board of Directors, Manhattanville College of the Sacred Heart, Purchase, New York, October 6–7, 1967, in "Board Meetings 1965–1967" File, Box 4, CTS Collection, ACUA.

9. Passed as a resolution as found in the SCCTSD Minutes of the Business Meeting, Sheraton-Jefferson Hotel, Saint Louis, Missouri, April 20, 1965, "Board Meetings 1965–1967" File, Box 4, CTS Collection, ACUA. Dean of Sacred Heart University Bridgeport to house the service according to a memo from James Wieland, July 22, 1965. The placement service was officially ended in April 1971. See "Minutes of Meetings of the Board of Directors," the Saint Paul Hilton Hotel, St. Paul, Minnesota, April 12–14, 1971, "Board of Directors Meetings 1971–" File, Box 1, CTS Collection, ACUA. Teaching Opportunities Information Listing (TOIL) announced its beginnings in 1973 as part of CSR.

10. CTS Minutes of the Board of Directors, October 6–7, 1967.

11. "Fourteenth National Convention, College Theology Society, Draft of resolutions to be offered to the CTS membership by the Committee on Structures and Possible Constitutional Reform," "Secretary's Data 1968–1970" File, Box 2, CTS Collection, ACUA.

12. "Summary of Questionnaire Responses on Professional Status of C.T.S. Membership," "Secretary's Data 1968–1970" File, Box 2, CTS Collection, ACUA.

13. "Secretary's Data 1971" File, Box 1, CTS Collection, ACUA.

14. CTS [sic] in "National Meeting 1968" File, Box 1, CTS Collection, ACUA.

15. CTS Minutes of the Semiannual Meeting of the Board of Directors, Century Plaza Hotel, Los Angeles, California, September 2–5, 1972, in "Board of Directors Meetings 1971–" File, Box 1, CTS Collection, ACUA.

16. CTS Minutes of Semiannual Meeting of the Board of Directors, Philadelphia Marriott Motor Hotel, City Avenue off Schuylkill Expressway, Philadelphia, Pennsylvania, [10 a.m. Monday, April 23, 1973], "Board of Directors Meetings 1971–" File, Box 1, CTS Collection, ACUA.

17. College Theology Society, "Minutes of Semi-annual Meeting of the Board of Directors," Manhattan College, Bronx, April 22, 1972, "Board of Directors Meetings 1971–" File, Box 1, CTS Collection, ACUA.

18. Rodgers, *A History of the College Theology Society*, 31.

19. Report "Should the College Theology Society Publish a Journal?" by Rodger Van Allen, Villanova University, Member/CTS Committee on Publications [no date], "Board of Trustees, 1971–" File, Box 1, CTS Collection, ACUA.

20. Memo to Publication Committee, College Theology Society, from Thomas M. McFadden, February 15, 1973, "Board of Trustees 1971–" File, Box 1, CTS Collection, ACUA.

21. Thomas M. McFadden, Publication Committee Office to "Colleague," Saint Joseph's College, Philadelphia, Pennsylvania, nonarchived material.

22. Thomas McFadden, chairman of Publication Committee to "Colleague," Publication Committee Office, Saint Joseph's College, Philadelphia, May 7, 1973, nonarchived material.

23. College Theology Society, "Minutes of Semi-annual Meeting of the Board of Directors," Palmer House, Chicago, Illinois, November 10–11, 1973, "Board of Directors Meetings 1971–" File, Box 1, CTS Collection, ACUA.

24. College Theology Society, "Minutes of Semi-annual Meeting of the Board of Directors," Philadelphia Marriott Motor Hotel, April 23, 1973.

25. "SCCTSD Minutes of Meetings of the Board of Directors," April 18–20, 1965.

26. Richard W. Rousseau, S.J., "Report on the Theology Seminar Discussions" in *Proceedings of Society of Catholic College Teachers of Sacred Doctrine Eleventh Annual Convention* (Saint Louis, Missouri, April 19–20, 1965; Weston, MA: Published by Society at Regis College, 1965), 186–192.

27. "Minutes of Meetings of the Board of Directors," March 26–28, 1967.

28. "Call for papers and presentations for the 19th Annual CTS Convention," Sister Vera Chester, C.S.J., chairman, Program Committee CTS, the College of St. Catherine. CTS Min-

utes of the Semiannual Meeting of the Board of Directors (Century Plaza Hotel, Los Angeles, California, September 2–4, 1972) in "Board of Directors Meetings 1971–" File, Box 1, CTS Collection, ACUA.

29. "CTS Minutes of Semi-annual meeting of the Board of Directors," April 23, 1973.

30. "Minutes of Semi-annual Meeting of the Board of Directors," November 10–11, 1973.

31. "CTS Social" flyer, "Secretary's Data 1974" Box 1, CTS Collection, ACUA.

32. Sister M. Julie, C.S.J., SCCTSD secretary to fellow member, February 1965, Regis College, Westin, Massachusetts, "Secretary's Data April 1964–April 1965" Binder, Box 2, CTS Collection, ACUA.

33. Sister M. Julie, C.S.J., to fellow member, January 1966, Regis College, Weston, Massachusetts, "Secretary's Data May 1965–April 1966" Binder, Box 2, CTS Collection, ACUA.

34. "Minutes of Meetings of the Board of Directors," March 26–28, 1967.

35. "Secretary's Data 1968–1970" Binder, Box 2, CTS Collection, ACUA.

36. "Business Meeting and Reports" and "Resolutions" in *Proceedings*, 193–194 and 197.

37. Elizabeth Jane Farians to Sister M. Julie, C.S.J., secretary of SCCTSD, February 1, 1965, in "National Meeting 1965" File, Box 1, CTS Collection, ACUA.

38. "Society of the Catholic College Teachers of Sacred Doctrine Minutes of the Business Meeting," Sheraton-Jefferson Hotel, Saint Louis, Missouri, April 20, 1965, in "Secretary's Data April 1964–1965" File, Box 2, CTS Collection, ACUA. Cf. "Procedures for the SCCTSD National Business Meeting SCCTSD" in "Board Meetings 1965–1967" Binder, Box 4, CTS Collection, ACUA.

39. *Sacred Doctrine Notes* I, 1 (January 1966), "Secretary's Data May 1965–April 1966" Binder, Box 2, CTS Collection, ACUA.

40. "SCCTSD Resolutions, Twelfth National Convention, 1966, Denver, Colorado." "Board Meetings, 1965–1967" File, Box 4, CTS Collection, ACUA. See also "National Meeting 1966" File, Box 4, CTS Collection, ACUA.

41. "National Resolutions Committee: Master List, being a verbatim transcription of all resolutions in submission as of March 1, 1967," Thirteenth National Convention, SCCTSD [sic], Pittsburgh, Pennsylvania, March 26–28, 1967, in "National Meeting 1967" File, Box 1, CTS Collection, ACUA. See CTS Business Meeting Thirteenth National Convention, Penn-Sheraton Hotel, Pittsburgh, Pennsylvania, March 27–28, 1967, in "Board of Directors Meetings, 1971–" File, Box 1, CTS Collection, ACUA.

42. "Convention Rules," in "National Meeting 1968" File, Box 1, CTS Collection, ACUA.

43. Minutes of Meetings of the Board of Directors, March 26–28, 1967.

44. Gerard S. Sloyan, president of CTS to Alexander Zaleski, Lansing, Michigan, March 31, 1967; and Alexander Zaleski, bishop of Lansing to Gerard Sloyan, president of College Theology Society, April 8, 1967, "National Meeting 1968" File, Box 1, CTS Collection, ACUA.

45. Philip Gleason, *Contending with Modernity: Catholic Higher Education in the Twentieth Century* (NY: Oxford University Press, 1995), 309–314. See also Mary Jude Brown, "Souls in the Balance: The Heresy Affair at the University of Dayton, 1960–1967," (Ph.D. diss., University of Dayton, 2003).

46. "Agenda" in "Secretary's Data 1968–1970" File, Box 2, CTS Collection, ACUA.

47. CTS Business Meeting, Fourteenth National Convention, Hotel Saint Francis, San Francisco, California, April 14–16, 1968, in "Board of Directors Meetings 1955–1970" File, Box 1, CTS Collection, ACUA.

48. "College Theology Society: Office of the President," University of San Francisco, San Francisco, California 94117 [1969], nonarchived material.

49. "Revised Draft of Resolutions for College Theology Society, April, 1969" attached to College Theology Society Business Meeting, Fifteenth National Convention, Sheraton-Chicago

Hotel, Chicago, Illinois, April 6–8, 1969, "Board of Directors Meetings 1955–1970" File, Box 1, CTS Collection, ACUA. The resolutions had to be mailed out because of a lack of a quorum at the business meeting. The results attached indicate all received a majority of affirmative votes.

50. David Michael Thomas to Dr. James Biechler, Theology Department, St. Louis University, August 12, 1973, nonarchived materials.

51. "Agenda," in "Secretary's Data 1968–1970" File, Box 2, CTS Collection, ACUA.

52. "Consensus Report from February 2–3, 1968, Meeting of CTS Committee on Current Problems," "National Meeting, 1968" File, Box 1, CTS Collection, ACUA. [Agenda also attached]. This document was to be circulated by the members in their departments. No clear procedure was in place for acting on the items.

53. "Agenda for the Coordinating Committee for the Study of Religion," New York, May 10–11, 1969, in "National Meeting 1969" File, Box 1, CTS Collection, ACUA.

54. Brochure, nonarchived materials.

55. "Conference on Religion in Public Education," by John Hardon, S.J., West Baden College, West Baden, Indiana, November 15, 1955, "Current Problems Committee" File, Box 5, CTS Collection, ACUA.

56. "College Theology Society, Meeting with Regional Officers," Century Plaza Hotel, Los Angeles, California, September 3–4, 1972, submitted by Sister M. Gertrude Anne Otis, nonarchived files.

57. "College Theology Society—1974 Annual Convention, May 31–June 2, 1974, Proposed Resolution from the Committee on *Religion and Public Education*," "National Council on Religion and Public Education" File, Box 4, CTS Collection, ACUA.

58. "Minutes of Semi-annual Meeting of the Board of Directors, Century Plaza Hotel, Los Angeles, California, September 2–5, 1972, "Board of Directors Meetings 1971–" File, Box 1, CTS Collection, ACUA.

59. "Report of the President, 'College Theology Society, Minutes of Meetings of the Board of Directors'" Manhattanville College of the Sacred Heart, Purchase, New York, October 6–7, 1967, "Board Meetings 1965–1967" Binder, Box 4, CTS Collection, ACUA.

60. James Wieland, president to "Member of the College Theology Society," Sacred Heart University, Bridgeport, Connecticut, November 14, 1970, "National Meeting 1970" File, Box 1, CTS Collection, ACUA.

61. "Minutes of Semi-annual Meeting of the Board of Directors," Manhattan College, Bronx, New York, April 1, 1971, "Board of Directors Meetings, 1971–1972" File, Box 1, CTS Collection, ACUA.

62. Francis J. Buckley, S.J., president, College Theology Society to "Colleague," "Presidential Newsletter" (University of San Francisco, January 1974), nonarchived material.

63. Minutes of Semiannual Meeting, November 10–11, 1973, "Board of Directors Meetings 1971–" File, Box 1, CTS Collection, ACUA.

64. "Report of the Committee on Resolutions," CTS Annual Meeting, Dayton, Ohio, May 31–June 2, 1974, submitted by James E. Biechler, chairman, Ronald Mizen, S.J., and Rachel Reeder, nonarchived material.

65. Memo "To: Members of the Board of Directors, CTS, [From: Sister Miriam Ward, office of the secretary, Trinity College, Burlington, Vermont], Date: May 31, 1974, Board Meeting University of Dayton, Dayton, Ohio, Re: Brochure revision." "Secretary's Data 1974" File, Box 1, CTS Collection, ACUA.

66. "College Theology Society, Minutes of Semi-Annual Meeting of the Board of Directors," University of Dayton, Dayton, Ohio, May 31–June 2, 1974, "Board of Directors Meetings 1971–" File, Box 1, CTS Collection, ACUA. No account was found as to why the change did not take place.

• 4 •

Theology as Liberation, Revolution, Freedom (1965–1974)

The Society's annual publications tell much about the "living intellectual background" that formed the theological preoccupations, concerns, and interpretive frameworks, not only among the Society's members who attended the national meetings, but also among those educated at Catholic colleges and universities in that remarkable span of years from 1965 to 1974.[1] The Second Vatican Council's work appeared in the foreground of the SCCTSD's concern in the beginning of its second decade. The council's effects remain important even in the fiftieth year, though gradually receding into the background and eventually into the undercurrents of the theological work displayed in CTS meetings and publications over the next four decades.

The words and phrases that appear with regularity in the annual volumes' titles, from 1965 to 1974, like "the other side," revolution, paradox, freedom, and liberation capture sentiments more intense than "change" implies. These choices connote ambiguity, upheaval or rupture, and a thrust into a new and bewildering reality. The titles also give evidence of that frequently evoked phrase in contemporary theology—"the turn to the subject" or the "anthropological starting point." Terms such as "religious secularity," "quality of life," "being a man" or "more human," "liberation," and even the question about Jesus making a difference are extensions of discussions from the preceding ten years about humanistic approaches to college theology, Catholic social action to reclaim the secular for Christ, or educating laity to serve as "pontifex," the bridge builder between the church and secular society. These views have been extended so far as to be turned inside out—the restoration is not of the secular to the Christian but of the Christian to its full experience of humanity, of Christianity/Catholicism to the world.

Some titles also suggest a newfound modesty. Rather than pinpointing the "finality" or "science" of college theology, the Society offers dimensions, reflections, and perspectives. This final observation is not intended to further a stereotype of the period preceding the council. The earlier chapters make it clear that enough creativity, experimentation, as well as critical questioning, existed around college theology to generate the founding of a professional society dedicated to fostering deeper levels of creativity, experimentation, and critical questioning. Nor did doctrinaire closed-mindedness evaporate after the council. Competition for the most doctrinaire could be just as fierce among and between those resistant to change and those utterly committed to its fullest implementation.

The following selections are taken from a small portion of the essays contained in the annual volumes. They are intended to convey something of the breadth of the subject matter covered in this ten-year period. The topics presented here include first, reflections on the council and then, assessments of theology teachers and their students. Examination of theological currents presents effects of an existentialist/personalist framework, the transformative impact of hermeneutics, and attempts to reconfigure ecclesial authority.

THE SECOND VATICAN COUNCIL: METAPHOR FOR CHANGE

The council awakened many Catholics to a reimagining of "Church." Without a trace of irony, the Jesuit John Powell characterized the church as "a magnificent structure, rated second only to General Motors as the most efficient organization in the world." He described its creed, canon law, papal authority as evidence of this highly organized structure. Then he asked, "is this highly elaborate organization really the Church of the Galilean fishermen?" His answer was a qualified yes as he provided an image of high contrast to the corporation—"a stumbling, battered pilgrim on its way to its destiny."[2] This "pilgrim church" serves as "the bride and body and presence of Christ in the world today, that is the avenue by which man goes to the encounter with God, and in which he is met by God."[3] In affirming the church as mediator of God, he used traditional ecclesial images affirmed in *Lumen Gentium* but read that mediation through a personalist, rather than scholastic lens, evident in the individual's "encounter with God."

Others conveyed the changes that the council effected with a little more dramatic flair. Sister Roderick O'Neil, R.S.H.M., in "Hermeneutics: The Encompassing-Which-Scripture-Is," confirms in the article's introduction what the daring title promises. She compares a Turner exhibit in the New York

Museum of Modern Art to the "science of interpretation" as it "invites us to think of Scripture in terms of personal revelation." A bolder comparison followed. The effects of the "Dogmatic Constitution on Divine Revelation" was likened to "LSD on human consciousness" in producing a "supersonic crack" centering on "salvific truth" in scripture.[4] Drawing from an eclectic mix of scholars including Carroll Stuhlmueller, C.P., Karl Rahner, S.J., Rudolf Bultmann, and the post-Bultmannians, Carl Jung, Marshall McLuhan, and Harvey Cox, O'Neil identifies "the elements of language, culture, distance, and time that vibrate in the written word of Scripture," as the hermeneutical task. For O'Neil, the exegete's historical-critical method unnecessarily constrained the interpretive process. "The synoptic problem is a pseudo-problem for the budding existentialist, who is so enamored of subjectivity that he would protest if the synoptics *had* come up with the same picture of Christ!" "'The Encompassing-Which-Scripture-Is" utilizes "a sociopolitically variegated key" to open "the revelation latent in the Denver Daily News or the New York Times," to discover "salvific meaning—that is, a potentiality for redemptive consequences—in the turmoil of a Selma or a Saigon." O'Neil wanted to form a student "much more responsive to the gospel-of-everyday that summons him [quoting Harvey Cox's *Secular City*] to 'imaginative urbanity and mature secularity.'"[5] Such a student has a task strikingly different from not only his or her parents but also an older sibling whose Christian maturity was measured only a few years earlier in the ability to withstand and eventually transform the secular order into a Christian one.

Revolution and redemption had, it seemed, broken into the world. Reverend Raymond A. Parr, president of the SCCTSD in 1965, called his fellow members to consider "the whole history of man . . . as a gradual and progressive liberation," identifying the twentieth century as "the century of liberations." Examples cited include medical advances, national movements of independence, and women's growing awareness of their freedom. Parr then turned to salvation history with liberations from Egypt and Babylon, and then to Christ where human freedom found its ultimate expression. Parr included those in his audience as agents in that salvation history. "We, the Society of Catholic College Teachers of Sacred Doctrine, have just moments ago, in Eucharist assembly extended in this agape, chosen to be the sign of freedom to each other, to this community, and to the whole world. Our very presence here in the freedom of the Risen Lord makes a demand upon us: it demands that we be prophets of human freedom." Describing those before him as choosing to be signs and as being called to be prophets on behalf of human freedom reoriented the focus away from the message to the messenger, the college theology teacher who instigates the "personalist revolution."[6]

TEACHING COLLEGE THEOLOGY
IN A TIME OF REVOLUTION

What had not changed were the great expectations laid upon the college theology teacher. With council-generated enthusiasms abounding, demands on theology teachers intensified. Raymond Parr, in that same presidential address, called for the "teacher-prophet" who "must take his student to the very root of his being." Such a teacher "takes his utterance from the heart of God to the heart of his student." To obey this utterance, this "law" creates a "vision" of humans in God's image and a "competence in freedom and in being human." Parr charged each "teacher-prophet" to conduct "his charismatic search" through attentiveness to student "demands and needs," parents' expectations, and the church's call for "Christian leadership" from "Catholic college graduates."[7] The prophet here acts as God's messenger delivering good news about human living.

Sister Anita Caspary, I.H.M., delivered a similar challenge in a 1968 presentation on "The Self-Image of the Contemporary Young Adult." She calls upon the theology teacher to be "poet" as well as "prophet." In this dual role, the teacher discloses "alternatives for young adults, to assure them by his living testimony that the important words—truth, faith, and above all, hope—are realistic." Like Parr's teacher-prophet, the poet-prophet "translate[s] the Word God into the here and now, to break into the world of man meaningfully, to permeate the lives of men with the content of the Word." Poetic translations might include creating or discovering "new myths, analogues, out of film and folksong, out of dance and pop art." In both, the teacher must not only convey something of God's Word but do so in a way that is experientially gripping, transforming, and meaningful. Whether such effects were possible on a regular basis in any formal setting let alone a college classroom received little serious examination, but then such were the enthusiasms of the time when sweeping changes intensified even the most ordinary of classroom meetings.[8]

In "The Psychology of Communication to a University Mind," Brother C. R. Wilson, F.S.C., offers a less glamorous emphasis: the college theology professor's role as "an authority." From a student's perspective, the "professional theologian" is now viewed "as a spokesman for the church, a representative of official teaching" regardless of "the instructor's personal competence." Effective communication requires "relevance, relativity, and naturalness" to be credible with students. All three are grounded in assumptions about the students' desires and predilections. He concludes that "the modern demands are such that theology will have to be creative or it will not survive as a field of knowledge" and praised those contemporary theologians who appear to be meeting that challenge.[9] Wilson's essay highlights the other side of the theology teacher's challenge in being "an authority"—sorting out the relationship to church teaching authority.

In examining "The Challenge of Religious Studies in State Universities," John Hardon introduces two more complicating factors in teaching college theology—laity teaching and teaching "religious studies" at secular institutions. Rather than the token priest or religious, Hardon advocates "training competent laymen for teaching positions in secular colleges" and criticized "Catholic universities [that] still fear to give laymen advanced degrees in the sacred sciences." He notes that "seminaries are even more intransigent."[10] Not only secular institutions but also Catholic colleges ought to foster "a pluralism which respects the faith of others, studies different religious systems, and wrestles with alien modes of thought." A Catholic institution can certainly make its own philosophical commitment clear without compromise. "Until teachers are prepared to handle orthodoxy and heterodoxy and are willing to trust themselves and the faith they profess to contradiction from the best intellectual critics of 'Catholicism and Christianity,' they are open to invidious comparison with secular (especially state) university educators whose main boast is that they are free to examine what Catholic institutions dare not touch." In clarifying what he meant by "intellectual critic," Hardon names many a bête noire of Catholic thought from Freud to James to Dewey to Marx to Gibbon to Harnack to Altizer to Robinson.[11]

At the 1970 annual meeting, Matthew C. Kohmescher, S.M., provided a report on "College Theology Teachers: Status of the Profession." Demographics of Catholic institutions of higher learning provided further insight to the challenges of college theology teachers. Of the 137 responses from colleges and universities, over half had fewer than a thousand undergraduates, and forty-one had between one and five thousand. Fifty-six schools had a theology faculty of five or fewer; twenty-five schools had between six and ten. The most common semester teaching load was twelve credit hours, teaching between one hundred and 120 students. Hiring of "laicized priests" and "divorced persons" remained restricted with only 58% permitting such hires. Questions surrounding Catholic identity and academic freedom elicited Komescher's observations that bishops "were much more vocal in asserting the 'Catholic factor'" but "at the same time that the bishops were almost unanimous in expressing the need for academic competency." Academic freedom was generally affirmed.

Questions concerning the relationship to the magisterium generated many comments indicating "there is a lot of work to be done here." Approximately half of presidents and department chairs and even more deans and vice presidents recognized having a relationship to the teaching office. "All but one bishop saw such a relationship." Areas of agreement included "respect for the magisterium," recognition of "professional obligations when presenting the teaching of the magisterium," as well as an emphasis on theology as an academic discipline. The bishops recognized theology's academic character "but focused strongly on the teaching of 'Catholic' doctrine to 'Catholic' students at our 'Catholic' universities." Among the "Conclusions and Suggestions" were better prepared departmental chairs, more faculty involvement in hiring, increased student participation in a department's work, a "uniform policy" for lay and "clerical/religious faculty," and "study and clarification" of a theology department's and its university's relationship to the magisterium. The committee recommended the Society focus on "the topic of improving college teaching," create "a bureau" to provide theology departments "a committee of 'peers'" to adjudicate "some complaints," and in a similar fashion furnish "evaluators" of "local theology departments and programs."[12]

A NEW BREED OF STUDENTS

Expectations of the college theology teacher arose out of assumptions about the students. As one essayist, Rabbi Eugene Borowitz, noted in 1966, "Something has happened—and that something seems irreversible." Students appear in these volumes as quite different from their immediate predecessors. They no longer passively or piously accept what is taught since they have learned that maturity requires them to "criticize and challenge" so they might "exercise their autonomy." These students are "a new breed" who want to look at religion dispassionately with a critical stance, a reflection of "the secular style of our age" that requires an adequate response from theology professors.[13]

Evidence for these changes came as frequently from popular culture's renditions of youth as from actual classroom experience. In introducing the annual volumes from the 1968 and 1969 conventions, the editor, George Devine, invokes two popular songs, "Changes" (1968) and the musical *Hair*'s "The Age of Aquarius" (1969) to convey student sentiments and perspectives. The first song contributed ambience to a film featuring young people "frolicking among the trees," viewing Manhattan from the Jersey palisades, driving in the slums of Newark and New York, and protesting and confronting people. No words, only music conveyed the film's message. Shown in "an interdisciplinary course entitled 'Psychotheology,'" this film captured what Devine surmised to be this generation's struggles because they "have in many ways had the psychological rug yanked out from under them, and so have developed growing pains unlike those of other generations." Devine placed the church in a similar situation in relation to the psychological rug. The volume, *To Be a Man*, "represents the inner life of a scholarly community" whose "dialogue and self-examination" concerns "the existential needs and situations of those students whom we serve." Devine noted that such a discussion required more than the "gray, pedestrian reports of just what was said by a group of teachers to each other," a negative reference linking the muted color of pre-1966 *Proceedings* with the quality of their content.[14]

Cautious support for protesting generally prevailed in the few essays that specifically address the topic. Reverend Joseph Travers, O.S.F.S., counseled developing the virtue of prudence to militate against the danger of students transforming into an "inhuman herd."[15] On the other hand, Gerard A. Vanderhaar, O.P., found in student movements evidence of "genuine theological interest" in student questions "about values; they want to understand whatever meaning life has." Despite students' negative attitude toward "the institutional church," an updated theology has the potential to meet students' "hunger for deeper meanings and insights into life."[16] William J. Kelly, S.J., similarly asserted that the theology professor is uniquely attuned to those students seeking "to be brought into the decision making" at "the paternalistic and authoritarian university." His assertion was based on Marquette's faculty active engagement in raising "social consciousness" and developing "community and responsibility."[17] Results of Eugene F. Shaw's empirical study of Marquette students corroborated Kelly's claims. "The theology department contributed the most militant students and the most militant faculty members to the Movement, according to the respondents, who conceded, however, that neither were 'actually too militant.'"[18]

For those who understood the primary agents of change to be the younger generation, the students had a distinct advantage over the professors. In "Where, How, and Why You Think Is What You Think," John H. Westerhoff describes himself as "an immigrant to a new age" in which the younger generation "teach adults the issues and questions, which must be addressed." In theology, "the people of God and theologians" must focus on "the process of reflection and discourse related to human life and action" rather than on "doctrine." Theology must "enable people" to live in "a world of change" instead of indulging in "long tirades on yesterday's pieties and the puzzles of antiquarian thought." To teach "living" requires engagement beyond the classroom confines. Westerhoff illustrates with a vivid account of what is surely a classic "experimental liturgy" held at the house of a young priest, who is described as "wearing sports clothes." The full effect requires a lengthy quote.

The house had a festive atmosphere. Large colorful paper flowers and birds hung from the ceiling. I was greeted with a bag decorated on the outside with large dayglow colors which read, "We Care." Opening the bag, I found a large red and yellow sheet of tissue paper with a hole in the middle and a variety of other things. We each picked a partner to dress in the paper costume. We read our partner part of an E. E. Cummings poem found in the bag: "I love you most beautiful darling, more than anything on earth, and I like you better than anything in the sky." We fed each other a Hershey kiss. Together, we stuffed a balloon with confetti, blew it up, tossed it into the air, punctured it with a pin. As the confetti fell over us, we blew party horns. The daily news programs, blaring from the two television sets in the room, were turned down as someone began to strum a guitar. Everyone joined in the folk song, "Turn, Turn, Turn," as we made our way to the table.

Given that the priest then blessed bread and wine, one can presume the celebration was some form of a Eucharistic liturgy. The participants ate the blessed food with cheese and fruit as they discussed "how to address racism in one's own particular place. Two hours later, after making definite resolves for action, we sang, 'We Shall Overcome,' and with the kiss of peace, departed into the night." Clearly those who participated had moved beyond "yesterday's pieties and the puzzles of antiquarian thought."[19]

The student in many of these essays takes on an exotic quality—the stranger or other who now escapes the grasp of modernity just as Catholic college theology teachers finally had permission to embrace it. In describing "The Crisis in American Culture—A Religious Interpretation," William Murnion describes young people's "exalting art over science, intuition over calculation, involvement over detachment, subjectivity over objectivity." He attributes experimentation with "drugs," love of "rock," wearing "exotic clothing," and explorations of "Eastern religions and occultism" as a desire for "escape from Western culture," as a means of freedom. Murnion then identifies "women's liberation and gay liberation" as a more positive and lasting means to freedom "because they affect the psyche at its profoundest depths."[20] Freedom appears in several essays like a code word for a conscious focus on the individual whose autonomy and personal choice define authentic human life.

TURNING TO THE SUBJECT

The "turn to the subject" provided the methodological sanction for this embrace of "the human"—a seemingly abstract idea undergirded by philosophical concepts borrowed from existentialism and personalism. Freedom and autonomy defined values for "the human" celebrated within the "secular city" made famous or perhaps infamous through Harvey Cox's book of that title. Katharine Hargrove, R.S.C.J, informed her reader of "the principle that unites" the essays in *The Other Side*, the 1966 *Proceedings*. It was the "existential emphasis on the freedom of the individual in the mature structuring of faith to choose for or against the Church, for or against commitment to God, for or against involvement in the society of man."[21] What is striking is the absence of any warnings about the consequences of choosing "against" especially when compared to earlier discussions fretting about teaching that might endanger students' faith. The silence reflects the changing understanding of the college theology teacher's role and responsibility to confront the world as it is in 1966, a secular city rather than a potential Christian social order.

The 1967 *Proceedings*, aptly entitled *The Paradox of Religious Secularity*, provided Hargrove with an opportunity to present the results of those for and against choices in the secular realm. To clarify the phrase, "religious secularity," Hargrove's preface evokes the memory of Judith, "a religious secularist who accepted the risk of autonomy" within her own situation. This woman of the Bible exemplifies the power of "free choice, free decision, and free involvement in the human situation" for understanding "what it is to live a divine milieu."[22] Such enthusiasms had their more temperate counterparts in assessing secularity's impact on religion. The already mentioned Rabbi Borowitz cautioned against an unfettered optimism in confronting "secular triumphalism." Most contemporaries "find it as natural to ignore religious coffee houses, theological folk singers, and jazz liturgy as conventional religious activities." The "outreach" may trigger "a speedy return to religious reaction, a post-postconciliar stance, so to speak."[23] This prediction's merit lies in its recognition of the power not only of secular influence but also of long-formed religious commitments in the face of a hyperrelativism.

Robert Michaelsen, by way of contrast, seemed to concede victory to the secular in identifying "experience" as replacing "belief" or "faith"—"experience in love" and "experience of life—especially the joyous, festive celebration of life." He took his cue from the "hordes of healthy, zesty . . . bumptious youngsters [who] dig life." A religion that attracts the young "celebrates life, which helps them live" though he conceded that such religious expression "might just add up to one big pagan ball of wax." In light of young people's interests, Michaelsen advised the "Christian theologian" to "describe faith as intimately related to life" and avoid "normative terms, realizing that words, while useful and necessary, must be related dialectically to experience."[24]

Andrew Greeley simply confirmed and then affirmed the younger generation's turn to the personal—"personal love, personal fulfillment through love, love as a condition for fulfillment" as the day's "primary and essential ethical and religious issues." He named "Freud, Kierkegaard, the existential-ist, Paul Tillich," as "the prophets of the personalist revolution . . . a revolu-tion which may be one of the greatest cultural breakthroughs, the greatest leaps forward the human race has ever made." It promotes "openness, honesty and authenticity." The most authentic personalist must be the Christian whose belief in resurrection allows a complete confidence in ultimate "self-fulfillment." "The promise of the Resurrection not only underpins personal-ism but personal growth anticipates the Resurrection." Greeley insisted that this personalism only occurs "in relationships," with marriage serving as "a paradigm of death and resurrection."[25] He chided Roman Catholic officials including theologians for "losing our nerve." They have ignored "the sign of the times" and failed to recognize how "their own tradition can speak directly, brilliantly, inspiringly" to young people's questions and desires.[26]

PERSONALIST TOUCH, EXISTENTIAL QUANDARY

The influence of personalism and a distilled form of existentialism on theo-logical discourse cannot be underestimated. From the 1970 annual meeting came an entire volume entitled, *New Dimensions in Religious Experience.* Twenty-three essays, over three hundred pages of text, examined various as-pects of "religious experience" beginning with that of "Man." The opening es-say by Gregory Baum declares that "traditional worship and piety have be-come more difficult, more problematic, and for some Christians an empty form." They do have resources for "new (religious) experience" in "conversion" and "reconciliation" that is "a touching of the mystery alive in oneself and in others as source of new consciousness."[27] Consideration was then given to the "religious experience" as found in a wide variety of sources including Pauline literature, Friedrich Schleiermacher, Confucianism, Buddhism, Judaism, and even atheism. Essays chosen for consideration of the Catholic communal ex-perience focused on papal infallibility and John Henry Newman, the former having to do with reassessment of ecclesial authority in light of the Second Vatican Council and *Humanae Vitae*; the latter because of the cardinal's unique role in theological discourse concerning doctrinal development and conversion through a complex intellectual-affective assent to faith. The final section focuses upon students' religious experience and "the responsibility of theologians." Here the essays affirm "theology class" as "a forum" for the stu-dent to "articulate his search for the religious experience."[28] Others assume an ability to connect with and redirect the students' search for meaning made ev-ident in everything from their exploration of Eastern religions to their exper-imentation with drugs.

The 1972 convention placed the existential squarely in the theological tradition by posing the question: Does Jesus make a difference? This particular question would have never occurred to the vast majority of the Society's founders. Perhaps they would have posed the question more like "How does Jesus make a difference?" Yet, the essays themselves left little room for doubt that the contributors assumed a difference exists, though each in his or her own way reflected the need to re-examine the issue under the new methodological conditions of theology. "The question has become 'existential'—a shift entirely consonant with the contemporary emphasis on the subjective meaning and significance of the realities Christians have chosen to live by."[29] The annual volume features essays from a wide range of perspectives including those of the early church to contemporary systematic approaches identifying "the uniqueness of Jesus," or "Jesus as the Horizon of Human Hope," or "Jesus as the Presence of God in Our Moral Life," or Jesus as inspiration to "Political Christians," or "Death and the Meaning of Jesus."[30]

The personalist perspective had another spokesman whose presentation at the 1973 meeting did not appear in the annual volume. The *Philadelphia Inquirer* provided some information in its Saturday, 28 April 1973 edition entitled "'Godspell' Author Sings Out," concerning John Mitchell Tebelak's presentation at the College Theology Society's convention. "The shaggily bearded figure tugged sheepishly on the faded blue overalls that sparkled with rhinestones as he stood before the group of nuns and clergymen." He described himself as "terrified" in a later interview. The article notes that despite the fact that "his play is an attack on organized religion, the audience welcomed Tebelak enthusiastically and praised him for finding a new way to spread the Word." The play came to Tebelak after a snowy Easter Sunday when he "was stopped and searched (presumably for drugs) in the church vestibule" as he was leaving Mass. "The show is Tebelak's view of Christ as a happy, lovable person rather than a gloomy serious teacher." He also notes that "I am finding the church is not the bugaboo I thought it was," adding that "nuns and priests are his best audiences. 'They know the Bible so well, thye [sic] get the jokes the best.'" The article makes no mention of the conference theme, "Does Jesus Make a Difference?" or of other major presenters.[31]

The personalist approach appeared in more than popular culture's rendition of religious faith. The exceptionally influential Catholic intellectual, John Noonan, gave a presentation at the 1972 international meeting. His essay, "Making One's Own Act Another's" deftly combines his legal and theological knowledge to consider the humanizing potential of church law in so far as one dominant strand of "Christian thought has stressed the unique character of each life on earth, and perceived each unique being here as linked to others by the bonds of love." In and through Christ, "our acts are acts of another's not by legal fiction but by likeness."[32] The result is a theological vision that determines the legal construction of the person—a Christian personalism.

Another influential figure, in this case in biomedical ethics, Daniel Callahan opened the volume *That They May Live: Theological Reflections on the Quality of Life* with an examination of what "quality of life" means in an age of affluence. His reflections outline a future "in which life will be weighed in terms of benefits." The young here are not Michaelsen's "bumptious youth" or even Greeley's self-possessed personalists. They are the alienated who find themselves in "a crisis of meaning and value." Those materially secure discover "that quantity does not insure quality" given the unhappiness among the affluent.[33] The search for meaning had taken on a more somber intensity.

THE QUESTION

The de rigueur of existentialism and personalism was "the question"—why do I exist, who am I, what does "it" mean, how do I live authentically. Catholic theology had certainly known the "quaestio," but these questions were of a different order. In discussing the "Freedom to Question as a Necessary Condition for Theological Questioning," Sister Ann Patrick Ware, S.L., from Webster College, describes the new circumstances of the Catholic college teacher. "Our problem, then, is not whether freedom to question is a necessary condition to theological learning, but *what* within the scope of theology is to be questioned."[34] Her essay ends with a plea for a thorough understanding of the relationship between the theologian's teaching and that of the magisterium, including the ordinary magisterium. She envisioned theologians doing more than posing questions. If unable to effect a positive role, Ware warns, Catholic theologians will be singing along with Robert McAfee Brown a new version of a familiar Christian hymn:

> Faith of our fathers, once so great,
> We must revise or be out of date,
> We must distinguish kerygma from myth,
> Or they won't be worth bothering with.
> CHORUS:
> Faith of our fathers we accept,
> Save for the parts that we reject.[35]

Five years later, John J. Mawhinney seemed to have joined McAfee's chorus with his message concerning "the ethics of belief." He described a "new morality of knowledge" that demands "a Roman Catholic Christian . . .

be willing to question any and every dogma—the divinity of Christ, eternal life, the infallibility, indefectibility and perpetuity of the Church and the existence of God." Mawhinney's ethics permitted a theologian "to work within the confines of a particular religious tradition" as long as the person engaged "in open communication with those who pursue the study of religion from a broad cross-cultural (and I should add, cross-disciplinary) approach."[36]

If Mahwhinney attempted to dislocate the theologian to expand his or her knowledge, then Nathan R. Kollar, in "The Hermeneutic of the American 'Now,'" attempts to pinpoint the scholar's exact location to highlight the inevitable limitations in perspective, in this case, "the American 'now.'" From his analysis of "the present hermeneutic," Kollar asserts some "very concrete, practical consequences for the academic study of religion," including the influence of the scholar's "own personality," the limits of "historical research" in so far as "the meaning" of the past work is defined in terms of the questions put to it from "the present," and the "chaos" inherent in "the interpretative process." Attempts to produce "a systematic unity of answers to one question" are futile.[37] Mahwhinney's and Kollar's essays appear in the same volume and represent two basic tendencies in recent theological discourse. The former tends toward a more abstracted, universalist position; the latter a more located, particularist position. Variations on these two perspectives animate much of the debate within the CTS and other sites of theological discussions for at least the next forty years.

METHOD: HOW TO GET THEOLOGY RIGHT

Mahwinney and Kollar, like Ware, represent the widespread preoccupation with how to do theology correctly, in other words, a concern for method, in part to fill the void left by neo-scholasticism's collapse. One of the late twentieth-century's Catholic masters of method, Bernard Lonergan spoke to this "Revolution in Catholic Theology" at a CTS session during the 1972 international meeting of learned societies in the study of religion. Bernard Lonergan located the methodological revolution in hermeneutics and history emerging from an empirical awareness of culture as context for all knowing coupled with the end of speculative theology in light of science and contemporary philosophy. He predicted the focus to be "conversion, intellectual conversion, moral conversion, religious conversion."[38] Both commentators challenged Lonergan's analysis as too abstract. William Murnion situated the revolution in the "practical" through religious leaders like the Berrigans, Dom Helder Camara, and Bishop Gumbleton.[39] Austin B. Vaughan doubted the lasting influence of methodological changes and suggested paying more attention to the "life of the Church" rather than the "mental processes of theologians."[40]

The two tendencies displayed in Lonergan and his commentators are evident in every field of theology but perhaps nowhere so clearly as in ethics. Attendees of the 1970 convention had an opportunity to see a foremost representative of each position. Charles E. Curran, priest from the diocese of Rochester, had recently been reinstated as a professor at Catholic University of America after being fired for dissenting from the teaching on artificial means of birth control. He took for his task tracing "some changes and developments . . . in the methodological approach to [Roman Catholic] social ethics," particularly as related to natural law now and in the future. Curran called for a "sound theological and philosophical methodology" able to "grapple with change" from a critical vantage point. Recent magisterial social teaching reflects "an insistence on both the dignity and freedom of the person and the complexities of contemporary existence calling for a correspondingly larger role of the state in social life." Curran's Roman Catholic social ethics situated its analysis around "man's life in society" based upon a complex balance of relations among "truth, justice, love, freedom and power."[41]

It is this situating social ethics in society rather than the church that Stanley Hauerwas objected to in his response, "The Future of Christian Social Ethics." He describes Curran's ethics as requiring "the Church and Christians to pay more attention to the necessities of power and the 'operational' (how to) means of the implementation of social justice." With this as the focus, "the Christian . . . must exercise power, he must coerce, he must finally kill . . . only then [the Church's] social ethics will be more than 'platitudinous.'" His stark commentary is intended to highlight that "the question of violence is *the* question of Christian social ethics" for those who wish to "become the world." He offers an alternative, "a distinctively Christian social ethic." It is "the Church" whose "primary ethical responsibility is to be herself" which means "refusing to take up the ways of the world even in the name of a good cause."[42] These two positions remain among the most influential in theological discourse on "church" as it relates to "world."

College theology curricula reflected the influences particularly in generating theological explorations in areas that had previously received little or no attention. The desire to break with the immediate past and seek the new is an undercurrent evident throughout the period's annual volumes. In the 1967 volume on religious secularity, Mary Eileen Paul took her inspiration from the "Council Fathers," who had the "courage" to consider "these very practical dimensions of our eucharistic life." She, in turn, speaks of a eucharistic-informed curriculum to "reveal us as present to the creative center of our culture" and an "open institution, present to ourselves as ongoing event, present to the *present* of our students, our faculty, our immediate social community, our Church community, and the world."[43]

This presence to the "present" quickly translated into reflections on political, cultural, and social engagement. Rosemary Radford Ruether examines Gabriel Vahanian and Thomas T. Altizer in "Two Types of Radical Theology." She commends Vahanian's theology in which "'death of God' [is used] prophetically to break apart our sterile and empty cultural symbols of the divine."[44] Richard Shaull found his theological inspiration in the renewed emphasis on eschatology through the Kingdom of God image to engage in transforming a technology-dominated society through "the formation of small groups of people who are free to search for new perspectives and new solutions, . . . a *political* equivalent to guerilla warfare."[45] The previous year, John Cogley professed his belief in a "post-modern revolution—[that] is worldwide in scope; it is Universal in its grasp; and it is profoundly rooted in the human personality." He chided theologians along with priests and bishops for their failure to teach "the social meaning of faith" but did not exclude the possibility that "theology has something to offer the political enterprise" if and only if it frees itself from its past.[46] Those at the 1968 convention where Cogley spoke could have begun by listening to Jack Vaughn talk about the Peace Corps "attempting to deal with reality, not images."[47]

The final example that Jack Vaughn used concerned the "long and hallowed tradition" of women's "almost complete subjugation." This treatment of women "not only constitutes an unpardonable affront to their dignity, not to say their humanity, but seriously retards the process of development."[48] Women's subjugation appeared as a problem not just in some distant developing nation. Sister Jane Stier, O.S.U., provided what is now a familiar historical account of women's religious communities as male dominated. She wondered whether the male domination of their communities "is largely the fault of us women" who are not "simply subordinating the structures of their lives to the needs of the apostolate." Similar to other strategists of the CTS conventions, Stier called for small, incremental changes "until the time when a woman or her work or her ideas can be chosen not because she is a woman but because she has a contribution to make in a particular area." Subordination to the apostolate appeared to include all the major events culminating in ordination itself, since Stier asserted that the poor wanted the Gospel preached whether the priest be male or female.[49]

One also finds here the beginnings of an ecological ethic. Two examples appear in *That They Might Live: Theological Reflections on the Quality of Life*. Hugh McElwain considers "Anthropocentricity: New Ways of Theologizing in an Evolutionary Context." He urges better understanding of a "man-centered cosmology" to ensure "that proper attitudes can be fostered for the acceptable and harmonious ordering of *all* the elements in our eco-system, *including* man."[50] Robert L. Faricy in "Faith and Ecology" insists that any "Christian ethic of involvement in environment change" must be "a theological understanding" centered in faith in the Risen Christ.[51]

THEOLOGY AND ITS AUTHORITIES

The fundamental question that runs like an undercurrent through all of these theological explorations, occasionally rising to the surface, concerns the source of authority in judging theological matters. Bernard Häring, C.Ss.R., in his 1965 talk on "The Constitution *De Ecclesia* and Freedom," illustrated the optimistic anticipation of the council's impact on lay participation in the church. He spoke of "the *sensus fidei*, the discernment of the faith which is given to the whole people of God." He imagined collegiality to involve not only dialogue among the bishops but a bishop's "patient dialogue with his priests and with all the faithful of his diocese." Häring emphasized the difference from the lay movements identified with Catholic Action. "This is an application of collegiality, not just a lay apostolate under a *mandatum*, as executors of the pastors' initiatives." He chose an example, the irony of which could not possibly have been anticipated. "The classical application of this principle is the papal commission on responsible parenthood. Two-thirds of this commission are lay people, so whatever advice the Pope receives from its members, married people cannot complain that decisions have come from priests who have no competence."[52]

Gabrial Moran, F.S.C., hinted at potential conflicts that the Christian's newfound freedom might generate. A Christian enjoys the freedom to "live the truth as he sees it while working with whatever intelligence and love he finds among superiors and equals." The commitment may require the Christian "to oppose a human authority" as the apostles did—an opposition arising out of "genuine respect and love for authority." Moran made crystal clear that "God is speaking to his church. Freedom is alive and growing and there is no force on earth that can stop it." The force behind this growth is "the charity of Christ [which] presses us."[53] Optimism remains even in the face of conflict.

Russell Barta, Ph.D., spoke of "Freedom as a Condition for the Lay Apostolate" and reflected an optimism similar to that of Bernard Häring and Gabriel Moran. He noted that the "American hierarchy," though clear on "gospel norms," has "respected freedom of laity" in "specific determinations of their actions in the temporal affairs of their community or profession." The shift that Barta identified was "the presence of more and more laymen who are asking for greater responsibility for the common good of the church, and with responsibility, greater freedom." Toward the conclusion of his remarks, Barta mentioned the birth control controversy, indicated the outcome remains unclear, and that the concern about losing authority because of change in teaching does not indicate much confidence in the laity. He ended on an up-beat note with the hope of an increase of creativity within the church as laity are given more freedom and responsibility.[54]

The birth control issue proved to be a source of controversy that few could have fully anticipated. *To Be a Man* was the first *Proceedings* to include essays not delivered as convention papers because of the decision to include essays specifically addressing the controversies surrounding *Humanae Vitae*. The essays were guarded in their criticism. Vincent Zamoyta observed in his opening remarks on the ethical issues of "the near future which will make the problem of artificial birth control almost ridiculously insignificant." He read Paul VI's position as a caution to those entering into control of "human life." The theologian's obligation is to complete a "careful and thorough study" in conversation "with his scientific peers" to contribute to the church's "deeper understanding of truth." Where Zamoyta parted company with many of his colleagues was in their advising "the faithful that they can opt noncompliance for their own reasons." Zamoyta furnished a logical extension of such advice. "The Pope's authority is binding only to the extent that we agree with his reasons." He used the analogy of a teenager no longer required to obey his or her parents unless in agreement "with their reasons for their commands." Zamoyta argued that even more is at stake in the theologian's "challenging the *authority* involved." In "challenging the authority itself which gives him his premises, he pulls the rug out from under his own feet. He destroys himself as a theologian."[55]

The other two essays only indirectly address *Humanae Vitae*, and neither exhibits a direct challenge to the document. One is in fact a homily delivered in the midst "of the initial explosion over the encyclical *Humanae vitae*." Father Kohli refused to celebrate a liturgy as planned by members of the college community. His reasons centered on the Eucharist as a sign of unity with the whole church. To celebrate "the Eucharist in the way prescribed for us by the Council, the rubrics, and the Bishop, we are set free from many limitations of our own into the dynamic life of the universal Church, the vine and Body of the Lord Jesus." For him, "the identity crisis is what is expressed in the privately created liturgy," which is different from the new liturgical rites in the vernacular. He refused to celebrate the liturgy as representing that identity crisis given that it is intended as a sign of unity in Christ's Body.[56]

The following year, Avery Dulles tried to sort out in a more systematic fashion the issues surrounding "The Magisterium and Authority in the

Church." He admitted "that theologians, as a class, have traditionally experienced an ambivalent relationship toward higher teaching authority—a mixture of love and hate, respect and resentment." The magisterium sometimes protects against "unfair charges," and other times acts as judge against the theologian who as "the critic, the innovator, the explorer . . . is likely to chafe under the curbs of authoritative teaching, especially when the authorities decide against his own opinion." Dulles alluded to recent controversies over *Humanae Vitae* as "a certain 'spice of martyrdom' . . . added to the lives of some theologians in recent months."

Despite these difficulties, "the times call not for a dismantling but for a rehabilitation of the *magisterium*." Key to this task is determining "a proper relationship between the juridically supreme teaching power of the bishops and the equally undeniable right of the faithful in general, and competent experts in particular, to exercise their doctrinal responsibility." The bishop's teaching responsibilities are "to give public expression to the doctrine of the Church." The theologian, also a teacher, examines "the present situation of the Church and of the faith, with a view to deepening the Church's understanding of revelation and in this way opening up new and fruitful channels of pastoral initiative." That process, at times, requires raising difficult questions that may be in tension with the bishop's teaching responsibility. Yet, like Zamoyta, Dulles cautioned against theology so independent that it "weaken[s] the corporate witness of the Church. While preserving its scientific integrity and autonomy, theology should be conscious of its ties with the *magisterium*." To adjudicate these difficulties, Dulles advocated some institutionalizing of "the participation of theologians in the Church's decision-making processes" as found in the Middle Ages where theologians had a "quasi-hierarchical status." Prelates alone cannot teach church doctrine effectively. "They must 'tune in' on the theological wisdom that is to be found in the community, and bring it to expression. Thus the theologians are not totally external to the *magisterium*, considered as a function or process."[57] When not in the foreground of theological reflection, these concerns about teaching authority remained ever present in the background as theological trends continued to change.

FROM PERSONAL FREEDOM TO POLITICAL LIBERATION

In the twentieth year of annual meetings, the College Theology Society turned once again to considerations of freedom, though in a new context of political and liberation theology. Francis Fiorenza provided the annual volume's opening essay—an examination of political and liberation theologies using German theologians including Johannes Metz, Dorothee Sölle, and Jurgen Moltmann and Latin American theologians such as Gustavo Gutiérrez, Juan Luis Segundo, and Leonardo Boff to represent the two types respectively. What is most interesting relative to a historical account of the College Theology Society is each one's critique of those theological movements that had informed much of what the Society imbibed and produced in the previous decade. "Political theology" stands against "the consequences of the enlightenment and secularization as they have been spelled out in existential, personalistic, and some strains of transcendental theology." It critiques religion's privatization and individualistic focus "by elaborating a new hermeneutic of the relationship between theory and praxis." The primary focus of "Liberation theology" is "the oppression and injustices within the Latin American scene." It highlights "the inadequacies of the models of Catholic liberalism as well as the theology of social action or the lay apostolate" and clarifies "the meaning of the symbols of the Christian faith for the concrete situation and praxis in Latin America."[58] The turn to the political, whether in theory or practice, stands in sharp contrast to the existential/personalist focus on finding one's "self" in personal religious experience.

The second portion of the text: "Liberation Theology and the Contemporary Search for Freedom" illustrates the contrast, though the illustration is probably unintentional. In a remarkable essay, "Freedom, Hope, and History," James H. Cone provides a theological account of liberatory praxis. "Human freedom is grounded in God's freedom to be with us in history, disclosing that our future is to be found in the historical struggle against human pain and suffering." Appealing to the spirituals, Cone then weaves his theological reflections on freedom within the experience of African American enslavement and the ongoing commitment to the struggle for freedom. These spirituals serve as illustrations of the struggle for freedom grounded in a hope in "what God has done and will do to accomplish liberation both in and beyond history. Indeed, because we know that death has been conquered, we are set free to fight for liberation in history—knowing that we have a 'home over yonder.'"[59]

T. Richard Schaull's essay stands in contrast giving a highly personal account of "my struggle for liberation" as "a white, middle class, male, North American." His self-description reveals "his involvement in the construction of prisons for the great mass of human beings living in the world today" despite living in Latin America for twenty years. His self-referential discussion focuses on imprisonment in institutions from marriage to education. Previous mediations of grace seem no longer available. He looks to an "experience of grace" manifest in "the creation of a new individual and group identity over and against the dominant system." An effective theology must be "incognito" in the contemporary situation.[60] Letty Russell provides an overview of "Liberation Theology in a Feminist Perspective." The essay presents a fairly moderate "feminist theology" defined "as reflection on the meaning of God's will to bring about full human liberation and the partnership of women and men in church and society."[61] Other essays explore freedom in American Indian religion and Zen Buddhism and raise questions concerning the use of violence as a means to liberation, and the final three offer Christian-based critiques of liberation theology.

As the second decade of the Society began, Catholic college theology seemed to be on the cutting edge but which side of that edge was not entirely clear. In "Dimensions of Theology in a Catholic College," presented at the 1966 convention, Christian brother, C. Stephen Sullivan ruminated on a *Look* magazine article "which suggested that the end of Catholic education's reason for existence in this country is in sight." Yet, in the postconciliar era, college theology had more reasons to exist then than before. Any adequate curriculum ought to "include a study of the Church, revelation, personal freedom, and the social questions facing the world today" in addition to now standard "biblical, liturgical, and ecumenical" studies. He called for a "fearless openmindness" in this pursuit. The council produced "a magnificent experience, a thrilling spectacle" and a tumultuous future, by Brother Stephen's account. The council, with all its greatness, "has violently changed our way of life and thinking" whose full effects have yet to be realized. Teaching theology, as a faith-based discipline, becomes even more critical at this juncture. "The next phase of the Council's accomplishments is beginning—and I believe it will be an arduous period of uncertainty and confusion."[62] The essays that fill the annual volumes for the next ten years (1975–1984) give witness to the magnificent, the arduous, the uncertain, and occasionally the confused as college theology continued to unfold in this period. Experiences bearing similar descriptions give shape to the life of the Society itself during that same period.

NOTES

1. A list of the themes and accompanying publication serves as an overview for a selective account of the theological discussions recorded in the annual volumes. The themes and annual volumes appear here in chronological order: "Freedom and Responsibility," *Proceedings of the Society of Catholic College Teachers of Sacred Doctrine*, Eleventh Annual Convention (1965); "The Relevance of Theology for the University World," *On the Other Side: Proceedings of the Society of Catholic College Teachers of Sacred Doctrine* (1966); "The Church in the Modern World," *The Paradox of Religious Secularity* (1967); "Images of Man," *To Be a Man* (1968); "The Teacher in

the Church," *Theology in Revolution* (1969); "Religious Experience," *New Dimensions of Religious Experience* (1970); "The Quality of Life," *That They May Live: Theological Reflections on Quality of Life* (1971); "Religion and the Humanizing of Man" [International Congress of Learned Societies in the Field of Religion], *A World More Human; A Church More Christian* (1972); "Does Jesus Make a Difference?" *Does Jesus Make a Difference* (1973); and "Liberation, Revolution, and Freedom," *Liberation, Revolution, and Freedom: Theological Perspectives; Proceedings of the College Theology Society* (1974). The dates reflect the year of the annual meeting rather than the publication date of the annual volume.

2. Reverend John J. Powell, S.J., "Ecclesial Dimension of Faith," in *On the Other Side: Proceedings of the Society of Catholic College Teachers of Sacred Doctrine*, ed. Katharine T. Hargrove, R.S.C.J., (Englewood Cliffs, NJ: Prentice Hall, 1967), 47.

3. Reverend John J. Powell, S.J., "Ecclesial Dimension of Faith," in *On the Other Side*, 56.

4. Sister Roderick O'Neil, R.S.H.M., "Hermeneutics: The Encompassing-Which-Scripture-Is," in *On the Other Side*, 61. The artist is probably J. M. W. Turner.

5. O'Neil, "Hermeneutics: The Encompassing-Which-Scripture-Is," 62, 65.

6. "SCCTSD Minutes of Meetings of the Board of Directors," Sheraton-Jefferson Hotel, Saint Louis, Missouri, April 18–20, 1965, "Secretary's Data April 1964–April, 1965" File, Box 2, CTS Collection, ACUA.

7. "Presidential Address," in *Proceedings of Society of Catholic College Teachers of Sacred Doctrine Eleventh Annual Convention* (Saint Louis, Missouri, April 19–20, 1965, Weston, MA. Published by Society at Regis College, 1965), 7–12 passim.

8. Sister Anita Caspary, I.H.M., "3. The Self-Image of the Contemporary Young Adult," in *To Be a Man*, ed. George Devine, the *Proceedings of the College Theology Society* (Englewood Cliffs, NJ: Prentice Hall, 1969), 22, 23. Caspary was the mother general of the original I.H.M. (Servants of the Immaculate Heart of Mary) community in Los Angeles (1963–1970). She became the first president of the new Immaculate Heart lay community (1970), made up of the vast majority of the I.H.M. community who left the I.H.M. rather than concede their reforms when ordered to do so by the directives of Los Angeles Cardinal McIntyre. The fact that the artist, Corita Kent, was also a member of her community may have influenced Caspary's perspectives.

9. Brother C. R. Wilson, F.S.C., "The Psychology of Communication to a University Mind," in *On the Other Side*, 19, 27.

10. Reverend John Hardon, S.J., "The Challenge of Religious Studies in State Universities," in *On the Other Side*, 86.

11. Reverend John Hardon, S.J., "The Challenge of Religious Studies in State Universities," in *On the Other Side*, 90–91 passim.

12. Matthew C. Kohmescher, "18. College Theology Teachers: Status of the Profession," in *That They May Live: Theological Reflections on the Quality of Life*, ed. George Devine, Annual Publication of the College Theology Society (Staten Island, NY: Alba House, 1971), 297, 298, 302, 303, 304.

13. Rabbi Eugene B. Borowitz, "1. Confronting Secularity," in *The Paradox of Religious Secularity Proceedings of the College Theology*, ed. Katharine T. Hargrove, R.S.C.J., (Englewood Cliffs, NJ: Prentice Hall, 1968), 3–5.

14. George Devine "1. Changes," in *To Be a Man*, 5, 6, 7.

15. Reverend Joseph A. Travers, O.S.F.S., "The Limits of Student Protest for Peace, and Freedom for Clergy and Religious," in *On the Other Side,* 44.

16. Gerard A. Vanderhaar, O.P., "5. The Peace Movement, the Draft, the New Left and the College Theologian," in *Theology in Revolution*, ed. George Devine (Staten Island, NY: Alba House division of the Society of St. Paul, 1970), 97.

17. William J. Kelly, S.J., "6. Student Power and the Theology Professor," in *Theology in Revolution*, 112, 114.

18. Eugene F. Shaw, "7. Student Power at Marquette University: An Empirical Analysis," in *Theology in Revolution*, 138.

19. John H. Westerhoff, "8. Where, How, and Why You Think Is What You Think," in *Theology in Revolution*, 149, 150, 154, 162–163, 164.

20. William E. Murnion, "9. The Crisis in American Culture—A Religious Interpretation," in *That They May Live*, 153.

21. Katharine T. Hargrove, R.S.C.J., "Introduction," in *On the Other Side*, 3, 4.

22. Katharine T. Hargrove, R.S.C.J., "Preface," in *The Paradox of Religious Secularity*, vi.

23. Rabbi Eugene B. Borowitz, "1. Confronting Secularity," in *The Paradox of Religious Secularity*, 7.

24. Robert Michaelsen, "2. How Much Can Today's College Student Believe?" in *To Be a Man*, 13.

25. Reverend Andrew Greeley, "1. Dynamic Theology—Today and Tomorrow," in *Theology in Revolution*, 15, 16–17.

26. Greeley, "1. Dynamic Theology—Today and Tomorrow," 28.

27. Gregory Baum, "Religious Experience and Doctrinal Statement," in *New Dimensions of Religious Experience: Proceedings of the College Theology Society*, ed. George Devine, (Staten Island, NY: Alba House, 1971), 7–9 passim, 11.

28. Marcia McDermott, "The Religious Experience of Students as the Starting Point for Teaching Theology," in *New Dimensions of Religious Experience*, 256.

29. Thomas M. McFadden, "Introduction," in *Does Jesus Make a Difference? Proceedings of the College Theology Society*, ed. Thomas M. McFadden (NY: A Crossroad Book, Seabury Press, 1974), iii.

30. Seely Beggiani, "Mythological and Ontological Elements in Early Christology"; Monika Hellwig, "The Uniqueness of Jesus in Christian Tradition"; Andrew Maloney, " Jesus as the Horizon of Human Hope"; William E. May, "Jesus as the Presence of God in Our Moral Life"; John A. Gray, "The Apolitical Jesus but Political Christians"; Joseph A. LaBarge, "Death and the Meaning of Jesus" in *Does Jesus Make a Difference?*, 30–43, 81–98, 113–128, 186–208, 209–229.

31. NC News Service piece dated 4/26/73, "Secretary's Data 1973" File, Box 1, CTS Collection, ACUA.

32. John T. Noonan Jr., "Making One's Own Act Another's," in *A World More Human; A Church More Christian*, ed. George Devine with Thomas McFadden and Thomas L. Sheridan, S.J., editorial board (NY: Alba House, 1973), 156–157.

33. Daniel Callahan, "The Quality of Life: What Does It Mean?" in *That They May Live*, 5.

34. Sister Ann Patrick Ware, S.L., "Freedom to Question as a Necessary Condition for Theological Learning," in *Proceedings of Society of Catholic College Teachers of Sacred Doctrine Eleventh Annual Convention* (Saint Louis, Missouri, April 19–20, 1965). (Weston, MA: Published by Society at Regis College, 1965), 94.

35. Ware, "Freedom to Question," 103.

36. John J. Mawhinney, "5.The Ethics of Belief: Methodological Implications," in *That They May Live*, 84–85.

37. Nathan R. Kollar, "8. The Hermeneutic of the American 'Now,' "in *That They May Live: Theological Reflections on the Quality of Life*, 142–143.

38. Bernard J. F. Lonergan, "Revolution in Catholic Theology," in *A World More Human*, 134.

39. William E. Murnion, "Commentary on 'Revolution in Catholic Theology,'" in *A World More Human*, 138, 139, 140.

40. Austin B. Vaughan, "Commentary on 'Revolution in Catholic Theology,'" in *A World More Human*, 144.

41. Charles E. Curran, "6. Roman Catholic Social Ethics: Past, Present and Future," in *That They May Live*, 87, 112, 120, 121.

42. Stanley Hauerwas. "7. The Future of Christian Social Ethics," in *That They May Live*, 129–131.

43. Mary Eileen Paul, "3. The Future of Eucharistic Life in the College," in *The Paradox of Religious Secularity*, 33–34.

44. Rosemary Ruether, "9. Two Types of Radical Theology," in *The Paradox of Religious Secularity*, 65.

45. T. Richard Shaull, "11. Confronting the Power Structures: Cooperation or Conflict?" in *The Paradox of Religious Secularity*, 96–97.

46. John Cogley, "11. The Image of Political Man," in *To Be a Man*, 110, 113, 119.

47. Jack Vaughn, "12. Tilting at Treadmills," in *To Be a Man*, 123.

48. Vaughn, "12. Tilting at Treadmills," 130.

49. Sister Jane Stier, O.S.U., "14. Women in the Church," in *The Paradox of Religious Secularity*, 121, 122.

50. Hugh McElwain, "2. Anthropocentricity. New Ways of Theologizing in an Evolutionary Context," in *That They May Live*, 17.

51. Robert L. Faricy, "3. Faith and Ecology" in *That They May Live*, 29, 43.

52. Bernard Haring, C.Ss.R, Lateran University, Rome. "The Constitution De Ecclesia and Freedom," in *Proceedings . . . Eleventh Annual Convention*, 45, 48, 55, 56.

53. Brother Gabriel Moran, F.S.C., "Freedom in Christian Revelation," in *Proceedings . . . Eleventh Annual Convention*, 77.

54. Russell Barta, Ph.D., "Freedom as a Condition for the Lay Apostolate," in *Proceedings . . . Eleventh Annual Convention*, 119, 123, 125.

55. Vincent Zamoyta, "9. On Humanae vitae: A Search for Human Understanding," in *To Be a Man*, 83, 87, 88, 89, 90.

56. Reverend Charles Kohli, "13. A Time To Be at One," in *To Be a Man*, 137, 140.

57. Avery Dulles, "2. The Magisterium and Authority in the Church," in *Theology in Revolution*, 29, 30, 35, 37, 40–41, 44.

58. Francis P. Fiorenza, "Political Theology and Liberation Theology," in *Liberation, Revolution, and Freedom: Theological Perspectives; Proceedings of the College Theology Society*, ed. Thomas M. McFadden (NY: A Crossroad Book, Seabury Press, 1975), 5.

59. James H. Cone, "Freedom, History, and Hope," in *Liberation, Revolution, and Freedom*, 62, 73.

60. T. Richard Shaull, "Grace: Power for Transformation," in *Liberation, Revolution, and Freedom*, 76, 85–86, 87.

61. Letty Russell, "Liberation Theology in a Feminist Perspective," in *Liberation, Revolution, and Freedom*, 95.

62. Brother C. Stephen Sullivan, F.S.C., "The Dimensions of Theology in a Catholic College," in *On the Other Side*, 30, 31, 32, 33.

· 5 ·

Defining Membership, Defending Members of the College Theology Society (1975–1984)

The College Theology Society had successfully negotiated its way through a time of enormous change in the discipline of theology and its sometimes competitor and other times collaborator religious studies. Upheavals in church, society, and university, all had a role in the changed circumstances of the Society. Now approaching its silver jubilee, the CTS turned its attention once again toward self-assessment. It hoped that reorganization might attract more members and entice current members to greater participation. The "Task Force on Membership and Objectives" proposed in 1976, eventually distributed an "80-item opinion questionnaire" to gather information about members' professional status as well as perspectives on the Society's nature and purpose. The task force described the questionnaire as an "honest solicitation of membership opinion" and "an exercise of democratic process," which contrasts with the church's official responses to current ecclesial crises.[1] Like most "democratic processes," this one proceeded slowly. Five years elapsed between initial discussion and final report. Conjecture as well as empirical analysis of the Society's perceived decline and potential for resurgence abound. Most observers returned to two of the Society's original defining characteristics. First, the Society focused on teaching undergraduate theology with a notable increase of emphasis on the scholarly demands on those who teach theology. The second concerned the Society's Catholic identity, a focus that mirrored the reassessments occurring in Catholic colleges and universities.

RECLAIMING THE SOCIETY'S IDENTITY

Accounts of the Society's history noticeably shaped expectations for the future. A relatively common account had evolved that depicted a society founded to fill in gaps among learned societies—gaps that no longer existed in those other societies. Charlie Brannen, S.J., a frequently frustrated organizer of Chicago's region, appealed to his "fallible understanding" to provide a historical account, that he attributed to Sister Assunta Werner, C.S.C., from Saint Mary's College, South Bend. "Barney Cooke and others organized it twenty years ago because CTSA did not admit women." The older theological society had also failed to "address itself to college problems" and "was snobby toward college people." The major goal of the "founders" was "to professionalize college people." Brannen observed "that professionalization has been achieved in great part. ERGO, our better members are into AAR, SBL [Society of Biblical Literature], SSSR, CTSA, Biblical, Canon Law, Moral, Patristics, Oriental . . . associations." In a world of limited time and scant financial resources, according to Brannen, the CTS offered little to make it stand out compared to the other professional societies. "Many of the historical reasons for founding the CTS no longer prevail." The Jesuit admitted that his "analysis may be wrong." Besides the possibility that a Holy Cross sister overlooked one of her own as the Society's founder, the further irony is the historical account appeared in a letter accepting nomination to run in the next board election.[2]

Brannen had one critical detail correct. The Society had been founded to address the challenges of teaching college theology, a discipline that still eluded precise definition. In a cover letter accompanying brochures mailed to colleges and universities, the secretary Richard L. Schebera, S.M.M., insisted that "the College Theology Society has a unique role to play in the complex world of contemporary theology." The Society's commitment to fostering "scholarly research as an essential element of effective teaching" continued to make it distinctive. The letter identified the "annual convention, regional meetings, publications, and informal exchanges" as the means for examining "contemporary issues in theology, creative teaching methods, class curriculum, bibliography, and teaching techniques." Concluding remarks highlighted the Society's unique focus on "how to communicate scholarly theological research in an actual teaching context."[3] Yet, in reviewing recent volumes, teaching appeared only occasionally as the explicit focus of selected essays.

Articulating strategies for attracting more members and encouraging an increase in active members became a major focus of the leadership. President James Flanagan, in his February 1977 letter, cast the Society in the role of being "notorious for innovations which have since become common practice in the fields of theology and religion." The CTS is credited with having "influence in establishing theology and religion departments on Catholic campuses" and ensuring "that professors have degrees in these disciplines." The CTS rightly received praise for granting women an opportunity to be "full members of a professional society in theology at a time when they usually received denials or restrictions." The letter linked CTS's success to its ability "to utilize the talents of *all* its members."[4] Yet, like Brannen, Flanagan was describing a society of the gaps.

Other emphases concerning the Society's identity appeared in correspondence among those serving on the Members and Objectives (M&O) Committee. Mary Lea Schneider observed that when the CTS functioned "as a distinctly RC organization," it simplified "distinguishing goals, etc." She acknowledged mitigating factors like finances and competition with professional organizations that complicated the situation. AAR and CTSA, in particular, served as "primary sources for those needs which CTS addressed on a more supplemental basis." She cautioned against attempts to "compete with these two groups" with concentration on "more 'abstract' and 'high-powered' theological interests" and wondered whether the problem lies in "the loss of the teaching emphasis" rather than too little or too much Catholic identity.[5] Another board member, Richard Schebera, S.M.M., described the Society as "basically a R.C. Group," but not one espousing "a narrow Catholicism." He illustrated his point with a fascinating distinction. "The attitude of many members is one of Christianity without an ecclesiastical influence."[6] Sister Maura Campbell, O.P, on the other hand, simply accepted the Catholic character as "adequate for now," noting how "like attracts like." Protestants have comparable societies; such "is the way of pluralism." The Society's male chauvinist tendencies concerned her more. Describing the CTSA as "male for the most part," Sister Maura wondered whether "we could move out of this and attract more females." For those who doubted the male dominance, she suggested reviewing "our publications."[7]

The September 1978 newsletter outlined a six-point "consensus" about what made the Society attractive. "Familial collegiality" with an emphasis on "interpersonal exchange" remained the key to the Society's distinctive character. Regional meetings lent themselves to the personal approach, but the "opportunity for exchange" even at the annual meetings helped "to keep this tone." The national working groups and relevant publications "are our most striking and visible contributions to members." The committee also reasserted "an obligation to young teachers to encourage scholarly growth and teaching ability," especially through maintaining active regions. Given that "the majority of CTS members are catholic, undergrad teachers," rather than leading researchers, the Society needs to make special efforts to avoid being "sectarianly

[sic] catholic" or "simply pedagogical." Taken together, these commitments enable the Society to "remain distinctive and valuable" as long as it continues "the effort to serve the college teacher," cognizant "that most CTS teachers work within the 'catholic' tradition, however loosely defined."[8] The stated consensus reinforced the significance of a Catholic identity connected to teaching undergraduates in defining the Society's distinctiveness as a professional society.

In the same newsletter, William Cenkner, the current president, announced the leadership's intention to proceed with organizational initiatives begun by James Flanagan, the preceding president. Coordinating "annual meetings, publications, and committee work" received special mention. Establishing new standing committees and ensuring organizational "flexibility" required another round of constitutional amendments. Cenkner also affirmed the CTS's unique "educational focus" among learned societies and the potential benefit to novice as well as experienced teachers. "Part of this focus is the development of that unique personality of teacher." In his "33rd semester" of teaching, Cenkner reflected on theology's transformative impact on the teacher both personally and professionally.

The activist president, James Flanagan had been less sanguine in his appraisal, attributing "many CTS problems" to "a schizophrenic self-understanding" whose "two poles" are the "academic" and the "Catholic." Flanagan claimed "no contradiction" between the two but still found it necessary to state the obvious. "A learned society" must be "academic." During his time as president, he attempted "to move the society away from a narrow, 'Catholic' identity," which he judged "not Catholic at all." A series of Society firsts provided evidence for the widening perspective. "Neither the president nor the vice-president held appointments at Catholic institutions, the annual meeting is being held at a public institution, and modifications have been made in some of the symbols of the society." He characterized these firsts as signs of "diversity" and expanded "boundaries" rather than "a struggle between Catholic and public." Marge Reher, in a letter to Bill Cenkner, offered her perspective on the Society's identity with a focus on changes in demographics. She observed that when she "joined in 1964, the CTS was priest-dominated in our region. As more lay people joined, the clergy withdrew." She interpreted "the recent increase in clerical attendance as a very healthy sign."[9] Taken together, Reher's and Flanagan's observations indicate complexities of changes in Catholic college theology after 1964. Enough time had passed for clergy to dominate, leave, and return to a Society whose theological commitments principally as Catholic academics had changed dramatically.

Correspondence between William Cenkner and some of the Society's founding mothers and fathers substantiate the complexities of change, demographic and otherwise. Most charter members sent regrets because other duties prevented their attending the Society's silver jubilee celebration. Urban Voll had to attend an ordination at the Seminary of St. Vincent de Paul, Boynton Beach, Florida, where he was teaching. He sent "the Society all good wishes and prayers" and remarked how he happened to be "perusing your Proceedings last night and this morning and profiting thereby." His optimism was circumscribed in looking toward an unknown "future . . . for the Church, the University and the Seminary, as well as ourselves." What exactly will transpire "is mercifully obscured." He did have "high hopes for a Hispanic apostolate."[10]

Bernard Cooke sent his regrets from distant Western Canada where he taught at the University of Manitoba. His departure from the Jesuits and subsequent marriage combined with his prominence as a postconciliar U.S. theologian no doubt complicated his securing another position. One can recollect Charlie Brannen's account of "Barney Cooke" as the Society's named founder to understand his significance. In a fashion similar to Voll, Cooke indicated how he had "kept abreast of developments in the Society." He mentioned his pleasure in observing "its constant progress—above all the *emergence of highly competent* and *imaginative 'second generation'*."[11] John Harvey simply informed Cenkner that his teaching in Australia prevented participation.[12]

Another founding member, Brother Luke Salm, had to withdraw from being the banquet emcee because of an obligation to his religious community. He suggested Gerard Sloyan, whom he described as "a charter member." Salm rightly recollected Sloyan's being "in the middle of the theology/religion controversy" as well as his pivotal role "(President, I think) in effecting change from SCCTSD to CTS." According to Salm, Sloyan "represents the old and the new (as I like to think I do)."[13]

Sister Mary Rose Eileen Masterman expressed an alternate view of the shift from the old to the new—negative—especially in accommodating to the secular forces an earlier generation had been charged to resist. She wrote a lengthy letter in part to correct certain details of the Society's history. She insisted "that in any statement relative to the JUBILEE of the Society, mention should be made that the organization was known as the SOCIETY OF CATHOLIC COLLEGE TEACHERS OF SACRED DOCTRINE from 1953 to 1967 when its title succumbed unfortunately to the mistaken ecumenical emphasis and secularistic influences of its leadership at that time." She believed the historical "records documented evidence for the broader perspective of *Catholic* higher education in its most important function of communicating the theology of divine revelation which, in turn, provides most valuable insights into the history of the Church in the U.S., during the past quarter of a century!" She correctly assessed "the valuable historical documentation" offered in twenty-five years of annual publications. They trace the "trends affecting the communication of authentic theology in higher education" in that period of significant change. Despite her misgivings, Sister M. Rose Eileen planned to attend the banquet.[14]

THE STEEMAN REPORT: SURVEYING MEMBERS

The Steeman Report, based upon the data collected from the 1976 questionnaire and tabulated in 1977, provided another valuable account of the Society now so unfamiliar to its founding mother, Sister M. Rose Eileen. Steeman described "a professional society of undergraduate theology/religion teachers, which enjoys considerable support from a rather strong core of its membership." The 413 who responded "broke down into 116, 28% female, 297, 72% male." Steeman lamented the absence of clerical status data but noted that from "the 297 male respondents 117, or 60%, are recent joiners." With nearly three times the number of male to female respondents, and over half of those relatively new to the Society, Steeman observed "that there are, proportionally, very few women in the 30–40 age group, while women are slightly overrepresented in the age bracket over 50." This differential suggested "that the C.T.S. missed out on a whole generation of female members because of the exodus of women religious on the one hand, and because of the slowness with which women are joining the men in the professional pursuit of theological and religious studies." The data indicated "an increasing sense of professionalism, and that, in that respect, the C.T.S. ranks as a second choice" especially "among the respondents in the 30–40 age bracket and recent doctorates." Oddly enough, even though most respondents identified "undergraduate teaching" as CTS's "most important focus," only nineteen of those indicated that the Society helped them considerably with teaching, and thirteen of those were over fifty.[15]

Steeman located the difficulties not in the Society but in the changing discipline itself. Colleges and universities were reconfiguring requirements allowing students to choose among a variety of courses. Since the Society's founding, college theology no longer existed necessarily as "a core requirement" intent on "Catholic orthodoxy." Students now chose among "a bewildering variety created by *de facto* theological pluralism" in an "elective system" with no guarantee of receiving "a well-rounded introduction to the theological enterprise." This shift has multiple causes including rapidly "increasing specialization and professionalization." More significant, in Steeman's understanding, the Second Vatican Council implicitly granted permission to re-examine "problems which an earlier generation, still present in the membership of the Society, thought had been settled once and for all." College theology has further challenges with integrating "the recently accepted sister discipline of religious studies into our college curriculum." With all these changes occurring simultaneously, the discipline faced "a problem of major magnitude."[16]

As if to corroborate Steeman's conclusions, William Cenkner, in one of his 1980 presidential letters, expressed concern about the status of "religion/theology in the college curriculum." Since the late 1960s, religion/theology courses "have moved from the center of the curriculum to a place sometimes close to the periphery of college education" with almost no protest. Cenkner challenged the CTS to create "some mechanism within the society" to situate the Society to "take a more explicit role in directing the future of the discipline as it unfolds on the college campus." Given how "few professional societies are concerned with undergraduate education" the College Theology Society can remain "singular in the field of religion and theology in this matter."[17]

Cenkner's vision of the Society's unique role may explain his reaction to the AAR's offer to serve as the oversight organization for the CTS. In his 5 March 1980 progress report, the president first mentioned AAR's intention to sever its affiliation with CSR. "AAR is also raising the question whether they have the capacity to become the 'umbrella' that CSR has become"—a proposal that Cenkner "categorically" rejected.[18] Four years later, in October 1984, Len Biallas, the CTS representative to CSR, reported to a newly elected William Shea, that both the Society of Biblical Literature and the American Academy of Religion withdrew CSR funding.[19] Steeman's assessment of the changing discipline seemed confirmed in the withdrawal.[20] The AAR and SBL had emerged as the more influential arbiters within the academy among those who studied religion.

The College Theology Society remained a small, learned society of teacher-scholars, most of whom now identified themselves as "theologians." In responding to the Steeman Report, the Membership Committee, under Vice President Keith Egan's leadership, sought to establish "opportunities for highly professional involvement by the membership in activities that lead to better scholarship and more effective teaching." Such "an on-going effort" posed no threat to the Society's "most distinctive and rewarding assets, opportunities for close and friendly interaction." The committee also wanted to identify "energetic leadership" to reinvigorate inactive regions and to "explore the significant character of the teaching of theology to undergraduates" but offered no specific actions for implementation.[21]

RECONFIRMING THE SOCIETY'S EXISTENCE

Sister Vera Chester, in her inaugural year as the Society's first woman president, continued to focus on membership with a report on the basic failure of the brochure mailing recruitment strategy. The board advised current members with "good will and energy" to offer personal invitations to "new faculty at your own or neighboring schools to become CTS members."[22] Chester's advice highlights the personal dimensions of members' commitment to the Society.

The professional identity of the CTS members seemed less clear. At least as suggested by the discussion of a proposal from the early 1980s to alter the president's term to one year, with the vice president becoming president elect in the previous year. In polling of past presidents (Buckley, Flanagan, Kohmescher, and Van Allen), the committee received several responses indicating some merit in the change. The most intriguing came from Mark Heath, O.P., whose long absence from the Society was due to his work as a seminary administrator. In considering "the two-year presidency," he identified the "first question" to be whether this "unique" structure ought to remain. He asked quite bluntly: "Is this structure a relic, a semi-extinct species, surviving from the past?" Perhaps the two-year term reflected the Society of the 1950s that no longer existed. Up to "the early seventies, the program roster of the annual meeting was all invited scholars." A general "call for papers" did not exist. Ten years later, "all the papers, or most of them, are offered by the membership; and the purpose of the meeting is to offer these scholars a chance to present a developed paper for peer and colleague reaction, etc." This change reflected members' very different sense of their work. According to Heath, the "CTS has moved from being an *apostolate* or Church related group into being a *professional* or academy related group." Though many members "may be something of both," Heath insisted that both existed in the "shift in the society from the apostolate to the professional section of the continuum." Heath identified the one-year presidency as more suitable to an academy-oriented group since the office becomes a matter of prestige. The two-year presidency suited the more church-oriented group because of the greater time of service demanded.[23] Heath's assessment of changes in the Society highlight the ongoing tensions in the Society's identity that seem to have little to do with a one- or two-year presidency.

The president's term remained two years with an additional year of service on the board. A candidate for vice president, William Portier, articulated the Society's nature and purpose in ways utterly familiar. He made three points. "First, I applaud and affirm our 'substance without pretense' approach as one of our distinguishing marks among professional societies. The relaxed and cordial atmosphere which characterizes CTS activities is one of our greatest strengths." He reaffirmed the Society's "historical commitment to support undergraduate teaching as well as research and publication" and attested to his support of "strong regional organizations" as best able to serve college theology teachers, the Society's "primary constituency." In other words, he was willing to accept "one of the chief responsibilities of the Vice President," coordination of regional activities.[24] For all the changes in the Society's membership, a certain recognizable identity continued into 2004. The Society remained a relatively small, close-knit, predominantly Catholic organization, dedicated to the undergraduate teacher of theology as pedagogue and scholar.

Certain changes in wording and a few omissions in the CTS constitution reflected the kinds of shifts in the discipline's transformation that Steeman and Heath mentioned. Rev. James Flanagan had mentioned "modifications . . . in some of the symbols of the society." Certainly, the apparently quiet omission of "Mary Seat of Wisdom" as the "Society's patroness" bore some symbolic significance. Accounts of the amendments made no mention of debating the change (Article I). Other notable changes occur with the substitution in the "academic discipline" from "theology" to "religion (theology, religious studies)," though the descriptor, "on a high professional level" remained. Omitted is "solid and effective" as the kind of teaching that the Society hopes to help the members gain. Added as a primary objective is "a concern for relating religion to life." The eight secondary objectives became six, principally through new combinations. The six objectives touched on pedagogical concerns from developing "effective teachers" and "effective ways of teaching" to "keeping abreast of current developments" in the field through publications and meetings to curricular and interdisciplinary concerns and ecumenism (Article II). Associate membership disappeared in a 1975 draft and reappears in the constitution's final form (1976). The category allowed participation of a burgeoning group, graduate students working on "degrees in religion," as well as the familiar group of "those engaged in college teaching in the field." Campus ministers and "others interested in the work of the Society" were also eligible for associate membership. The absence of a record of debate suggests that concern about membership had finally subsided with the vast majority of members assuming professional degrees as a standard qualification.

The basic organizational structure remained unchanged. The vice president no longer coordinated national meetings but continued to oversee the regional work and now served as "*ex officio* chairman of the standing Committee on Membership and Objectives" (Article V, VI [1975]). Evidence of longtime inclusion of men and women in leadership was found later in a word change under "regions" where "chairman" became "chairperson" (Article X).

All but one of the five standing committees were eliminated or renamed. The committees had been Admissions, Nominations, Budget and Auditing, Current Problems, and Sacred Doctrine Studies. The only survivor was Nominations. An Awards Committee attended to the CTS work of judging outstanding scholarship in religion. The "Academic Study of Religion Committee" signaled, first and foremost a recognition of the change in the academic discipline, formerly called "Sacred Doctrine Studies." The final two, Membership and Objectives as well as Publications, made minor, practical adjustments in those areas that had most preoccupied board members in recent years (Article VII).

The document left little doubt that the CTS's long tradition of publications was going to continue (Article IX). The constitutional section, "Publications" reflected several changes, most notably the definitive shift from *Proceedings* to an "annual publication." Omitted was the caveat, "so long as their publication of a separate volume continues to be economically feasible." The information about a "quarterly newsletter" was omitted and added was "editor(s) of *Horizons*" and a "correspondent to the *Bulletin*." Earlier, the document had identified the *Bulletin of the Council on the Study of Religion* (Article IV) as the members' principal source for information about the national meeting.[25]

Arguments for further changes in committee structures arose in 1977 with the recent constitutional amendments barely a year old. The president, Rev. James Flanagan, outlined a very specific argument about the interrelationships between the annual meeting, committees, and publications. "Contradictions among the committees, annual meeting program, and publication programs indicate a faulty sociology of knowledge (or none at all!)—and will lead to the weakening and failure of each, and eventually the demise of the Society." The argument then was laid out based upon how ideas gain influence in the academy. A scholar's ideas migrate from a paper to an article to a monograph to a scholarly book to normative idea accepted and discussed in other papers whose ideas will follow a similar trajectory. The learned society supports this development through its annual meeting, committee structure, and publications.[26] Flanagan suggested forgoing specifics in the constitution. Instead he advised only acknowledging the existence of committees, publications, and annual meetings guided by the bylaws.[27]

The standing committees did change and award specific names. The standing committees included three new ones for the Annual Meeting, research added to Publications, and Financial Planning; those retained included Awards, Membership and Objectives, and Nominations. All committee members were to be "elected by the membership upon the presentation of the President and the recommendation of the Board of Directors." The one committee eliminated was the Academic Study of Religion. All standing committees had as their principal focus the Society's internal affairs—an orientation that coincided with the Society's desire to delineate more clearly its own self-understanding. These changes were approved at the national convention in June 1979.[28]

A WHOLE NEW ANNUAL MEETING

The annual meetings remained the central communal activity of the Society and as such provided a glimpse at the changing understanding of college theology's role as a profession. In keeping with his "sociology of knowledge," James Flanagan encouraged viewing the annual meeting no longer "as a chance to 'get away for a few days' or as a respite from academic labors." Even those days of attending "to hear a 'big name' are gone forever, thank God." The focus ought to be on the members "planning [an] agenda for our discipline, of testing and refining ideas, and of agreeing about directions and areas of research, which of course includes development of teaching resources and techniques."[29] The 1977 convention saw a new variation for encouraging such exchange. Ten working groups with conveners appear for the first time with multiple papers in multiple sections. The groups bear the following names: Academic Study of Religion (method, goals, introductory course, etc.); Church and Sacraments; Ethics; History of Christianity; Philosophy of Religion; Religion and Culture; Scripture; Systematics; Women and Religion; World Religions and their Scriptures.

The board took the concrete steps necessary to ensure a permanent reorganization outlined in the "Annual Meeting [AM] Structure and Regulations." The document describes in detail the work of the organizing committee under the guidance of the AM chairperson. Every meeting was to consist of plenary sessions, interest sections with conveners who reassess every three years, groups that have working projects, seminars, and the even more focused consultations that last only a year or two. The guidelines also restricted individual participation to one paper and one chairing of a session. Program unit chairs must be CTS members. The first AM chairperson was to be Joseph LaBarge of Bucknell University; his successor was Mary Lea Schneider, from Michigan State University.[30]

The 1979 convention, marking the twenty-fifth year of annual meetings, opened a day earlier than normal, a Thursday evening, rather than a Friday, with dinner and a plenary address. The reasons given included alleviating the "frenzied pace of the convention and providing some time for seeing the sights in Washington."[31] The Thursday evening convention opening remained through the fiftieth year, 2004. Another change, determined at the fall board meeting in 1980 was expecting the president to give an address only every other year—an accommodation to the two-year presidency.[32] This decision also remained through 2004.

The Society instituted concrete activities to demonstrate its practical commitment to improving the academic status of college theology for student and faculty. Nearly twenty years after Sister M. Rose Eileen had championed the establishment of a student honor society, the CTS board unanimously passed a resolution approving "the concept of a National Honors Society for Professors and Students of Religious Studies to be called Theta Alpha Kappa." A statement about Theta Alpha Kappa (TAK) printed on Manhattan College letterhead ascribed its conception to Manhattan College in the 1975–1976 academic year. Its Greek letters stand for "Theos Anthropos Koinonia" to reflect "three areas of primary concern to students of Religion: God, Man, Community." Membership was to be through election based upon "excellence in the study of Theology or Religious Studies." The process was described as "highly democratic" given the merit-based admission open to all students of religion or theology. Encouraging student-delivered papers became a unique feature. An annual award including a "monetary stipend" and possible publication would recognize "an outstanding manuscript." To provide leadership, the CTS board agreed to appoint a "National Advisor." This professor from an active local chapter "shall serve as an animator and consultant for national activities and shall make an annual report to the College Theology Society on the activities and status of Theta Alpha Kappa."[33] The CTS allowed its mailing list to be used to contact prospective members. In 2004, TAK, now affiliated with the AAR, had more than two hundred chapters at religious and secular institutions in the United States.[34]

Another innovation was the teaching workshop first introduced in 1979. Leonard Weber from Mercy College of Detroit made the suggestion to Keith Egan.[35] "On teaching workshop, a memorandum," dated 14 August 1979, suggested having at least two teaching workshops each year as a response to observations made in the Steeman Report. The first workshop on teaching ethics in college was to be at the University of Scranton with Stephen Casey, professor of ethics, as organizer.[36] The workshop had no connection to the annual meeting in time or location. In a lengthy letter to President Vera Chester, Stephen Casey analyzed why the teaching workshop failed to get enough participants but offered no definitive conclusion except the conviction that the workshop remained a good idea.[37]

The solution came two years later. Immediately prior to the 1982 annual meeting, at Mercy College, Detroit, a "Workshop on the Teaching of Ethics," featured Daniel C. Maguire as the keynote speaker. With the timing settled to immediately prior to the annual meeting, Steve Casey and Len Weber continued developing the content.[38] The March 1984 newsletter outlined an elaborate program for the third workshop. Ethics once again served as the focus. The line-up featured two plenary sessions, the first with Leonard Weber, from Mercy College of Detroit, "Ethics and the College Curriculum" and the last with Matthew Lamb, from Marquette University, "The Relationship of Ethics and Systematic Theology." Six smaller groups, repeated three times, featured "Biblical Roots of Ethics" (Anthony Tambasco), "Faith Development as Related to Ethics" (Paul Philibert), "Medical Ethics" (John Gallagher), "Sexual Ethics" (Christine Gudorf), "Business Ethics" (Patricia Werhane), and "Contemporary Thinking on War" (Daniel Di Domizio).

Renewed enthusiasm for the annual meetings seemed more evident even in official announcements. President Vera Chester announced the 1983 annual meeting would be held at Cabrini College and in 1984 at Cardinal Stritch College with a friendly suggestion. "Mark your calendars now to save the dates—the CTS is still the liveliest and friendliest meeting around—and the best bargain going!"[39] Rodger Van Allen's report of the Detroit-Mercy meeting portrayed a lively meeting with plenary sessions featuring Rev. Richard P. McBrien and David J. O'Brien. Two more involved panel discussions: one on "Writing and Publishing in the Field of Religious Studies/Theology," with John Loudon of Harper & Row, David Toolan of *Commonweal*, and Robert Heyer of Paulist Press and *New Catholic World* and the other a symposium discussion on "Religious Literacy in the Catholic College," with Bernard J. Cooke, Pheme Perkins, Keith J. Egan, and Lawrence Cunningham. A total of eighty papers were presented during the convention, and "discussions and renewal of friendships filled the evening social hours." Thanks went to local organizer, Len Weber and his Mercy College colleagues plus "the Committee on the Annual Meeting and its Chair, Mary Schneider."[40] At the June 1982 board meeting, a report highlighted the activity of fifteen regions. Topics for regional meetings included "the transition from pre-Vatican II college teaching of religion to present professionalization," "the degree of authority given the scriptures in the theologizing process," and "freedom and authority in theological academe."[41]

Discussion of the 1984 annual meeting eventually "turned to the matter of liturgy: the need to pay more attention to liturgy in general." Questions raised included who to make responsible "for planning the liturgy," whether an "alternate liturgy" should be celebrated, and who could attend to details. The board determined "*For this year only*" to permit "Richard Sklba, auxiliary bishop of Milwaukee" to celebrate the Saturday Eucharistic liturgy. Surprisingly, given its significance in the life of the church, almost exactly twenty years after the implementation of the Vatican II liturgical reforms, CTS board minutes reflected the Society's addressing its own liturgical celebrations for the first time since those reforms.[42]

The March 1984 newsletter, announcing the annual meeting at Cardinal Stritch College, with its theme "The Future," also included a report from the vice president concerning the formation of "an ad hoc committee" for planning "liturgical celebrations for the 1984 Annual Meeting." Its duties included a careful "study of the role of liturgical celebration at the Annual Meeting" taking under consideration "the needs and interests of various groups within the Society." Its charge included implementing "a comprehensive liturgical program for the Annual Meeting." The members were to report to the vice president and call a meeting at the 1984 annual meeting.

The 1984 Saturday evening liturgy itself generated at least one response, a letter written to William Shea, newly elected president. It chided the CTS for failing to take up a collection at the liturgy on behalf of the poor. The letter mentioned an aside of Bishop Richard Sklba "that every liturgical ecclesial gathering should express itself in an 'outreach' to the poor. The most obvious way to do this is by a monetary collection." He noted that the meeting offered little benefit to the poor, a situation "perhaps more to our detriment than to theirs." Shea acknowledged the letter, promised to pass it on to the liturgical coordinator, Ron Pachence, and suggested that the members "should be provoked to reform by next year's topic, 'Religion, Economics, and the Social Order.'"[43]

THE CTS AS PUBLISHER

As noted in the opening chapter, the Society had always considered publishing in areas apropos of college theology to be one of its primary purposes. Volume editors, with the support of the officers and board members, had overcome many obstacles to maintain the annual publication since the first annual meeting. From 1955 to 1975, not only had college theology been redefined but the publishing industry had also transformed itself to respond to a burgeoning knowledge class. The demands for college textbooks, however, had diminished after the baby-booming sixties.

The ever-energetic James W. Flanagan selectively circulated a "white paper," entitled "The CTS as Publisher." The paper's heading made clear that it was "for private use only." Flanagan argued for the increasing necessity of connecting between "futures of learned societies and of scholarly publishing." He placed his proposal in the context of colleges' declining enrollments combined with increased expectations on faculty. He warned of an uncertain future that "cannot be guaranteed by institutions, religious groups, and even professionals from outside the field. Religionists are responsible for their own destinies." The destiny of "the academic study of religion" appears to be intimately linked to the favorable judgment of "an audience who judges without 'religious' motives. To realize this can be frightening or it can be freeing." The remainder of the paper discussed how a learned society could prepare a text for publication "in return for less expensive, short run, publications." Flanagan pointed to "the publishing of journals" as illustrative of what a learned society can produce as a matter of course. "What remains is to extend the lessons learned there to other areas of Publishing [sic]." Unless a learned society, regardless of size, is publishing, "it is not serving its members or its discipline fully. Bread and butter issues such as tenure and promotion, to say nothing of intellectual integrity, are being neglected."[44] The CTS intended to provide a means for making its members not only better teachers but also published and thus tenurable scholars.

Expanding CTS's publications had champions besides James Flanagan. In 1978, the board discussed the possibility of producing a "Classroom Series." As a member of the board, Lawrence Cunningham from Florida State University cautioned against duplicating efforts such as those of Scholars Press or of textbook publishers. He suggested publishing "primary sources for the teacher's use in the classroom." His example was Mariological sources from the early church through the early modern period. He also advised polling members to get a better sense of classroom needs.[45]

In a letter to "Colleagues," dated March 1979, CTS president William Cenkner lauded the Society for its publishing successes noting that the Society's jubilee year "marks the fifth year in the life of HORIZONS." Like its sponsoring society, *Horizons* "has rapidly taken on a personality distinct from other journals." Under "SCHOLARSHIP AND WRITING," Cenkner reflected on "the public nature of theologizing and what this means for our theological/religious articulation." Different teaching "publics," such as "the college classroom, the seminary hall, and the graduate school lecture or seminar," require distinctive "academic writing." Cenkner praised the wide-ranging talents of Society members, displayed in "articles for scholarly journals but also other pieces for a broader audience." Still "undergraduate education in religion and theology" remained the primary public venue among members, who generated "more classroom contact hours than the research scholar or the graduate school lecturer." The newly proposed "SOURCE BOOK SERIES" intended to speak to that public by "cultivat[ing] those skills which most directly benefit the college student."[46] In the next year's preconvention letter, Cenkner announced the first in the "Source Book Series," *Issues of Peace and*

Social Justice, by William Oesterle, would be available at the annual meeting.[47] Vera Chester, in her presidential letter dated March 1981, indicated the volume was "selling steadily" bolstered by good reviews. A second, by Nathan Kollar, was in process. Other encouraging news included the bishops' interest in such endeavors indicated in their providing $2,700 to support the series.[48]

Publication plans expanded further in the next few years. At the 1982 preconvention board meeting, members voted to publish Rosemary Rodgers's *History of the CTS* through Scholar's Press.[49] At the end of 1982, the board discussed another publishing opportunity. Rodger Van Allen, president, and Robert Masson, chair of the Publications Committee, informed CTS members of "a co-Publishing Program with the University Press of America." Their letter described "careful preliminary work" that included "discussion at the December 1982 Board Meeting, and discussion and approval at the June 1983 Board Meeting." The venture would have no impact on *Horizons,* the annual volume, or the *CSR Bulletin* since it involved publishing monographs, textbooks, and reprints. Using a production process similar to the one used for *Foundations of Religious Literacy* and *A History of the College Theology Society,* the Society could publish a limited quantity, as few as eighty-five, "for a fee of $4.50 per page for copy editing." The intent was to "greatly expand our publishing program in the years ahead" following in the tradition of *Horizons.*[50] The following year, 1984, Robert Masson reported that the copublishing project had already produced "two books in the monograph series, Joe Bracken's *The Triune Symbol: Persons, Process and Community* and Vernon Gregson's *Lonergan: Spirituality and the Meeting of Religions.*" Two more were soon to appear in the "Resource Series": *Newman and the Modernists,* edited by Mary Jo Weaver, and "a translation of *The Spiritual Exercises* by Elisabeth Tetlow."[51]

The Society had more than survived its period of self-examination. It showed all the signs of thriving. From 1983 to 1984 membership numbers reached 808, up from 734, with 111 new members and only thirty-seven withdrawals. Forty-three student and associate members also belonged to the Society. In his account of his two years as president, Rodger Van Allen could "look back" and "see many projects that have come to fruition during this time." Some had come to completion after years of work; others "have been initiated during this time to be carried on by others." He mentioned the several publication successes including the "co-publication program," the Society's history, an "upgrading" of the annual volume's published form, and the flourishing *Horizons.* He also specified projects other than scholarly publishing. "An annual fund raising campaign has been organized, a grant proposal is in the process of development by CTS, a new logo has been adopted, records are being computerized, and a *Directory* progresses toward publication." As if to reiterate the Society's vitality, a notice for Rosemary Rodgers's

A History of the College Theology Society was attached to the letter. The notice described how the completed work made "a valuable contribution to understanding the intellectual history of Catholicism in America. The book also offers perspectives on religion in higher education and in Catholic colleges and universities in particular. Finally, it helps explain the history and development of Catholic theology." Academic libraries are urged to order their own copy.[52]

MORE RESOLUTIONS

The Society, of course, gave its attention to many other issues beyond their own continued existence. Resolutions once again provided clues as to what preoccupied CTS leadership and members. The production rate of resolutions had significantly diminished when compared to the previous decade. Resolutions passed at Boston included one in support of hiring "women as full-time faculty members" especially given "the number of women competent in theology and religion is increasingly significant."[53] Another more controversial resolution concerned the status of Quentin Quesnell, a tenured scripture professor dismissed from Marquette University after leaving the Jesuits and marrying. The board voted unanimously to omit a portion of the resolution identifying the "notion of conditional tenure by reason of considerations extraneous to professional fitness" to be "a serious threat to academic freedom in all Catholic colleges and universities."[54] The final resolution objected to Marquette's treating Jesuit faculty differently from "academic colleagues." Such inconsistency threatened "the good reputation of Catholic higher education." The Society used the resolution to "go on record as urging the administrative representatives of the aforementioned university [Marquette] to seek an amicable resolution of this conflict over tenure rights in light of the traditions of academic freedom and due process affirmed by the AAUP and reaffirmed in specific terms with regard to dispensed priests by both the CTS (1972) and the CTSA (1974)."[55]

The "aforementioned university" failed to achieve the prescribed "amicable solution" and came under AAUP sanctions for violating the former Jesuit's "tenure rights." So when the offer came from Marquette to host the 1981 convention, the Society declined. Board members evidently shared no common view on the situation given the vote was "6 against and 5 in favor" with the executive officers split "2 against and 2 in favor." Unanimous in their opposition was the "Committee on the Annual Meeting" with all four members voting against the offer. A letter, dated 10 December 1979, was sent to Father William Kelly informing the department chair of the decision.[56]

Attendees of the twenty-fifth convention's annual business meeting approved not only proposed constitutional amendments and bylaws but also two resolutions. "William Frost (University of Dayton) introduced and Sonya Quitslund (George Washington University) amended the following resolution which was approved unanimously: "'Be it resolved that the CTS urges the American hierarchy to promote continued theological investigation of the question of the ordination of women to the priesthood.'" Lawrence Cunningham introduced the second resolution permitting the CTS president to "send a protest telegram" to "Florida's governor" if he issues "death warrants."[57] Three years later, the March 1982 newsletter featured a lengthy resolution (consisting of eleven statements) condemning the arms race. The statement made clear that the authors were "theologians and religious educators" and their statement came out of a deep respect for life and that "nuclear war constitutes the greatest contemporary danger to the future of humanity." The resolution endorsed disarmament, and nonviolent alternatives to war.[58] The scope of these three resolutions encapsulates the challenge to anyone who self-identified as a college theology teacher charged with the responsibility of introducing students to an academic discipline that concerned itself with women's ordination, the death penalty, and nuclear proliferation. The topics suggest that far more was at stake in theological studies than any final exam could communicate, no matter how comprehensive.

CHALLENGING, SERVING, AND COLLABORATING WITH THE EPISCOPACY

The CTS's concern about its influence in the academy was matched by its concerns about its status in the church. In the period from 1975 to 1984, the relationship between the church's officials and CTS leadership precluded a simple characterization. Times of disagreement and collaboration frequently overlapped. Issues concerning women's relationship to the church continued to receive special attention. William Cenkner, acting in his capacity as CTS president, wrote a letter of support for "Theresa Kane who invited Pope John Paul to dialogue, at the convocation for religious women in Washington."[59] The Society also put forth a resolution in support of Sr. Agnes Mary Mansour who resigned from her community due to "the authoritarian exercise of administrative power on the part of the Vatican officials and their representatives." At question was her refusal, as director of the Michigan Department of Social Services, to "publically repudiate the use of Medicaid funds for abortions." The local ordinary, Archbishop Edmund Szoka, Detroit, demanded the repudiation, for her to receive the canon law required permission to serve in a public office and remain a member of her religious community. The resolution was to send a "release to the press and send to the Sister of Mercy officials and to Ms. Mansour a statement of support for the position taken by NETWORK, [a] Washington-based lobbying group." The primary reasons were "the issues as outlined by Network are those of due process and the American Catholic experience of freedom of conscience, matters of concern to the society and to its members."[60] The public nature of theology took on new meaning in this political context.

President William Cenkner, after consulting with the board of directors, sent yet another letter concerning violated rights, but unlike Mansour's, this case involved academic rights. The addressee was Dr. Aldolp Theiss, president of the University of Tübingen, and the subject was "the academic rights of Professor Hans Küng." Cenkner quoted at length from "A Statement on the Nature of the Contemporary Catholic University" (July 1967); published under the auspices of the International Federation of Catholic Universities, a long excerpt from the "Land O'Lakes Statement," October 1968, and the CTS resolution, May 1969. Each defended the Catholic university's overriding commitment to protecting "autonomy" and "academic freedom" against all authorities external to the academy, whether secular or ecclesial. Cenkner reasserted the "basic norm" that the College Theology Society embraced. When "questions of orthodoxy" arise, "academic competence is the proper concern of the college and university." Given this competence, "the institution has a responsibility to defend the academic freedom of the theologian in face of accusations and imputations concerning orthodoxy."[61] No response appears in the available files.

The Society's members frequently diverged from church officials on fundamental issues. The divergence was startlingly evident when CTS members served on a committee to review a 1974 draft (second consultation) of the National Catechetical Directory. They made a report to the "Board of Directors and Members from the Committee on the National Catechetical Directory."[62] The report offered thirteen pages of detailed, section-by-section, mostly negative, commentary ending with an additional four pages entitled "a thematic critique." Taking a cue from Bernard Lonergan's claim about a radical shift in perspective, the major criticism revolved around still "*advocating a single 'world-view'* namely a classical, static world-view" with no "hint of an 'evolutionary world-view.'" Since the contemporary world will not return to the classical worldview, the review committee noted, "the need is for Christian tradition to re-articulate itself from within the contemporary world-view and culture and language." The Directory failed to meet this "challenge for our time."[63]

Other matters of more direct concern to college theology teachers garnered far more attention than any catechetical directory. In the fall of 1975, the board discussed "with Msgr. John Murphy from NCEA who was serving on the 'Purposes and Identity' Committee dealing with the Catholic University in the modern world especially in relation to teaching Theology to undergraduates." NCEA hoped to form "a single, united voice" at a 1976 meeting in Rome concerning teaching theology-related subjects in Catholic educational institutions. Possible topics for the 1976 meeting included whether all biblical studies must be at pontifical or Roman academies and whether the church ought to grant "permission for ex-priests to teach."[64] Here began a nearly thirty-year saga concerning the official status and authority of anyone claiming to teach Catholic theology in any academic setting.

An early form of this discussion centered on a "canonical mission" for the "teaching of the sacred studies and those connected with them" within the institutional context of "academic centers of the Catholic Church," i.e., papal institutes. The "canonical mission" had a fairly circumscribed audience, those who taught theology in seminaries or other pontifical institutes. It is worth noting, however, that the appearance of theological studies in U.S. colleges and universities was a relatively new phenomenon, and those involved had little clarity on what church officials might claim as under their jurisdiction in the teaching of the sacred science.[65] An undated document entitled "Relations of American Catholic Colleges and Universities with the Church" exemplified early and often repeated attempts to profess loyalty to the church while insisting upon the university's autonomy from church authority. Part of the argument, soon to become standard, was the unique United States civil context in which episcopal interference in the institution's academic freedom might jeopardize the current governmental financial support provided Catholic colleges and universities.[66]

Debates about impending enforcement of these new ecclesial requirements for college theology teachers still did not eliminate cooperative engagement with the hierarchy. William Oesterle served as the CTS representative to the Call to Action conference in Detroit, 20–23 October 1976 and offered a report filled with enthusiasm for "a wholesome process" that involved the "listening and dialoguing by bishops and people." He characterized the conference's "operations" as "unfamiliar and strange." He concluded wondering whether it was "too far-fetched to say that Detroit was *and is* where the theological action of the Church is today." His characterization of CTS involvement bears some irony, but only in hindsight. He conjectured whether "CTS members have not only an opportunity, but a mandate to answer this 'call.'" He could not have anticipated another episcopal "mandate" that would preoccupy much time and energy of CTS members in the near future.

Another, more ongoing cooperative effort between bishops and scholars was the Joint Committee of Catholic Learned Societies. In a "Report to the NCCB [National Conference of Catholic Bishops] Administrative Committee" under Archbishop Quinn's name, the College Theology Society was identified as one of the eight societies. The others were the Catholic Biblical Association, the Catholic Theological Society of America, the American Catholic Historical Association, the American Catholic Philosophical Association, Canon Law Society of America, Mariological Society, and North American Academy of Liturgy. According to Quinn's official report, the committee sought to foster "an attitude of mutual confidence between the Catholic scholarly community and all parts of the Christian community" and to promote scholarly work "to understand and respond to problems in contemporary society." The first "consultation held in June of 1975" examined possible content for "the proposed pastoral letter on moral values." Another possible project, a "white paper," was to explore the "tradition and practices governing relations between the intellectual communities and the institutional Church."[67]

The CTS representative, Mark Heath, O.P., explicitly recommended remaining active in the work despite the slow deliberation with "no great external results" in evidence for the Society. He urged greater familiarity with the Society's pool of scholars "to give young and professorial talent an opportunity" to participate in the Joint Committee of Catholic Learned Societies and Scholars (JCCLS).[68] In a subsequent memorandum on the JCCLS, Heath provided a brief history beginning with the CTS's Committee on Relations with Bishops (1972). According to his account, in 1974, the bishops sought assistance "in the aftermath of the polemic carried on in the right wing Catholic press against Catholic Biblical Scholarship." By organizing "members representing the several Catholic learned societies," the bishops could establish "a liaison" that might "provide a mechanism and a forum for handling problems similar to the biblical one." The committee contributed to the 1981 Synod Agenda, a Colloquium of Scholarship in the Church, and an Inventory of Catholic Scholars (to know who was available for what kind of research). Despite the proposed "white paper," Heath observed that "in the aftermath of the *Humanae Vitae* controversy, bishops were not attracted to discussions of freedom or dissent in the Church."[69] In his report on JCCLS, William Loewe, Mark Heath's successor, mentioned that the "'white paper' on scholarship in the Church seems to have been scotched, but there is enthusiasm for continuing the colloquium for at least another year."[70] Even with no "white paper," in a period fraught with conflict, the organization gave opportunities for dialogue between two of the parties in conflict, church officials and theologians.

The variance in the Society's efforts to maintain its integrity as a learned society in religious and theological studies is quite evident in considering that during the same period of JCCLS interaction, the Society appointed Dolores Greeley, R.S.M., to serve as a liaison to women's groups in the profession. At the 1976 preconvention board meeting, she reported on interactions with several distinct groups. The AAR/SBL Women's Caucus "supports women's participation in professional meetings and publications" and explores alternative approaches to theological studies including a "rejection of competition and alienating models of research, in favor of a learning community." The caucus affirmed the value of "journal work, fantasy writing, spontaneous theater." Another group, the "Office of Women's Affairs" at GTU, Berkeley, served as "an information source for women's consciousness raising." A third, the "Association of Women Aspiring to the Presbyteral Ministry," supported the international movement among "women who have discerned in their lives a 'call' to the priesthood." A "task force" from this group organized the "Ordination Conference" in Detroit in November 1975, attracting 1,000 religious, 100 men, and 100 laywomen. The NCEA Department of Religious Education, "under the inspiring leadership of Alfred McBride" offered informative sessions such as Loretta Girzaitis' "Equality: Women in the Church." Finally, the National Association of Women Religious was mentioned as cooperating in the U.S. bishops' bicentennial initiative "Liberty and Justice for All"—a five-year social action plan.[71]

Raised consciousness concerning women's exclusion from so many areas of public and professional life gave the Society a certain place of pride for its inclusion of women from its inception. As noted elsewhere, the CTS's story of its origins gradually came to emphasize women's exclusion from other societies as motivation for the Society's founding. Rodger Van Allen emphasized the Society's exceptional record in a 1983 letter to Sister Fidelia McDonough, R.S.M., from the Women's Ordination Conference. "As you may know, the CTS has more women theologian members than any other essentially Catholic theological organization. In fact, one reason for the initiation of CTS in 1954 was the exclusion of women at that time from the Catholic Theological Society of America."[72] Debating the statement's accuracy misses the point. What this rendering highlights is a changed understanding of women's exclusion as well as inclusion in theological studies.

A year later, Rodger Van Allen received a letter from Bishop Joseph Imesch, chairman of the "Bishops' Committee for the Pastoral Letter on Women in Society and the Church." On behalf of the committee, Imesch requested identification of "consultants proficient in the following areas: Systematic Theology, Sacred Scripture, Anthropology/Philosophy, Women's Studies and Social Psychology." He specifically requested giving "particular consideration to women who would have a competence in these areas."[73] The bishops' attentiveness to "Women in Society and the Church," however ill-fated, indicates that the episcopal interests were not entirely divergent from those of the Society. Of course, the bishops had to contend with a much wider range of perspectives and more vocal rejection of second-wave feminism.

Other concerns directly related to the theologian's teaching authority in the church arose even as bishops sought their expertise on difficult issues such as women's participation in the church's life. Sister Vera Chester, CTS president, received a letter from CTSA's new president, Thomas F. O'Meara, regarding the membership and board members who "passed a resolution expressing their reserve towards canon sixty-four of the section on 'The Church's Teaching Office' in the forthcoming Code of Canon Law" at the 1980 convention in San Francisco. "The canon reads: 'Those who teach any theological courses or courses connected with theology in institutions of higher learning require a canonical mission.'" O'Meara found in this canon: "A new kind of law" unparalleled in the 1917 code. "It is sweeping in its application; teachers of any area related to theology in all institutions of higher education are embraced by it." The local bishop must "approve or disapprove" every Roman Catholic teacher in his jurisdiction. He continued with the soon to be standard plea about the unique circumstances in the North American context. O'Meara asked the CTS to make its membership aware through discussion of the implications of canon 64.[74] At the fall board meeting, those present passed a motion "that Vera Chester write a response to the presidents of NCCB, NCLS, IFUP; raising grave concern about the change in Church law as found in canon sixty-four of the section on 'The Church's Teaching Office.'"[75] No such letters are found among preserved documents, perhaps because "Canon 64" per se was no longer at issue since it no longer existed as "Canon 64."

The fall 1983 newsletter described the last convention "on the beautiful campus of Cabrini College." After listing the plenary speakers, the "banquet session" receives special notice. "William Byron, the President of the Catholic University of America spoke on 'The Canonical Mandate and Teaching Theology in Catholic Colleges.'"[76] Canon 64 had disappeared in the 1983 code revision, and canon 812 had, in fact, appeared as part of the preconvention board meeting during the discussion of resolutions. Sister Alice Gallin, executive secretary of the Association of Catholic Colleges and Universities (ACCU), informed the board and executive officers that a committee of canon lawyers had begun to review the canon. The ACCU recommended maintaining a "low key." The association's "public statements" stressed two points: "1) that the full implications of the canon are not clear and 2) that each college and university is a separate autonomous institution. They are not part of a group." The CTS board appointed Bill Loewe, Bernie Prusak, and Bernard Cooke to serve on a committee that would maintain the Society's relationship with the ACCU in light of the concern over canon 812.[77]

Concern over changes in canon law did not dissuade the CTS leadership from continuing to solicit funds from bishops as well as college presidents. Father Matthew Kohmescher served as the Society's agent and met with some modest success, receiving $1,765 from bishops and $950 from college presidents. In a letter justifying the need, the Society's former president described the increasing difficulty of funding "worthy projects" despite careful spending including the use of college campuses for annual meetings. Kohmescher's letter reminded potential donors—"The study and teaching of religion is a most challenging and necessary task today." Gifts ranged from the "CTS Supporter (gift of $25.00)" to the "CTS Associate (gift of $100 or more)." Recipients received assurance that "any financial help, along with your prayers and personal support of our ventures is most graciously appreciated."[78] Father Kohmescher reported a single episcopal request, in this case, "to bring out Mary's role in the redemptive work of Christ." He advised the board to "mention projects that we have undertaken as a result of the success of our solicitation" in the future.[79]

The bishops' generosity did not allay fears about *mandatum*. The following year, the CTS ad hoc committee on canon 812 and related matters reported on ACCU's efforts to secure the services of a reluctant Charles Wilson "to head a task force or provide much public information at this stage." Bill Loewe also reiterated that Father Byron's remarks still apply, "namely, that the matter is a delicate one, that the hope is that no explosive incidents occur, and that the less public attention is drawn to the matter, the better."[80]

For those prone to worry about the effects of implementing canon 812, they could point to the successful attack on Anthony Wilhelm's *Christ Among Us*, in a review, first published in *Reflections*, a supplement to *The Wanderer*, by James Likoudis, vice president of Catholics United for the Faith. This text's imprimatur was retracted. The review highlighted those places where the text allegedly dismisses traditional Catholic catechesis, e.g., on angels, original sin, etc.[81] At the annual board, in discussing the Wilhelm text, the Resolutions Committee became "the Ad Hoc Committee on Resolutions and Current Issues." Kathleen Gaffney was asked to chair the committee with two other members, Bill Portier and Len Weber. Discussion about introducing a resolution concerning the Vatican's censorship of the Wilhelm book was delayed to allow the committee to "study and make recommendations on this and other issues." The board announced at the business meeting their intention of following up on this issue and instructing the representative to the Joint Committee of Catholic Learned Societies and Scholars to place the item on their agenda.[82]

The various incidents of conflict that occurred between 1985 and 1994, though different in kind, contributed to the air of uncertainty about what the future held for Catholic theologians. The deleterious effects of modernism's condemnation had become emblematic, in many postconciliar minds, of any Roman interference in academic endeavors, especially given the secular academy's lingering suspicion against Catholic scholars. The potential for controlling theologians through the revision of the code of canon law became the repeated focus of "study" and "recommendations" over the next twenty years as the CTS board attempted to stop its enforcement.

NOTES

1. "Task Force on Membership and Objectives: Report to the Board of Directors," James E. Biechler, chairman, Sister Fara Impastato, C.P., Thomas J. Ryan (undated), nonarchived materials.

2. Charles J. Brannen, S.J., to James W. Flanagan, Loyola University, Chicago, September 25, 1976, "Secretary's Data 1976" File, Box 1, CTS Collection, ACUA.

3. Richard L. Schebera, S.M.M., to "Colleague" (no date), in "22nd Annual Convention (1976)" File, Box 1, CTS Collection, ACUA.

4. "Minutes of Annual Meeting of Regional Representatives of CTS," Saint Mary's College, Indiana, June 4, 1977, Richard Schebera, secretary, nonarchived materials.

5. Mary Lea Schneider to Jeremy Miller, Michigan State University, January 10, 1978, nonarchived materials.

6. Richard L. Schebera, S.M.M., to Reverend Jeremy Miller, Maryknoll Seminary, Maryknoll, New York, February 23, 1978, nonarchived materials.

7. Maura [Campbell], O.P., to Jeremy [Miller], Caldwell College, Caldwell, New Jersey, February 28, 1978, nonarchived materials.

8. William Cenkner, College Theology Society, office of the president to "Colleagues," Catholic University of America, September 1978, nonarchived materials.

9. Marge [Reher] to William Cenkner, Cabrini College, Radnor, Pennsylvania, November 5, 1978, in "Committee on Annual Meeting, 1978–1980" File, Box 1, CTS Collection, ACUA.

10. Urban Voll to Reverend Cyprian Cenkner, O.P., St. Vincent de Paul Seminary, Boynton Beach, Florida, April 30, 1979, "Committee on Annual Meeting, 1978–1980" File, Box 1, CTS Collection, ACUA.

11. Bernard Cooke to Father Cenkner, the University of Calgary, Calgary, Canada, April 10 [no year], "Committee on Annual Meeting, 1978–1980" File, Box 1, CTS Collection, ACUA.

12. John F. Harvey, O.S.F.S., to Reverend William Cenkner, O.P., Oblates of Saint Francis de Sales, Hyattsville, Maryland, February 21, 1979, in "Committee on Annual Meeting, 1978–1980" File, Box 1, CTS Collection, ACUA.

13. Brother Luke Salm, F.S.C., to Professor Joseph A. LaBarge, March 8, 1979, "Committee on Annual Meeting, 1978–1980" File, Box 1, CTS Collection, ACUA.

14. Sister M. Rose Eileen Masterman, C.S.C., to Dr. William Cenkner, Saint Mary's Convent, Notre Dame, Indiana, February 28, 1979, "Committee on Annual Meeting, 1978–1980" File, Box 1, CTS Collection, ACUA.

15. One hundred and twenty of the respondents indicated that the CTS had assisted them in teaching "somewhat" but a significant number, 189, answered that the CTS had "no significant difference" on their teaching.

16. "The College Theology Membership Poll—Analysis of the Responses," by Theodore M. Steeman, O.F.M., in "Membership Poll Results Poll, 1977—1979" File, Box 4, CTS Collection, ACUA. A 1990 AAR task force "observed that the 1970s had witnessed a 'time of pedagogical experimentation, curricular innovation of many kinds, revisionist scholarship, some confusion and a great deal of intellectual ferment.'" Quoted in D. G. Hart, *The University Gets Religion: Religious Studies in American Higher Education* (Baltimore: Johns Hopkins University Press, 1999), 230.

17. William Cenkner, president to "Colleague." Catholic University of America, April 1980, nonarchived materials.

18. "To: Board of Directors College Theology Society, From: William Cenkner, Re: Progress Report # 9," Catholic University of America, March 5, 1980, nonarchived materials.

19. "SBL and CSR: A Report to CSR Delegates," Kent Harold Richards, executive secretary-treasurer, Society of Biblical Literature, October 16, 1984, and "Views from the AAR Regarding Issues Raised in Documents Circulated for October 19–20 CSR Meeting," James B. Wiggins AAR executive director and CSR delegate in "CTS-CSR" File, Box 7, CTS Collection, ACUA.

20. Len Biallas to Bill [William Shea], Quincy College, Quincy, Illinois, October 30, 1984. Attached appear to be the minutes of the 1984 meeting that took place October 18–19 in Washington, D.C., in "CTS-CSR" File, Box 7, CTS Collection, ACUA.

21. "To: Board of Directors, College Theology Society; [From] Members of the Committee on Membership: Sr. Vera Chester, Fr. William Frost, Dr. Frank Maguire, Dr. Mary Lea Schneider, Dr. Leonard Weber, Dr. Keith J. Egan, chairperson; Subject: Report of the Committee on Membership"; Date: May 15, 1980. "Recommendations to the Board of Directors," nonarchived materials.

22. Newsletter, Sister Vera Chester, CSJ, to "Colleague," office of the president, Theology Department, the College of St. Catherine, St. Paul, Minnesota, March 1981, nonarchived material.

23. Mark Heath, O.P., to Dr. Rodger Van Allen, College Theology Society, Dominican House of Studies, Washington, D.C., February 15, 1983, nonarchived materials.

24. "Policy Statement," William Portier, nonarchived materials.

25. "Constitution," nonarchived materials, and "Revised Constitution" in *Bulletin of the Council of the Study of Religion* (February 1975): 9–12.

26. "Draft of Proposed Constitutional Amendments Arising from Deliberations of the Subcommittee on Committees," Meeting held in Atlanta and Philadelphia, March 18–19, 1977, James W. Flanagan, Jeremy Miller, Thomas Ryan, William Oesterle, nonarchived materials.

27. "To: Regional Chairpersons and/or Contact Persons, From: Jeremy Miller, Re: Regional Issues," February 15, 1977, nonarchived materials.

28. "CTS Annual Business Meeting, Trinity College, Washington, D.C.. June 2, 1979," "Board of Directors Meetings 1971–" File, Box 1, CTS Collection, ACUA.

29. "To: CTS Board (General Comments), From: J. W. F. [James W. Flanagan], Re. Windsor Meeting," office of the president, University of Montana, May 21, 1978, nonarchived materials.

30. "Annual Meeting Structure and Regulations," office of the program director, CTS Annual Convention, Bucknell University, Lewisburg, Pennsylvania, October 27, 1978 (Joseph A. La Barge).

31. "To CTS Members—Call for Papers for the 1979 Annual Convention," From: Joseph A. La Barge, program director, Bucknell University, Lewisburg, Pennsylvania, September 11, 1978, nonarchived materials.

32. "To: CTS Officers, Members of the Board and Program Chairman for AM," From: Dolores Greeley, CTS secretary, "Re: Minutes of Semi-Annual Meeting, 1980," Thursday, November 6, 1980, at the Loewe Anatole Hotel, Dallas, Texas, nonarchived materials.

33. "Theta Alpha Kappa" in "Secretary's Data 1976" File, Box 1, CTS Collection, ACUA.

34. "To: Board of Directors College Theology Society; Re: Progress Report #7," From: William Cenkner, September 28, 1979, nonarchived materials. William Collinge provided the updated information on TAK.

35. To: Keith Egan, from: Leonard Weber, Date: November 13, 1978, "Topic: Response to Memorandum of November 6, 1978," Mercy College of Detroit, nonarchived materials.

36. William Cenkner to "Colleague," office of the president, Catholic University of America, December 13, 1979, nonarchived materials.

37. Stephen J. Casey to Sister Vera Chester, C.S.J., president, College Theology Society, University of Scranton, October 23, 1980, nonarchived materials.

38. College Theology Society "Newsletter," Rodger Van Allen, president, to "Colleague," office of the president Religious Studies Department, Villanova University, Villanova, Pennsylvania, September 1982, nonarchived materials.

39. Newsletter, Vera Chester, C.S.J., president, College Theology Society, to "Colleague," Theology Department, the College of St. Catherine, St. Paul, Minnesota, March 1982, nonarchived materials.

40. College Theology Society "Newsletter," Rodger Van Allen, president, to "Colleague," office of the president Religious Studies Department, Villanova University, Villanova, Pennsylvania, September 1982, nonarchived materials.

41. "To: CTS Board of Directors, June 1982, From: Len Biallas; Re: Vice-president's Report," Quincy College, Quincy, Illinois, nonarchived materials.

42. "To: CTS Officers, Members of the Board and Program Chairperson for AM, From: Suzanne C. Toton, CTS Secretary; Minutes of Board of Directors Meeting—Tuesday, December 20, 1983, Dallas, Texas," nonarchived materials.

43. Edward L. Hamel, O.S.A., to Professor William Shea, president, College Theology Society, Villanova University, June 20, 1984; William M. Shea to Edward L. Hamel, O.S.A., [response], June 18, 1984. How Shea managed to respond before the letter was sent is hard to explain.

44. James W. Flanagan, "The CTS as Publisher" (For Private Use Only—Not for Circulation), "Secretary's Data 1977" File, Box 1, CTS Collection, ACUA

45. "To: Bill Cenkner; From: Larry Cunningham; Re: 'Classroom Series' for C.T.S.," Florida State University, Tallahassee, Florida, October 20, 1978, nonarchived materials.

46. William Cenkner, president, to "Colleague," College Theology Society, office of president, Catholic University of America, March 1979, nonarchived materials.

47. William Cenkner, president to "Colleague," Catholic University of America, April 1980, nonarchived materials.

48. Newsletter, Sister Vera Chester, C.S.J., to "Colleague," office of the president, Theology Department, the College of St. Catherine, St. Paul, Minnesota, March 1981, nonarchived materials.

49. "To: CTS Officers, Members of the Board and Program Chairperson for AM; From: Dolores Greeley, CTS Secretary; Re: Minutes of Annual Meeting, 1982 Thursday, June 3, 1982, at Mercy College, Detroit, Michigan," nonarchived materials.

50. Robert Masson, chairman, Publication Committee and Rodger van Allen, president, College Theology Society, to "Colleague," College Theology Society, Villanova University, no date, nonarchived materials.

51. "Report of the Research and Publication Committee," CTS Board of Directors Meeting, May 31, 1984, "Board Meeting 5-31-84" File, Box 1, CTS Collection, ACUA.

52. College Theology Society Newsletter, March 1984; Rodger Van Allen, president, to colleague, Religious Studies Department, Villanova University, Villanova, Pennsylvania, nonarchived materials.

53. Presidential Newsletter, Father Matthew F. Kohmescher, S.M, president of CTS, University of Dayton, Dayton Ohio, August 1975, nonarchived materials.

54. "COLLEGE THEOLOGY SOCIETY: Minutes of Annual Meeting of the Board of Directors, June 3–6, 1976, 22nd Annual Convention, Rosemont College, Philadelphia," "Board of Trustees—" File, Box 1, CTS Collection, ACUA.

55. "Resolution Passed at the Business Meeting of the Annual Convention of the College Theology Society," Rosemont College, Rosemont, Pennsylvania, June 5, 1976, nonarchived materials.

56. William Cenkner, president, College Theology Society, to Father William Kelly, S.J, December 10, 1979, "Committee on Annual Meeting, 1978–1981" File, Box 1, CTS Collection, ACUA.

57. William Cenkner, president of College Theology Society to "Colleague," office of the president, Catholic University of America, September 1979, nonarchived materials.

58. Newsletter, Vera Chester, C.S.J, president, College Theology Society to "Colleague," Theology Department, the College of St. Catherine, St. Paul, Minnesota, March 1982, nonarchived materials.

59. "To: Board of Directors College Theology Society; Re: Progress Report # 8," From: William Cenkner, November 5, 1979, nonarchived file. Theresa Kane, R.S.M., was president of the Leadership Conference of Women Religious. In her greeting to John Paul II, "she felt obliged to advert to 'the intense suffering and pain which is part of the life of many women in these United States.'" Being barred from ordination was a primary source of this pain. Quote from Rosemary Rodgers, *A History of the College Theology Society* (Villanova, PA: College Theology Society, 1983), 84.

60. Mansour was a Sister of Mercy who after thirty years of religious life chose to leave her religious community rather than resign as director of the Michigan Department of Social Services. The point of contention was the department's funding of abortions. A packet of materials with the resolution stapled on to the materials with the letterhead, "Network, A Catholic Social Justice Lobby."

61. Dr. William Cenkner, president, College Theology Society to Professor Dr. Aldolp Theiss, president, University of Tübingen, Catholic University of America, January 8, 1980. Copies sent to Most Reverend George Moser, Professor Dr. Helmut Engler, and Professor Dr. Hans Küng, nonarchived materials.

62. Chairman of committee, Dr. Michael Donnellan, University of Dayton, members include Sr. Mary Barbara Agnew, C.PP.S., Villanova University; Msgr. Seely Beggiani, Our Lady of Lebanon Maronite Seminary, Washington, D.C.; Dr. Richard Boulet, University of Dayton; Sr. Jeanette Stang, O.P., Ohio Dominican College; and Sr. Mary Catherine Vukmanic, OSU, St. Mary's College, Kentucky; nonarchived material.

63. Report: Part Two "Thematic Critique" in Report to the Board of Directors and Members from the Committee on the National Catechetical Directory (NCD), College Theology Society Convention 1975, 14, nonarchived materials.

64. College Theology Society, "Minutes of the Semi-Annual Meeting of the Board of Directors," Palmer-House, Chicago, November 1, 1975, "Board of Trustees 1971–" File, Box 1, CTS Collection, ACUA.

65. "Preparation of Definitive Academic Legislation for the Church, May 31, 1975," "NCEA-CTS Liaison" File, Box 4, CTS Collection, ACUA. A document with the heading "INSERT II: Preparation of definitive academic legislation for the Church COMMENTS ON SOME ASPECTS of the academic laws contained in *Normae quaedam*, proposed to universities and individual faculties of ecclesiastical studies for the study of certain points pertaining to the law: either matters to be considered as already in possession or those which require further study," May 31, 1975. Including under "II. CHANCELLOR AND LOCAL ORDINARY (Nq 3)" A) Agreed norms.

66. "Relations of American Colleges and Universities with the Church," "NCEA-CTS Liaison" File, Box 4, CTS Collection, ACUA.

67. "Report to the NCCB Administrative Committee," by Archbishop Quinn, "NCCB Liaison with the Joint Committee of Catholic Learned Societies," February 1976, "22nd Annual Convention—1976" File, Box 1, CTS Collection, ACUA.

68. "To Board of Directors, College Theology Society, From Mark Heath, O.P., Representative of the Society to the Joint Committee of Catholic Learned Societies, Annual Report 1975–76," Washington Theological Union, May 21, 1976, in "22nd Annual Convention—1976" File, Box 1, CTS Collection, ACUA.

69. "To: Officers and Board of Directors, the College Theology Society, From: Mark Heath, O.P., Washington-Baltimore Representative of the Society to the Joint Committee of Catholic Learned Societies, and Scholars, Subject: Report of Activity in the Joint Committee 1976–1978," May 20, 1978, in "Jiggles: 1976 Report, Mark Heath" File, Box 7, CTS Collection, ACUA.

70. William P. Loewe, Ph.D., to Sister Vera Chester, C.S.J., president, College Theology Society, Catholic University of America, May 10, 1981, nonarchived materials.

71. "Report on Liaison with Women's Groups," Dolores Greeley, June 1976, "22nd Annual Convention—1976" File, Box 1, CTS Collection, ACUA.

72. Rodger Van Allen to Sister Fidelia McDonough, R.S.M., Women's Ordination Conference, February 21, 1983, attached to information about the "Report of the ad hoc Committee on the Role of Women in Society" draft, November 10, 1982, in "CTSA, ACCU, CCMA, 1982–84" File, Box 4, CTS Collections, ACUA.

73. Most Reverend Joseph L. Imesch, bishop of Joliet to Dr. Rodger Van Allen, president, College Theology Society, Diocese of Joliet, May 8, 1984.

74. Thomas F. O'Meara, O.P., president, Catholic Theological Society of America, to Sister Vera Chester, president, College Theology Society, Washington, D.C., September 19, 1980, nonarchived materials.

75. "To: CTS Officers, Members of the Board and Program Chairman for AM, Re: Minutes of Semi-Annual Meeting, 1980." The acronyms NCLS and IFUP may refer to the Canon Law Society of America and International Federation of Catholic Universities respectively.

76. "College Theology Society Newsletter," Rodger Van Allen, president to "Colleague," Religious Studies Department, Villanova University, October 1983, "Board Meeting June 1983, Cabrini" File, Box 1, CTS Collection, ACUA.

77. "To: CTS Officers, Members of the Board and Program Chairperson for AM; From: Suzanne C. Toton, CTS Secretary; Re: Minutes of Annual Meeting, 1983," nonarchived material.

78. Reverend Matthew F. Kohmescher, S.M., Finance Committee, CTS, to [no name], University of Dayton, February 28, 1983, nonarchived materials.

79. "1983 CTS Solicitation to Bishops and Presidents," Matthew F. Kohmescher, S.M., May 15, 1983, nonarchived materials.

80. "Subject: Ad Hoc Committee on Canon 812 and Related Matters, From: William Loewe, To: CTS Board," Catholic University of America, April 27, 1984, "Board Meeting 5-31-84" File, Box 1, CTS Collection, ACUA. Charles Wilson is a lawyer who has represented Catholic colleges in cases involving governmental funding and separation of church and state.

81. "Christ Among Us . . . Or the Devil?" by James Likoudis, "CTS Ad-hoc Committee" File, Box 7, CTS Collection, ACUA. William Collinge provided detailed information on the incident.

82. "To: CTS Officers, Members of the Board and Program Chairperson for Annual Meeting, From: Suzanne C. Toton, CTS Secretary; Re: Minutes of Annual Meeting, 1984," nonarchived materials.

Group photo of the first Annual Meeting, 1955, Trinity College, Washington, D.C. (See page 15.) Photo courtesy of Archives of Catholic University of America.

The meal served as an admirable opportunity for conversation and informal discussion. Annual Meeting, Philadelphia, 1958. (See page 15.) Photo courtesy of Archives of Catholic University of America.

Sister M. Rose Eileen Masterman, C.S.C., the Society's founding mother with Cardinal Cushing and Bernard Cooke at the Annual Meeting of the Society of Catholic College Teachers of Sacred Doctrine, 1961, Boston. (See pages 12 and 52.) Photo courtesy of Archives of Catholic University of America.

A 1961 version of a special interest session with the focus on practical teaching problems and techniques in the various branches of sacred doctrine. Annual Meeting, Boston, 1961. (See page 55.) Photo courtesy of Archives of Catholic University of America.

Group photo of the Fiftieth Annual Meeting, 2004, Catholic University of America. The original panoramic photo is displayed in three parts. (See page 257.) Photo by Terrence W. Wiley.

Mary Ann Hinsdale, I.H.M., Michael Barnes (far right), and company dancing to the "Vatican Rag" at the postbanquet party, Fiftieth Annual Meeting, Washington, D.C., 2004. (See page 301.)

· 6 ·

The Hermeneutical Circle: Location! Location! Location! (1975–1984)

If the preceding decade had brought into focus "the person" by turning to "the subject" in all of her or his existential desire for freedom and autonomy, then the CTS's third decade sought to understand that person, on the one hand, as interpreter of texts, transmitter of traditions, historical agent and, on the other, as the interpreted subject of texts, the recipient of tradition's formative power, and history's subject. This "existential self," this "person," interprets, transmits, acts out of a particular social location, in several instances in these volumes identified simply as "America." Volume titles, taken together, suggest a widening role for the theologian as the "pontifex," bridge builder between religion and culture, between church and academy, and from religious traditions to contemporary sensibilities. Theology now "confronts," interprets, imagines, creates its own literacy claims, engages in critical history and rises above it.[1] Contributors to the CTS's annual volumes identify many of the unresolved issues left in the wake of the postconciliar euphoria from the most basic, such as language about God, to the more particular Catholic embrace of American social and political culture.

The 1975 meeting anticipated the United States bicentennial celebration with a focus upon *America in Theological Perspective*. The humiliating retreat from Vietnam of only two years earlier and the widespread opposition to the war remained fresh in most people's memory. The Watergate scandal culminating in Richard Nixon's resignation in 1974 further complicated the "state of the nation" with bitterness and pain giving way to cynicism toward the federal government and its politicians. The U.S. Catholic community experienced its own divisions, bitterness, and pain. Catholics had been in the forefront of support for the war as well as antiwar protest, most evident in the radical actions identified with the Berrigans and their compatriots. Yet, the church had other struggles in the aftermath of the exodus of thousands of priests, sisters, and brothers from religious orders and diocesan service and the ongoing challenges to a host of issues, including sexual morality, women's ecclesial roles and rights, and demands for more democratic processes in the church.

GOING NATIVE WITH AN AMERICAN-BRED THEOLOGY

Reading through the annual volume, *America in Theological Perspective*, one can discern a narrative of encroaching declension marked by glimmers of hope for those willing to embrace new or, in a couple of cases, overlooked traditions. The first section, entitled simply "The American Catholic Experience," affirms Catholicism's integration into the American community. James Hennesey, S.J., used the phrase "square peg in a round hole" to describe the U.S. Catholic experience up until very recently, but admitted in his conclusion that this image is like the "Puritan-inspired images of God's New Israel and manifest destiny [that] are wearing out." The eminent historian of U.S. Catholicism called for "a new and necessary liberation from a foreign philosophic and theological imperialism." True to his vocation as historian, Hennesey predicted only what knowledge of the past ensures—that "new images will replace the old."[2] His call for a liberation from European theological influences added yet another wrinkle to theology taught in U.S. universities and colleges.

Two subsequent essays offer examples of American-bred theology. According to Joseph Gower, a native-born American, theology had appeared long before the 1970s. Convert Isaac Hecker found in Catholicism's more positive understanding of human nature the necessary theological starting point for a defense of democracy as a viable political system. Also assuming humans' inherent goodness, the contemporary moral theologian Daniel C. Maguire offered his own version of Hennesey's "new and necessary liberation" in his "distinctively Catholic ethic of the American variety." He appealed to abstract referents such as "Catholic hopefulness," Catholicism's "Dionysian element" manifest in liturgy, the lost moral tradition of "probabilism," and "Thomas Aquinas," who had evidently suffered as "a victim of bad companions." Replete with these resources, Catholicism offers "genuine possibilities" that, unfortunately, must fight against a "management" that "de facto" excommunicates intellectuals, fixates on abortion, neglects women's liberation, insists on celibacy, and remains mired in its "whiteness."[3] Maguire's selected conflicts certainly locate his ethics clearly in America, where the theologian serves as liberator against a native-born but foreign-formed oppressor, the U.S. episcopacy.

The following year, in the edited volume *Theology Confronts a Changing World*, Norbert J. Rigali, S.J., like Daniel Maguire, described a "Moral Theology in Transition," in a section whose title, "Confronting a New Morality," follows the volume's theme. His is a very positive read of moral theology's developments. "Whatever aberrations of the inchoative new age may have to be corrected by subsequent theological reflection, its remarkable energy and intensity are a prima facie indication that moral theology is developing toward a higher stage of truth." Three sources of this positive change are situation ethics with its focus on "persons, not laws," the challenge to the idea of a "distinctively Christian ethic," and changes in anthropology under the influence of personalism and existentialism as well as psychology, so that the subjective and objective are not as easily demarcated and the focus on acts is overshadowed by interpersonal relationships.[4]

The CTS's emphasis on ethics reflected American preoccupation with the practical and the applied. Three years later, the Society dedicated an entire volume to *Essays in Morality and Ethics*. As if to highlight the growing interest in a changing field, the editor, James Gaffney, explained that a minority of the featured scholars "would locate their main academic specialty within the field of ethics." The essayists examined "specific areas of morality or ethics that have impinged forcefully on their more habitual fields of interest, widely distributed among the theoretical, historical, and practical subdivisions of religious studies." Gaffney offered two justifications for the selection of nonspecialists' work. First, professional ethicists themselves tend to focus upon ethical theories rather than moral problems. Second, a trend exists in which those in other fields including "religion" delve into moral issues. The collection "exemplifies also the interdisciplinary sensitivity typical of modern religious moralizing, which makes increasing use of theories as well as facts derived from secular humanistic and scientific undertakings."[5]

The final result displayed a wide range of topics and concerns. The opening essay, a philosophical and theological meditation on evil, argued that an "other face of evil" exists. This "other face" manifests itself as "the test of love, the challenge of love, the very food of love . . . best understood when we contemplate the Son of God on the cross as he lays down his life for his friends."[6] Other essays considered adaptation of comparative religious ethics to criticize multinational corporations, an interchange between moral development theorists like James Fowler, Jean Piaget, and L. Kohlberg and traditional theological perspectives as found in thinkers like Aquinas. Two final essays found their inspiration in the controversial CTSA volume, *Human Sexuality: New Directions in American Catholic Thought*. The first, by longtime member Luke Salm, considers the methodological difficulties of the work; the other, from Mary Lou Grad, identifies human sexual intercourse as the most profound manifestation of *homo ludens*, an anthropological starting point Hugo Rahner developed.[7]

Two other essays present East Asian alternative ethical frameworks read through contemporary American concerns. Silvio E. Fittipaldi considers "The Zen of Ethics," in which he equates Zen ethics with Zen art, by which he means the "art of living"; hence the article is not "Zen Ethics" but "the Zen of Ethics." The person formed by Zen "is relating directly to the life situation, and enters into it thoroughly and creatively" rather than subjecting it to external principles as found in Western traditions.[8] The next essay explores Confucian approaches to ethics through "benevolence" or the concern for the other or, in the more familiar Western parlance, the common good.[9]

OTHERS AND THEIR THEOLOGIES

Concern for the "other," especially the marginalized, appeared in various volumes throughout the Society's third decade. A theology too narrowly identified with those in power received scrutiny. Maria Augusta Neal, S.N.D., spoke forcefully on religion's cooptation for oppressive purposes in her plenary address, "Civil Religion, Politics, and Theology in America," at the 1975 annual meeting. The sociologist's primary example was not American but Afrikaner use of religion to justify apartheid. She also cited Mary Daly for her fierce criticism of theology's complicity in women's oppression. Neal took a dim view of current theology, i.e., "language about God," since it "does not yet reveal space and hope for the oppressed people of the world." The marginalized "experience" theology as "a political act" benefiting "middle and upper classes, whites and males."[10] Mary L. Schneider assessed civil religion in more benign terms. She appealed to Catholic traditions found in Thomas Aquinas and then John Courtney Murray that emphasized participation in American civil society but from the critical stance that theological analysis provides.

Both Schneider and Neal assumed an obligation exists for theologically committed scholars to examine the implications of social ethics in which the right and duty to participate fully in the many dimensions of contemporary society, from the political to the cultural, is central. Other colleagues in later volumes shared in this assumption. In the 1976 volume already mentioned, the opening section, "Confronting Social Upheaval," offers the essay, "Beyond Moralism: Ethical Strategies in Global Development." Denis Goulet brought his direct experience in developing nations and among diverse peoples who suffer poverty, combined with his formal studies in the "ethics of development," to consider "strategies for change."[11] He identified the source of change not in the professional classes, such as college professors, even those who teach theology, but in "the struggling deviants, the social prophets" actively accepting "the vulnerability of the oppressed." He used examples like Martin Luther King Jr. and Dorothy Day to illustrate his point. Goulet challenged "every teacher of college theology in the 'developed' world" like every Christian to make part of his or her "noble mission" a commitment to implanting hope that such global development among the poor is attainable.[12]

The opening essay in the twenty-fifth annual volume offers as the single entry in a section, entitled "Introduction: The Challenge," Richard L. Rubenstein's "Reason's Deadly Dreams." His intellectual impetus is to understand "the *full* implications" of the Holocaust, the obliteration of European Jewry, including "the death of God" as "*Sovereign Lord of covenant and election.*" This essay warned against the triumph of "functional rationality," here defined as "the methodical attainment of a practical end by means of a precise calculation of adequate means." Such practical reasoning permits, as one logical outcome, mass murder to achieve particular social ends, the elimination of unwanted populations or those who have little monetary value. His bleak depiction of contemporary culture began with the Holocaust and ended with a reflection on religious cults, in particular the mass suicide of the Jim Jones cult. Only in the very last paragraph did Rubenstein offer any hope, with a suggestion that Christianity's own millenarian beginnings may provide resources for "socially constructive long-range results."[13]

The "other" is not limited to persons but includes the cultural movements from modernity to postmodernity. Still, many explicitly future-oriented essays offer more than a modicum of hope with appeals to diverse, often nontraditional sources. *America in Theological Perspective* offered intriguing examples. David M. Thomas found technology to fit well within a Christian eschatology where hope arose from humans participating in their own fulfillment. In more apocalyptic fashion, Thomas warned that religion's failure to connect with America's technological aspirations would ensure religion's extinction.[14] Henry David Thoreau served as Russell Jaberg's theological guide in exploring "planetology" as a constructive response to "the death of man," since "man" no longer functions as the "principle of our culture." This essay provided the volume's concluding thought. "This paradigm of nature which can be learned from Thoreau may remind Christian protagonists of their obligations and opportunities in a culture turned earthward."[15] In this final sentence one reads yet another theological reorientation found neither in the "finality of sacred doctrine" nor in the existential quest for autonomy.

The Society marked the twenty-fifth year of its existence, as already noted, with an "earthward" convention theme focusing on religion and culture. The annual publication bore as its title *the bent World* taken directly, with full acknowledgment, from Gerard Manley Hopkin's poem "God's Grandeur." In the preface, the volume editor, John R. May explained the choice. First he acknowledged that Hopkins' own focus was on "the interaction of *God* and world rather than *religion* and world or culture." Though "*not* God," religion often represents "the God-oriented aspect of culture." The "bent world" of this collection therefore—not unlike Hopkins'—is that contemporary intersection of religion and culture that is both an indictment of the detritus of civilization and a stimulus to the quickening of the human spirit."[16] The "world" here is not Russell Jaberg's planet but the situated human.

The bent World essays placed immediately after Richard Rubenstein's ominous warning reflect a more hopeful account of the relationship between "technological society and theological method." Martin C. Kastelic argued for a mutually beneficial dialectical relationship between technology and Christian mysticism. Relying on Jacques Ellul's critique of technology's emphasis on technique at the expense of the human person, Kastelic attributed to "mysticism" an ability to provide "a much-needed critical edge" and a "creative thrust" that might also "stimulate the development of those techniques necessary for our continued stewardship of creation." The ultimate goal of the dialectic between the imaginative creativity of mysticism and the creative techniques of technology is "to make our technological society a human society." In so far as the contemporary society has moved away from Christianity, Kastelic asserted, it is also failing to enter fully into the technological.[17]

Theology's reorientation also had an earthward movement in its grappling with various liberation movements captured in the 1976 convention's already cited volume: *Theology Confronts a Changing World*. The editor, Thomas McFadden, noted that the ten selections were chosen among "literally scores of manuscripts," and those not given at the convention were submitted by CTS members. "The book demonstrates, therefore, the growing competence of college teachers of theology and religious studies, and their commitment to appropriate research and publication."[18] According to the editor, the volume's more accurate title might have been "the Catholic Church confronts a changing theology in a changing world and is not changing in the ways that it ought to change." The choice of the verb, "confronts" suggested that "growing competence" had emboldened the theologian to seek engagement with the world even when faced with opposition from the church as well as the world.

IMAGINING A FUTURE FOR THE CHURCH

Theology's attentiveness to the world is easily matched by its attentiveness to another critical social entity, the church. Richard McBrien examined "The Church and Social Change: An Ecclesiological Critique." Using his own clear delineations of the topics under consideration led McBrien to his inevitable conclusions. The church as an institution ought to work for justice through social services and specific political actions. Given the variety of legitimate responses, particular political actions cannot constitute a test of fidelity. On the other hand, the church must "subject itself constantly to the demands of God's justice" to "be a credible sign of the divine redemptive presence in our midst."[19] McBrien insisted that the church must engage in self-criticism.

Such a demand for openness to further reforms in the church served as the central focus of other essays in this volume. "Confronting Future Needs" took its cue from an unusual mix of sources. Geffrey B. Kelly looked to "Futurists and Reformers" to understand "the Shape of the Future Church." A reformer, according to Kelly, frequently "comes across only as provocative bad news to 'status quoers' who resent that theologians should rock boats that still slide around in brackish ecclesial swamps, places like Tridentine marsh or Vatican I creek up which a futurist would not like to be caught without oars." His candidates for effective "futurists and reformers" include Avery Dulles, who offers a "superbionic church from the best of five basic models," Hans Kung, with his church focused on service, Richard McBrien, who calls for "a thorough democratization of church structures," and Gabriel Moran, who promotes religious education that nurtures communal relationships. All four, if implemented together, have the potential to form a "movement," a sociological term Gregory Baum uses to describe a mechanism for reform. This "movement" could utilize "what Rahner calls the formation of open, declericalized 'basic communities,'"—a term made familiar in Latin American liberation theology. Vibrant small communities require "personal action, particularly in the interaction of community and education at its most effective level, the unsanctioned but ever innovative roots of the church." Kelly offered no speculation on the actual future of his envisioned reform of the church.[20]

Two more essays in the 1976 volume focus on specific ecclesiastical issues, in this case "Confronting Sexism" within the church. Robert Kress argues for an "androgynous Church" as the "Church of the Future." Kress appealed to scripture, arguing that Jesus "is and acts androgynously" and to Paul who works with women as well as men. He made several "practical proposals"— avoid using sexist language in "church writing" (not in rewriting traditional hymns and prayers), renew Mariology, and ordain women.[21] In the subsequent essay, Sonya Quitslund examines the 1973 *Theological Reflections on the*

Ordination of Women. Her title indicates her intention to make "A Theological Case for the Ordination of Women." Quitslund was one of the "core commissioners" at the Women's Ordination Conference that met in Detroit in November 1975. She appealed to the "New Testament" message concerning those transformed in baptism, women's ministerial roles, and the church understanding itself as changing over time. Quitslund directly countered the document to demonstrate inconsistencies in its arguments concerning women's participation in Christ's redemption and challenged the claim that women's exclusion from ordination is clearly defined as dogma. In her relatively modest proposals, she suggests adopting process philosophy to support a more dynamic view of God's interactions and changing relationship with the world.[22]

Six years later, another Richard McBrien essay on the church appeared in the annual volume on religious literacy. Featured at the 1982 convention, McBrien in this case considered "the function of the Church as context and matrix for reading and interpreting the Christian classics in particular, and every classic in general." "Classic" refers to David Tracy's concept developed in *The Analogical Imagination.* The ecclesial matrix emerges through a gathering of disciples who are formed in a tradition manifest in its "public worship" composed of "word, sacrament, and apostolic ministry." This community is pluralistic, clearly evident among contemporary Christians but even within Roman Catholicism. The "distinctive context and matrix" with Roman Catholicism arose from "the principles of sacramentality, mediation, and communion." These three principles, of course, loom large in McBrien's influential work, *Catholicism.*[23]

THE BIBLE: BEYOND THE HISTORICAL CRITICAL

The annual volumes offer essays from other influential scholars in various fields of religious studies and theology including biblical related studies. Elisabeth Schüssler Fiorenza provides a preview of what has proven to be a groundbreaking work, *In Memory of Her.* The essay's title, "The Study of Women in Early Christianity: Some Methodological Considerations," made clear the focus. This essay, along with Wayne A. Meeks's sociological approach to the study of the Pauline communities, was delivered at the 1977 annual meeting and appeared in the annual volume, *Critical History and Biblical Faith: New Testament Perspectives.*[24] Fiorenza's article reveals the challenges for those focusing upon women in their theological research. She related how a fellow scholar had "remarked about a professor who wrote a rather moderate article on women in the Old Testament, 'It is a shame, she has ruined her whole scholarly career.'" She told how each semester she had to convince her chair that focusing a course on women in the Bible can serve as an introduction to scriptures. She found that any mention of "women" in a course title automatically made the course suspect intellectually and theologically. After these remarks, she provided a brief overview of the argument soon to appear *In Memory of Her*. She introduced the hermeneutics of suspicion concerning the androcentric interpretations of the biblical authors themselves and the patriarchalization of the egalitarian Jesus movement.[25]

Essays with scripture as their central focus frequently exhibited interests well beyond historical-critical exegesis of the text. In the volume featuring Fiorenza and Meeks, an entire section is devoted to accepting the traditional theological category of resurrection without abandoning modern biblical scholarship and critical history. All the authors affirmed "resurrection" interpreted existentially or eschatologically and thus as ahistorical, an event that transcends history. A commitment to theological ethical traditions in light of contemporary biblical scholarship is also found in Robert Daly's essay, "Toward a Christian Biblical Ethics." How satisfactory the results are is not the point here. Rather the point here is a complex commitment to scriptures' normative theological role.[26]

Essays using scriptures as their principal source to reflect on other convention themes appear in subsequent volumes. At the University of Windsor, Ontario, meeting in 1978, Leander Keck considered "Ethos and Ethics in the New Testament" as his contribution to the thematic focus on ethics. He first had to justify the possibility of identifying an "ethos" or "ethics" in the New Testament. He argued that "ethics concerns not only the question, What is to be done? But also the question, Who is the doer and what are his or her communities?" If these claims are true, "then it is difficult to exclude anything in the NT from an analysis of its ethics." Keck described the other term, "ethos," as "a customary way of thinking and acting, a pattern of values, a style." Then, similar to Meeks and Fiorenza, he drew upon sociological approaches to scripture and concluded that "Jesus was trying to purify an ethos. Paul was trying to shape a new one." His approach avoided a proscription of particulars in favor of a way of understanding "the doer" and "the community."[27]

The essay immediately following Keck's attempts to identify "The Foundations of Paul's Ethics." The author, Al Hiebert, opened with a contemporary observation—"we live in an age of 'residual Christianity' when many who do not go to church still acknowledge certain moral standards that depend on Christian roots." He also acknowledged a contemporary assumption of "the possibility and validity of moral systems independent of God."[28] Hiebert then focused on identifying specific Pauline principles which guide particular actions such as patterning oneself after Christ or embracing agape as the primary Christian motive for action. In light of the waning Christian influence in contemporary society, the author sought to establish in this essay common ground among Christians to unify and thus strengthen influence.

Other readings of biblical texts, especially as the 1980s began, feature discussions of hermeneutics, both specific and general. In *Foundations of Religious Literacy*, for example, Jeanne Evans specified Paul Ricoeur's "biblical hermeneutics" as her interpretative framework for a "Taunt Song" in Isaiah 14. What she noted is the difference between the historical-critical approach which "tends to move in back of the text in search of original sources" to "literary criticism" with its interpretive focus "*in front of* the poem to the world of the text."[29] Alice Laffey, in the 1983 volume, *Interpreting Tradition*, extended the interpretive focus "beyond the hierarchical-patriarchal culture which produced them" to ensure their "meaning today—for the twentieth century believer, for advocates of peace, as well as for women." She identified this work as "a contemporary hermeneutical task, for both scholars and teachers of the Scriptures," that entails accounting for the "time and culture conditioned" quality of the texts' "prejudices." Laffey refused to stop with a collection of problematic texts concerning "political and religious power" or featuring "female biblical characters who are victimized by male dominance." She "sought out, in addition, those texts which point toward a new way of relating to power as well as a new way of relating to women." From Old through New Testament the methodology is applied to reveal "a vision of a peace-filled global village and a truly just Church." Such a utopian vision might serve in turn as a motivating factor for twentieth century believers to work toward a peace-filled world and "just Church."[30] Such an interpretive frame of reference further highlights a dialectic of normativity between sacred text and contemporary culture.

TRAVELING IN HERMENEUTICAL CIRCLES

Wrestling with hermeneutical questions preoccupied many others besides biblical scholars. In the introductory paragraph of his essay on Christology, John McCarthy quotes David Tracy, "All contemporary systematic theology can be understood as fundamentally hermeneutical.'" McCarthy then demonstrates this point with a critical consideration of what one is doing in creating a Christology with special attention given to Johann Metz, Jozef van Beeck, and David Tracy. McCarthy attributes to these three authors an emphasis on "an authority that questions the claim to adequacy of any proclamation."

These authors communicate "this authority which fails to authorize by numerous critical categories: dangerous memory, narrative, analogical and dialectical language, relative adequacy, rhetoric as opposed to concepts, imitation as opposed to knowledge or confession." Each one serves as a "proclaimer of a proclamation that is never complete, that is filled with blanks and negations."[31] McCarthy focused on Christology as an exercise in method rather than as engagement in constructive theology.

Among the essays included in *The Pedagogy of God's Image* is Walter Ong's "The Psychodynamics of Oral Memory and Narrative: Some Implications for Biblical Studies." The CTS presentation anticipated his *Orality and Literacy*. Ong moved from the contemporary reader in front of the text to far behind the text past any written sources to the oral culture that created and transmitted these communal texts. "Memory, in its initial role and in its transformations, is in one way or another a clue to nearly everything that went on as discourse moved out of the pristine oral world to literacy and beyond." In a literate culture, memory is greatly altered.[32] Despite its written form, the Bible must be understood as reflecting primarily the mindset or "psychodynamics of oral culture." Unlike the "'analytically linear,' forms of written expression, oral thought is highly redundant and echoic: this is the only way it can proceed, by feedback loops out of and into itself." Jesus as itinerant preacher reflects oral culture just as the traveling in the Gospels provides a flexible framework for carrying the narrative.

Interest in the interpretive dynamics of transmitting and receiving scripture and tradition arose out of broader explorations of human knowing and the possibilities for religious experience. In considering the "psychodynamics of oral culture," Ong made clear the layered complexities of interpretation, transmission, and reception of religious faith. His talk enriched the discussions of the 1981 convention theme, "symbol and the religious imagination." Symbolic expression, in fact, became a common starting point for several students of religion in the early 1980s. The 1981 volume, bearing the title, *The Pedagogy of God's Image: Essays on Symbol and the Religious Imagination*, reflects this interest. The 1981 volume's editor, Robert Masson, explained the appearance of apparently disparate essays in a single volume. "If we ask, where is God's image to be found?, we will not hear one answer, nor will we find a single response to the question, how does the image get us from here to God and back?" Masson expressed confidence that responses, even "complementary" ones, to both queries, exist.[33] Imagination served as the epistemological key to responding.

John Hogan produced the volume's very first essay, a critical analysis of Wolfhart Pannenberg's adaptation of R. G. Collingwood's philosophy of history. Hogan challenged history as factual with his emphasis upon imagination in constructing historical narratives. He expanded Tracy's to-do list for systematicians. "Relating the 'subjective,' 'present' and hermeneutical with the 'objective,' 'past' and historical is emerging as a focal task for Christian theologians. Increasingly, imagination appears essential to that task."[34] Hogan's reading of Pannenberg makes clear how much present considerations shape not only philosophical commitments to hermeneutics and historical consciousness but imaginative constructions of history.

Continuing explorations of the subjective, situated dimensions of human knowing, Mary Aquin O'Neill, R.S.M., concentrated on Paul Ricoeur's influence in understanding the ambiguity of "human existence" which "is open to several interpretations, to multiple and conflicting readings." The *imago Dei* offers the imagination a hopeful vision of humans without dismissing the human capacity for evil.[35] The role of imagination and symbol also appear in William Shea's revisiting "religious experience." Roberto Goizueta argued that "symbol" rather than "concept" serves liberation theology as found in Enrique Dussel's approach. Paul Knitter reflected on imagination's importance in "interreligious dialogue."

Essays relying upon symbol and imagination for exploring hermeneutical questions are not limited to the 1981 volume. Morny Joy's comparison of Gilbert Durand and Paul Ricoeur on "the Philosophy of Imagination" appeared in the 1982 volume. Like Hogan, Joy placed her analysis in an intellectual movement involving a significant shift "from an exclusive emphasis on logical and propositional formulations as the sole criteria of truth." The shift emerges from "an existential notion of truth that refers to a type of ontological resonance which underlies an experientially grounded model of knowledge." Imagination plays "an integral role" in these experiential ways of knowing first encountered "in imagistic form."[36]

THEOLOGY'S PRIMARY SOURCE:
AN EXPERIENTIAL GROUND

Anthropology as a theological starting point often relies upon "an experientially grounded model of knowledge" in which humans engage the transcendent through symbols such as biblical narrative, liturgical ritual, and religious art. So, for example, Marchita B. Mauck considered "The Liminal Space of Ritual and Art." She defined "liminality" as a particular relationship to "space/time in which we allow mystery to unfold." Openness to mystery allows "the power of symbol to penetrate our being and lead us deeper into mystery. Liturgy and art function most effectively in such a space/time." The desired effects of entering mystery through symbol include receptivity to "the world of myth, story, ritual, and at the same time the secular, technological world." For Christians, Christ is the "primal symbol," providing the "root metaphor," namely "the process of death and resurrection." Mauck appealed to both Paul Tillich and Karl Rahner to support her argument that symbol mediates being.[37]

Mary Collins also explored ritual's significance in theological reflection. Rather than relying upon theologians like Rahner and Tillich, Collins turned to cultural and social anthropologists, most notably Clifford Geertz, and to the field of "ritual studies" to examine the relationship "between symbol and power." In part, such an examination provided a basis for her trenchant criticism of current Roman Catholic ritual practices, particularly their exclusion of women. Rites reveal theological commitments as well as cultural practices. "For religious ritual, like religious literature, is a cultural artifact, expressing transcendent meaning through non-verbal limit language—a language of acts which press participants beyond the world of ordinary human existence."[38]

Mary Jo Weaver relied upon religious literature read through a Rahnerian framework to shape her essay, "Quest for Self/Quest for God." From Rahner, Weaver took as her guiding principle "the fundamental, dialectical unity between the experience of God and the experience of the self." She drew the logical conclusion that one could produce "a table of correspondences between the history of one's self-experience and one's God-experience." Using "pilgrimage" to frame the quest, Weaver appealed to both classic literature, namely Dante's *Divine Comedy*, and contemporary literary selections to illustrate this dialectic.[39]

The image of journey shapes the organization of the 1980 convention volume. In *The Journey of Western Spirituality*, Thomas Berry appeared as author of the final essay and perhaps, from the editor's point of view, his thought serves as final destination of Western spirituality's journey. This volume seems to have a fairly clear organizing principle. After the first essay, in which Silvio E. Fittipaldi reflects on "Teaching Religion as a Spiritual Process" using Chuang Tzu's story of the wood-carver as the central meditation, the next ten essays appear in a kind of chronological order, beginning with an essay on Christian prayer's grounding in Judaism to a meditation on and analysis of Gethsemane in Mark's Gospel then a look at the Gnostics, Celts, Julian of Norwich, and Thomas Traherne. The next three may be construed as contemporary approaches comparing Buddha and Christ, examining Progoff's "intensive journal approach" and considering a spirituality of peace and justice. Berry's essay argues that the combination of "Classical Western Spirituality and the American Experience" has unleashed a destructive pattern evident in the life of the planet itself. The alternative offered is his now familiar "new story of the universe." Berry rehearsed major philosophical shifts in Christian thought from the early church adoption of "Platonic philosophy" to Augustine's use of "Neoplatonism," to Aquinas's reliance upon "Aristotle." Today's philosophical resource is "our modern understanding of the origin and development of the universe and the emerging ecological age." Berry identified "creating this new cultural coding of the ecological age" as potentially "the next phase of the American experience," and suggested that "creating a spirituality integral with this coding may well be the next phase of the Christian tradition."[40]

The volume also features a unique concluding section. Entitled "End papers," it showcases five pieces of creative or meditative writing. In "The Unlived Life of St. Thérèse," for example, Virginia J. Knight created a series of imagined correspondence in which Thérèse experiences a miraculous cure, leaves the convent, and joins forces with Edgar Cayce who becomes her master, goes to Holland and lives in the same house as Anne Frank, ends up in India protesting with Gandhi, suffers a stroke in 1956 that leaves her paralyzed, and dies six years later in a nursing home in Bayeux, France. Her final words are "Oh! I love Him . . . My God . . . I love You," but the story's final entry is from the Vatican Observatories: "One of the black moments of the Church's history and an embarrassment in modern times, has ended. The former Sister Thérèse of Lisieux, Carmelite, has died. . . . The Church must counsel its nuns to beware of examples like this. It is felt that if she had remained in her Order, she might have become a modern saint." The text does not make it entirely clear how these "End papers" illustrate or illumine the *Journey of Western Spirituality*.[41]

THEOLOGY IN HISTORY

The organization of the CTS's twenty-sixth annual volume on spirituality highlights the impressive developments in theologically related historical studies. Every volume from 1975 through 1984 features some explicitly historically framed essays. In *the bent World*, for example, in a section entitled, "Scripture, Tradition, and Wholeness," one can read a comparison of Saint Paul and Sigmund Freud as well as Keith Egan's guide to reading Teresa of Avila and Lawrence Cunningham's reappropriation of hagiography as a window onto "heroic sanctity." Reflections on religious literacy in 1982 include several historical essays. Paul Misner examines religious literacy in light of John Henry Newman's attempt to establish a curriculum for a liberally educated individual. This volume includes more than the usual historical suspects. William Shea examines Jonathan Edwards' life with particular attention to his relationship with his wife, Sarah. William Grosnick provides an account of his own Irish-American family's reunions as exemplifying how "family ritual" effects a kind of literacy. Joan Leonard turns to Muriel Spark's *The Prime of Miss Jean Brodie* and *Momento Mori* to consider their parabolic effect. William J. O'Brien rereads Samuel Beckett's *Waiting for Godot* as a modern rendering of "Holy Saturday among the dead," who remain uncertain of the cross's meaning for their own life and death.[42] Diane Apostolos-Cappadona renders the Magdalene tradition from scripture and in Christian art. The figure who emerges "incorporates several of the paradoxical images and characteristics of woman within the framework of Christian traditions." Every symbolic rendering "explicates *that* particular cultural understanding of woman and her societal role."[43]

Interpreting Tradition, as might be expected, includes a sizeable section on historical explorations, titled, à la David Tracy, "Classics Revisited." Through a careful study of primary sources, J. Patout Burns countered the "received interpretation of Augustine" that makes him responsible for "the dualism of body and soul" in Western Christianity.[44] Gary Macy examines an eleventh century example of "statements of the official church that embarrassed theologians when they were written and have haunted their successors down through the centuries" concerning the Eucharist. Through his historical analysis, Macy illustrates the church's long history of pluralism. "Pluralism is not a twentieth century idea which somehow challenges a monolithic tradition, but rather the history of the church, and especially the history of the medieval church, is a history of pluralism." Historical work, therefore, offers a variety of theological perspectives. "Tucked away on the back shelves of Wisdom's great storehouse, many such treasures await discovery."[45]

William Loewe extends Macy's point back into the early church with an examination of Irenaeus's salvation history narrative, a theological response to the contemporary problem of Gnosticism. The finished work displayed "Irenaeus' own creative originality," weaving "notions of dispensation, recapitulation, and the Pauline Christ-Adam typology" into a coherent narrative. Loewe argues that current theological advances result in "a clearer, more adequately differentiated grasp" of those early Christian theologians whose work comprises the current tradition. "Hence the history of theology remains an unfinished tale, needing constantly to be recast."[46] Theology's progress reaches backward as well as forward in an imaginative process of reappropriation in light of changing circumstances.

Ewert H. Cousins, an established historian-theologian of Christian spirituality, spoke to the "Interpretation of Tradition in a Global Context." Tradition, Cousins wrote, ought to be "evoked and cultivated by an attitude of reverence and respect" accompanied by an awareness of its "dark side." It can become "heavy and oppressive, a dead weight, a lifeless corpse, a prison of the human spirit." Cousins cautioned, "Even at its best, when it is alive and nourishing, [tradition] can present obstacles to innovation and stifle creativity." Appealing to Jean LeClercq, Cousins described tradition's "organic unfolding" as occurring at times as "a quantum leap in which a new context is produced by a break with the past and a leap into the future." LeClercq had identified the postwar period as such a leap into "a global consciousness: . . . open to traditions other than our own and, in fact, to the traditions of the entire human community." Cousins used the sixty-volume Paulist Press series, "The Classics of Western Spirituality" and the twenty-five volume Crossroad Publishing reference, *World Spirituality: An Encyclopedic History of the Religious Quest,* to illustrate the new consciousness. Borrowing from Karl Jaspers, Cousins identifies the present as "a Second Axial Period," imaged in the astronauts' view of earth—"the beautiful blue globe shining against the black background of space." This new image of the planet serves as "symbol of the archetype of the common tradition that underlies all diverse traditions." The astronaut view finally provides the perspective necessary to comprehend this "global context."[47]

Quantum leaps notwithstanding, it was only a matter of time before Thomas Aquinas would receive an invitation to return to that familiar space, the classroom. In the 1983 convention volume on *Interpreting Tradition,* Keith J. Egan characterizes Thomas's absence from the undergraduate religion curriculum as an "impoverishment." He questions whether "the laity or the clergy [could] be theologically literate if they have no familiarity with the thought of the man whom Paul Tillich has referred to as 'the classical theologian of the Roman Church.'" In teaching Marquette undergraduates, Egan emphasized "the process of Thomas' inquiries," encouraging students "to ask questions with him, to explore the meaning of the Christian message in the company of master explorer." Thomas returned to the classroom not as the one who provides all answers but as the master of the question, whose text now serves as a classic in theological inquiry.[48]

Earlier in that same volume, Monika Hellwig returned the Society to the classroom to consider the teaching of "Theology as Fine Art." Like Egan, she wanted to involve the students in "the reading of the masters." Learning theology becomes "an apprenticeship in thought." Its finality comes from "an attempt to find ultimate meaning in life" not through inventing but through "discovery." The process of theological reflection involves three moments. One is contemplation or an openness to what is; another is empathy or a linking with the past, tradition, and the experience of others. The third and most demanding is reason which calls for "discerning and eliminating all unnecessary vocabulary, evasive citation of authorities, and the smoke screen of convoluted arguments, in order to come to the real human issues because it is these that open to the revelation of the divine." She then describes studying of a particular doctrine in which the biblical narrative, historical investigations and contemporary questions contribute to a student's "apprenticeship of thought."[49]

AMERICAN CATHOLICS SEARCH FOR THEIR IDENTITY

The College Theology Society had done enough historical investigating and contemporary questioning to feature in several volumes self-conscious reflection about "America" as the context of their theological work and their understanding of their Catholicism. The 1975 volume, as already noted, had situated *America in Theological Perspective*. In that volume, Elizabeth McKeown probes how an American Catholic identity had emerged out of America's religious pluralism. At the beginning of the twentieth century, Catholic University's William Kerby offered an astute analysis of forging an identity. He understood that "belonging" required more than assent to dogma or sacramental and liturgical activities; it "was also a matter of 'feeling,' of inspirational leadership, a sense of history, evocative symbols, mass demonstrations of group strength, and even common experience of attack or antagonism from the outside world." In Kerby's time, a national Catholic movement suffered from lack of coherent episcopal support. With the U.S. entrance into World War I, the bishops forged a unified Catholic effort to demonstrate the immigrant community's national loyalty. World War II reinforced this equation of Catholicism with the U.S. political and military commitments, and the strong loyalty to church and country remained "until the events of Vatican II and Vietnam shook the church and country to their very roots."[50] Such an uprooting triggers renewed interest in forging an American Catholic communal identity that avoids cooptation or withdrawal from society.

The post-1960s "uprooting" evoked a variety of responses. Just as the second generation of the immigrant church made concerted efforts to forge a national identity, so some of their children sought to reclaim what consensus Catholicism had obscured. The 1976 convention's volume, *Theology Confronts a Changing World*, included Ronald Pasquarriello's "Theological Considerations on the American Experience of Ethnicity." He relied upon an understanding of theology "as 'reflection upon the meanings present in human experience and the meanings present in Christian tradition.'" Based upon that definition, "the renewed American emphasis on ethnic identity" requires the theologian's attention. Ethnicity affirms "primary relationships—of compassion, intimacy and friendliness—over against dominance, competitiveness, and mere efficiency." Ethnicity becomes a theological resource for consideration of concerns like "cultural justice," "personal identity" arising out of experience of self, a commitment to "life," pluralism within church and society that also mediates "unity through diversity." In ethnicity, "universality is mediated through particularity."[51]

A self-conscious focus upon U.S. Catholicism appears in the opening essay of *Foundations of Religious Literacy*. David O'Brien presented themes now very familiar to those who have read his other works. He rehearses the familiar story of Catholicism's growth from a minority to a large and vibrant community in the United States. O'Brien attributed the success to a strategy, in part, of remaining separate from the wider culture and, in part, of utilizing the opportunities offered in the U.S. context of religious liberty. The brief historical overview served only as a prelude to the challenge that O'Brien laid before the Society's members. He asked his audience to consider their own role as Catholic educators in the present context—"to regard the world as our world, to recognize the religious dimensions of the world and the worldliness of the church, and to renew religious studies in the concrete settings in which we work and live." In the face of failed "secular theologies" and America's loss of "moral attractiveness," and desirous of a "personal faith and community experience, Catholic intellectuals seem to be retreating into a new ghetto, no matter how prophetic its terminology or how universal its so-called 'concern.'" Beyond the chiding, O'Brien called upon the teachers of college theology to seek "common ground." "If, somehow, we could combine the intelligence of our scholars, the courage of our ministers, the goodness of our people, the richness of our tradition, and the networks of our church, we could in fact make a difference in this land of ours."[52]

The decade seems to end where it began seeking to place America in theological perspective. "*Rising from History* describes the kind of house it is, and *U.S. Catholic Theology Looks to the Future* are apt words to inscribe over its portal. They who choose to enter will be able to find their way comfortably, will find a good place in which to dwell for a while."[53] David O'Brien returned after a year's hiatus to acknowledge once again the difficult challenges in the current U.S. Catholic community, rehearsing a frequent triad that dissolved the identity found earlier in the twentieth century—"the gradual collapse of the American Catholic subculture," the church's changed stance toward modernity after Vatican II, and the "massive cultural upheaval in the sixties." O'Brien noted a plurality of views existed long before the Second Vatican Council and that the postwar period was an anomaly. O'Brien's hope remained in a liberal American Catholicism, now with "a more chastened appreciation of the demonic potential of power and deeper concern for the personal, spiritual and organizational dimensions of church life and ministry." Chastened does not mean "withdrawal to some mountaintop of biblical prophecy" or "a new conservatism of Catholic power and doctrinal orthodoxy." Like his 1982 essay, O'Brien challenged his audience to reclaim "a sense of mission, inspired by contemporary church teaching and rendered operative by close attention to the specifically American character of our own situation." He called for a mission-oriented theology that embraces the mundane, that "gives a central place to the laity, to politics, to work, to neighborhood life, and an approach to pastoral planning which is participatory and democratic." O'Brien conveyed clearly his enduring conviction that such organizing remains a possibility for those who have the will to do it, and that such organizing could become a means to effect change.[54]

The explicit American focus of *Rising from History* continues with an entire section in the thirtieth volume given over to an analysis of "Americanism." William Portier introduces the four essays connecting a century-old episode with the future. "As Americanism was about a vision of where the world was going and the place the United States had in that movement, so, at the end of the 'American century,' Catholics in the United States must have a vision of history to guide their actions with respect to their nation and with respect to what Karl Rahner called the emerging 'world Church.'"[55] Portier identifies three myths that provide a "narrative structure" for how Catholics understand their relationship to American history. One he identifies with the "Catholic left," which defines "America" as "the evil empire" evident in its militarism, particularly its nuclear weaponry. This position shares characteristics with the "apocalyptic and sectarian." Another reads "America" through "messianic symbols of scriptures." Both are dualistic, with the former setting the true Christian community against America as the evil empire and the latter setting "America" as Christian nation against evil empires, e.g., the Soviet Union. The final is an "enlightenment faith in reasoned public discourse as it comes to us from the founding fathers." It is pluralistic rather than dualistic but also tends to secularize politics and stands in tension with scriptures' proclamation of "God's sovereignty over history." According to Portier, only a variation of the third option "allows the prophet to warn that this is not true peace, this is not true freedom, without setting him or her at mortal odds with history." This "liberal myth" advocates entering "the market place" of ideas where sound arguments of "law and reason" may "engender political conflicts" but not "cosmic battles." Admitting liberal myth's Pelagian tendencies, Portier also maintains that "the doctrine of creation does not allow one to equate government with the demonic." A Catholic historical perspective "cannot end in dualism."

What follows are three papers and a critical response to various facets of Americanism. William Portier examines first and second generation Americanists in Isaac Hecker and John Keane, with an emphasis on Keane's more direct attempts to push the Americanist program. Thomas Wangler considered the Americanist worldview as manifested in the diverse interests of men like Isaac Hecker, John Keane, John Ireland, and Denis O'Connell. Robert C. Ayers considered the concerted efforts of the Americanists in Europe and the reactions due to European rifts. Marge Reher comments on each essay, observing in her concluding remarks the differences in interpretations in "some aspects of Americanism," which she finds hardly surprising given that "reading contemporary 'signs of the times' is subject to divergent interpretation."[56]

THE FRUIT OF COLLEGE THEOLOGY

One also begins to see, in the third decade of the Society's existence, the intellectual fruit of a second generation of U.S. Catholic theologians schooled in the theology of Karl Rahner and Bernard Lonergan and seeking to read their own "sign of the times." A most notable example is Catherine Mowry LaCugna, whose essay, "Re-conceiving the Trinity as Mystery of Salvation" serves as preview of coming attractions, namely her book *God-for-Us*. Karl Rahner proved pivotal in LaCugna's own account of her systematic exploration of Trinitarian doctrine. "'The "economic" trinity is the "immanent" trinity and vice versa'" is the Rahnerian "axiom" that provides "a grammatical and theological perimeter within which one may re-conceive the relationship between God and all that is other than God ('the world')." LaCugna clarifies her point that "what one says about God's economic-historical activity is true as well of God's 'inner' history or immanent life." The implications for the theological task, as LaCugna explains, are significant. Theology "will not imitate the modern *scientia* which equates 'objectivity' with personal distanciation, nor will it surrender its passion for rigorous logic and precision. In a contemplative-speculative theology, the theologian will be engaged with God affectively as well as cognitively, imaginatively as well as discursively, silently as well as expressively, doxologically as well as academically." In the specific focus on the Trinity, by "conceiving of God as 'God for us' in such a way that 'God for us' is 'God as God,' trinitarian faith might once again be restored to the center of Christian doctrine and spirituality."[57] LaCugna's goal perhaps does portend theology's "rising from history" into a new period of constructive Christian theology.

Denise Lardner Carmody places Bernard Lonergan's "dynamic view of human consciousness" in dialogue with Eric Voegelin's on human conscious-

ness and Karl Rahner's on humans' relationship to God as Mystery to lay out
a theological context for considering a feminist spirituality. Works like Carol
Gilligan's examination of women's moral decision making help to concretize
the feminist dimensions of her analysis. Carmody identifies two basic principles in her Christian-inspired spirituality, love and freedom. She also displays
the growing variations within Christian and post-Christian feminism, noting
that once-defended CTS member Mary Daly had made the correct decision
"to write herself out of the Christian camp." Carmody admits that Daly's accounts of "the injuries that women in several cultures have suffered from men
makes Daly's position understandable, but they also color her care splenetic."
Carmody identifies her position as similar to Schüssler Fiorenza. Both reject
"cheap grace that would erase the evils of past history without repentance and
reparation" but also find hope in "shafts of forgiveness and new starts." Carmody wonders, "Where would any of us be without forgiveness?" given our
common identity as sinners and our "need to be freed by her careful love." A
feminist spirituality has much in common with other Christian spiritualities,
as made clear in her concluding remark. "In that careful love, finally, lies our
freedom. In our freedom lies our true spirituality."[58]

Fran Leap, in a subsequent section entitled "New Visions and Challenges," considers ethical "decision-making" and "decision-living" in light of
"the slow progress of the vision we presently call feminism." She first provides
an overview of the religious feminist vision emphasizing its dynamism, "the
movement of revolution" in response to "the experience of Presence" as "definitive, efficacious, powerful, propitious." Response to presence is twofold:
"reverence and rage," which provide the dynamism of the revolution. The
movement eschews destructiveness in the feminist commitment to an ethical
"wholeness" in which means are not divorced from ends. Unlike Carmody,
Leap draws upon Mary Daly's work as helpful guidance in critiquing the
Christian past. "As Mary Daly has pointed out, the notion of *imitatio Christi*
as used by moral theology is especially devastating to feminists today who are
living and becoming in ways unimaginable to even their mothers and grand-
mothers, let alone Christ and his blessed mother!" Though acknowledging
the contribution of past "experiences, strategies, and skills," Leap emphasizes
emerging "feminist 'models'" that display "enspiriting courage; strong women
who influence us with infectious freedom." Leap, in the second part of the article, provides a basic framework for "moral decision-facing and decision-living" from a disclosure to a discernment to an embodiment phase dependent
upon the formation brought through participation in the feminist movement
or "dance."[59]

Rodger Van Allen's presidential address appears in the 1984 annual volume, a volume that marked the thirtieth anniversary with little said about the
milestone. His address focused upon the "Chicago Declaration," a statement

produced at a 1977 meeting in the city from which the document received its title. The declaration revisited a topic that had inspired an earlier generation of Catholic college theology teachers to educate the laity. "The signers feel that the welcome involvement of lay people in many church ministries has in fact upstaged, distracted and confused many laity into thinking that this was what religion was all about." Among the forty-seven signatures are familiar names to longtime members of the Society. These include Carroll Stuhlmueller and Russell Barta. Van Allen acknowledges the legitimate concerns of the document's critics but agrees with the declaration in its wondering "what went wrong in the last twenty years in the move to achieve some sense of worldy [sic] vocation?" His response, acknowledging only a partial answer, "is that the priesthood of all believers has been neglected." He argues that "even this single theme could easily be linked in a positive way to themes of work, family, liturgy, and more." His vision was not limited to "a merely individualistic kind of religious vocationalism but can and must include the knowledgeable structural analysis that comes from this kind of experience."[60]

The theologian's challenge, as reflected in these ten volumes and in the controversies that preoccupied the board and members of the College Theology Society, had to do with their interpretation of the tradition and theirs and others' interpretations of their authority in interpreting tradition. They had yet to settle on their place in the academy and their role in the church. Some sought to embrace the tradition in such a way as to transform it; others found too little, too late in the Catholic or even wider Christian traditions and were making their own way in uncharted territory. One can assume that through all of this, they continued to teach undergraduates, though the task had receded into the background in volumes and even in board meetings, with the exception of the teaching workshop. The fourth decade would prove equally distracting, uncertain, exciting, and enlightening, but the focus would be an even more resolute turn outward to the other.

NOTES

1. The third decade produced the following ten volumes: "America in Theological Perspective," *America in Theological Perspective* (1975); "Changing Church; Changing Society," *Theology Confronts a Changing World* (1976); *Critical History and Biblical Faith* (1977); "Ethics: A Contemporary Assessment of the Discipline," *Essays in Morality and Ethics* (1978); "Religion and Culture: Exploring the Interface," *The Bent World: Essays on Religion and Culture* (1979); *The Journey of Western Spirituality* (1980); "Symbol and Religious Imagination," *The Pedagogy of God's Image: Essays on Symbol and the Religious Imagination* (1981); "Foundations of Religious Literacy," *Foundations of Religious Literacy* (1982); "Traditions and Interpretations," *Interpreting Tradition: The Art of Theological Reflection* (1983); and "The Future," *Rising from History: U.S. Catholic Theology Looks to the Future* (1984).

The Hermeneutical Circle (1975–1984)   165

2. James Hennesey, S.J., "Square Peg in a Round Hole: On Being Roman Catholic in America," in *America in Theological Perspective: The Annual Publication of the College Theology Society*, ed. Thomas M. McFadden (NY: A Crossroad Book, Seabury Press, 1976), 11.

3. Daniel C. Maguire, "Catholic Ethics with an American Accent," in *America in Theological Perspective*, 13–31 passim.

4. Norbert Rigali, S.J., "Moral Theology in Transition," in *Theology Confronts a Changing World: The Annual Publication of the College Theology Society*, ed. Thomas M. McFadden (West Mystic, CT: Twenty-Third Publications, 1977) 188, 190, 191, 192–198 passim.

5. James Gaffney, "Introduction," in *Essays in Morality and Ethics: The Annual Publication of the College Theology Society*, ed. James Gaffney (NY: Paulist Press, 1980), 1, 2.

6. S. Youree Watson, S.J., "The Other Face of Evil" on *Essays in Morality and Ethics*, 24.

7. Roderick Hindery, "Applying Comparative Ethics to Multinational Corporations"; Paul J. Philibert, "Theological Guidance for Moral Development Research"; Luke Salm, "Methodological Issues in the Ethics of Human Sexuality"; Mary Lou Grad, "Play as an Ethical Paradigm for Sexual Intercourse" in *Essays in Morality and Ethics*.

8. Silvio E. Fittipaldi, "The Zen of Ethics," in *Essays in Morality and Ethics*, 64, 70.

9. Thaddeus J. Gurdak, "Benevolence: Confucian Ethics and Ecstasy," in *Essays in Morality and Ethics*, 76–85.

10. Maria Augusta Neal, S.N.D., "Civil Religion, Politics, and Theology," in *America in Theological Perspective*, 115.

11. Denis Goulet, "Beyond Moralism: Ethical Strategies in Global Development," in *Theology Confronts a Changing World*, 12, 13 [phrase appears in "Precis"].

12. Denis Goulet, "Beyond Moralism: Ethical Strategies in Global Development," in *Theology Confronts a Changing World*, 31, 34, 35, 36.

13. Richard L. Rubenstein, "Reason's Deadly Dreams," in *the bent World: Essays on Religion and Culture: The Annual Publication of the College Theology Society*, ed. John R. May (Ann Arbor, MI: Edwards Bros.; distributed by Scholars Press, Chico, CA, 1981), 8, 11, 20.

14. David M. Thomas, "American Technocracy and the Religious Spirit: An Unholy Alliance?" in *America in Theological Perspective*, 202.

15. Russell L. Jaberg, "Search for a Center," in *America in Theological Perspective*, 235, 236, 244.

16. John R. May, "Preface," in *the bent World*, v.

17. Martin C. Kastelic, "A Mysticism of Technology," in *the bent World*, 35, 36.

18. Thomas M. McFadden, "Introduction," in *Theology Confronts a Changing World*, 6.

19. Richard P. McBrien, "The Church and Social Change: An Ecclesiological Critique," in *Theology Confronts a Changing World*, 45–54 passim; quotes from 58.

20. Geffrey B. Kelly, F.S.C., "Futurists and Reformers: The Shape of Tomorrow's Church," in *Theology Confronts a Changing World*, 67–87 passim, long quote 87.

21. Robert Kress, "The Changing Church of the Future: The Androgynous Church," in *Theology Confronts a Changing World*, 138–152.

22. Sonya Quitslund, "A Theological Case for the Ordination of Women," in *Theology Confronts a Changing World*, 161–178.

23. Richard P. McBrien, "The Classics in Their Ecclesial Context: Ecclesiological Principles of Interpretation," in *Foundations of Religious Literacy:The Annual Publication of the College Theology Society, 1982*, ed. John V. Apczynski (Chico, CA: Scholars Press, 1983), 31, 33–43 passim.

24. *Critical History and Biblical Faith: New Testament Perspectives*, ed. Thomas J. Ryan (Villanova University: College Theology Society, *Horizons*, 1979).

25. "The Study of Women in Early Christianity: Some Methodological Considerations," in *Critical History and Biblical Faith: New Testament Perspectives*, ed. Thomas J. Ryan (Villanova University: College Theology Society, *Horizons*, 1979), 32.

26. *Critical History and Biblical Faith: New Testament Perspectives*, 208–236.

27. Leander Keck, "Ethos and Ethics in the New Testament," in *Essays in Morality and Ethics*, 29, 30, 37, 45.

28. Al Hiebert, "The Foundations of Paul's Ethics," in *Essays in Morality and Ethics*, 50.

29. Jeanne Evans, "Paul Ricoeur's Biblical Hermeneutics: An Application to the Text Isa. 14:4b–20b," in *Foundations of Religious Literacy*, 60.

30. Alice Laffey, "Biblical Power and Justice: An Interpretive Experiment," in *Interpreting Tradition: The Art of Theological Reflection: The Annual Publication of the College Theology Society, 1983*, vol. 29, ed. Jane Kopas (Chico, CA: Scholars Press, 1984), 55, 56, 69.

31. John McCarthy, "Reading and Proclaiming the Text: Christology as Literacy and Rhetoric," in *Foundations of Religious Literacy*, 79, 100.

32. Walter Ong, S.J., "The Psychodynamics of Oral Memory and Narrative: Some Implications for Biblical Studies," in *The Pedagogy of God's Image: Essays on Symbol and the Religious Imagination: The Annual Publication of the College Theology Society, 1981*, ed. Robert Masson (Chico, CA: Scholars Press, the College Theology Society, 1982), 57, 64, 69–70.

33. Robert Masson, "Introduction," in *The Pedagogy of God's Image*, 2.

34. John P. Hogan, "The Historical Imagination and the New Hermeneutic: Collingwood and Pannenberg," in *The Pedagogy of God's Image*, 25.

35. Mary Aquin O'Neill, R.S.M., "The Anthropology of Ambiguity and the Image of God," in *The Pedagogy of God's Image*, 31.

36. Morny Joy, "Explorations in the Philosophy of Imagination: The Work of Gilbert Durand and Paul Ricoeur," in *Foundations of Religious Literacy*, 51–52.

37. Marchita B. Mauck, "The Liminal Space of Art and Ritual," in *the bent World*, 149, 150, 151.

38. Mary Collins, "Critical Ritual Studies: Examining an Intersection of Theology and Culture," [given as a plenary address] in *the bent World*, 133, 129.

39. Mary Jo Weaver, "Quest for Self/Quest for God," in *the bent World*, 177.

40. *The Journey of Western Spirituality: The Annual Publication of the College Theology Society 1980*, ed. A. W. Sadler (Chico, CA: Scholars Press, the College Theology Society, 1981), 190, 191.

41. Virginia J. Knight, "The Unlived Life of St. Thérèse," in *The Journey of Western Spirituality*, 208.

42. William Shea, "Jonathan Edwards and Sarah Pierpont: An Uncommon Union"; William Grosnick, "Literacy in Family Ritual: An Examination of an Irish-American Family Reunion"; Joan Leonard, "Muriel Spark's Parables: The Religious Limits of Her Art"; William J. O'Brien, "To Hell with Samuel Beckett" in *Foundations of Religious Literacy*, 172 [quote].

43. Diane Apostolos-Cappadona, "Images, Interpretations, and Traditions: A Study of the Magdalene," in *Interpreting Tradition: The Art of Theological Reflection*, 117.

44. J. Patout Burns, "Variations on a Dualist Theme: Augustine on the Body and the Soul," in *Interpreting Tradition*, 13.

45. Gary Macy, "The Theological Fate of Berengar's Oath of 1059: Interpreting a Blunder Become Tradition," in *Interpreting Tradition: The Art of Theological Reflection*, 27, 35.

46. William P. Loewe, "Myth and Counter-Myth: Irenaeus' Story of Salvation," in *Interpreting Tradition: The Art of Theological Reflection*, 40, 39.

47. Ewert H. Cousins, "Interpretation of Tradition in a Global Context," in *Interpreting Tradition: The Art of Theological Reflection*, 95–97, 106, 107.

48. Keith J. Egan, "The Return to the Classroom of Thomas Aquinas," in *Interpreting Tradition: The Art of Theological Reflection*, 150–151.

49. Monika Hellwig, "Theology as Fine Art," in *Interpreting Tradition: The Art of Theological Reflection*, 3, 5, 9.

50. Elizabeth K. McKeown, "Catholic Identity in America," in *America in Theological Perspective*, 58, 66.

51. Ronald Pasquarriello, "Theological Considerations on the American Experience of Ethnicity," in *Theology Confronts a Changing World*, 117, 118–127 passim, 127 quote.

52. David O'Brien, "Literacy, Faith, and Church: An American Religious Perspective," in *Foundations of Religious Literacy*, 19, 20, 25.

53. Robert J. Daly, "Preface," in *Rising from History: U.S. Catholic Theology Looks to the Future: The Annual Publication of the College Theology Society, 1984*, vol. 30, ed. Robert J. Daly (Lanham: University Press of America, 1987), vii.

54. David O'Brien, "Choosing Our Future: American Catholicism's Precarious Prospects," in *Rising from History*, 18, 41.

55. William Portier, "The Future of 'Americanism,'" in *Rising from History*, 49.

56. William Portier, "Two Generations of American Catholic Expansionism in Europe: Isaac Hecker and John J. Keane"; Thomas E. Wangler, "Myth, Worldviews and Late Nineteenth Century American Catholic Expansionism"; Robert C. Ayers, "The Americanist Attack on Europe in 1897 and 1898"; and Marge M. Reher, "Americanism and the Signs of the Times: Response to Portier, Wangler, and Ayers" in *Rising from History*, 97.

57. Catherine Mowry LaCugna, "Reconceiving the Trinity as Mystery of Salvation," in *Rising from History*, 125–126, 133, 134.

58. Denise Lardner Carmody, "Feminist Spirituality as Self-Transcendence," in *Rising from History*, 139, 153–154.

59. Fran Leap, "Feminist Movement: The Ethics of Revolution," in *Rising from History*, 193–200 passim, 200 [quote].

60. Rodger Van Allen, "The Chicago Declaration and the Call to Worldly Holiness," in *Rising from History*, 157, 159, 165, 166.

• 7 •

Maintaining Identity, Drawing Boundaries, Fighting Battles (1985–1994)

$\mathcal{T}$hose who attended the College Theology Society's 1985 convention's business meeting at Salve Regina College could reasonably conclude their beloved Society remained robust with 853 members, according to secretary Suzanne Toton's report, and, as treasurer George Gilmore announced, a total income of $50,130.76 and total expenses to date of $41,241.23, leaving a respectable margin of $8,889.53. Bernard Prusak reported that forty nine participated in the preconvention workshop on teaching Christology with an approximate $700 profit to the Society.[1]

The minutes from the board meeting just prior to the convention leave a different impression. The board enumerated "concerns" in a "discussion of [the] CTS Present and Future." The first item on the list called attention to external threats that created "the need as a professional society to deal with the repression experienced by a number of theologians today from church, society and the academic community."[2] Over the next ten years, the board, along with other CTS members, invested much time and effort in defending embattled theologians and delineating clearer boundaries between church and university, even as commitments to both remained. As with the previous accounts of the Society's internal business, much of what the CTS discussed from 1985 through 1994 reflected wider concerns of Catholic colleges and universities and the theologians who taught in these institutions. Of particular concern were the implications of *Ex corde Ecclesiae* for the university's Catholic identity. Theologians perceived their own ambiguous status relative to church and academy to be the real heart of the matter in John Paul II's working document on Catholic higher education.

CREATIVE MAINTENANCE

Strengthening the Society's role in dealing with "the repression" of theologians like Kung and others had an effect on the board's reading of internal challenges to the Society's vitality. The board worried about its ability "to hold the Society together and be creative" especially in "the program of our annual convention." The emphasis on creativity served as a counter to the perceived external strictures. An obvious source of creativity would be new members, especially younger ones. A May 1985 report of the "Standing Committee on Membership," chaired by Dolores Greeley, identified several recruitment strategies, from the ongoing "regional activities," to serve "the professional needs of scholars," to the "Graduate Student Essay contest," recently established to attract younger scholars.[3]

Greeley also mentioned distributing a brochure to promote the Society. Its effectiveness in attracting new members is difficult to discern, but its message indicates what CTS's leadership thought most attractive about the Society of 1985. The message had a familiar ring even as it incorporated new emphases reflecting the changing discipline of university theology. "Purposefully and increasingly ecumenical in its membership and concerns," the CTS boasted one thousand members "devoted to developing the academic disciplines of theology and religious studies, to assisting college and university teachers to teach their discipline effectively, and to relating religion to life." The Society offered "opportunities" for the "study of religion" in relationship to "other academic disciplines," examination of "teaching religion effectively," and "development of programs which are genuinely intellectual, value oriented, and realistically designed to meet students' needs." The annual convention, "a forum for the exchange of interests and ideas on a national level," featured awards for scholarship, including recognizing an outstanding graduate student essay. The brochure touted the Society's publications: *Horizons*, the annual volume, and other series.[4] The brochure's depiction of a mix of teaching, scholarship, pastoral concerns, and special recognition of colleagues honored the CTS members, "college theology teachers," who are located on the fluid boundaries between church and academy, teaching and scholarship, the pastoral and the theological.

The Society embraced its liminal identity with its "CTS Presidential Award for Outstanding Service to Religion and Society," announced in the April 1986 newsletter.[5] In his call for nominations in January 1988, Michael Barnes explained the award's distinctiveness. It recognizes not necessarily scholarship but "service to the Church, to religion, or to the larger community. The service could be related intimately to academic work or it could be far removed from it. The award can give recognition to those whose work is valuable but nonetheless easily overlooked and unacknowledged."[6] The description seemed to mirror the CTS's own sense of itself as making valuable, but too often overlooked, contributions to the field.

The selection of Joe and Sally Cunneen to receive the first CTS Presidential Award demonstrates the CTS's willingness to recognize Catholic intellectuals serving the church outside the confines of academia. The citation described "a felicitous choice." The Cunneens' journey as "Catholic intellectuals" parallels that of the CTS. The couple, like the Society, began in the "heady days in the immediate post war period through the halcyon period of the Second Vatican Council to these days when, in the decades since the council, the American church has attempted to grow into the maturity which was heralded by the great events in Rome in the 1960s." The thirty-seven-year-old *Cross Currents* magazine recorded many of these intellectual shifts. The Society declared the Cunneens to be "prophets" for "their faith which weds intellectual rigor, love of God, and passion for justice into a whole and in their ability to see the future clearly." Sally Cunneen published *Sex: Female; Religion: Catholic* in 1968 and became one of the "first women to raise the feminist issue in the Catholic church in this country."[7] Subsequent recipients of the presidential award included Brother Albert Clark, F.S.C., "as founder, nurturer and president of THETA ALPHA KAPPA"[8] and publisher Michael Glazier, who received it in 1993. As part of the Society's fortieth anniversary celebration, Gerard Sloyan received a special recognition award for his years of service to the Society and the profession, and Sebastian Moore received the presidential award.

CTS presidents had many demands on their time and effort in leading the Society. Their leadership truly affected the Society's direction. By the fourth decade, women were regularly elected to the presidency. Dolores Greeley, R.S.M., succeeded Bill Shea. Mary Lea Schneider, O.F.M., followed Greeley; then came Keith Egan, Joan Leonard, O.P, and Brennan Hill.

The annual meeting still served as the Society's principal venue for member interaction and scholarly exchange. The program's complexity continued to rival those of any learned society of comparable size. The thirty-first annual convention, for example, held for four days (30 May–2 June), at Salve Regina College, Newport, Rhode Island, featured forty-six sessions with two papers in each session. In announcing the thirty-third annual convention in the April 1987 newsletter, President Dolores Greeley wrote, "If you have not recently attended a national meeting of the CTS let me assure you of the warm, welcoming atmosphere which prevails as well as the highly professional competent scholars and educators who come to share, discuss and learn one from the other."[9] Joan Leonard's February 1994 presidential newsletter lifted up "the excellent quality of our conventions, the stimulating conversations, and the inclusive community spirit" and encouraged members to convey to "colleagues and graduate students" the annual meeting experience.[10]

College campuses remained the preferred location. Not only were they more affordable but they also facilitated CTS's "warm, welcoming atmosphere." One has only to note the sharing of meals in a common dining hall. Yet, even colleges became increasingly expensive venues. At the 22 November 1986 board meeting, members learned of the difficulty in negotiating a reasonable price for facilities. "Negotiations have again made it clear how important it is to 'write the book' on all the CTS jobs: officers' job descriptions, publishing the Annual Volumes, hosting the convention, et al."[11] This task remained incomplete for another decade.

Such complications did not dampen the board's enthusiasm for improving the annual meeting. Terry Tilley, convention director beginning in 1989, developed strategies for using the plenary sessions to stimulate intellectual engagement on the selected theme. In a 1990 letter to potential volume editor Peter Phan, he explained, the first (Thursday) evening session "is a 'table-setter.'" The second "can be almost anything," with recent ones being "controversial" and others being "horizon-expanding." Wide variations are also possible for the third but "it should provoke discussion."[12]

Themes selected reflected current developments in theological and religious studies. Some choices required more defense than others. At the 27 May 1987 board meeting, Bill Shea proposed the theme "'Fundamentalism and Modernist Thinking'" for 1989. It proved "both problematic and immediately provocative of discussion."[13] The teaching workshop was to be "the impact of world religions on the teaching of theology." A suggestion for 1993, "The Nature and Future of Religion," was to rely on "theologians, historians of religion, anthropologists, and philosophers, some of them favoring religion and others not." The actual selection for 1993, "Religion and the Body," was noted to be "provocative" and "important" given its impact on various theological and religious studies disciplines.[14] The selected theme for the fortieth convention at Saint Mary's College, South Bend, was "Women and Theology." Given that CTS had a founding mother in Sister M. Rose Eileen Masterman, C.S.C., it seemed especially fitting that the College Theology Society met at the site of innovation in women's theological education fifty years earlier. Admittedly, the convention's feminist emphasis reflected little of Sister M. Rose Eileen's own perspective.

One aspect of the convention that had not changed since Sister M. Rose Eileen's time was the Society's reliance on competent volunteers. The preconvention teaching workshops that flourished in the late 1980s were prime examples since they depended upon members' willingness to offer their time and organizational talent with only minimal compensation, usually remuneration for convention expenses. Bernard Prusak's report on the teaching workshop emphasized the importance of a "permanent coordinator" to work with the "program chairperson" whose expertise coincided with the workshop topic. Steve Casey was named coordinator and remained in that role until 1989.[15] Diminishing attendance in the early 1990s led the board to review whom the workshops served. The minutes named "1) small college teaching types, 2) particular topics—interest types, and 3) graduate students looking ahead to teaching."[16] The minutes offered no record of a debate about these conclusions or any arguments to forgo the workshop.

Workshop topics, like the convention themes, reflected the changing focus in theological and religious studies as taught to undergraduates. The 1985 workshop, "Teaching Christology" included an impressive array of presenters: "Lucien Richard (Weston), Pheme Perkins (Boston College), John Galvin (St. John's Seminary), Stephen Duffy (Loyola, New Orleans), Paul Knitter (Xavier, Cincinnati), Jane Kopas (University of Scranton), Frank Fiorenza (CUA) and Bill Loewe (CUA)."[17] The 1987 workshop focused on "Recent Approaches to the Biblical Text: The State of the Question."[18] Two years later, "The Feminist Perspective in Religious Studies Curricula" utilized "standard course descriptions" to communicate "mainstreaming . . . as the goal . . . so that non-specialists in feminist theologies will feel welcome."[19] The 1991 workshop considered "Culture, Class, Gender, and Race: Educating for Diversity." In 1992, Islam was the focus—coordinated by Dan Sheridan. The 1994 offering, initially called "Teaching Spirituality: A Challenge for Women"[20] appeared in the September 1993 newsletter as "Teaching Spirituality: Women and Men Collaborating."

The board's multiple efforts to emphasize the Society's academic persona found another mode of expression in the revised policies and procedures for the book and published essay awards, approved at the 26 May 1994 board meeting. The revisions eliminated internally driven criteria to assert the Society's role as arbiter of scholarly excellence. No longer were criteria based on "the ideals of the College Theology Society" in its support of undergraduate theological education. The committee simply gave the award to "the 'best' book and article each year." Committee members chose "winners" who "manifest excellence in scholarship and represent a significant contribution to the field." Omitted was the acknowledgment that "criteria will vary somewhat depending upon the make-up of each year's committee and depending upon the nature of the works submitted in a particular year." Eligibility for either publication award remained limited to members in good standing. Limiting eligibility to members coupled with identifying "significant contribution"[21] as a principal criterion for the award made clear the CTS's academic credibility.

The board's emphasis on the CTS's academic character did not diminish the Society's distinctiveness among learned societies. The 1993 preconvention board meeting revealed how self-consciously protective the board was of the annual convention's character. In addition to the usual discussion of future meetings and possible sites, the 1993 preconvention board meeting considered possible "joint meetings" with various groups including "ACTHUS [Academy of Catholic Hispanic Theologians of the United States], several women's groups, Islamic groups, and a Baptist group." Consensus allowed for possible joint sessions but ultimately the board supported "separate" meetings to preserve "the ethos of the CTS convention."[22] The subsequent November meeting's discussion sparked little enthusiasm for joint meetings with the CTSA and CBA "because of the different ethos of these groups."[23] The National Association of Baptist Professors of Religion (NABPR) eventually decided to meet at the same time and place as the CTS, beginning in 1996, at the University of Dayton, but that story is in chapter 9.[24]

SPEAKING ITS MINDS

The Society's alternating focus between academic and ecclesial concerns reflected ambiguities among Catholics about the theologian's role in church, academy, and society. The resolutions produced for the 1985 CTS business meeting revealed these multiple theological identities in distilled forms. Resolutions, expressing political positions, ecclesial and civil, reappeared briefly. William Portier, as chair of the Resolutions Committee, presented five resolutions at the business meeting. The first announced, "Whereas we are saddened by our nation's failure to respect the rights of Central Americans to self-determination" and concluded with a call to end mining Nicaraguan harbors. The second protested the Vatican characterization of liberation theology. Both were tabled. A third did pass. The U.S. bishops, praised for past leadership in examining modern warfare, were asked to "re-evaluate the 1983 conditional acceptance of nuclear deterrence" and make the results public.

The "scholars of religion" per se appeared in the fourth resolution. The resolution's discussion and approval represented ecclesiastical politics in its more fractious form dividing not only episcopal leaders from theologians, but also CTS members from each other. It addressed the negative impact on those who signed the "Catholic Statement on Pluralism and Abortion." Marjorie Maguire, CTS member and signer of the "Catholic Statement," had amended the resolution to clearly identify some of the signers as "members of the College Theology Society," who "have suffered reprisals or threats of reprisal from Church authorities and institutions." The resolution expanded its concern to include those whose "writings on diverse topics" have faced censure or "threats of repression from Church authorities." In the face of such "repression," the Society "affirms for scholars of religion—the right to free inquiry in the pursuit of truth,—the duty of responsible expression of legitimate dissent from official ecclesial affirmations,—the right and duty to engage in honest discussion of controversial issues." The relatively close vote, 38 in favor, 30 against, and 9 abstentions, highlighted a divided membership about the appropriate response in this case. With no time for the fifth resolution, the results of the four votes would be communicated to appropriate parties.

The business meeting minutes ended with a laconic declaration. "The president agreed to review the procedures under which resolutions are presented to the membership and voted on at the semi-annual meeting of the board in November."[25] Vice president Kathleen Gaffney had already presented "preliminary changes" for the "Procedure for Proposing Resolutions," at the 1985 preconvention board meeting. By establishing an April 15th deadline for all member proposals, the Committee on Resolutions and Current Issues (CRCI) could present the board resolutions with "comments and recommendations," prior to the annual meeting. The board functioned as first arbiter with members attending the convention receiving the board-approved resolutions one day prior to the business meeting. A two-thirds vote of attending members could move a resolution to the floor.[26]

The 1985 resolutions tabled as well as those narrowly passed make clear that the College Theology Society, like much of the Catholic world, included members with widely divergent views in politics, both ecclesial and civil. While it would be difficult to imagine members defending "repression" of their peers, it is not as difficult to imagine CTS members unwilling to defend a Catholic theologian who maintains abortion to be a permissible act consonant with Catholic moral teaching. The new procedure limited the scope of resolutions and reflected the more circumscribed perspectives on the Society's official role in theological controversies.

Two years later, three resolutions received unanimous approval at the business meeting, 30 May 1987. In the first, the Society "endorsed the call for a 'new American experiment'" as found in the U.S. Catholic bishops' economic pastoral and encouraged members to promote the pastoral's "educational goals" according to their "own academic speciality." The second commended Justus George Lawler for his "vigorous support of scholarly publishing" as editor of *Continuum* and *Jubilee*—a role ending after thirty years. The third thanked Robert Masson for his work as chair of the Research and Publication Committee.[27] In 1989, a similar resolution thanking Mary Ann Hinsdale and Michael Barnes for their service as board members passed unanimously. The resolutions had come full circle—serving as expression of public gratitude for those who served the Society rather than as political protests or theological stands.[28]

The CTS's Women's Caucus offered another venue for engaging in conversations on some of the more controversial issues in Catholicism—those involving women's full participation in the ministry and life of the Catholic Church. The May 1987 meeting marked its fifth anniversary.[29] The following year, the Women's Caucus discussed students' and professors' responses to the 1988 draft of the National Conference of Catholic Bishops' (NCCB) controversial and ill-fated pastoral addressing women's role in the church. The report of discussions provides a glimpse of the generational differences and similarities in women's perspectives on the church. Students observed "a preference for 'style' rather than 'substance'" in the document that evoked their suspicion of "the document's commitment to *real* change regarding women's role in the church." Descriptions that construed women's comments as "negative" or as "voices of alienation" rather than simply as "true" elicited their criticism. Ordination received mention, as one would expect. "Some students did not think that ordination would solve all of the problems women had in the church, but women students in particular said that they needed role models at the altar—and not just in serving positions!" CTS members noted the differences in expectations between them and the students. "Because of our experience and background, many of us were better able to appreciate some of the courageous elements of the draft," including condemning "sexism as sinful" and the call for "further study" of women's ordination.

The Women's Caucus reserved its final comments on sexism for the College Theology Society. Acknowledging its "commendable record towards women," the caucus members "reluctantly" called attention to "how few women theologians are involved in substantive dialogues between the bishops and theologians" except when an officer happened to be a woman. They then appealed to the now common account of a Society whose "very origins, in part, stem from the exclusion of women from full participation in an association of Catholic theologians." The Society as much as the bishops must attend to "the role of women as theologians in service to the church."[30] Three years later, at the 1991 convention business meeting, "the Women's Caucus of the College Theology Society" announced that the group had produced a press release expressing "serious reservations concerning the content and adequacy of a pastoral letter on women's concerns issued by an all-male body." The bishops' "consultative process" did receive their praise. The following day, the board endorsed the caucus's statement at a special meeting.[31]

The pervasive influence of feminist consciousness is evident in the 1994 board meeting minutes. Discussions about changing a section's name from "Symbol, Ritual and Sacrament" to "Symbol and Ritual" caused some board members to worry about participants' objections. One board member "suggested that, as a feminist, the proper procedure would be to go back to [the] group and ask what they wanted." A motion on that point followed and passed unanimously.[32]

PLAGUES AND OTHER PLEASANTRIES

The impact on theological studies of the AAR's and SBL's growing dominance among the learned societies in religious studies has yet to be fully examined. These two societies' ability to act independent of the smaller learned societies becomes clearly evident in a CSR controversy. CSR had originally provided a framework for learned societies in religious and theological studies to collaborate in various projects to promote the development of religion as an academic discipline. A letter to CTS president William Shea from Leonard J. Biallas, dated 15 November 1984, discussed AAR's and SBL's desire to claim "the best projects" in a move to "deregulate" the CSR.[33]

Combining wit with ire, William Shea, in his capacity as president, wrote to SBL's representative. He left little to the imagination for SBL representative Kent Richards in protesting CSR's moving to Mercer University in Georgia. Shea wrote that despite Richards's efforts "to educate me. . . . I am still in the dark" and expressed "regret that SBL has found it necessary to its own interests to pick up its marbles and go home." Asserting CTS's basic satisfaction with "CSR staff and leadership," Shea wondered about CSR's ability "to continue its services to the societies which need it." Shea then referred to his prayer "for an infestation of ravenous fleas" in an earlier letter. He described "the remark" as "in fact true to my best spirit. It is only my present eminent rank that restrains my worst spirit in this case" and invoked "the spirit of my Irish ancestors who were experts at curse prayers and who never managed to take pomposity seriously." He promised to desist if "the SBL decides to change its ways" and warned that "flea powder has disastrous side effects."[34] Though he later sent a written apology, Shea's humor displayed an ironic distance in his response to elitism, a stance familiar to many a U.S. Catholic.

Sardonic perspectives on the CSR reconfiguration appeared in Gerard Sloyan's letter to William Shea about a meeting at a Chicago O'Hare airport hotel, 11–12 October 1985. SBL's Kent Richards focused on ineptness of leadership and delivery of services, and AAR's James Wiggins denounced CSR for its failure to keep "pace with the changes." Sloyan then enumerated the changes: "grant-getting capability, AAR's and SBL's recent admission to ACLS [American Council of Learned Societies] (spoken of in awe as the anteroom to the beatific vision), the need for a complete computerization of the data on academic religion study, the need for a more sophisticated appearance of TOIL [Teaching Opportunities Information Listing] and the *Bulletin*." Sloyan then observed that neither representative "said a word to indicate that AAR and SBL together could do the job better as sun in our little solar system. I suspect that everyone thought this was their game." Sloyan astutely noted the "psychic distancing" between SBL and AAR that led him to conclude: "we were not to understand them as Tweedledum and Tweedledee, only partners in the new publications *Openings* and *Newsletter* out of Scholars Press, Decatur GA, at Emory, but also as intending to give aggressive leadership in the field."[35] CTS's own frustration with the performance of the now Council of Societies for the Study of Religion (CSSR) soon emerged. In 1991, Gary Macy made a motion to "sever our relationship" as soon as "we have gotten our own list and the appropriate software to do the mailings." The motion carried but did not go into effect for over a decade.[36]

STRUGGLES AS PUBLISHER

Publications remained a source of pride and of consternation for the Society's leadership, especially given the transformation of publishing's role in academic culture. Despite progress on individual monographs, publication coordinator Robert Masson had to report several obstacles to CTS publications. In 1985, he spoke of a lack of funds for the various "publications [sic] projects" and received $1,000 "to use as the need arises."[37] One year later, Masson reported publication completion falling behind, and in 1987, the lack of minimum subscriptions for publications of the UPA (University Press of America). The latter required "another subscription publicity drive."[38] He also sought to rectify the lack of scholarly review of the annual volume. With a pending move to Marquette University, Masson announced his resignation.

Bill Shea, Bill Portier, and John Apczynski coordinated the selection of John McCarthy as chair of publications and research in June 1987. About a year and a half later, McCarthy provided a "report and observations" about the Society's publication woes, including inadequate scholarship in submissions and the existence of only fifteen library subscriptions to "the various CTS series (Annual Volume, Reprints, Monographs, Resources)." Besides "declining library acquisitions budgets," McCarthy mentioned the perception of UPA as a "vanity press" contributing to the low number of subscriptions.

McCarthy's final reason resurfaced a familiar issue—"the identity of the CTS" as academic. The Society is "still perceived by many within and outside the membership as being an organization of Roman Catholic teachers in small denominational colleges concerned primarily with teaching." Such perceptions complicated the "publication program" because of "an increasingly blurred identity." If the CTS embraced its teacher persona, then publications should focus on "classroom material." To take on "publishing original research of substantial quality then we may be better identified as a society for college and university theological education."

McCarthy's report also acknowledged publications' changing role "as a category of evaluation or prestige." Among scholars, especially younger ones, CTS publications simply did not carry "clout." McCarthy also observed in amazement that he knew of no other "theological society of our size which mounts an effort to publish a journal, an annual volume and three separate manuscript series, with a goal of six publications a year, and to do it all on the basis of volunteer effort."[39] The report generated serious discussion at the 1987 preconvention board meeting about the Society's publishing mission including concern that McCarthy "wants us to define ourselves in terms of CTSA, etc." At some subsequent point, the "CTS constitution was read" in response to the question about whether "quality teaching" is the Society's "primary purpose." Walter Conn reminded the board "that the original idea of publishing was to have the opportunity to publish books that might not have broad appeal."[40] The minutes reported no definitive decisions.

Whatever the "original idea" for CTS as publisher, the May 1991 report from the Research and Publications Committee provided a more detailed account of increased publication costs. "The actual price per volume to the membership rose from $7.20 for Prusak in '88 to $9.52 for Apczynski in '90 and $12.76 for Gower in the same year." Despite the increase, John McCarthy assessed the UPA relationship as positive and then proposed "a serious review of the Annual Volume" to determine "whether it is of service to the Society." Suggestions included charging additional fees to members for the volumes or continuing "a Theme Volume without the commitment to publish a yearly volume."[41]

The May 1991 report from the Research and Publications Committee also presented an alternative publishing venue. Bill Shea was to edit "'Catholic' material" for a Scholar's Press series, "Religion and the Social Order," with Jacob Neusner as general editor. Questions about the limits of such a series were quickly raised. Attention then turned once again to the "quality" of CTS publications. "Are we a vanity press? The marketability and competitive angle raise questions. Are we serving ourselves as undergraduate teachers?" Later a discussion of the annual volumes included their value "to the membership in terms of promotion, tenure, etc."[42] Others wondered about rarity of citations in other publications. Terry Tilley, in a separate report as convention director, addressed quality control. He argued that the volume editor ought to choose the plenary speakers, given that the editor is chosen for his or her scholarly expertise.[43] His proposal points to the annual volume's complex history with its origins as the annual meeting's proceedings that eventually became a thematic volume that included the plenary addresses. But, as McCarthy had predicted, finances determined the decisions made. A motion to discontinue a "complimentary" annual volume with membership passed 12 to 2. A "straw vote" on choosing UPA or Shea's offer found 9 in favor of UPA and 5 for the other.[44]

John McCarthy announced at the November 1992 board meeting that the Society had entered into a new contractual arrangement with UPA to produce camera-ready copy. The agreement "allows us to regain financial footing." McCarthy focused on the risk for UPA that obligated the Society to ensure the volume's marketability.[45] At the June 1993 meeting, he warned that without a subsidy "the Annual Volume will be in danger of extinction."[46] The board meeting minutes simply reported "some new contract problems" and that "UPA is trying to work these out."[47] Dennis Doyle volunteered to succeed John McCarthy as chair of research and publications for a period of three years.[48] In assuming McCarthy's position, Doyle committed himself to restoring the annual volume "to all the members as part of dues." He had gained permission to talk with XXIII Press and Orbis, both of whom were interested in publishing the materials. Orbis requested the Mary Ann Hinsdale and Phyllis Kaminski volume on women in theology as their first.[49]

BALANCING ACT

Finances emerged as a growing problem, with costs exceeding income, beginning in 1982. For the next few years, a deficit, ranging from about $300 to nearly $4,000, occurred off and on. Then, in 1990, a deficit of $19,000 appeared, which decreased to $18,401 in 1991. Several factors contributed to the deficit and mirrored challenges facing higher education throughout this period. The rise in operational costs exceeded revenue. The already mentioned increase in academic publishing costs drained surplus, and the convention was not paying for itself. In spite of the deficit, board member Mary Lea Schneider cautioned against disrupting the convention's success. "It has never been in better shape nor with greater promise for continued growth in the future."[50] Even though she praised *Horizons* and the annual volume, she warned against raising dues to support the annual volume for fear of losing members or affecting the convention's success. The board did approve raising dues from $25 to $30 in 1990.[51]

The following year, the board discussed appealing, as in past years, to the U.S. episcopacy. The response was noticeably less than enthusiastic even though the need was greater than before. Theresa Moser expressed discomfort "asking the Bishops for money." John McCarthy suggested separating the "relationship to Bishops from fund-raising." Moser "moved that we set aside fund-raising for the present." The board accepted the motion.[52] With the financial problems remaining, the board raised dues at the June 1993 meeting, this time to $40.[53]

With controversies in teaching and writing theology escalating, finances were not the only matter requiring balance. Walter Conn must have queried CTS president William Shea about *Horizons's* responsibility for defending a specific position. Shea counseled Conn to respect the journal's primary purpose, not as "a political mouth for the CTS" but as "a religious studies journal sponsored by the CTS." Other venues existed for the CTS to display its positions, "publicly and directly in its statements and in its choice of theme and speakers for the national convention, and indirectly by choice of materials for its annual volumes and the Resources series." Shea qualified his advice noting that the "journal is not aloof, theology is not only historical and systematic but it is also a practical and political way of being." In concluding his correspondence, Shea depicted a relatively bleak picture in the Catholic theological world with only a glimmer of hope in "that Armageddon has been averted" at the recent synod, "but the sniping, the isolate-and-destroy missions, the creation of an anti-creative atmosphere will undoubtedly continue."[54]

THE CURRAN AFFAIR

William Shea may have had in mind the Congregation for the Doctrine of the Faith's (CDF) "isolate-and-destroy mission" to remove Charles Curran from Catholic University's theology department.[55] Only a year earlier, in the March 1985 newsletter, the CTS president had sounded upbeat. He encouraged members to maintain relationships with their "religious and educational communities" and to provide "our faithful and sustained support" to Roman Catholic bishops and other ecclesial leaders. The latter faced the contentious issues of "academic freedom," "censorship," and the "equality of women and men in the church," as well as general "efforts to promote a genuinely American Catholic church with its special gifts to contribute to the universal church."

The Society had a significant role in fostering this relationship. "From the beginning the society took responsibility for pedagogy as well as research, and pedagogy is inherently political, . . . meant to change the world (and the church)." He assured members "that the church needs our brains, our enthusiasm, our support, and our criticism, and it needs them from us as individuals, in our regional organizations, and nationally."[56] Such assurance proved less convincing over the coming years.

The April 1986 CTS newsletter featured William Shea's strong support for Charles Curran in his conflict with the Congregation for the Doctrine of the Faith. He reiterated his "conviction" of being responsible for taking an active role in the "life of the Church" and a less pleasant "recognition of conflict between theologians and office holders in the church."[57] Shea noted a letter from him and Frank Fiorenza "which solicits your support for a solution that will protect Charlie's academic freedom and his status as a Catholic theologian." The compromise, approved by Cardinal Bernadin and outlined in the letter would allow Curran "to retain his tenured professorship on the theological faculty in exchange for an agreement not to teach a course in sexual ethics."[58] Shea offered a personal tribute to Curran as "a responsible, loyal, and decent man" who served as "a prudent and careful advisor" during Shea's decision concerning leaving the priesthood and CUA. On the other hand, the CTS president also wrote of defending the Catholic University of America against a "bigoted" Florida colleague's denunciation.[59] At the 22 November 1986 meeting in Atlanta, the board echoed Shea's sentiments and affirmed two major points: "a) the need to support Curran specifically and concretely at the time of his hearing; b) the need to make a positive statement on the place of open debate and discussion in the doing of theology." An "ad hoc committee" received the charge to write "a fuller, positive statement on academic freedom and the importance of open debate for theology in the university," based on John Apczynski's previously approved statement.[60]

In the extant material, only one disapproving note to the CTS president appeared. The note, from a Jesuit theology professor, expressed difficulty imagining Curran directing graduate students except "on *his* version of the foundations of morality, *his* ideas on medical ethics, *his* concept of the magisterium, dissent, etc." The priest expressed concern for "God's people, who are genuinely scandalized (in the technical sense) and greatly confused by people like Curran."[61] He called for prayers "for the unity and peace of the Church." In responding, Shea complimented the author for "stating your views calmly and clearly and without rancour," a position that "probably reflects very well the sentiments and conviction of most bishops." He enclosed his "presidential address" described as "diametrically opposed" and "not so calm" to explain the deep convictions among Curran's supporters.[62]

The CTS was hardly the lone voice of Curran support. Graduate students at Catholic University organized into a group called FACT (Friends of American Catholic Theology) to bring to attention Curran's "educational work and Christian witness" and how it had "enriched the lives of American Catholics."[63] They sent 751 signatures to Cardinal Ratzinger, bishops on CUA's board of trustees and on the doctrinal commission, "as well as six other bishops designated by Charlie." The memo was signed by Sally McReynolds, an active CTS member in 2004. The CTSA board also submitted a statement of support to the CUA's academic senate. It featured Charles Curran's prominent role in their society, including serving as president (1969–1970) and receiving "the John Courtney Murray Award for outstanding achievement in theology." The CTSA accounted for the current objections to Curran's disagreements with "present formulations of the church's official teaching" as due to Ratzinger's blurring distinctions between "infallible and non-infallible teaching." The letter mentioned the threat to the "academic integrity of Catholic institutions of higher learning."[64]

A CTS statement produced by the committee of John Apczynski, Michael Barnes, and Marie Anne Mayeski opened with identifying concern "as college teachers of theology" who strive "to stimulate the intellectually honest and critically reflective appropriation of the religious heritage of our students." It also affirmed Charles Curran's status as "a Roman Catholic theologian." To suggest otherwise "is in effect to deny the legitimacy of the theological enterprise for Roman Catholics."[65] In the February 1987 newsletter President Dolores L. Greeley instructed members to send their "statement of support for our testimony or to write your own" to Dr. Andrew C. Favret, chairman of the Academic Senate at Catholic University of America.[66] "Our testimony" referred to the CTS statement. The Curran case received a hearing in the DC Superior Court, 28 February 1988. The court found in favor of Catholic University of America.

Curran's earlier skirmish with Roman officials in 1967 had symbolized a victory for academic freedom in theology among students and faculty who organized against official authorities. This time, however, similar strategies failed to get the results most CTS members had sought. To show continued solidarity, the board determined that Curran was to "be invited publicly to celebrate the Eucharist and preach at the 1989 Annual meeting."[67] Terrence Tilley recollects the designation given to Charles Curran was "chaplain," an honorary title he gladly accepted.

MORE CONTROVERSIES; MORE RESPONSES

Curran's difficulties appear as the proverbial tip of the theological controversy iceberg.

With a postcouncil incubation period of twenty years, many other controversies erupted in 1985. The withdrawal of imprimaturs for three popular texts: *Christ Among Us* (Wilhelm), *Human Sexuality* (Keane), and *A Challenge to Love* (Nugent) became the focus of the College Theology Society Ad Hoc Committee on Resolutions and Current Issues under the leadership of vice president Kathleen Gaffney (21 June 1984). Another controversy previously discussed concerned those, like Dan and Marjorie Maguire, who signed a *New York Times* ad, claiming that Catholics could legitimately defend a spectrum of positions on abortion. Still a third concerned Cardinal Ratzinger's sharp criticism of liberation theology.

These controversies led the various Catholic learned societies to make common cause. Kathleen Gaffney, CTS vice president, reported her work on an ad hoc committee that included representatives from the Canon Law Society of America, the CTSA, and the NCDD (National Conference of Diocesan Directors of Religious Education) to formulate a response to CDF's demand of rescinding the imprimatur from Keane's, Nugent's, and Wilhelm's texts. The committee met with "the National Conference of Catholic Bishops' Committee on Doctrine in Washington on November 11, 1984." The CTS minutes listed nine points for the discussion from the very broad—"Doctrine, Magisterium, Pluralism, Dissent"—to a focus on the imprimatur, its purpose, and procedures for gaining or losing it. Other concerns included "Subsidiarity and the role of the Bishops' committee" as well as the CDF's authority in relation to "rights for authors, publishers, bishops, scholars" and the role of scholars in judging "catechetical materials." According to the bishops, the CDF considered the imprimatur important for responding to the "needs of the local church" in guiding their judgment of a text's suitability for religious instruction. Despite the contentious topics, discussions were "cordial."[68]

All of the scrutiny, and at times censure, of Catholic theologians elicited strongly felt emotions among several CTS members, including the president, William Shea. His numerous and varied extant correspondence with bishops marked a new level of a CTS's president engaging directly and actively in intraecclesial controversies. William Shea had submitted a piece to *National Catholic Reporter* in September 1985 that situated the censure of dissenting theologians in a wider context. He focused on "the silence of American Catholic theologians about the two-tiered altercation between Daniel Maguire and several Catholic colleges and universities, and between the religious women signers of the statement of pluralism on the issue of abortion"

(*New York Times*). Shea stated clearly his unwavering opposition to abortion but defended "the rights of theological inquiry and of responsible dissent from the teaching of bishops." He invoked the "silence of theologians" during the modernist controversies that "made them accessories to the wrecking of scholarly careers and of the lives of the modernists." Shea insisted that such silence is untenable "no matter the cost to ourselves."[69]

Bishop James D. Malone, Youngstown, Ohio, received a letter dated 18 September 1985 in which Shea protested Cardinal Ratzinger's criticisms of liberation theology as "an attempt by one theological faction to control or, indeed, stamp out another." He warned Malone against initiating a "dangerous game . . . in a post-Vatican II church where theological pluralism and governmental subsidiarity are supposed to be accepted facts of church life." The "hearts and minds" of certain Roman officials remain unconvinced of their inability to "rule the church's intellectual life any longer." The response among American theologians may very well become "militant opposition."[70]

In a lengthy letter to Bishop Raymond Lessard, D.D., bishop of Savannah, on his election to "chair of the Doctrinal Committee," Shea emphasized the good working relationship between the CTS and the bishops. Distinct from the CTSA was the attention the CTS paid to "college teaching and interdisciplinary research in the study of religion." Shea described a society having "a valuable and enjoyable time growing toward middle years." As in other correspondence, Shea aligned the membership with those who "have made a substantial contribution to the present health of the American church" out of "the extraordinary grace given the church in the person and influence of Pope John XXIII as well as our American heritage."

The letter then identified three problematic areas in the relationship between bishops and theologians. Shea mentioned specifically "the final adjudication of the cases of the religious women who signed the advertisement of *Catholics for Free Choice*," an event from fall 1984. Shea reiterated his hope for an equitable solution that allowed "bishops to teach and Catholics to speak their minds openly without fear of repression." The second concerned "the actions of Cardinal Ratzinger against Father Charles Curran" as only a sample of "his increasing collection of information to be used against other American theologians" that will negate "academic freedom" and "responsible dissent from noninfallible teachings." The final concern was "the norms for colleges and universities proposed by Cardinal Baum's Congregation," especially in the United States. He forecasted, correctly one could add, several years of tension between U.S. theologians and the Vatican with bishops attempting to mediate.[71] Shea's correspondence reflects the growing concerns among a generation of Catholic theologians who imagined the fruit of John XXIII's "extraordinary grace" to include a freedom to explore and even dissent.

The tensions not withstanding, the CTS sought various means of communicating with bishops. A unique example is "the Commission of Bishops and Scholars," whose "Statement of the Purpose" dated 19 November 1987, explained its commitment to fostering "interaction and collaboration between bishops and scholars" on selected topics judged to be "of serious concern and ecclesial import." A revived Joint Committee of Catholic Learned Societies and Scholars (JCCLSS) worked with the NCCB's Committee on Doctrine to facilitate exchanges.[72] A letter, dated 16 May 1989, to CTS president Mary Schneider from Bill Loewe requested a $200 contribution in anticipation of a commission colloquy: "The Bishop Then and Now: The Contemporary Significance of the Origins and Early Development of the Ministry of Bishop." Loewe later reported that the October 10–12 meeting, at Los Altos, California, proved to be "rewarding and enriching." Only California's bishops and those on the Committee on Doctrine [Raymond Lessard, Savannah, Georgia, and Oscar Lipscomb, Mobile, Alabama], plus selected "scholars" from the San Francisco Bay area attended. Because of the positive experience, planners thought such colloquies "should take place in other areas of the country."[73]

THE CHALLENGES OF *EX CORDE ECCLESIAE*

The correspondence and meetings proved to be warm-ups for intensive discussions of the "Statement on the Nature of Catholic Colleges and Universities," what eventually appeared as *Ex corde Ecclesiae* (*EcE*). An earlier version, dated 9 June 1986, appeared in a CTS file. The document's treatment of "The Task of Theology" seemed to highlight more than resolve the tensions surrounding theologian as academic persona. The document placed "Christian faith" in "the academy as a subject of critical investigation." To be transmitted effectively theology had to inculturate its work whether through "evangelization and preaching," "liturgy and devotion" or "moral decision and action, faith must be expressed in the language and concepts of particular cultures." The New Testament served as an example. The document placed on "Catholic scholars . . . a double fidelity: to the Church and to the academy." It affirmed "responsible academic freedom" as "essential to the research and teaching of a Catholic institution" and insisted upon responsible theologians who must be willing to "state the Church's belief accurately and to interpret it systematically" though their "theological investigation does not fall under the direct supervision of the hierarchy." The bishops maintained their roles as judges of the "adequacy . . . [of] expression . . . in a particular culture." These normative judgments depended on determining "the sense of the faithful" and working "through procedures appropriate to the gravity of the task." Besides a commitment to justice, a Catholic college or university was to "be a community of scholarly investigation and critical evaluation inspired by faith shared in reflection, by hope celebrated in liturgy, and by love working in service."[74]

The specter of a Roman document on Catholic colleges and universities motivated still more unified efforts among Catholic learned societies including the Association of Catholic Colleges and Universities (ACCU). ACCU's importance in organizing a unified response to *EcE* had much to do with the leadership of its executive director, Sister Alice Gallin, O.S.U. The "Minutes [of the] CTS Board Meeting—May 29, 1986" reported unanimous support for Alice Gallin's "proposal to organize a National Committee of Catholic Theologians."[75] With Curran's situation still fresh in his mind, William Shea wanted a well-established committee "to provide the societies with a mechanism of communication and reflection, and aid to members, on the difficulties inherent in the work of educators, of exegetes and theologians, of educational and church administrators." He had described this committee to the convention attendees in his presidential address and offered concrete procedures for its establishment. He envisioned a pledge of $10,000 divided evenly among the three societies, the CTSA, CLSA, and CTS. "We should not leave the discussion to bishops and the official church bureaucracy—it must be informed in the most direct and profound manner by our own collective wisdom, experience, and love of the gospel and the church."[76] The CTS board meeting, 5 December 1988, recorded approval of a $3,000 allocation pending matching funds from the other societies.[77]

Shea also wrote to William Cardinal Baum, secretary, of the Sacred Congregation for Catholic Education to communicate the board's "deep concern" about "the consequences of the enactment of the *schema* on American Catholic education." He described it as "disastrous, a decisive set back for our colleges and universities in the American education and political world and a cause of widespread confusion and conflict in departments of theology and religious studies."[78] Shea wrote in the April newsletter, "I continue my novena that the draft disappears. I remain skeptical and fearful, however, since my last novena was for Walter Mondale's victory."[79]

Alice Gallin, O.S.U., agreed to Shea's request and organized a 19 August 1986 meeting where Bill Shea and Rodger Van Allen represented the CTS.[80] It marked the founding of the short-lived "Intersocietal Committee on Ecclesial Responsibility and Academic Freedom." A report from a 13 December 1986 meeting indicated that the CLSA declined to participate[81] and less than a year later, in October 1987, the board of the CTSA decided to withdraw its representative.[82] The report of December 1986 summarized a discussion on the "context of freedom and responsibility." The summary offers insight into how *EcE* was viewed as discussions began in earnest. One strategy was to define "ecclesial responsibility" on its own terms as "pastoral," encompassing "fidelity both to the tradition of the Church and to its growth as life giving knowledge in the Christian community." Such "responsibility" would require "freedom" to engage in "the pastoral task of listening to the people of God and to the tradition." A subsequent paragraph upheld the importance of "academic freedom" to ensure "the healthy development of the academic discipline of theology."[83]

A 9 May 1988 "Report" of the Intersocietal Committee served as summary of "the main issues" discussed over the last two years and echoed conversations occurring in many Catholic colleges' departments of religious studies and theology. The committee voiced concern for a "disheartened" membership due to "restrictions imposed on some of their colleagues and about the general failure of the Church to understand the pastoral task of theologians in the Church." They identified two consequences: "alienation from the Church" and "abandonment" of controversial research topics. The report then reiterated freedom in a pastoral context, concern over "the dramatic increase in papal and Vatican documents," and consideration of media coverage's impact.[84]

The perceived onslaught of threats to theologians' freedom of inquiry, exemplified for many in the Curran case, motivated Michael Barnes to produce a statement on "freedom of public discussion by theologians." He wanted CTS members to discuss and amend the content and send the amended document to the U.S. bishops if a majority of members approved. The April 1989 newsletter announced that a vote was to be taken at the next annual business meeting during the convention. Those unable to attend the meeting could vote using the postcard included with the newsletter.[85]

The preserved archival documents offer no example of a direct challenge to Barnes's statement. In a 14 May 1989 letter, Fr. Matthew Lamb, from Boston College, raised more basic questions about contemporary Catholic scholars' expertise in Catholic theology, especially "pre-modern Catholic classics," given their lack of language proficiency and perhaps more troubling to Fr. Lamb, their education in "Protestant programs." Lamb cited inadequate work of "conservative" as well as "liberal" scholars to demonstrate his point.[86] Lamb's point received a courteous response, and Barnes's proposal an overwhelming affirmative vote. Mary L. Schneider reported in the September 1989 newsletter that of the 281 postcards returned (at least a third of total members), 248 or about 88% had voted in the affirmative for the statement. "The statement, with the voting results included in a cover letter, had been sent to the American bishops, to all ACCU presidents, directors and seminary Rectors and officers of professional societies in theology for their information."[87]

The final version opened with the following statement: "The College Theology Society urges that free and public expression of careful theological reflection be promoted as a positive good for the life of the Church in its mission to humanity." It mentioned the "current active discussions" concerning "the degree of freedom that is appropriate for the individual theologian to exercise in public discussions of the teachings of the official magisterium of the Church." The statement then expressed, on the one hand, respect for the role of the magisterium as "guide and guardian of the tradition" and, on the other hand, the necessity of "searching the tradition for new possibilities, by the work of the theologian." The statement also defended "the value of public disagreement in the Church" especially as a testimony to "the dignity of the person according to Vatican II in its declaration of religious freedom." Again expressing the College Theology Society's self-understanding, the document turned to the role of teacher as, in this case, the model of "honesty of inquiry and reflection appropriate to the work of theology." Such a teacher "cannot do less than encourage students to learn to reflect critically for themselves even on matters of faith in order that they may grow more fully into conscientious and responsible persons."[88]

The overwhelming support for Barnes's statement coincided with the emergence of a new and seemingly more dangerous threat to the theologian's freedom—requiring an Oath of Fidelity (canon 833, 1983 revised code of canon law). The possible requirement sparked intense discussion at the CTS's 1989 open forum (Rochester). The specific occasion for concern was the publication in *L'Osservatore Romano* (25 February 1989) "of a new formula for profession of faith with an additional text for an oath of fidelity." Three additional paragraphs followed the Nicene Constantinopolitan Creed. The first professed belief in "everything contained in the Word of God, written or handed down in tradition and proposed by the church—whether in solemn judgment or in the ordinary and universal magisterium—as divinely revealed and calling for faith." The second expanded on the first to ask the oath taker to "embrace and hold each and everything that is definitively proposed by the same church concerning the doctrine of faith and morals." The language of "definitively proposed" seemed to create an "'in-between' category" difficult to distinguish from the "everything" contained in the preceding paragraph. The third paragraph attested to an adherence "with religious 'obsequium' of will and intellect to the doctrines which either the Roman Pontiff or the college of bishops enunciate when they exercise the authentic magisterium even if they proclaim those doctrines in an act that is not definitive."[89] The forum produced a proposal to establish a committee "that would deal with theological, moral and philosophical issues related to the Oath the Vatican may require of theology professors, Catholic College presidents and seminary faculty."[90] The five-person committee consisted of Francis J. Buckley, S.J., Joseph A. Grau, M. Theresa Moser, R.S.C.J., William M. Shea, and Paul Surlis. Moser served as chair.

At the November 1989 board meeting, Theresa Moser presented a twenty-two page "Preliminary Report" from the "Committee on Profession of Faith/Oath of Fidelity," dated 18 November 1989, with a cover letter (dated 6 November 1989) to the president, Mary Schneider. Each committee member offered her or his contribution based upon consultation on canon 833 with a different canon lawyer. The CDF's "new formulation" of the oath, according to the report, "sent shock waves through the ecclesiastical world." Its appearance in *L'Osservatore Romano* rather than *Acta Apostolicae Sedis*, raised the question: "'What is the CDF up to now?'" Board members offered their own conjectures as to why the oath had become an issue. "Theresa thinks that the 'Humanae Vitae' connection is important here."[91] But the more critical question was who had to take the oath given that, in the canon's seventh section, the phrase "'teachers in any university whatsoever who teach disciplines which deal with faith or morals'" excluded very few. The board's discussion emphasized the unique situation in the United States where Catholic institutions are not established canonically. Though some variance existed among canon lawyers, the general conclusion placed "the burden of proof . . . on those who claim that canon 833 does apply to Catholic colleges and universities in the United States." The report depicted a "deep and profound disquiet" among "theologians, pastors, and bishops" concerning the oath's "new formulaes" and invoked the "excesses of [the] modernist era" with its "atmosphere of suspicion, intimidation, and fear." The "'loyalty oath', as interpreted in *L'Osservatore Romano*, seems to require assent to integralist versions of what constitutes doctrinal orthodoxy."

The ability to produce a report in less than six months highlighted the perceived urgency of the issue. The "collaboration of the canon lawyers consulted and of Charles Curran, who checked the text for accuracy with a 'fine tooth comb'"[92] received the committee's public gratitude, and the board agreed that "Theresa did a great job, and it was professionally done." The board thanked Theresa Moser and the committee for the work completed in a short time and for the professional quality of the final report. The report was unanimously accepted.

The board then considered several options for the document's distribution. Theresa Moser suggested that the report be sent to the NCCB through their Committee on Doctrine. Some members thought the best strategy was actively lobbying bishops and college and university presidents. Others thought the wiser course was to "let sleeping dogs lie." A few board members noted that silence can mean assent. Questions arose about whether such distribution would have a public element or be handled through internal channels. The minutes suggested that at least four board members favored the internal approach. The full report was to be published in the spring 1990 *Horizons*, with a copy placed in every convention packet. A strategic mailing to a few bishops was also thought to be a good idea.[93]

One year later the board gave support to circulating among CTS members a CTSA statement: "Do Not Extinguish the Spirit." It dealt with issues similar to those treated in the report on the oath. The board also voted to send a letter congratulating Alice Gallin and the ACCU for the developments in the "document 'Ex Corde Ecclesiae.'"[94] At the May 1991 board meeting, the board again discussed approving "Do Not Extinguish the Spirit," this time in response to CTSA president Walter Principe's request "to show a united front, especially on the oath." After lengthy discussion, "George [Gilmore] made the following motion: 'The officers and Board of Directors of the College Theology Society in solidarity with the Catholic Theological Society of America endorse, share the concerns and affirm the intentions of the document: "Do Not Extinguish the Spirit" of the Catholic Theological Society of America.'"[95] At the subsequent business meeting of 1 June 1991, CTS president Keith Egan "announced that the CTS board sent a statement of support to the CTSA" on the document.[96]

The CTS participated in the issuance of more statements reiterating Catholic theologians' principal identity as academics in relation to the church. The "Joint Committee of the Catholic Theological Society of America, the Canon Law Society of America, and the College Theology Society" met on 27 February 1993. The minutes included a clear statement that "taking the Oath of Fidelity and even the Profession of Faith in its present form is repugnant to people in American Catholic higher education." The record of the discussion conveys a myriad of emotions from fear to defiance. Some expressed worry about the effects on younger theologians who had no experience of oaths. Others warned that the current "good will . . . toward the hierarchy" would be lost though someone observed the episcopal suspicion of theologians and theologians' "impression that their *scholarly* work is not read or studied by bishops" hardly described a relationship of good will. Questions emerged about the "ambiguity" in a theologian's "teaching function" given its questionable status as "an ecclesiastical office." Expressions of fear included the specter of "certain groups or individuals" adapting "the Oath of Fidelity and Profession of Faith for other purposes (e.g., ideological, proving they are 'super' Catholics)." Such uses "could lead to further disruption in the community."[97]

The concerns about the oath quickly migrated to concerns about the implementation of *Ex corde Ecclesiae.* Theresa Moser dedicated herself to discussions concerning *EcE* in a fashion reminiscent of her work on the oath. She provided a "report and update" on the U.S. bishops' *EcE* implementation document. Based in part on Moser's report and on subsequent discussion, the board decided at the November 1993 meeting to send the CTS response "to all the members in the February mailing." The sentence "This ordinance does not contribute to realizing the goals of *Ex corde Ecclesiae* and therefore we recommend that it not be implemented." replaced "This ordinance is not acceptable."[98] The extended commentary on the unacceptability of the "proposed ordinances" from the "Board of Directors of the College Theology Society" (22 November 1993) was a ten-page document. Its "Introduction and Statement of Position" emphasized the importance of "American autonomy" as critical "for the flourishing of our institutions and for the general recognition by the larger American society of their excellence as institutions of higher learning with a Catholic character." So the basic recommendation to "the Committee on Education of the NCCB" was that "*Ex Corde Ecclesiae* remain the exhortatory and inspirational document that it is." Implementing the ordinances "would undermine the identity of our institutions and threaten their existence as Catholic institutions."

Four of the ten pages considered Ordinances 5 and 6 having to do with *mandatum.* The discussion of Ordinance 5 described *mandatum* "as recognition by the *competent ecclesiastical authority* of a Catholic professor's *suitability* to teach theological disciplines." The written analysis focused on the lack of a clear definition of "mandate" and of its distinction from "canonical mission" or what constituted competency and suitability. The sixth ordinance concerned university officials' role in informing "*Catholic* professors of theological disciplines" of the "Church's expectation that they *request the mandate.*" The italicized terms as in the discussion of Ordinance 5 received attention. In this case, raising questions of the university's involvement in what "is described in canon law as a private matter between the individual and the bishop." Further arguments against *mandatum* included the possibility of losing federal funding because of violation of separation of church and state.

The document then focused on the impact in theology's current academic culture. "Catholic members of theology departments are aware of the fact that they will lose the respect of their peers in the Academy if they are required to have a mandate." The document asserts that "colleagues" will perceive theologians "as 'agents of the bishop,' inferior scholars with no freedom of inquiry." It will "reinforce the view that 'Catholic' and 'University' are mutually exclusive terms." The document predicted a deterioration in "the quality of professors of theological disciplines in Catholic universities." The future was depicted in bleak terms with "promising young Catholic scholars" choosing "non-theological fields where academic freedom is not threatened" and completing doctoral studies as well as seeking "teaching and research positions in State and private, non-sectarian institutions." The final warning concerned "harassment not only of individual Catholic faculty members, but also of university and church officials by extremist groups and self-appointed guardians of orthodoxy."[99]

Joan Leonard's February Presidential Letter mentioned the acknowledgments received from CTS members and Gerard Sloyan, representing the CTSA, on "the quality of the CTS response to the 'Proposed Ordinances' of the NCCB." "Some indicated that they were proud to share the document with other colleagues and administrators in their respective institutions."[100] A CTSA response, dated 15 December, 1993, stood in contrast. It read more like an invitation to "a process of conversation and dialogue lasting for three years" between bishops and Catholic colleges and universities that could be facilitated by the ACCU and attended by representatives of Catholic learned societies, rather than the extensive analysis of the CTS.[101]

In May 1994, news came of another Vatican Commission investigation, in this case, of Father Robert Nugent and Sister Jeannine Gramick concerning "New Ways Ministry," serving gays and lesbians. A "Memorandum" from Paul Albergo, Chair of New Ways Ministry requested a "public statement of support for their 24 years of ministry in this area, and the need for the Church to allow it to continue." Albergo characterized the ministry as "prophetic" and raised concerns about the consequences when a religious community's ministry is "unjustly suppressed because of healthy tensions between religious charisms and Church hierarchy."[102] An undated resolution from the CTS Board of Directors offered Archbishop Maida or another "appropriate authority" the Society's expertise "to ensure adequate and just review of the case" including suggestions of theologians to add to the committee. A second resolution allowed the board to copy the letter to Nugent's and Gramick's religious communities and to contact the principals directly. A third resolution proposed establishing a CTS committee to review other possible actions by the CTS.[103] The resolution was discussed and approved.[104] The next day, Sunday, a "Special Board of Directors' Meeting" was held. The board appointed a five-person committee, chaired by the new president, Brennan Hill, and included "Alice Laffey, William Shea, James Gaffney, and one further theologian from the gay community. The three competent theologians to be recommended to Archbishop Maida [were] Norbert Rigali, Theresa Moser, and John Hanigan."[105] The president, Brennan Hill, reported at the November 1994 board meeting that Maida had "declined the Society's offer of professional help" and the situation indicated that Nugent and Gramick would be removed from their ministry.[106] The report from the investigatory meetings appeared to be unfavorable.[107]

Little evidence exists to suggest that the CTS changed episcopal minds in their treatment of individuals. The discussions themselves highlighted the very different contexts in which the CTS and the bishops express themselves. The CTS expressed their pastoral concerns through an academic lens, and the bishops defined their pastoral duties through the prism of the church's doctrinal articulations. Responding to "proposed ordinances" had only just begun as the next decade resembled a wild roller coaster ride with steep ascents, rapid descents into unexpected twists and turns, and the final coast to the end, only to find oneself beginning the ride again.

NOTES

1. Suzanne C. Toton, CTS secretary, to CTS officers, members of the board, and program chairperson of the annual meeting, "Re: Minutes of the Business Meeting, 1985," Salve Regina College, Newport, Rhode Island, June 1, 1985, "CTS Correspondence" File, Box 7, CTS Collection 178, ACUA.

2. Suzanne C. Toton, CTS secretary, to CTS officers and members of the board of directors, "Re: Minutes of the Annual Meeting. May 30, 1985, Salve Regina College, Newport, Rhode Island," "CTS Correspondence" File, Box 7, CTS Collection, ACUA.

3. "Annual Report to the Board of Directors, [College Theology Society]," Salve Regina College, Newport, Rhode Island, May 30, 1985, nonarchived material.

4. Application for membership, College Theology Society, "CTS Board Meeting May 1990" File, Box 3, CTS Collection, ACUA.

5. William M. Shea to colleague, College Theology Society Newsletter, April 1986, nonarchived material.

6. Mike Barnes to the members of the College Theology Society, "Concerning: Nominations for the biannual Presidential Award," January 30, 1988, nonarchived material.

7. "Citation; the Presidential Award for Joseph and Sally Cunneen," May 30, 1987, "Presidential Correspondence 1986–87" File, Box 7, CTS Collection, ACUA.

8. Mary L. Schneider to colleagues, "[College Theology Society] NEWSLETTER, September 1989," nonarchived material.

9. Dolores L. Greeley to colleague, "[College Theology Society] NEWSLETTER, April 1987," "CTS Correspondence with CTS President 1986–88" File, Box 3, CTS Collection, ACUA.

10. Joan A. Leonard, "[College Theology Society] Newsletter February 1994," 1993 Binder, Box 1, CTS Collection, ACUA.

11. "CTS Minutes: Board Meeting, November 22, 1986, Atlanta Hilton, Atlanta, Georgia," "CTS Annual Board Meeting Minutes 1986–87" File, Box 3, CTS Collection, ACUA.

12. Terrence W. Tilley to Peter Phan, March 20, 1990, "CTS Correspondence with CTS President 1988–1990" File, Box 2, CTS Collection, ACUA.

13. "Minutes Board of Directors Meeting, May 27, 1987," "CTS Annual Board Meeting, 1986–1987" File, Box 3, CTS Collection, ACUA.

14. Terry Tilley, executive director of national conventions, to CTS Board of Directors, "Re: Report on upcoming conventions with points for discussion and decision bolded," November 1991, "CTS Convention 1991" File, Box 2, CTS Collection, ACUA.

15. Suzanne C. Toton, secretary, to CTS officers and members of the board of directors, "Re: Minutes of the Annual Meeting. May 30, 1985, Salve Regina College, Newport, Rhode Island," "CTS Correspondence" File, Box 7, CTS Collection, ACUA.

16. "CTS Board Meeting—May 31, 1990, Miller Hall, Mezzanine Meeting Room, Loyola of New Orleans," "CTS Board Meeting May 1990" File, Box 3, CTS Collection, ACUA.

17. William M. Shea, "[College Theology Society] NEWSLETTER, March 1985," "CTS Correspondence" File, Box 7, CTS Collection, ACUA.

18. Dolores L. Greeley, "NEWSLETTER, April 1987."

19. "Agenda for the Meeting of the CTS Board," May 26, 1988, "CTS Annual Board Meeting May 1988" File, Box 2, CTS Collection, ACUA.

20. "Acting Secretary's Report, Board of Directors' Meeting, St. Mary's, Moraga, June 3, 1993," 1993 Binder, Box 1, CTS Collection, ACUA.

21. "Policy and Procedures for College Theology Award Committee Revisions," 1993 Binder, Box 1, CTS Collection, ACUA. The finished changes appear in a document entitled "Job Description for the Awards Committee Chair; Policy and Procedures for College Theology Society Award Committee" dated May 26, 1994.

22. "Acting Secretary's Report," June 3, 1993.

23. "Secretary's Report, Board of Directors' Meeting, AAR Convention, Washington, DC, November 20, 1993," 1993 Binder, Box 1, CTS Collection, ACUA.

24. "College Theology Society, Board of Directors' Meeting, 4–9 p.m., November 19, 1994, Chicago Hilton Conference Room 5G," 1994–1995 Binder, Box 1, CTS Collection, ACUA.

25. Suzanne C. Toton, "Re: Minutes of the Business Meeting, 1985."

26. Suzanne C. Toton, "Re: Minutes of the Annual Meeting. May 30, 1985."

27. Dolores L. Greeley to colleague, "[College Theology Society] NEWSLETTER, September 1987," "CTS Annual Board Meeting Minutes 1986–87" File, Box 3, CTS Collection, ACUA.

28. "Minutes of the Business Meeting (Nazareth College, Rochester, NY, June 3, 1989)," "CTS Board Meeting Minutes Extra Copies May 1989" File, Box 2, CTS Collection, ACUA.

29. "College Theology Society Annual Meeting, Concerns of Women Caucus, May 30, 1987," "CTS Annual Board Meeting Minutes 1986–87" File, Box 2, CTS Collection, ACUA.

30. "Draft: Women's Pastoral Response," November 19, 1988, "CTS Annual Board Meeting Nov. 1988" File, Box 2, CTS Collections, ACUA.

31. "Business Meeting, College Theology Society, Crown Center Auditorium, Loyola University, Chicago, 3:30 p.m., June 1, 1991" and "Special Meeting of the Board of Directors, Sunday, June 2, 1991," "CTS Board Meeting Nov. 1989" File, Box 3, CTS Collection, ACUA.

32. "Uncorrected Minutes, Board of Directors' Meeting, St. Mary's, Notre Dame, May 26, 1994," "1994–1995" Binder, Box 1, CTS Collection, ACUA.

33. Suzanne C. Toton, CTS secretary, to CTS officers, members of the board and program chairperson [sic] for annual meeting, "Re: Minutes of Semiannual Meeting, December 10, 1984," "CTS Correspondence" File, Box 7, CTS Collection, ACUA.

34. William M. Shea to Mr. Kent H. Richards (SBL), February 26, 1985, "CTS-CSR" File, Box 7, CTS Collection, ACUA.

35. Gerard S. Sloyan to Dr. William Shea, October 18, 1985, "November 1985 Meeting" File, Box 7, CTS Collection, ACUA.

36. The Council on the Study of Religion changed in 1986 to the Council of Societies for the Study of Religion and began publishing its Bulletin again in 1988. "College Theology

Society Board of Directors Meeting, Hussey Lounge, Damen Hall, Loyola University of Chicago, 9:00 a.m. May 30, 1991," "CTS Board Meeting Nov. 1991" File, Box 3, CTS Collection, ACUA.

37. Suzanne C. Toton, "Re: Minutes of the Annual Meeting, May 30, 1985."

38. "Minutes Board of Directors Meeting May 27, 1987," "CTS Annual Board Meeting 1986–1987" File, Box 3, CTS Collection, ACUA.

39. "Report and Observations, John McCarthy, CTS, October 29, 1988," "CTS Annual Board Meeting Nov. 1989" File, Box 2, CTS Collection, ACUA.

40. "Board Meeting of the CTS, Thursday, June 1, 1989, Casa Italiana Room, Nazareth College, Rochester, N.Y.," "CTS Board Meeting Minutes Extra Copies May 1989" File, Box 2, CTS Collection, ACUA.

41. "Board Report: Research and Publications, May 1991," "CTS Board Meeting May 30, 1991" File, Box 2, CTS Collection, ACUA.

42. "College Theology Society Board of Directors Meeting," May 30, 1991.

43. Terry Tilley, "Re: Report on upcoming conventions," November 1991.

44. "College Theology Society Board of Directors Meeting," May 30, 1991.

45. "College Theology Society Board Report, Chair, Research and Publications, November 21, 1992," "CTS Convention, Nov. 21, 1992" File, Box 2, CTS Collection, ACUA.

46. "CTS Board Meeting, June 3, 1993, Research and Publication," 1992–94 Binder, Box 1, CTS Collection, ACUA.

47. "Acting Secretary's Report, Board of Directors' Meeting," June 3, 1993.

48. "Uncorrected Minutes, Board of Directors' Meeting," May 26, 1994.

49. "College Theology Society, Board of Directors," November 19, 1994.

50. Mary S[chneider] to Keith [J. Egan] and other board members, November 17, 1990, "CTS Board Meeting 1990" File, Box 3, CTS Collection, ACUA.

51. George Gilmore to members of the CTS board, no date, and "CTS Board Meeting, Nov. 17, 1990, 5:00 p.m. Iberville Room, Marriott Hotel, New Orleans, LA," "CTS Board Meeting Nov. 1990" File, Box 3, CTS Collection, ACUA.

52. "College Theology Society Board of Directors Meeting, Heartland Room, Radisson Suite, Kansas City, MO 5:00 p.m. November 23, 1991," "CTS Board Meeting Nov. 1989" File, Box 3, CTS Collection, ACUA.

53. "Acting Secretary's Report, Board of Directors' Meeting," June 3, 1993.

54. William Shea to Walter Conn, January 3, 1986, "CTS Correspondence" File, Box 7, CTS Collection, ACUA.

55. Friends of American Catholic Theology [FACT] to Professor William Shea, "Re: Enclosed listing of signers of CTSA/CTS Past Presidents' Statement concerning Charles Curran's investigation by the CDF," "Curran" File, Box 7, CTS Collection, ACUA.

56. William M. Shea, "NEWSLETTER, March 1985."

57. William M. Shea, "April, 1986."

58. Francis Schüssler Fiorenza, president of CTSA, and William M. Shea, president of CTS, to colleagues, April 4, 1986, "Curran" File, Box 7, CTS Collection, ACUA.

59. William M. Shea, "April, 1986."

60. "CTS Minutes: Board Meeting, November 22, 1986."

61. Name withheld to Dr. William M. Shea, April 26, 1986, "Curran" File, Box 7, CTS Collection, ACUA.

62. William M. Shea to name withheld, June 16, 1986, "Curran" File, Box 7, CTS Collection, ACUA.

63. FACT to friend, "Curran" File, Box 7, CTS Collection, ACUA.

64. No title, no date, "Curran" File, Box 7, CTS Collection, ACUA.

65. "Testimony from the Officers and Board of Directors of the College Theology Society Regarding the Case of Professor Charles Curran," no date, "Presidential Correspondence 1986–87" File, Box 7, CTS Collection, ACUA.

66. Dolores L. Greeley to colleague, "[College Theology Society] NEWSLETTER, February 1987," "CTS Correspondence with CTS President, 1986–88 (Mayeski)" File, Box 3, CTS Collection, ACUA.

67. "Agenda for the Meeting of the CTS Board," May 26, 1988.

68. Suzanne C. Toton, "Re: Minutes of Semiannual Meeting, December 10, 1984."

69. No title, the first line reads "The silence of American Catholic theologians about the two-tiered . . ." "CTS Ad-Hoc Committee" File, Box 7, CTS Collection, ACUA.

70. William M. Shea to Bishop James D. Malone, September 18, 1985, "CTS Correspondence" File, Box 7, CTS Collection, ACUA.

71. William Shea to Most Reverend Raymond Lessard, D.D., December 13, 1985, "CTS Ad-Hoc Committee" File, Box 7, CTS Collection, ACUA.

72. "Report of the Joint Committee of Catholic Learned Societies and Scholars," signed by William Loewe and Donald Buggert, O.CARM., January 18, 1988, and "Appendix A, Statement of the Purpose of the Commission of Bishops and Scholars (Provisional Constitutions)," November 19, 1987, "Presidential Committee 1987–1988" File, Box 7, CTS Collection, ACUA.

73. William P. Loewe to Professor Mary L. Schneider, May 16, 1989, and "Report on Colloquy of Bishops and Scholars" submitted by Donald W. Buggert, O.CARM., secretary, Commission of Bishops and Scholars, no date, "CTS Annual Board Meeting June 1989" File, Box 2, CTS Collection, ACUA.

74. "Statement on the Nature of Catholic Colleges and Universities; Draft Version: 9 June 1986," nonarchived material.

75. "Minutes CTS Board Meeting May 29, 1986, Xavier University, Cincinnati," nonarchived material.

76. William Shea to Dolores Greeley, November 3, 1987, "Presidential Committee 1987–1988" File, Box 7, CTS Collection, ACUA.

77. "MINUTES: DECEMBER 5, 1988; Tufts Suite, Boston Marriott Copley Place Hotel," nonarchived material.

78. William M. Shea to William Cardinal Baum, January 22, 1986, "Baum document" File, Box 7, CTS Collection, ACUA.

79. William M. Shea, "April, 1986."

80. Dolores L. Greeley to colleague, "[College Theology Society] NEWSLETTER, September 1986," nonarchived material.

81. "Intersocietal Committee on Ecclesial Responsibility and Academic Freedom," no date, "Presidential Correspondence 1986–87" File, Box 7, CTS Collection, ACUA.

82. Richard J. Clifford, S.J., to the executive committees of the Catholic Biblical Association of America, the Catholic Theological Society of America, and the College Theology Society, "Re: Final Report of the Committee," March 17, 1988, "CTS Annual Board Meeting May 1988 (Mayeski)" File, Box 2, CTS Collection, ACUA.

83. "Intersocietal Committee on Ecclesial Responsibility and Academic Freedom."

84. "Report of the Intersocietal Committee on Academic Freedom and Ecclesial Responsibility," May 9, 1988, "Presidential Committee 1987–1988" File, Box 7, CTS Collection, ACUA.

85. Mary L. Schneider to colleagues, "[College Theology Society] NEWSLETTER, April 1989," "CTS Correspondence with CTS President 1988–1990" File, Box 2, CTS Collection, ACUA.

86. Fr. Matthew L. Lamb to Professor Michael Barnes, May 14, 1989, "CTS Annual Board Meeting June 1989" File, Box 2, CTS Collection, ACUA.

87. Mary L. Schneider, "NEWSLETTER, September 1989."

88. "Statement of the College Theology Society on Freedom of Public Discussion by Theologians," Revised example of a possible statement, for consideration by the CTS board at its December meeting, October 9, 1987, "CTS Annual Board Meeting Minutes 1986–87" File, Box 7, CTS Collection, ACUA.

89. "College Theology Society, Preliminary Report, Committee on Profession of Faith/Oath of Fidelity, November 18, 1989," M. Theresa Moser, R.S.C.J., chair; Francis J. Buckley, S.J.; Joseph A. Grau; William M. Shea; Paul Surlis, "CTS Annual Board Meeting Nov. 1989" File, Box 2, CTS Collection, ACUA. 1, 14, 19.

90. "Minutes of the Business Meeting (Nazareth College, Rochester, NY, June 3, 1989)."

91. "Board Meeting, College Theology Society, November 18, 1989, 5:00 p.m., Anaheim, California," "CTS Board Meeting, May 1990" File, Box 3, CTS Collection, ACUA.

92. M. Theresa Moser, R.S.C.J., to Dr. Mary Lee [sic] Schneider, November 6, 1989, and "College Theology Society: Preliminary Report: Committee on Profession of Faith/Oath of Fidelity, November 18, 1989," "CTS Annual Board Meeting Nov. 1989" File, Box 2, CTS Collection, ACUA.

93. "Board Meeting, College Theology Society," November 18, 1989.

94. "CTS Board Meeting, Nov. 17, 1990."

95. "College Theology Society Board of Directors Meeting," May 30, 1991.

96. "Business Meeting, College Theology Society," June 1, 1991.

97. "CTSA-CLSA-CTS Joint Committee on the Profession of Faith and Oath of Fidelity," February 27, 1993, "1993–94" Binder, Box 1, CTS Collection, ACUA.

98. "Secretary's Report, Board of Directors' Meeting," November 20, 1993.

99. "Response to Proposed Ordinances of the Committee on Education of the NCCB on *Ex Corde Ecclesiae*, Board of Directors of the College Theology Society," November 22, 1993, nonarchived material.

100. Joan A. Leonard, "Newsletter February 1994."

101. Board of Directors of the Catholic Theological Society of America, "Response to Request for Comments on the Proposed Ordinances for the Implementation of *Ex Corde Ecclesiae*," submitted by Gerard S Sloyan, president, December 15, 1993, nonarchived material.

102. Paul Albergo to leadership of national Catholic organizations, "Memorandum, RE: Public Statements on Vatican Commission Investigating Fr. Robert Nugent and Sr. Jeannine Gramick," May 18, 1994, "1993" Binder, Box 1, CTS Collection ACUA.

103. No title, the first line reads "Mindful of the great values of the 24 years of ministry of . . ." "1993" Binder, Box 1, CTS Collection, ACUA.

104. "Uncorrected Minutes, Annual Business Meeting," May 28, 1994.

105. "Uncorrected Minutes, Special Board of Directors' Meeting, St. Mary's, Notre Dame, May 29, 1994," "1994–1995" Binder, Box 1, CTS Collection, ACUA.

106. "College Theology Society, Board of Directors' Meeting," November 19, 1994.

107. Brennan R. Hill, "[College Theology Society] Newsletter February 1995," "1994–1995" Binder, Box 1, CTS Collection, ACUA.

· 8 ·

Theology in Local and Global Perspective (1985–1994)

$\mathcal{E}$ssays from the Society's fourth decade of annual volumes suggest a preoccupation with theology's varied locales from its immediate American social and culture surroundings to its world context in relation to the "other." The thirty-first annual convention took its inspiration from the first draft of the U.S. bishops' pastoral on the economy. The next three address theology's situatedness in the church, in the university, and in the world. The specific themes were "Authorities and Structure in the Churches" (1986), "Theology in the University" (1987), and "Theology in World Perspective" (1988). In 1989, the Society turned to examine "fundamentalism" as a modern religious movement and its role in shaping theological discourse, expressed in the theme, "Fundamentalism in the Modern World" (1989). The cosmos provided the context for considering "Ecology in Theological Perspective," the 1990 convention theme. The next two annual meetings appealed to more local and particular contexts. In 1991, the impact of ethnicity and nationality on religious experience was considered under the heading, "Ethnicity, Nationality and Religious Experience." "Descendants of Abraham: Judaism, Christianity, Islam" appears as the theme of the following year with the three traditions united in their distinctiveness as the "religions of the Book." Religion as an embodied reality was the contextual theme of 1993 and women's important influence in shaping contemporary theology served as the decade's closing theme. The final convention, held appropriately enough at Saint Mary's College, South Bend, celebrated the fiftieth anniversary of the Graduate School of Sacred Theology that educated many of the women instrumental in the Society's founding. *Horizons* celebrated its twentieth year of publication the same year.

Self-conscious reflection on distinctive and disparate social locations did not preclude aspirations toward a studied unity within a pluralistic context—a unity that recognized common cause with the poor, the cultural or religious other, and with the very cosmos. The desire for theological studies to be relevant also continued in many essays throughout this decade. Willing to grapple with issues broad in their scope, the Society considered fundamentalism as a global movement, environmental denigration in its cosmic context, globalized economic disparity, gender in its cross-cultural context, interreligious dialogue, and intercultural exchange. Such complex conversations manifested the fruition of theological movements long in gestation and now intertwining: liberationist, ecological, interreligious and intercultural, and feminist. Here were further iterations of biblical and historically oriented theological studies as well as methods identified with Karl Rahner and Bernard Lonergan sometimes placed against their counterpoint, identified with Karl Barth, particularly, in the U.S. context, with the work of Stanley Hauerwas and his theological associates.

This chapter's review of the fourth decade's volumes begins with the College Theology Society's members' assessment of the teaching authority granted the theologian, especially in light of Charles Curran's removal from the Catholic University of America. Then the review turns to essays featuring scripture and historical methods, then to those utilizing now familiar theological approaches, especially Rahner's and Lonergan's thought. The final sections review developments in liberation theology, interreligious and intercultural dialogue, and ecological theology, ending with an examination of the extensive influence of feminist theology and a charge for the future.

TEACHING THEOLOGY: BY WHOSE AUTHORITY?

A U.S., or more accurately, an increasingly self-conscious "American" perspective on the teaching and transmission of theology remained central to several essays throughout this decade's volumes. Development of a nationally informed theology was nowhere more evident than in discussions regarding the U.S. bishops' attempts to shape social policy. The thirty-first annual volume, *Religion and Economic Ethics*, received its impetus from "the Catholic bishops of the United States" who had recently published the "first draft" of their "pastoral letter on the U.S. economy." Joseph Gower, the volume's editor, described economic ethics as an emerging field, with a growing concern for business ethics and comparative "moral evaluations of economic systems."[1] The U.S. bishops seemed to be in the forefront with their moderate critique of capitalism. In the volume's opening essay, Douglas Sturm supports the episcopal effort. Borrowing language from U.S. culture, Sturm champions a "social covenant," that ordered "economic growth and distribution" to the "interests of commonwealth" as the ultimate end "most to be cherished" in this economic system.[2]

Others, like plenary speaker Rebecca Chopp, showed little hesitancy in criticizing the U.S. bishops regarding their account of the "option for the poor." She wanted "some substantive content and transforming vision of the common good" and gave the bishops a "mandate." They ought to emulate "an uniquely American tradition, the tradition of social theologians such as Reinhold Neibuhr and Martin Luther King, Jr., who used the biblical vision to critique and transform the reason and experience of our culture." Chopp believed that for the "common good" to exist, Americans need "a change of heart and a change of mind" to "correct our ways."[3] William Murnion critiques the bishops' "creative dialogue" concerning the free market economy. In contrast to Chopp's call for moral conversion, Murnion faults the bishops' refusal to champion a more overtly socialist response to economic justice. He describes the economic pastoral's "theology of the preferential option for the poor" as "an ideology in support of the convergent interests of the majority of the Catholic laity, of the American system, and of liberal capitalism."[4]

James Heft, S.M., uses the mixed responses to the U.S. episcopacy's pastoral letters on war and economic justice as an entrée into a different arena of the debates, that of "non-infallible teachings." Heft outlines the possibility of "episcopal conferences" having authority to "exercise a *mandatum docendi*" that lies between the teaching authority of the local ordinary and that of the pope and bishops together. In drafting these letters, the U.S. bishops seemed to appreciate the authority in the *sensus fidelium*, exemplified in their broad-based consultations. The "new dialogical mode" clearly admits to a fallibility of conclusions and "is perplexing for those who prefer their bishops to speak in absolute ways or to remain silent."[5]

The right for other teaching authorities, i.e., theologians, to engage in the "new dialogical mode" through public dissent from "non-infallible teaching" stood at the heart of the controversy between the Congregation for the Doctrine of Faith (CDF) and Charles Curran. Curran's dismissal, as already noted, carried great symbolic weight among Catholic theologians. The resolution of the controversy served as foreground and background for CTS discussion of canon 812 concerning *mandatum* for theologians and intensified anxiety over theologians' future in the academy and the church. In the 1986 annual volume, *Theology and the University*, Charles Curran provided his account of the Congregation for the Doctrine of the Faith's investigation. Initiated in 1979, the investigation concluded in 1986 when Joseph Cardinal

Ratzinger informed Curran that he could no longer "'exercise his function as a Professor of Catholic Theology.'" Curran's written account, based on a 1986 convention plenary address, became an occasion to see the remarkable development in theologians' understanding of their work in the church, the academy, and the wider society since the Society's founding in 1954. The five salient points Curran identifies in his own situation are "the role of the theologian, the possibility of public theological dissent from some noninfallible, hierarchical church teachings, the possibility and right of dissent by the Christian faithful, the justice and fairness of the process, and academic freedom for theology and Catholic institutions of higher learning." The focus on dissent, academic freedom, and due process is striking in light of the members' questions concerning development of doctrine thirty years earlier.

Fr. Curran assumes a measured approach, invoking "creative fidelity" to describe the theologian's role. It allowed preservation "in its own time and place [of] the incarnational principle" and furthered the church's work of "bearing witness to the word and work of Jesus." Like "the majority of Catholic theologians," he views the theologian's position "as somewhat independent and cooperative in relationship to the hierarchical office and not delegated or derivative from the role of pope and bishops." The position requires recognizing "the teaching of the hierarchical magisterium" as one of the important "*loci theologici*," but not the only one. Only after these preliminary comments did Curran identify "the central issue" in his own situation. His case raised questions about "the possibility of public theological dissent from some noninfallible teaching which is quite remote from the core of faith, heavily dependent on support from human reason, and involved in such complexity and specificity that logically one cannot claim absolute certitude." Ratzinger would have probably described "the central issues" in very different terms.

Curran admits to inevitable "tensions" between bishops and theologians that require establishing "norms or criteria governing public dissent." The key for Curran was the academy as the theologian's principal site. Any norm must account for "being Catholic and being American" in higher education which requires affirming academic freedom. Though granting "due weight to the teaching of the hierarchical magisterium," a theologian establishes academic credibility through the judgment of "peers in the academy." Theological "errors and ambiguities" can be addressed by the "hierarchical magisterium" as they "deem it necessary" but can have no "direct juridical effect in the academy." Curran concludes with a warning to the complacent. "According to canon 812, teachers of theological disciplines need a mandate from a competent ecclesiastical authority. Thus the decisions of ecclesiastical authority can have a direct effect in the hiring, promotion, and dismissal of faculty members." The "Schema for Catholic colleges and universities" displayed a similar "structural understanding" though U.S. "Catholic leaders of higher education" strongly criticized the schema and canon 812.[6] Curran suggests that his fate may be only a precursor for more widespread removals.

James Heft, S.M., in an essay immediately following Curran's, also affirms that a "Catholic may dissent from noninfallible teachings," but notes that the practice of responsible public dissent remains undefined. Heft cautions that a responsible dissenter must be "docile, that is, has done his or her best to accept the teaching." Other theologians also bear responsibility for correcting their peers' errors—a task rarely done, according to theologians like Joseph Komonchak and John Boyle. Heft's tempered view of dissent was in the context of his confidence in "the *sensus fidelium*, or the 'sense of the faith,' possessed by the entire people of God." The "sense of faith" requires "laity, theologians and the bishops . . . to be docile, to be taught by the Lord, and to be led by the Spirit." Docility does not, however, preclude "speak[ing] with confidence about those matters within our competence, even though at times we may find it necessary to disagree in a responsible way with certain teachings not infallibly taught."[7] In a subsequent volume, Heft examines the intricacies of academic freedom and concludes again on a positive note. He invites Catholic institutions to reject the "ghetto" by remaining an "open circle," i.e., a "community of scholars who are committed to the Catholic tradition, and others who are committed to engaging it and the religious and moral issues raised by it and by modern society."[8] The "open circle" image is suggestive of the challenge for theologians trying to negotiate the complex relationship between fidelity to Catholic tradition and responsiveness to modern circumstances in the academy.

Heft might have found in the work of his colleagues at the University of Dayton justification for his confidence in the "sense of the faithful." Under "Charting a Nuanced Theological Course," Dennis Doyle, Michael Barnes, and Byron Johnson present survey results that indicate most Catholic theologians assent to basic Christian doctrine and most "people in the pew" have a more "nuanced" understanding of those same doctrines. William Shea challenged the sanguine interpretation, admitting no gap "between the desk and the pew" but rather "an abyss in the church between the old and new principles for theology."[9] This somber view appeared as an extension of that found in his presidential address from the same volume.

William Shea began his presidential address professing deep love for the Catholic Church. He conveyed this love with poignant recollections of his boyhood parish, St. Raymond's in the Bronx, his father at prayer, his serving at Mass, his formation in the seminary, both the uninspiring and the inspiring. The scripture scholar Myles Bourke provided the seminarian with an "intelligence and utter honesty in his approach to a text" that "woke me to the role that intelligence, free and dedicated, could play in the religious life." Shea also conjured less benign ecclesial images—specific incidents like two archbishops refusing to say Mass for leaders of women's religious congregations or John Paul II publicly rebuking Nicaraguan Ernesto Cardinale. He also invoked the church's long, bloody, and oppressive history recently manifested in such disparate events as the Holocaust and the suppression of intellectual life, including the teaching sanctions against Hans Küng and Charles Curran. Shea distributed the blame widely to include theologians.

The theologians, excepting birth control, have failed to respond "corporately with Rome, with our local hierarchies, with our local bishop" and now exist as "a politically marginal group in the church—utterly essential to the Catholic way of life and just as utterly powerless." Canon lawyers, by comparison, have recognized the need "to act politically in the church if the mountain is to be moved." Theologians must do the same, securing their discipline's autonomy if it is "to exist at all, in any university and even in any church." To assist in establishing this autonomy, Shea proposed organizing "an ecclesiastically independent national theological commission," funded and supervised by professional theology societies. It could serve the "individual theologian" as well as the "American bishops on issues and events bearing on academic freedom and theological responsibility." The commission would first compose a "statement of principles on freedom and responsibility for the use of bishops, university administrators, and theologians" and then offer a much needed collective "voice" for promoting "the intellectual and spiritual health of the church." CTS members passed Shea's resolution.[10] The short-lived Intersocietal Commission was the fruit of that suggestion.

TEACHING THEOLOGY:
EDUCATING FOR TRANSFORMATION

The CTS, despite tensions with church officials, maintained dialogue with willing bishops. In a section entitled "The Dreams and Vision of Leadership" are two essays: Archbishop Pilarczyk's "The Bishop as Pastoral Teacher: Implications for Theologians" followed by William Shea's previously described presidential address. Pilarczyk, recalling a Perry Como hit, asked the CTS members "to dream along with him"—a kind of "wouldn't it be nice" exercise, though without a nod to the Beach Boys. Pilarczyk hoped undergraduates who study theology have a firm grasp of "what the Church teaches in some depth and some detail," and that, through this study, they come to love the church, enough to serve "the Lord and the Church in the world." He acknowledged his echoing the Baltimore Catechism's answers on knowing, loving, and serving.[11]

Although Pilarczyk's dream for theology is far more explicitly ecclesial than that of most theologians featured in these volumes, many shared his hope for students transformed through their theological studies. Three examples must suffice. Father David Tracy offered the "Plato-Socrates" dialogue as a model for educating "the soul." In describing "Timaeus" as Socrates' credible "teller of tales," Tracy observed that the "curious combination of myth and dialectic in mutually critical correlation is an odd genre, to be sure: it is sometimes called theology." "Conversation" in theology involves "continuous searching of the Christian classics, especially the Bible" that encompasses "retrieval, critique, and suspicion." Tracy saw himself retrieving "how theological education began." Theology as conversation allowed not simply instruction in "values" and "character-formation" but also critical reflection on "the Christian soul as the subject-in-process of the Christian identity."[12]

Alice Gallin's emphasis on theology's integrative role in a liberal arts curriculum serves as the second example. Rejecting a replication of the 1950s' quest for integration, Gallin maintained that the discipline still has a critical role in the mission of a Catholic institution of higher learning. Accepting Father William Cenkner's "two constants" in theology: "'the interpretation of tradition, and the interpretation of contemporary experience,'" Gallin envisioned an integration inclusive of "exploration in other fields" that provides students the basis for creating "a better human community for the 21st century."[13]

William Portier recognized that Catholic colleges have been "born into a conversation which has been going on for centuries." In this context, "to think at all" requires being "active participants in that conversation. To think critically is to become systematically aware of that fact." This centuries-long conversation seeks "ultimately the integration of faith and reason," which thereby grants philosophy and theology a special role. Faculty in these disciplines offer "the public vocabulary or form of discourse in which the conversation about values can take place," so that their students acquire not only "methodological competence in their respective disciplines" but also an ability "to raise and answer the inevitable value questions of their disciplines from within the perspective of Christian humanism." In concluding, Portier argued that academic freedom frequently functions as an "empty absolute," a defense of "critical thinking . . . as an end in itself," which he contrasted to the medieval *disputatio*, whose participants engaged in critical inquiry confident in truth's ability to withstand every scrutiny.[14] The visions of Tracy, Gallin, and Portier make clear that dreams of theology's transformative role remained a part of the Society's conversations.

Sandra Schneiders offered another theological venue for transformation—the academic study of spirituality. Drawing upon her sixteen years of experience as founder and director of "a Ph.D. program in Christian Spirituality at the Graduate Theological Union in Berkeley," Schneiders described an "anthropological approach" that relies upon an "inter-disciplinary, cross-cultural, and inter-religious methodology." The academic approach does not, however, preclude the scholar's engagement in spiritual practice. Schneiders "doubt[s] that anyone who is not involved in her or his own spiritual life will have the insight and sensitivity to the subject matter necessary for first-rate research in the field of spirituality." In fact, the dedicated scholar of spirituality often experiences "the transformative effects of deeper understanding in her or his own spiritual life." The effects are indirect since neither ought to be the "direct objective of the academic study of spirituality" and the spiritual formation ought not to be conflated with the academic approach.[15]

Theology received a different kind of scrutiny from Catholic women engaged in transforming the discipline to ensure the students' transformation. Jane Kopas agreed with Catherine LaCugna's wry observation that exclusion from ordination gave Catholic women an opportunity to focus on theological work that "has proven to be revolutionary in its own way." In this case, Kopas considered developments "in theological anthropology" that certainly challenge official Catholic theological anthropology as in *Inter Insigniores* but has even "moved beyond mere gender issues. They have envisioned the body more holistically, recognized that culture creates gender, challenged the sharp distinction between male autonomy and female relationality, re-integrated theology and ethics, and gravitated toward the metaphor of transformation as a sign of inclusivity."[16] In the thirty-ninth volume, *Broken and Whole: Essays on Religion and the Body*, the editors, Maureen Tilley and Susan Ross, as if to pick up where Kopas leaves off, assured the "gentle reader" that choosing "Religion and the Body" for the 1993 convention theme is "no disengagement from the intellectual life, no retreat into sentiment and sensuality." In fact, "controversial religious issues in Catholicism are all issues of embodiment: women's ordination, priestly celibacy, abortion. Authority is primarily in relationship to body issues."[17]

Ann O'Hara Graff, as if to prove Kopas' point and operationalize Tilley's and Ross's observations about authority, described an internationalized process of "ecclesial discernment" that is practically organized around local churches and ever mindful of the incarnational character of Christian belief. "My vision is that local churches might come together in regional areas to discern together, and that the Vatican might become a center of international ecclesial discernment, challenge and support." In this discernment process, "local churches" might experience being "both one and catholic" through "the commerce of conversation about the narratives and symbols we all share" in and through "the necessary mediation of our constructed cultural and social worlds, which continue to interpret, and be interpreted by, the central narratives and symbols of Christianity." Such an inclusive discernment process provides "experiential starting places" that span the globe, even as the discernment begins in the local churches.[18]

Several entries in the fourth decade's volumes feature theologians looking for new "experiential starting places" to foster a transformative experience. Perhaps none so dramatically illustrate this wanderlust as Matthew Fox. In "Creation Mysticism and the Return of a Trinitarian Christianity," he identifies "at least nine ways" for theology to transform itself in response to "the ecological crisis of our time." The key to all nine is engagement in cosmological reflection since it generates new understanding of mysticism, leading to new images of God and thus new ways of relating to God. Changed views of God call for different worship practices, a deeper engagement in eros, "earthiness," new approaches to "justice and compassion," including receiving the wisdom offered by "people of color and people of the land," and an education of the young that brings hope.[19]

Apparently not as enthusiastic about transforming theological discourse as he proved to be about transforming society, the respondent, J. Patout Burns, first transposed Fox's "message into another form of discourse, the more formal language of the academy," to allow discussion "at least by the likes of us." According to Burns, Fox exhorted his listeners to "recognize the error of Platonic theism, cast off the chains of an anthropocentric fall-redemption theology, and embrace this creation centered spirituality" resulting in a "mystical sense of interdependence and thereby inspire an ecologically sound economy and life-style." Burns found neither in scripture nor in tradition support for the concept of a "living cosmos" or a "Cosmic Christ" Christian. He judged Fox's position not only theologically groundless but "impotent in the face of contemporary social and ecological problems." By way of ending on a hopeful note, Burns appeals to a unicorn of sorts, the rhinoceros, "an apt symbol for the Christian belief of God living and working in human history and society" in the "mysticism of the church as the Body of Christ and the living Temple of the Holy Spirit." This "sacrament of God's presence" might prove useful in "a renewed mysticism of the church and indeed of human culture or society" not only because of its symbolic power but also because "we have some evidence for believing that it might be true."[20] Whether Burns's response was the corrective among theologians that Heft had in mind, those who attended the talk probably recall that his comments were not entirely welcomed by Matthew Fox or his ardent supporters. Its impact, at least on Matthew Fox, appeared to have been negligible as suggested by reliable reports of a very contentious breakfast conversation prior to his departure for the airport. Despite Burns's strong challenge to Fox, both shared an assumption that theology has the power to mediate transformation.

READING SCRIPTURE—BEYOND
THE HISTORICAL CRITICAL

Across the volumes, many essays seeking new perspectives in Catholic theology drew upon the biblical narrative though rarely featuring a strictly historical-critical exegesis of a text. Most often scripture, as Christianity's normative text, provided a narrative framework for theological reflection. William McInerny, for example, made explicit his intention to use "biblical stories" to develop "paradigmatic construals" that engage the "creative moral imagination" in the "formation and development of moral character." He borrowed from Walter Rauschenbusch, who used such "paradigmatic construals" in developing his theology of the Social Gospel. In the contemporary context, the method allowed one "to incorporate critical, historical exegesis but . . . to go beyond the results of that kind of analysis."[21]

Most essays used scripture as a normative resource in addressing contemporary theological questions. Rev. Richard Dillon examines the term authority, *exousia*, in the New Testament and concludes that "*authority* means *freedom*." This charism-based authority contrasts with contemporary appeals to "the teaching of the Church"; charismatic authority "cannot be kept under control by the institution." In particular, the charism of "*critical intelligence*"— the charism of "the Church's prophets, teachers, even theologians"—encourages asking "does this teaching or discipline really pertain to the core of the gospel?" Such a gift proves "the most troublesome, and the most unwelcome at chancery and curia."[22]

Dillon was hardly alone in finding important lessons in scripture for contemporary theological concerns. In his essay, "The Historical Relativity of Jesus' Experience of God," Bernard Cooke offers an optimistic assessment of "the careful and extensive scholarly work of the past century" that provided a more complete "knowledge of [Jesus] as he actually was." Cooke focuses on Jesus's experience beyond the "prior unstructured and immediate exposure to the reality of God as his ABBA" to consider it "*at the level of structured understanding* quite limited and relativized by his Jewish culture." To comprehend more fully what Jesus learned of God from prior experience and what he learned from the culture requires not only academic study but also "prayer and contemplation and experience of liturgy." Cooke understood such a process of comprehension to lead toward an awareness of "God's self-giving to humans" that exceeds "even Jesus' experience." His expansive vision moves into the deeper level of Jesus's experience to encompass "the entirety of human history."[23]

Alice Laffey contributed two essays featuring liberationist-advocacy readings of scripture that highlighted the limits of historical-critical methods. In the 1988 essay, "A Liberation Perspective: Patriarchy, Monarchy, and Economics in the Deuteronomistic History," Laffey's reading overtakes the "paradigm of domination-subjugation with the paradigm of interdependence-mutual respect." Such a reading was possible since "there is no 'objective meaning' in a text apart from its reader/interpreter." The much-touted "historical criticism" is now recognized as a product of "the Enlightenment, which was the historical milieu of the historical critics."[24] A 1991 essay espouses the biblical demand that readers "must remember their experience of being that stranger and, consequently therefore, love the 'strangers' in their midst and treat them with equality; whether the stranger is Palestinian, or gay or lesbian, or elderly, or African or African-American, or female, or a victim of AIDS, or a refugee, or a parolee, or a combination thereof."[25] Biblical studies here serve a purpose beyond simply a close textual analysis.

John McCarthy, like Laffey, followed a postmodern cue though he focused on the hermeneutics that guide biblical interpretation. In one essay, he utilizes postmodern literary criticism to read the Gospel narrative, particularly Mark's account of the Eucharist and resurrection in which the name Jesus "recedes" and the pronoun (he) "takes precedence." He found in the narrative's gaps a "transformed presence, a presence that disrupts the expectations of personality" and elicits "new readings" of the "character of Jesus."[26] In the volume on fundamentalism, McCarthy produces a "fundamentalist biblical hermeneutics" to provide a basis for a "more fruitful exchange with critical biblical scholarship." Fundamentalists rely upon a "hermeneutics of trust" in the Bible as "the inspired Word of God." Trust, as distinct from "certainty," can prevent "premature closures to the truth of the text and a betrayal of the trust and hope demanded" in interpreting the text.[27] Whether the fundamentalist's trust could be extended to the biblical scholar was left to others to discover.

Ann Clifford also engaged the fundamentalist perspective to delineate more clearly the fault lines between a fundamentalist perspective and the historical-critical, social-scientific approach to scripture and religious commitment in general. She characterizes "creation science" as "a popular, positivistic model of science [combined] with a simplistic Biblical religion." Science also received a negative assessment for venturing beyond its scope "into a speculative world view and humanistic faith with its own quasi-religious myths." Fundamentalists, just like their scientific rivals, seek "to actively participate in and shape our academic culture." Clifford pleads for dialogue between the mainline denominations and the fundamentalists in the hope that mainlines might recognize how their accommodation leads to moral relativism, and fundamentalists might realize a more nuanced position on creation and science.[28]

CTS members also considered the different relationships Christians and Muslims have to their sacred texts. William Cenkner, O.P., describes a meeting with "two Muslim educators from Egypt" in which they conversed about scripture's role in their respective traditions. "Long before our visitors left it was clear to me that as 'People of the Book' my understanding and use of scripture was significantly different from theirs. It demonstrated to me the distinction between a recitation experience and a narrative experience." Cenkner then explores what an interreligious dialogue requires including a description of "the other that the other recognizes as true" and an appreciation of the how "the other" experiences "the mystery of God."[29]

Elizabeth Newman, member of CTS and NABPR, explores the "narrative experience," in considering whether one can claim "'God was in Christ reconciling the world to himself' in ways comparable to declaring 'E=MC^2 or 2+2=4?'" In developing her argument, Newman quotes Joshua Lederberg, a scientist, whose discovery came when he imagined himself to be "one of the chemical pieces in a bacterial chromosome." The use of both the mathematical formula and biblical statement is rooted in our "incorporation of particular stories and metaphors drawn from a deep and complex linguistic and cultural history." Both speak to "what is and is not the case" because both "speak forth worlds in which we live and dwell, the full reality of which depends on our responsibly laying claim to those worlds. When we imagine otherwise, then a picture has indeed held us captive."[30] The varied approaches to scripture are striking if one considers the uncertainty that greeted David Stanley when he introduced SCCTSD members to form criticism not even three decades earlier. Yet, in this volume, the Biblical texts appear in some sense more central as source and norm of every Christian narrative.

HISTORY AS THEOLOGICAL ENTERPRISE

Historical studies prove to be another rich repository on almost any convention theme. No volume is without historical essays; several include sections providing historical perspectives on the topic at hand. Historical investigation becomes a vehicle to explore theological alternatives. It functions somewhat like a thought experiment where fidelity to the tradition can be found in a variety of expressions. The systematician's viewpoint often turns to some forgotten resource that suggests the past "to be more open, dynamic, and pluralistic sort of inquiry than it frequently is presumed to be—by academics as well as ecclesiastical authorities."[31]

The opening essay in *Theology and the University* featured the noted historian of U.S. Catholicism, James Hennesey, S.J. In his essay, "The Scholar in the Church," he considers, quoting Walter Kasper, how "'we are experiencing a radical historicization of all reality,' marked by 'metamorphoses and developments in the church's pattern of faith' taking place 'not only in accordance with the laws of organic growth,' but proceeding 'by leaps and bounds, shifts, anticipations and retardations.'" Hennesey attributes many positives to historical research's effects. The "uses of history in the theological enterprise are many. Its service is to assist the community, its theologians, its leaders, to know more accurately, to sense more faithfully, what has been, down the centuries, the life, the thought and the worship of the Christian community, the 'tradition' on which Catholic Christianity places such reliance."[32]

As if to illustrate Hennesey's point, in the very next essay, Gary Macy provides a "case of theological diversity in the thirteenth and fourteenth century," concerning what "unbelievers and animals ate" in consuming consecrated bread and wine. Such medieval notables as Alexander of Hales, Peter Lombard, Albert the Great, Bonaventure, and Thomas Aquinas offered diverse opinions on the issue. None was condemned. Macy observes that the disagreements demonstrate that "the history of theology is at its best a history of toleration and diversity; and even such disputed issues as the real presence have a tradition of more breadth than a narrow reading of post-Reformation theology would lead one to believe."[33] In the next essay, Lillian Bozak-DeLeo retrieves an alternative to Anselm's soteriology from Julian of Norwich, whose image of "a God of love who is involved with us as a mother is with her own child, corresponds much more closely to current theological emphases."[34] Macy's and Bozak-DeLeo's emphasis on diversity brings their medieval sources into contemporary conversations.

The volume on economics contains two essays that illustrate two other basic historical approaches to theological exploration. The first traces a specific intellectual movement over time. In an overview of Adam Müller's "Romantic-Catholic Response to Modern Economic Thought," Paul Misner identifies Müller among the Catholic "pioneers" who, "with a mixed record of insight," identified "some intrinsic flaws in economic liberalism."[35] William L. Portier sought to understand "the context of a thinker's concrete subjectivity in all its dimensions." In this case, Portier provides a "social and economic portrait" of John R. Slattery as a necessary prelude for understanding his missionary work with emancipated slaves and the Modernist trajectory of his thought that eventually led to his leaving Roman Catholicism."[36]

The early church frequently provided the theologian with alternative traditions for adaptation in the contemporary context. Aaron Milavec looked to Origen to consider qualifications for the "office of the Bishop."[37] According to Milavec, the "bishops assembled during Vatican II" decided "to reintroduce the early patristic tradition wherein the episcopal office was principally ordained toward the service of studying, of teaching, and of exemplifying the Gospel of Jesus Christ." Milavec found in Origen an affirmation of such episcopal authority.

For others like Maureen A. Tilley, the early church provides a window onto Christian practices, sometimes exotic and other times familiar. One essay explores the "early Christian attitude toward the natural world" through stories of ascetics' relationships with animals. Lest the reader think such depictions are the quaint beliefs of benighted antiquity, Tilley compares them with contemporary tabloid accounts in which "animals have positive relationships only with good or innocent people" such as children. The "commonplace" of "Late Antiquity" linked ascetics with animals in their cooperating "to recreate Eden in this life."[38] In the volume on ethnicity, nationality, and religious experience, Tilley provides a detailed analysis of a third century (ca. 203 CE) written account of the martyrdom of Perpetua and Felicity, two North African Christian converts. The original story featured these two women's bodies as "the locus and instrument of holiness"—Perpetua as a nursing mother, Felicity in giving birth. Subsequent "ecclesiastical authorities" awarded both the identity of "virgin" concealing the redemptive dimensions of their maternal bodies. Tilley countered with an appeal to the heart of the tradition. "Salvation for Christians was and is in the body, the human body which hung on the cross."[39] Martyred mothers as much as virgins join in this embodied reception.

The nineteenth century serves as another historical locus especially concerning ecclesiastical authority. Jo Ann Eigelsbach characterized the nineteenth century as "a critical period for church authority as the Papacy struggled for power and identity in the social upheavals and political realignments of Europe." Wilfred Philip Ward, a "disciple of Newman and key English Roman Catholic writer and editor at the time of the Modernist Controversy," was her subject. In choosing Ward, Eigelsbach wanted to challenge the "romanticism" that perceives "the Early Church as a 'Golden Age.'" The essay explains how Ward's historical approach to "authenticity" in ecclesiastical authority allowed him to see an alternative to a "monarchy/anarchy model, more akin to 'syn-archy.'" Drawn from Matthew Lamb's work not Wilfred Ward's, "'Syn' here refers to 'pluralist cooperative' and 'arche' to 'principles.'" Reminiscent of Lamb's "syn-arche," Ward's work from the nineteenth century allows for the possibility of "responsible human freedom" in its principles of pluralist cooperation.[40]

The awakening of feminist consciousness refashions not only systematic theology as Jane Kopas described but also historical work. Essays display these effects in two distinct but interrelated ways. Margaret R. Miles's "new reading of Augustine's *Confessions*" exemplifies textual analysis "necessarily and inevitably directed by the specificity of my own social location as a late-twentieth century Anglo Saxon woman." The consequence in part was that her reading brings to light things that elude an ancient reader or even modern male reader. Miles notes this text's "role in the social construction of desire" as it carried forward "the gender socialization planted deeply in his [Augustine's] society and his own psyche," gave "theological validation to beliefs about women's and men's 'natures'" and thus renders a "female-gendered reading" as a "ravaging—rather than a ravishing—experience." She calls upon the reader to "take up Augustine's task of strenuous critique and reconstruction rather than his conclusions" and to "allow Augustine's intense vision of the Great Beauty to alert us to its presence" not above the mundane but "*within* the sensuous sensible world."[41]

Other essays recover women's theological agency in the midst of marginalization. Caritas McCarthy vividly describes the spirituality of Cornelia Connelly, foundress of the Sisters of the Holy Child. She had in her life an "affective, imaginative contemplation of Jesus in the Gospels," that fostered a "deeply incarnational spirituality." Adapting the *Spiritual Exercises*, Connelly "situated herself and her sisters, not on the Ignatian battlefield, but in the home, the garden and the school. Elements of the *Exercises* recognized today as inappropriate and even negative for women were apparently, in her misogynist era, overshadowed by their clearly positive effects."[42]

Maisie Ward provides a twentieth century exemplar of a theologically engaged woman. Dana Greene describes Ward with vivid language typified in the following two sentences. "As biographer, historian, preacher, teacher, social critic and activist Maisie Ward was Vesuvius-like—erupting in many directions, dynamic because she was connected through subterranean routes to a center which was vital. Like a volcano Maisie Ward changed a theological landscape and bedded down a rich lava soil from which new life and thought could grow."[43] Like Connelly, Ward's biography is not about a career but of a life responding to what lay before her.

The third example is Helen Marie Ciernick's historical review of women's presence at the Second Vatican Council—a presence that depended upon bishops who chose to respond to women's demands to participate. Ciernick writes, "By reconstructing—not recreating—women's history at Vatican

II, we see that the council becomes more fully an empowering moment in church history." Her reason for such a positive assessment came from demonstrating how "women moved beyond the roles prescribed for them by the council leaders. . . . They were active agents and not just passive victims." Their achievements in the face of resistance point to possibilities for women's "full participation" in the life of the church.[44]

Susan Marie Maloney examines the inadequacies of past histories of women's religious communities that have followed paradigms for histories of men's religious communities. Citing the work of Margaret Susan Thompson as a prime example, Maloney observes how feminist historians "give the feminist theologian new ground on which to construct a contemporary feminist theology of religious life." Such analyses eventually "reveal the universal struggle between clerical men and women religious: the contest for control and theological interpretation of the lives of women" as well as "uncover for the feminist scholar a rich theological source of pre-institutionalized commitment based in the practice and work of women religious."[45] Whether or not one agrees with Maloney's analysis, hers, like the other examples, highlight the role historical work has played in reshaping theological conversations as the twentieth century ended.

FUNDAMENTALISM, GLOBALIZATION, AND HISTORICIZING THE PRESENT

The immediate as much as the distant past receives historical analysis, coupled frequently with cultural and social analysis to shed light on contemporary phenomena. Even those religious expressions under a cloud of suspicion received a fair assessment from the College Theology Society. From the thirty-fifth annual meeting (1989) came an annual volume bearing the provocative title, *The Struggle Over the Past: Fundamentalism in the Modern World.* The essays viewed "fundamentalism" from multiple perspectives, critical in their assessment without forgoing a surprisingly irenic tone.

The volume's editor, William Shea, identifies two dangers that he hoped "the essays here escape. The first is the long-standing anti-fundamentalist bias of the academic community." The other is the long-standing animosity between Catholics and evangelical Protestants, among whom fundamentalists are a subgroup. Shea even suggests a certain affinity between Catholics and evangelicals in their interrogation of "modernity." Both groups share a "common unease" as they encounter "conditions that destroy community, weaken belief, eviscerate hope, undercut values, eliminate faith and trust, shred texts, corrupt freedom, water the milk of human kindness, and transmute culture into a playground for pornographic and lupine human imagination." Shea disparages "the secularist academic mill" where one witnesses the "objectification" of a "living tradition" and attests to knowing "first hand a variety of victims of what those academics call progress." Shea acknowledges a "sense of communion" with Muslims as well who have experienced the political and cultural exploitation that "Westernized political leadership" has wrought.[46]

R. Scott Appleby's opening essay in the volume presents religious fundamentalism as a worldwide phenomenon and serves as an implicit defense of the international scope of the "Fundamentalism Project" that he and Martin Marty had just begun. Appleby provides a masterful analysis of an array of Muslim, Jewish, Hindu, Sikh, as well as Christian movements. All have religious identities that are intertwined with militant resistance to modernity in its economic, social, cultural, and political forms. Fundamentalists adhere to an apocalyptic worldview in which "God has a plan and a blueprint for society" to which believers must commit themselves absolutely. Appleby cautions against underestimating fundamentalists' sophistication. They "are shrewdly selective, namely, in their evaluations and appropriations of modernity." Hardly "naifs: they know how the game is played, and they play it with increasing sophistication. Drawn from the university educated middle and upper middle classes, many have backgrounds in engineering and the sciences."[47] Appleby speculates on whether gaining political power will mitigate their extremism. While a possibility, it is not the inevitable outcome.

John Esposito's essay on Islam, that immediately follows Appleby's, illustrates the ongoing academic debates concerning the term "fundamentalism." He refuses to use "the term fundamentalism as too laden with Christian presuppositions and western stereotypes as well as implying a unity that does not exist" and opts for "revival (*tajdid*) and reform (*Islah*)." The worldview, as Esposito describes it, specifies Islam as a total way of life inclusive of political and social spheres, replacing Western civil law with Islamic law. Esposito emphasizes variety, experimentation, and development in Islamic revival, and, like Appleby, notes that "the leadership of both moderate and radical Islamic organizations are not uneducated, anti-modern reactionaries." Muslim activists, mostly laity, often "combine traditional backgrounds with modern educations at major national universities and international centers of learning."[48]

Three Protestant scholars offer their analysis of American forms of Protestant fundamentalism that extended well beyond biblical interpretations. Samuel S. Hill presents an overview of "the Spirit of Fundamentalism" in terms of what remains consistent. What perdures is a commitment to "truth" as "order, orderly, and ordered. It is not ambiguous or subjective or relative."[49] Bernard Ramm describes the fundamentalist "ethos," i.e., its "spiritual formation" in terms of a "devotional approach to Scripture" and "moral seriousness" with dangers coming from its legalistic tendencies, forgetfulness of Christian history as resource, and its overly simplistic assessment of the human person.[50] E. Glenn Hinson offers a prescient analysis in fundamentalism's resistance to "world consciousness" with a defense of America as "God's chosen nation" in the cold war context. He warns against "underestimat[ing] either the appeal or the peril in the nationalistic vision of the New Christian Right." Their issues are "close to the soul of American public life." Their solutions appear "reassuring to a vast number of thoughtful people, people who would again like to believe their country is at least as moral as they are privately."[51]

The fundamentalism volume followed its consideration of its American Protestant form with a section on "Fundamentalism and Catholicism." Francis Schüssler Fiorenza examines the challenges fundamentalism poses to theology as "both an expression of modernity and a reaction to modernity." Fiorenza refrains from providing a simplistic definition of Catholic fundamentalism that exchanges papal authority for scripture and Marian apparitions for premillennial expectations. Roman Catholic fundamentalists, located in the longer history of integralism, criticize selected papal teachings. In the essay's conclusion, Fiorenza notes the gap between academic theology and "the religious needs of popular culture" and acknowledges the legitimacy of popular religious concerns.[52]

The sociologist William Dinges emphasizes the difficulty distinguishing "Catholic fundamentalists" from their Protestant counterparts and other Catholic conservatives. As "a religious response to modernity, . . . Fundamentalism is also an innovative response to change." It fosters "a world-view orientation or habit of mind" that "manifests a highly cognitive, doctrinal form of religiosity characterized by exaggerated objectivism, by tendencies toward literalism and dogmatism, and by an elitist and exclusivistic ecclesiology." Lefebvre served as his example of Catholic Fundamentalism, a "schismatic conservatism" convinced in its own truth and willing to forgo charity for ideological convictions.[53]

In *Ethnicity, Nationality and Religious Experience* (1991), the editor, Peter C. Phan, turns to the contemporary situation with a historically minded focus on troubling world events, the Gulf War resulting from Iraq's invasion of Kuwait, "the doomed insurrection of the Kurds," the interethnic conflicts in the former Yugoslavia, the Middle East peace conference, and the Soviet Union's dissolution into distinct states. In light of "the new ethnic, national, and global conflicts,"[54] Robert Schreiter provides an overview of "Ethnicity and Nationality as Contexts for Religious Experience." "Ethnicity" in a postmodern world is "not a stage on the way to assimilation and modernization" but "often a protest against it"—an alternative to relinquishing "sources of identity for a dubious and even withheld mess of pottage." Religious expression and experience can foster ethnic identity through its "sense of community, moral authority and meaning." In its attempt to use religion, the nation-state "must worry constantly about evincing patriotism from its citizens" as well as "fear the subversive side of religion."

Schreiter warns against oversimplifying globality and its effects, given that "global culture has no context and no memory." The "religious experience" of the postmodern context may include "nostalgia" and a kind of postmodern baroque. For Roman Catholics, the sense of the ironic may serve as an alternative response—"more than our life vest"—especially for "non-Hispanic Roman Catholics" adapted to the "modernist mainstream" but discovering they actually travel "on the uncharted waters of postmodernity." Such a discovery may awaken a renewed "appreciation for ritual, myth, and the textuality of our stories without reverting to a simple romanticism." As a consequence of this renewed appreciation, Roman Catholics may come to a religious perspective in which "ethnicity, nationality and globality intertwine."[55] Such a perspective introduces a whole new set of challenges to theological work.

THEOLOGICAL TRAJECTORIES: LONERGAN, RAHNER, AND THEIR ALTERNATIVES

The legacy of Bernard Lonergan's and Karl Rahner's thought worlds remains evident throughout this decade's set of volumes. What is especially striking is the variety of contexts in which these mid-twentieth century "transcendental Thomists" serve as key referent points in late twentieth-century theology given its ever-expanding scope. Andrew Tallon relied on both Rahner and Lonergan to consider a more theoretical theological influence of "affectivity in ethics." Lonergan's understanding of "faith" as "'knowledge born of love'" confirms the centrality of the affective in ethical practice—practice that transcends knowing and willing when guided by a heart transformed by "God's gracious gift of Self in love."[56]

Rahner's thought has a wide range of other, more specific applications. Ronald Modras uses Karl Rahner's theological anthropology to place in relief the distinctive qualities of John Paul II's "anthropological starting point" and its implications for fashioning "economics and the social order." Wojtyla's "Thomistic personalism," according to Modras, leads to the pope's overemphasis on sexual ethics, self-control, and subordination. These emphases prove problematic "with regard to their respective implications for economic and the social order," especially when compared to Rahner's linking of love of God and neighbor.[57] Peter Phan also appeals to Karl Rahner's thought. He relies upon Rahner along with Thomas Aquinas, and the apophatic tradition to provide an image of God that contrasts with the fundamentalist image of "the God of Power and Might," knowable through the Bible. According to Phan, "the fundamentalist option for a strong national defense, law and order, and 'traditional family' reflects a view of God as all-powerful and all-knowing, patriarchal and dominant." The alternative view acknowledges God as "'Holy Mystery; we only know what God is not, but God's incomprehensibility *is* our blessed happiness.'"[58] Peter Phan also examines Karl Rahner's "dialogues with Judaism and Islam," especially since his engagement in dialogues with Jews and Muslims began long before it was "fashionable" and when in fact it was somewhat risky.[59]

Lonergan also has his share of disciples. William Shea invokes Bernard Lonergan's vision of education, the "constructing a world of meaning and value," combines it with John Dewey's education for a democratic society, to construct a "civic and ecclesial life" that moves "beyond tolerance." Shea found a "splendid example of this behavior in the American bishops' pastorals on peace and the economy," letters which are "clearly public in their intent, their temper, and their rationale, and consequently open to disagreement and the criticism of Catholics and others."[60] Cynthia Crysdale relies upon Bernard Lonergan's extensive treatment of conversion as inclusive of the subjective, cognitive, and affective dimensions to provide a case study of a young woman, "Sandra," whose experience of conversion through a Christian fellowship only began her Christian development.[61]

If Lonergan and Rahner are the "go-to" theologians, Stanley Hauerwas and his allies frequently serve as the point of contrast in several CTS essays. When James Donahue explores various theological frameworks as possible sources for environmental ethics, he excludes "confessionalists like Hauerwas" as being "unable to support an adequate environmental ethic" because "*at least in principle* [his thought] *is incapable of interrelatedness with other and all narratives.*" He identifies the work of Wendell Berry, Kathleen Fischer, and Philip Keane as possible resources.[62] Leonard Weber, in his "Public Policy: Reflections on the Role of Ethics and Ethicists," asserts that uncompromising "religious ethicists" have little effect on "public policy debates if they are constantly stressing the specifically Christian nature of our ethical beliefs." Weber identifies his position as neither like Hauerwas's nor Neuhaus's but akin to that in the Economic Pastoral Letter of the Bishops.[63] In the ethical considerations of "Ethnicity, Nationality, and Religious Experience," Sally

Ann McReynolds defends Paul Ricoeur's "theory of narrative approach" as surpassing those of Stanley Hauerwas, James McClendon, and Alisdair MacIntyre as a resource for Catholic ethics. She seeks a challenge to prejudice through a narrative that encourages conversion in stimulating the "metaphoric imagination."[64]

LIBERATING THE "OTHER": A WORLD MOVEMENT

Paul Knitter introduces the 1988 volume, *Pluralism and Oppression* with a call to CTS members to "get out of their backyards" so they might become more effective as contemporary theologians in a discipline now requiring an international awareness. "The *totaliter aliter* (totally other) is the *totaliter necessarium* (utterly necessary) for the job of being Christian and doing theology." The "other" is defined against white, male, economically privileged, educated in the West, and so on. From their privilege comes power to erase pluralism through colonizing, hence Knitter's choice of "oppression" as the companion concept to pluralism for this volume. "Only if we respect and nurture our differences and at *the same time* maintain our oneness through relatedness—only so can we have life and have it more abundantly." The producers of the volume—"the essayists, the blind readers of the 38 originally submitted manuscripts, the translators, the typists, and the editor—could ask for no greater reward."[65]

The preferential option for the poor beckons the liberation theologian into the world of the "other." In reflecting on "Theology in a Suffering World," Jon Sobrino imagines liberation theology as *intellectus amoris*, a theological knowledge born out of compassion, that "integrates and retrieves—but in a more radical way what is contained in theology understood as *intellectus fidei* and *intellectus spei*." He insists upon distinguishing the theology done within the context of "suffering" from that of cultural diversity and religious plurality considered in other sections of *Pluralism and Oppression*. Suffering reflects "the real world as such," and these "real world" dimensions lend a certain poignancy as well as power to Sobrino's analysis. He refers, for example, to his soon-to-be martyred Jesuit confrere I. Ellacuria's description of theology as "the ideological moment of ecclesial and historical praxis" where praxis is "understood as love, service, justice." Theology, Sobrino explains, comes to its own truth "in the crucified peoples of this world." The poor become the evangelizers of theologians in helping them "to realize (not just conceptualize) the realities fundamental to theology: real faith and hope, real Gospel values, and something that has often required of the poor their very lives—real love. Here we have the ultimate mediation of the truth about God and the truth about humanity."[66] The essay conveys its challenging vision of theology with a tone of genuine humility.

Susan Brooks Thistlethwaite takes a decidedly different tone in her fundamentally positive response to Sobrino's address. She brings a feminist liberationist reading to the talk and to the situation, calling upon women's anger rather than compassion and mercy, which have too often masked the domination of women. She demands of her audience recognition of "where in your social location is justice struggling to be born" followed by a practical answer to the question "how can you help."[67]

The thirty-fourth annual volume includes still another liberationist perspective. Argentinian-born Enrique Dussel directly addresses the thorny issue of Marxist influence on liberation theology. Offering a historical perspective, Dussel recalls how Christian theologians, like Thomas Aquinas, have always borrowed from their philosophical contemporaries. John Paul II's encyclical *Laborem Exercens*, "like liberation theology, uses Marxist categories in the same way that Saint Thomas used Aristotle." Dussel predicts that like Aquinas's thought, "the prophetic calls of liberation theology will be passed on as the 'common' and 'long established' beliefs of Christianity."[68] Making John Paul II an ally in this prophetic mission certainly made its identity as "common" seem possible if not probable.

William Portier offers another surprising pairing. He identifies "solidarity" as a practical site of common ground between two approaches usually considered at odds—the "contextual approach" of Edward Schillebeeckx's "*mysticism* and *politics*" and the "concrete anthropological approach" of Joseph Cardinal Ratzinger's "integral salvation." Schillebeeckx seeks "to overcome the dualism (between the private or spiritual and the public or political)" by fostering a "political holiness" arising out of a "love of God and love of neighbor," a "political love" linked to a "'spirituality of solidarity with the poor.'" Joseph Cardinal Ratzinger's "concrete anthropological approach" appeals to an "integral salvation" which can also be transformed into concrete "'political love'" through solidarity with the poor. Despite the disparate starting points in these two theologies, solidarity provides a point of unity against those definitions from "secular culture" that "divide the church according to its political categories" rather than theological commitments.[69] Taken together, these essays highlight in their variations the wide-ranging developments and creativity in liberation theology from Sobrino's *intellectus amoris* to Thistlethwaite's feminist anger to Dussel's Marxist analysis to Portier's "spirituality of solidarity with the poor."

COSMOS AS THEOLOGICAL STARTING POINT

Thomas Berry's site of solidarity is not human communities but the cosmic community. For Barry, the critical issue is fashioning religious expression commensurate with contemporary awareness of the universe's evolutionary story—cosmogenesis. In this context, the human rather than the earth is "derivative." Though no model exists, the one emerging "within the context of a spatial model of consciousness" must include "the perspective of a time-developmental mode of consciousness." Berry identified the Eastern religious traditions as the best sources currently available for such a model.[70]

Drawing from ecofeminist insights, Rosemary Radford Ruether provides a brief historical overview of culture that shows "some of the symbolic connections of domination of women and domination of nature in Mediterranean and Western European culture." She also challenges the Western conceptualization of immortality that refuses to accept participation in "the disintegration side of the life cycle." Under the pretense of immortalizing "ourselves, souls and bodies, we are immortalizing our garbage and polluting the earth." What Radford Ruether envisioned is conversion from patriarchy to overcome an "alienated, hierarchical dualism to life-sustaining mutuality." Such a transformation would demand radical shifts in conceptualizing "God, soul/body and salvation" resulting in coming "much closer to the ethical values of love, justice and care for the earth . . . proclaimed by patriarchal religion, yet contradicted by patriarchal symbolic and social patterns of relationship."[71]

Two years later, in introducing the Society's thirty-sixth annual volume, bearing the evocative title, *An Ecology of the Spirit: Religious Reflections and Environmental Consciousness*, Michael Barnes confirms Berry's observation about lack of models. "For the Christian this ecology of the human spirit is also an ecology of the Spirit, which seeks to locate cosmos, earth environment, society, and self in relation to ultimate value and beauty and truth." Work on this "theological task" has only begun, and the CTS volume adds "to that work." What remains is the need for changing perspectives and new stories to account more adequately for an evolving ecology.[72]

H. Paul Santmire provides the first account in the volume. Referring to Henry David Thoreau and all those who assert Christianity's ecological bankruptcy, Santmire counters "that the kerygmatic and dogmatic traditions of Christianity are better equipped to guide the faithful in this global, ecological era than the much heralded primal religious traditions themselves." To make his point, Santmire draws upon Augustine's view of creation to demonstrate "how a biblically inspired, traditionally conversant, narrative of creation, fall, redemption, and fulfillment can be historically viable and ecologically relevant theological project in our time." This choice is particularly interesting, since those most associated with ecological theology, particularly Matthew Fox, have depicted Augustine as one of the most egregious examples of Christianity's ecological bankruptcy.[73]

John F. Haught provides an alternate account, appealing to the Christian tradition's "sacramentalism," grounding for a "positive attitude toward nature." For Haught, "sacramentalism" provides a response to the central theological question of reconciling the religious sense of cosmic homelessness with a genuine concern for ecological well-being. Not only religion but also "scientism" and "scientific materialism" can contribute to a sense of cosmic alienation. Haught turns to Whitehead's depiction of nature as "creatively restless" to suggest that the "cosmos itself" is "an adventure" with an "aim toward novel forms of order, or toward increasingly wider beauty."[74] Herein lies a resource for a "positive attitude toward nature."

The volume's final essay features Sally Kenel's examination of another theological conundrum—the relationship between nature and grace, though in this case, as "an ecological metaphor." Appealing to "the metaphor of the world as God's body,"[75] Kenel considers how "the world serves as the medium of divine communication." Borrowing from "Marshall McLuhan that the medium is the message," she describes "the world" as "God's self-communication. Or, to put it even more pertinently, nature is grace." Dissolving this duality "enables a strong affirmation of the principle of sacramentality" and undermines other dualities including "church-world, individual-social, spiritual-political, eternal-temporal, to name a few." Such reflections as these three suggest how a theology for an "ecological age" sometimes utilizes and other times challenges and transforms classical theological categories.[76]

CULTURAL AND RELIGIOUS DIFFERENCE AS THEOLOGICAL STARTING POINTS

Honoring biodiversity within a cosmos marked in its creation as interdependent has an analog in embracing cultural and religious diversity of a human family unified in its created dignity. The missionary impulse of Christianity precipitated cultural encounters that have not always produced positive effects. Jill Raitt, in her address, "Christianity, Inc." offers perspectives on "Christianity as a body that are both political and mystical." Corporate Christianity, without a doubt, had destructive effects on indigenous religions and cultures in its missionary efforts. Yet, "the corporate church, the body of Christ" also exists when "folks like us" enter "into the Easter liturgy to be forgiven and renewed." Through these corporate moments of healing grace, "Christianity incorporated can turn its face to the God . . . in the image of all peoples. . . . In the many ways of being human, the face of Christ becomes at once more particular and more universal." Theology has an opportunity to benefit from the riches offered by "feminist theologies, African-American theologies, ecological theologies, and indigenous theologies" in understanding Christianity in all its corporate diversity.[77]

Raimon Panikkar highlights the challenges and contradictions inherent in bringing Christianity into cultures with well-established religious traditions. He identifies three approaches: supracultural, i.e., above all cultures; supercultural, i.e., inextricably tied to a superior culture, or transcultural. Panikkar champions the third option which he identifies theologically with a "cross-cultural Christian principle" that permits "a healthy pluralism" and abides "within a genuinely historical and incarnational spirit." The revelation in Jesus Christ remains at its center. "*The christic event has an inherent dynamism to take flesh wherever it can.* This 'can' is *ambiguous, ambivalent,* and *not apodictic.*"[78]

Examples of transcultural Christianity are highlighted in two essays from different volumes. In *Pluralism and Oppression,* Caritas McCarthy illustrates how "several images and figures proper to African life and worship" assist the contemporary African to "approach the mystery of Christ more authentically." Among these images are Christ as "proto-ancestor," Christ as "Elder Brother," "Savior/Healer."[79] Peter Phan briefly describes contemporary Asian theology—noting its critique of Western theology, its liberationist framework, its "comprehensive socio-cultural analysis of the Asian situation," the available resources for theology, and "a theological reformulation of basic Christian doctrines." A single example among many is C. S. Song's Christology, which poses the question "whether Jesus has been waiting for the past two thousand years to hear something different about himself from the parts of the world now called Third World, especially Asia." Song's answer emerges from "the stories of suffering and oppression of Asian peoples" that he uses "to construct a christology from below which identifies Jesus with the crucified people, men, and women" in Asia.[80]

A key theological issue in any consideration of pluralism concerns how to understand the unique revelatory significance of Jesus as universal savior and the claims of Christianity's exclusive normativity. Gerald F. Finnegan reviews the central theological issues following from religious pluralism. "The pluralist position is truly pluralist. All faiths are denied the right to claim normative validity." Those who reject pluralism to defend "the uniqueness of the incarnation of God in Jesus" must develop "better and fuller explanations." On the metaphysical level, pluralists ultimately choose "multiplicity over unity, whereas those who accept the traditional understanding of Christian faith seem to presume that unity exists at a deeper level of reality, indeed at the deepest level, and multiplicity is a phenomenon which arises from it and returns to it in the end."[81] To convince others of this deeper unity is the task of those theologians "who reject pluralism."

Other authors offer specific theological strategies for interreligious dialogue that refrain from completely abandoning Christianity's exclusivist claims. Ralph Del Colle made "Spirit Christology" the context for dialogue between Christians and Jews, and Christians and Muslims.[82] Terence L. Nichols considers the problems posed by "social and religious pluralism" as a threat to the "common good." He proposes "a theology of non-Christian religions based on the notion of the catholicity of the Church," confirmed in Vatican II's implicit recognition "that authentic revelation is given within non-Christian religious traditions." Nichols then appeals to a "catholicity" which precludes simple rejection of "what is true and holy, and perhaps revealed, in other religions" even while maintaining the "uniqueness of the incarnation." Catholicity becomes "a creative tension between unity and diversity (pluralism)" and allows for establishing some commitments to the common good in areas like the environment.[83]

Gerard Sloyan, the editor of *Religions of the Book* (1992), notes the deep misunderstandings and mutual animosity among Jews, Christians, and Muslims. With his usual charming bluntness, Father Sloyan describes "200 members of the College Theology Society (founded 1954) [who] met over four days at Allentown College of St. Francis de Sales in May, 1992 to reduce their common ignorance. These papers convey something of their intellectual and human exchange, but necessarily little of the many fruitful conversations that followed from them."[84] Jewish, Christian, and Muslim scholars reflected concerns from the perspective of their own traditions.[85]

Susannah Heschel provides perspective on Judaism read through feminist critique articulated, at least in part, in Mary Daly's *Beyond God the Father*. Heschel describes "women's experience" as "marginalization" that she links to "the experience of alienation" that remains "central to Judaism." Unlike Christians, whose faith has at its center the resurrection, the triumph over sin, death, despair, Jews believe "the redemption has not yet come, and the state of exile remains."

Joseph Devlin, a Christian voice in the trialogue, focuses on the possibility of dialogue on behalf of "world transformation." He appeals to the powerful, shared conviction that recognizes "God's image in every human being" and calls believers "not to rule over others—even theologically—but to empower others." Drawing from Michael Barnes' article, "Christian Identity and World Pluralism—Religions in Conversation," Devlin describes possibilities for dialogue that emphasize commonality though he admits the "three traditions' 'absolutist' claims makes a dialogical approach extremely difficult."[86]

Mahmoud Ayoub focuses on the relationship between religious convictions and "socio-political and state relations." This Muslim scholar observes "that religion in the Middle East has always been, and remains to this day, not merely a set of beliefs, or even a theological system. It is rather the framework of socio-political identity: a culture and way of life, a communion of worship and liturgy." He also offers a starting point for building positive relationships. "The qur'_nic emphasis on the centrality of the Book could help Jews, Christians, and Muslims become for the first time the reconciled children of Abraham to become one happy family."[87] As with other examples, the expanded discussions around difference are striking in their serving as the starting point for theological conversation toward understanding.

WOMEN'S EXPERIENCES AS
THEOLOGICAL STARTING POINT

Certainly one of the most influential alternative theological sources over the past fifty years comes from "voices of women" who "help us reframe our theological questions and call forth life-giving metaphors." Evidence of this reframing appears in every section of this chapter. Phyllis Kaminski's introduction to *Women and Theology* bears the subtitle "Theology as Conversation," taking its lead from David Tracy's assertion that "conversation is a rare phenomenon." It bears a dialogic character that privileges open-ended questioning over debate or exam. A plurality of voices, including diverse women's voices, are a necessary part of any theological conversation. "If theological conversation is to thrive, then it must be fully opened to women and it must be cured of its systemic biases." Kaminski recognized the College Theology Society's long-term commitment to considering "the problem of women's exclusion and issues of gender requiring critical scrutiny. Indeed, it has regularly provided a discursive space for authentic theological conversation." The fortieth annual volume provides a partial record of that conversation that allows its readers to "reflect a wide spectrum of questions about women and about theology."[88]

M. Shawn Copeland provides a fitting opening essay for the volume. She examines the theologies of liberation that feminists have adopted with a particular focus on feminist theologians' "rhetoric of solidarity" in contrast to the practice of actual solidarity. She critiques "Celtic-, Anglo-, European-American feminists" who appeal to solidarity even though "they ignore, and sometimes, consume the experiences and voices of the marginalized and oppressed, while, ever adroitly, dodging the penitential call to conversion." Copeland then offers a brief history of feminist theology now in a "fourth phase that will require a turn, a conversion among all theologians to engage difference in the work toward authentic solidarity in word and in deed."

For Christian theologians, "solidarity is grounded in the confession of Jesus as Lord," which entails "standing before the Cross of Jesus of Nazareth yearning to grasp the enormity of suffering, affliction, and oppression; to apprehend our complicity and collusion in the suffering, affliction, and oppression of others." It also means embracing Eucharist as "the heart of the Christian community. *Women and men must do what they are being made*: there are social as well as sacramental . . . consequences to the Eucharist." Such participation makes possible recognizing the "other . . . as 'sister,' 'brother,' 'neighbor,'" a "solidarity in word and in deed."[89]

A panel organized around "hearing one another into speech" instantiated what Copeland described as a key first step. The convention plenary featured the diverse perspectives of Mary Rose D'Angelo, Kwok Pui-lan, María Pilar Aquino, and Anne Patrick. D'Angelo reflected on her struggle to recognize silences in her own work, especially of lesbians as scholars of the Bible and history and as subjects of those texts.[90] Kwok Pui-lan described Asian women's theology with an emphasis on the "multi-racial, multi-cultural, and multi-religious world" of Asia, that is the home of "over half the world's population." Concentrating on Christology, Kwok noted "the maleness of Jesus is a problem only if one is assuming a Chalcedonian, substantive understanding of Christ. . . . Asian feminist theologians find Jesus liberating not as a male, but as a person who led a particular way of life." In confronting the ecological crisis, she invited use of "theological imagination to speak of God's incarnated presence in the trees, the rivers, the birds, and the stones as well." Those in the third world believe the "old style of doing theology is morally bankrupt" given its use "to legitimate cultural imperialism and exploitation of our inhabited earth." Theology must concern itself with the poor and marginalized, an experience common to women across many cultures.[91]

María Pilar Aquino offered "the standpoint of Latina/Latin American women." After enumerating the ways in which first world "consumerism" wreaks havoc on "the majority of the world's population located in the South," Aquino, identifying herself with "Latina/Latin American feminists," described "a life-giving logic presided by the ethical and theological principles of justice, wholeness of life for all, the social and political recognition of each one's subjectivity, true autonomy and self-determination, integral development, effective participation and ecological equilibrium." Promoting "women's full human integrity" must be integral to this logic.[92] Anne Patrick offered "three steps for a praxis of solidarity": "*contextualizing the voices*," in their "complex relational setting," "*internalizing the voices*," "hearing them regularly in one's own self-talk," and "*harmonizing the voices*," granting "the challenging protests and demands to play over a ground bass, or even better, a ground alto, of God's healing and empowering and justice-making love for us all."[93] The panel demonstrates how intertwined liberation and feminist perspectives have become and their impact upon Christian theological discourse.

Phyllis Kaminski provided an example of the "open-ended questioning" of women doing theology as described in her introduction to the volume she and Mary Ann Hinsdale edited. She examined Julia Kristeva's "Stabat Mater" as indicative that this "theorist and critic of culture" may provide "hidden sources for the transformation of theological discourse." Kaminski offered a close reading of the text, noting even Kristeva's splitting of the text into two columns lead to deeper insights. The left column provides "an account of the speaker's physical and psychic impressions of the birth of her [Kristeva's] son", the right "traces the development of Marian doctrine." As Kaminski explains, "the split text obliges the eye to cross the space between the columns in order to grasp the whole. From a feminist perspective, the full page reproduces visually the split/whole folds of the labia. The two-columns that form one essay thus produce meaning that cannot be understood by a reader who seeks only the message of the words." The ultimate impact of "Kristeva's crossed voices suggest new possibilities for redeeming love" in "the mother-child dyad" as "a foundation for all social relation," though Kristeva does not "deal with concrete dilemmas in sexual morality, reproductive technology, or medical and social ethics." Kaminski identified in Kristeva's work a "theoretical framework from within which feminist theologians can continue to re-interpret the cross as 'part of the larger mystery of pain-to-life, of that struggle for the new creation evocative of the rhythm of pregnancy, delivery, and birth so familiar to women of all times.'"[94] Kaminski's claim places women's experience of giving birth at the Christian theological center point.

BUILDING FROM STRENGTH TO STRENGTH

The afterword in *Women and Theology* is the presidential address of Joan Leonard, who died of cancer shortly after the convention. She began with reflections on the struggles of women and others to find their place in the academy, in their institutions, in theological discourse and the ongoing difficulties for those marginalized and for the planet under siege and called upon the College Theology Society to consider six strengths on which to build. First the Society's "tradition of expansive hospitality" provides a context for welcoming "a more diverse membership." Second, the practice of theology as interpreting "tradition" and "contemporary experience" makes possible more "interdisciplinary work." Third, this "professional society values teaching and participation in a community of relationships with other persons, things and ideas." It attends to "the viewpoints and writings of women and persons from other cultures in our courses and professional meetings" and encourages "development of cooperative learning styles and . . . diverse ways of related knowing" including "a study of the new cosmologies and epistemology." The account of the last ten years of theology corroborates Leonard's observation.

The next three strengths relate to the Society's current organization and constituencies. The fourth rejects "old hierarchical ways of doing things" as unworkable and encourages utilizing "the best of what we have learned from our experience in cooperative, mutual ways of leading our society and organizing our society." The CTS can be a model of leadership that counters "professionalism, political correctness, competition, Vatican assaults on academic freedom, Cartesian dualism, objectivism, and business management–style administrators." Fifth, the Society ought to "embrace the challenge for ecumenical and interfaith dialogue" with special attention to encouraging "the increasing role of women as participants and leaders" who are "consistently underrepresented in leadership and all too often ignored for their contributions." Sixth is making concrete a "commitment to peace and justice" that is "a special mandate" for those engaged in theological studies, "to make real the biblical vision of justice and shalom," and to commit to "a renewed spirituality" that can "enable students to understand and make decisions both in the classroom and outside." Leonard wondered "whether we will achieve a theology that has the potential to bring about a renewed community of women and men in church, society, and academy."[95] If remaining fully engaged in the struggle is any indicator, then in the final ten years of its half-century history, the College Theology Society achieved more than Leonard could have imagined.

NOTES

1. Joseph F. Gower, "Introduction," in *Religion and Economic Ethics: The Annual Publication of the College Theology Society*, vol. 31, ed. Joseph F. Gower, (Lanham, MD: University Press of America, Inc., 1990), xiii, xv.

2. Douglas Sturm, "Economic Justice and the Common-Wealth of Peoples," in *Religion and Economic Ethics*, 7, 27, 31.

3. Rebecca Chopp, "Making the Poor the Rich: Rhetoric vs. Strategy in the Pastoral Letter on the Economy," in *Religion and Economic Ethics*, 268–269.

4. William E. Murnion, "The 'Preferential Option for the Poor' in *Economic Justice for All*: Theology or Ideology?" in *Raising the Torch of Good News: Catholic Authority and Dialogue with the World: The Annual Publication of the College Theology Society*, vol. 32, ed. Bernard P. Prusak, (Lanham, MD: University Press of America, 1988), 232.

5. James Heft, "Episcopal Teaching Authority on Matters of War and Economics," in *Religion and Economic Ethics*, ed. Joseph F. Gower (Lanham, Md.: University Press of America, 1990), 280, 283.

6. Charles E. Curran, "Authority and Structure in the Churches: Perspective of a Catholic Theologian," in *Raising the Torch of Good News*, 83–84, 93, 96, 97, 99, 100, 101.

7. James Heft, "The Response Catholics Owe to NonInfallible Teachings," in *Raising the Torch of Good News*, 109, 116, 120.

8. James Heft, S.M., "Academic Freedom and the Catholic Community," in *Theology and the University: The Annual Publication of the College Theology Society*, vol. 33, ed. John Apczynski, (Lanham, MD: University Press of America, 1990), 235.

9. Dennis Doyle, Michael Barnes, and Byron Johnson, "Pluralism or Polarization? The Results of a CTS Survey"; William M. Shea, "A Response"; and "Authors' Responses" in *Raising the Torch of Good News*, 275–286, 287–290, 291–296.

10. William M. Shea, "Theologians and Their Catholic Authorities: Reminiscence and Reconnoiter," in *Raising the Torch of Good News*, 269, 270, 271 272.

11. Most Reverend Daniel E. Pilarczyk, "The Bishop as Pastoral Teacher: Implications for Theologians," in *Raising the Torch of Good News*, 254–259 passim.

12. David Tracy, "Can Virtue Be Taught? Education, Character, and the Soul," in *Theology and the University*, 135, 145, 148.

13. Alice Gallin, O.S.U., "The Place of Theology in the Liberal Arts Curriculum of the Catholic College and University," in *Theology and the University*, 202–203.

14. William L. Portier, "The Mission of a Catholic College," in *Theology and the University*, 241, 250, 252–253, 254.

15. Sandra M. Schneiders, "Spirituality as an Academic Discipline: Reflections from Experience," in *Broken and Whole*, 207, 218.

16. Jane Kopas, "Beyond Mere Gender: Transforming Theological Anthropology," in *Women and Theology: The Annual Publication of the College Theology Society*, vol. 40, eds. Mary Ann Hinsdale and Phyllis H. Kaminski, (Maryknoll, NY: Orbis Books, 1995), 217, 229.

17. Maureen A. Tilley and Susan A. Ross, "Introduction: Embodied Religion," in *Broken and Whole: Essays on Religion and the Body: The Annual Publication of the College Theology Society*, vol. 39, eds. Maureen A. Tilley and Susan A. Ross, (Lanham, MD: University Press of America, 1995), vi.

18. Ann O'Hara Graff, "Ecclesial Discernment: Women's Voices, New Voices, and the Revelatory Process," in *Women and Theology*, 208, 212, 213.

19. Matthew Fox, "Creation Mysticism and the Return of a Trinitarian Christianity," in *An Ecology of the Spirit: Religious Reflection and Environmental Consciousness: The Annual Publication of the College Theology Society*, vol. 36, ed. Michael Barnes, (Lanham, MD: University Press of America, 1994), 62, 69–71.

20. J. Patout Burns, "The Unicorn and the Rhinoceros: A Response to Matthew Fox," in *An Ecology of the Spirit*, 75, 76, 77, 82.

21. William McInerny, "Scripture and the Social Order: 'Paradigmatic Construals' of Walter Rauschenbusch," in *Religion and Economic Ethics*, 247–248.

22. Richard J. Dillon, "Speaking of Authority and Charism from the New Testament," in *Raising the Torch of Good News*, 8, 9, 10.

23. Bernard Cooke, "The Historical Relativity of Jesus' Experience of God," in *Ethnicity, Nationality and Religious Experience: The Annual Publication of the College Theology Society*, vol. 37, ed. Peter C. Phan, (Lanham, MD: University Press of America, 1995), 51, 54, 55.

24. Alice L. Laffey, "A Liberation Perspective: Patriarchy, Monarchy, and Economics in the Deuteronomistic History," in *Pluralism and Oppression: Theology in World Perspective: The Annual Publication of the College Theology Society*, vol. 34, ed. Paul F. Knitter, (Lanham, MD: University Press of America, 1991), 224, 225.

25. Alice L. Laffey, "'Love the Stranger; Remember When You Were Strangers in Egypt,'" in *Ethnicity, Nationality and Religious Experience*, 43.

26. John McCarthy, "'What If Jesus . . . ?' Narrative Naming and Theological Reflection," in *Theology and the University*, 128, 129.

27. John McCarthy, "Inspiration and Trust: Narrowing the Gap Between Fundamentalist and Higher Biblical Scholarship," in *The Struggle Over the Past: Fundamentalism in the Modern World: The Annual Publication of the College Theology Society*, vol. 35, ed. William M. Shea, (Lanham, MD: University Press of America, 1993), 123, 131, 136.

28. Anne Clifford, C.S.J., "Creation Science: Religion and Science in North American Culture," in *The Struggle Over the Past*, 105, 114, 116, 119.

29. William Cenkner, O.P., "People of the Book: Basis for Muslim-Christian Dialogue?" in *Religions of the Book: The Annual Publication of the College Theology Society*, vol. 38, ed. Gerard S. Sloyan, (Lanham, MD: University Press of America, 1996), 119, 125, 126.

30. Elizabeth Newman, "E=MC² and 'God Was in Christ Reconciling the World to Himself': An Unbridgeable Chasm?" in *Religions of the Book*, 254, 269.

31. John V. Apczynski, "Preface," in *Theology and the University*, xii.

32. James Hennesey, S.J., "The Scholar in the Church: An Historian's View," in *Theology and the University*, 5, 13.

33. Gary Macy, "Reception of the Eucharist According to the Theologians: A Case of Theological Diversity in the Thirteenth and Fourteenth Centuries," in *Theology and the University*, 36.

34. Lillian Bozak-DeLeo, "The Soteriology of Julian of Norwich," in *Theology and the University*, 43, 46.

35. Paul Misner, "Adam Müller and Adam Smith: A Romantic-Catholic Response to Modern Economic Thought," in *Religion and Economic Ethics*, 198.

36. William L. Portier, "Missionary as Philanthropist: A Social and Economic Portrait of John R. Slattery," in *Religion and Economic Ethics*, 200.

37. Aaron Milavec, "The Office of the Bishop in Origen," in *Raising the Torch of Good News*, 13, 17, 21.

38. Maureen Tilley, "Martyrs, Monks, Insects and Animals," in *An Ecology of the Spirit*, 99, 108, 109.

39. Maureen A. Tilley, "One Woman's Body: Repression and Expression in the *Passio Perpetuae*," in *Ethnicity, Nationality and Religious Experience*, 67–68, 68.

40. Jo Ann Eigelsbach, "The Historian and the Reformer: Gaining a Critical Perspective on the Issue of Authority," in *Raising the Torch of Good News*, 41, 42, 54.

41. Margaret R. Miles, "Desire and Delight: a New Reading of Augustine's Confessions," in *Broken and Whole*, 3, 4, 5, 15.

42. Caritas McCarthy, "'In this flesh'—Cornelia Connelly and the Incarnation," in *Women and Theology*, 39, 43, 48.

43. Dana Greene, "Maisie Ward as 'Theologian,'" in *Women and Theology*, 51, 60.

44. Helen Marie Ciernick, "Cracking the Door: Women at the Second Vatican Council," in *Women and Theology*, 77–78.

45. Susan Marie Maloney, "Historical Perspectives on Women Religious: Implications for Creating a Feminist Theology of Religious Life," in *Women and Theology*, 137, 149, 150, 151.

46. William M. Shea, "Preface," in *The Struggle Over the Past*, xii–xiii passim, xiv.

47. R. Scott Appleby, "Religious Fundamentalism as a Global Phenomenon," in *The Struggle Over the Past*, 15, 27.

48. John L. Esposito, "Revival and Reform in Contemporary Islam," in *The Struggle Over the Past*, 33, 40, 42.

49. Samuel S. Hill, "The Spirit of American Fundamentalism," in *The Struggle Over the Past*, 214, 215.

50. Bernard Ramm, "The Ethos of the Fundamentalist Movement," in *The Struggle Over the Past*, 217, 221, 222.

51. E. Glenn Hinson, "Fundamentalism and World Consciousness," in *The Struggle Over the Past*, 225, 227–228 passim.

52. Francis Schüssler Fiorenza, "Roman Catholic Fundamentalism: A Challenge to Theology," in *The Struggle Over the Past*, 232, 237, 239–240.

53. Willam D. Dinges, "Catholic Fundamentalism," in *The Struggle Over the Past*, 263, 271, 278.

54. Peter C. Phan, "Introduction," in *Ethnicity, Nationality and Religious Experience*, 1, 2.

55. Robert J. Schreiter, "Ethnicity and Nationality as Contexts for Religious Experience," in *Ethnicity, Nationality and Religious Experience*, 15, 20, 21, 24–25

56. Andrew Tallon, "Affectivity and Praxis in Lonergan, Rahner, and Others in the Heart Tradition," in *Religion and Economic Ethics*, 94, 121.

57. Ronald Modras, "Karl Rahner and John Paul II: Anthropological Implications for Economics and the Social Order," in *Religion and Economic Ethics*, 123, 125, 138, 139, 142, 150.

58. Peter Phan, "Might or Mystery: The Fundamentalist Concept of God," in *The Struggle Over the Past*, 90, 102.

59. Peter C. Phan, "Karl Rahner in Dialogue with Judaism and Islam: An Assessment," in *Religions of the Book*, 129, 144.

60. William M. Shea, "Beyond Tolerance: Pluralism and Catholic Higher Education," in *Theology and the University*, 255–256, 269.

61. Cynthia Crysdale, "Reason, Faith, and Authentic Religion," in *The Struggle Over the Past*, 157–180 passim.

62. James A. Donahue, "Environmental Ethics and Contemporary Moral Discourse," in *An Ecology of the Spirit*, 168, 173–175 passim, 173, 175 quotes.

63. Leonard J. Weber, "Public Policy: Reflections on the Role of Ethics and Ethicists," in *Religion and Economic Ethics*, 35, 41, 43.

64. Sally A. McReynolds, "Toward an Understanding of Prejudice: Contributions from Paul Ricoeur's Theory of Narrative," in *Ethnicity, Nationality and Religious Experience*, 104, 118, 119.

65. Paul F. Knitter, "Introduction: The Totally Other—The Utterly Necessary," in *Pluralism and Oppression*, vii, xii.

66. Jon Sobrino, "Theology in a Suffering World: Theology as *Intellectus Amoris*," in *Pluralism and Oppression*, trans. José Pedrozo and Paul F. Knitter, 154, 166, 167, 176.

67. Susan Brooks Thistlethwaite, "Suffering—Different Faces and Reactions: Response to Jon Sobrino," in *Pluralism and Oppression*, 184, 185–186.

68. Enrique Dussel, "Liberation Theology and Marxism," in *Pluralism and Oppression*, trans. Irene B. Hodgson and José Pedrozo, 208, 210, 213, 214.

69. William L. Portier, "Mysticism and Politics and Integral Salvation: Two Approaches to Theology in a Suffering World," in *Pluralism and Oppression*, 261, 262, 273, 274, 275.

70. Thomas Berry, "The Cosmology of Religions," in *Pluralism and Oppression*, 106, 112.

71. Rosemary Radford Ruether, "Ecofeminism: Symbolic and Social Connections of the Oppression of Women and the Domination of Nature," in *An Ecology of the Spirit*, 46, 55, 56.

72. Michael H. Barnes, "Introduction: The Task of this Volume," in *An Ecology of the Spirit*, 2, 8.

73. H. Paul Santmire, "Is Christianity Ecologically Bankrupt? The View from Asylum Hill," in *An Ecology of the Spirit*, 11, 21, 22.

74. John F. Haught, "Religion and the Origins of the Environmental Crisis," in *An Ecology of the Spirit*, 29, 30–31, 35, 36, 39.

75. Sallie McFague develops the metaphor in her book, *The Body of God*. Other CTS scholars consider this metaphor. In fact, three essays in *Broken and Whole* are dedicated to this topic. William C. French ("The World as God's Body: Theological Ethics and Panentheism") considers the ethical implications of panentheism. John P. McCarthy ("A Short Consideration of Sallie McFague's *The Body of God*") considers the need for "a more deeply articulated tragic vision, one in which confidence in a change of resistance to the crushing, maybe inevitable, greed and violence which humanity has so finely tuned in twentieth century." Susan A. Ross ("*The Body of God*: A Feminist Response") provides the third response to McFague's book.

76. Sally Kenel, "Nature and Grace: An Ecological Metaphor," in *An Ecology of the Spirit*, 235, 239.

77. Jill Raitt, "Christianity, Inc.," in *Broken and Whole*, 99, 104, 112.

78. Raimon Panikkar, "Can Theology Be Transcultural?" in *Pluralism and Oppression*, 14.

79. Caritas McCarthy, "Christology from a Contemporary African Perspective," in *Pluralism and Oppression*, 33–39 passim.

80. Peter C. Phan, "Ethnicity, Experience and Theology: An Asian Liberation Perspective," in *Ethnicity, Nationality and Religious Experience*, 257, 274.

81. Gerald F. Finnegan, "Jesus as Savior of the World," in *Pluralism and Oppression*, 148, 149.

82. Ralph Del Colle, "The Two-Handed God: Communion, Community, and Contours for Dialogue," in *Religions of the Book*, 36, 38, 39.

83. Terence L. Nichols, "Social and Religious Pluralism and the Catholicity of the Church," in *Religions of the Book*, 65, 73, 75.

84. Gerard Sloyan, "Introduction," in *Religions of the Book*, 2.

85. Susannah Heschel, "The Exile of Redemption in Judaism," in *Religions of the Book*, 3, 4, 9.

86. Joseph W. Devlin, "The Bridge of Partnership: Christians, Jews, and Muslims as Participants in the Struggle for World Transformation," in *Religions of the Book*, 13, 19.

87. Mahmoud Ayoub, "Islam and Christianity: Between Tolerance and Acceptance," in *Religions of the Book*, 23, 24, 31, 32.

88. Phyllis H. Kaminski, "Introduction: Theology as Conversation," in *Women and Theology*, ix, x.

89. M. Shawn Copeland, "Toward a Critical Christian Feminist Theology of Solidarity," in *Women and Theology*, 3, 5, 7, 8, 9, 10, 11, 23, 25, 29, 30–31, 32.

90. Mary Rose D'Angelo, "Hardness of Hearing, Muted Voices: Listening for the Silenced in History," in *Women and Theology*, 84, 85, 89.

91. Kwok Pui-lan, "Emergent Feminist Theology from Asia," in *Women and Theology*, 93, 96, 97, 98.

92. María Pilar Aquino, "Hearing One Another into Speech: Latin American Women," in *Women and Theology*, 99, 103, 104.

93. Anne E. Patrick, "From Hearing to Collaboration: Steps for the Privileged toward a Praxis of Solidarity," in *Women and Theology*, 106, 107, 108.

94. Phyllis H. Kaminski, "Kristeva and the Cross: Rereading the Symbol of Redemption," in *Women and Theology*, 235, 240, 249, 251, 252–253.

95. Joan A. Leonard, "Presidential Address," in *Women and Theology*, 261–270 passim.

· 9 ·

Negotiating the Golden Years (1995–2004)

$\mathscr{T}$he pattern for board meetings in content and form changed very little with the society's fifth decade. The board tended to those matters that comprised the society's institutional existence—annual meetings and the teaching workshops preceding the meetings, publications, financial health, and stable membership. What consumed far more of its attention were the various issues related to theologians' official relationship to the Roman Catholic Church. The principal topic of debates concerned implementing canon 812, that required theologians receive *mandatum* from their local ordinaries. Feeding concerns about implementation were conflicts between various church officials and specific theologians. The contentious circumstances included excommunication, termination of employment, and questions concerning theological content of specific publications.

BUSINESS AS USUAL

The annual conventions and the volumes produced from those meetings' papers remain the most visible expression of the society's existence as a learned society. Michael Barnes, in his capacity as local coordinator for the annual meeting at the University of Dayton (1996), laid out the scenario that every hosting institution hoped to provide. He assured members of "fine hospitality, air-conditioned meeting rooms and dormitory suites, good food, assistance from graduate students, and a pub for our own use." Among other attractions mentioned was CTS member and university provost, Jim Heft, as presider at the Saturday evening liturgy "assisted by a local liturgist."[1] One was not disappointed as Fr. Heft began the homily on Trinity Sunday—first holding up one finger, then three, then shrugging his shoulders. What followed provided a little more clarity on the doctrine the liturgy was celebrating.

Barnes's invitation is striking not only for the warmth it conveys but also for its similarity to Father Matthew Kohmescher's message of hospitality in CTS's visit to the University of Dayton in 1974. Consistency in hospitality is far from trivial in the life of the CTS; it highlights what was noted in the introduction about the Society's distinctive life analogous to that of an individual's. The CTS's annual meetings become occasions to meet up with friends of a particular kind. Friendships emerge out of a shared passion for theological studies not only in research and writing but in teaching—teaching hundreds of undergraduates who take these courses because they are required to do so. Even if not the explicit focus on the program, it remains a presence throughout the meeting in participants' conversations in and out of formal sessions. The Society provides the hospitable context for these conversations to continue.

Through the fifth decade, the convention appeared at sites across the country: the University of San Diego (1997), Saint Louis University (1998), St. Norbert College (1999), Villanova University (2000), the University of Portland (2001), St John's University (2002), Marquette University (2003), and the Catholic University of America (2004). The geographical range of locations, with only the Deep South not appearing on this list, highlights the national character of CTS membership.[2] Other specific points about location need also be noted. The San Diego annual meeting took as its theme "Theology: Expanding the Borders" and included for the first time a paper delivered in Spanish. The terrorist attacks on 11 September 2001 that destroyed the World Trade Center and damaged the Pentagon provided much food for thought in formal and informal conversation and for the Eucharist of the 2002 convention, the first after the attacks, but long planned to be held at St. John's University, who counted many alumni among those who died in the World Trade Center attack. On a less dramatic note, the acceptance of Marquette's offer to host the annual convention occurred with no mention of the earlier AAUP controversy, and the 2004 site, Washington, D.C., marked a return to the site of the first convention to commemorate the fiftieth anniversary of the annual meetings.

The themes for the conventions have the feel of a fifty-year reprise of themes previously explored but in light of the latest research in theology. Society members explored "the new histories" (1998), "lived Christianity" (1999), "the social sciences" (2000), and "scripture" (2001). In 2002, the focus was "Christology," and in 2003, it was "Spirit, Church and World." To culminate the fifty years of annual conversations, the theme chosen for 2004 was "Jubilee: New Horizons in Theology."

Teaching workshops also continued. Their focus varied widely, including such topics as "Teaching the Marriage Course" (1995) and "Teaching American Religions in the American Context" (1996). The remarkably dedicated coordinators were Gaile Pohlhaus and then Peter Beisheim. As with so many Society practices, discussions concerning the "informal policies surrounding the workshops" came up in the May 1996 board meeting. The concern arose in part as the new treasurer sought to understand the expense budget and, more troubling, because of the continuing decline in participants. Board members defended the workshop for its contribution to "the distinctive mission of the Society," particularly in assisting novices in teaching.[3] The coordinators made valiant efforts to provide interesting and timely workshops. Yet, despite all the efforts and fine programs, attendance remained relatively low.

At the meeting prior to the fiftieth annual meeting, the board reluctantly decided to "suspend the workshop for an indefinite period." To maintain the CTS's "distinctive mission," session conveners were to encourage "proposals on pedagogy" relevant to their sections. "In the November meeting (2005), the board will discuss how to assess the teaching component of future convention programs."[4] The minutes offered no systematic assessment of the decline in participation. Several factors probably contributed, including the number of members with extensive teaching experience, the diminishing importance of teaching for tenure, opportunities for teaching workshops at members' home institutions, unique department curricula, and increased demands of the professorate. Low attendance at workshops did not translate into similar drops in convention participation. Attendance at conventions varied depending on location but generally attracted from two to three hundred plus (around 20 to 30% of membership).

The challenges of regularizing and maintaining membership never subsided in the fifty-year history of the CTS. Members who failed to pay their dues contributed to the financial crisis that began in the late 1980s. Thomas Wangler, elected treasurer in 1995, reported a debt of $10,768.59 owed to *Horizons*, a debt incurred when publishing expenses exceeded projected costs coupled with delays in the timely completion of several volumes.[5] Upon further investigation, Wangler discovered a major discrepancy between the membership number of 956 and the actual dues-paying members who numbered around 700. The 250 person differential cost the society almost ten dollars per nonpaying member. Tracing the discrepancy proved quite difficult given the variety of membership categories and the inadequate record keeping of the CSSR (formerly the CSR) who collected the dues. In May 1996, Wangler concluded, "It does not appear appropriate to me to recommend another rise in dues at this time. We need to get clear what our actual income and expenses are, and to determine what the problems are in collecting dues.

If we really have only 700 or so paying members then we have to face that and possibly cut the others off."[6] The possibility of such a precipitous drop elicited a response from the society's president. In his September 1996 presidential letter, Terrence Tilley encouraged members to "'Invite a Friend,'" i.e., a colleague "who could benefit from joining the Society." Tilley noted that "we haven't had a 'membership drive' in many years."[7]

"CONTINUITY FROM GENERATION TO GENERATION"

Another recurring topic, the CTS regional meetings, made its appearance for discussion in November 1995. Mary Anne Hinsdale, in her role as vice president, "reported that few regions were active but those that were are strong." She had determined "not to push the regions but to allow them to develop naturally." The following year, Hinsdale, after informing the board that "there are only a couple of regions who are active,"[8] made the following observation. "I get the impression that we are trying to keep a corpse alive. Should we rethink the Regional set-up? Is it really meeting the professional needs of our members?"[9] No definitive response to the question appeared in the minutes.

In suggesting this break with the past, Hinsdale announced that she had "the original 'black book' which has been passed on from Vice President to Vice President and should go into the archives."[10] This explicit reference to archives also indicated a growing awareness of the historical import of the society's work. As the fiftieth anniversary approached, other officers made efforts to ensure better record keeping. In a letter dated 10 June 1997, Terry Tilley, now CTS president, asked Walter Conn's permission to place a "short report on the Annual Convention" in *Horizons* on an annual basis. Its author, the society's vice president, would limit the length to three to five pages. "In that way, a clear record would be developed and be easily accessible to scholars."[11]

Besides creating a permanent public record in its forty-third year of meeting, efforts were made to establish a permanent home for the extensive archive collection. Sandra Yocum Mize was appointed to find a place for the archives[12] but did not complete the task. In 1999, Thomas Wangler "volunteered to take on this first task of retrieving archival materials and finding a repository for them by November."[13] Wangler contacted Timothy Meagher at the Catholic University of America, who had an interest in accepting the CTS holdings at the university's archives.[14] In a letter dated 3 May 2000, William John Shepherd, assistant archivist at CUA, informed Sister Theresa Moser, R.S.C.J., president, College Theology Society, that the "Deed of Gift form" is enclosed. "We are honored to have these records among the many other important collections regarding the documentary history of the American Catholic Church."

Accompanying these attempts to order the CTS's past were efforts to regularize organizational procedures. In a memo to the board in preparation for the November 1996 meeting at the AAR, Terry Tilley, president, asked for authorization "to buy a 1" binder for each of the board members. The members would then begin to keep in it the various job descriptions, minutes of meetings, etc." His request reflected his desire to address "a serious lack of continuity from generation to generation" in the society. Job descriptions plus a record of the board's major decisions would begin to address these issues.[15] Tilley's generational reference, like the desire for archives, reflected longtime active members' growing awareness of their responsibility to pass on the CTS's traditions. Policies and procedures seemed the least problematic in passing on CTS traditions to its younger members formed in a church, an academy, and a culture quite different from those whose careers began in the 1960s and 1970s.

Responses to Tilley's request for job descriptions varied. Thomas Wangler's nine-point description of the treasurer's duties serves as an interesting example. His list included the obvious—maintaining the checking account and an investment account (if approved), reporting on revenue and expenditures, preparing and filing a tax return, and maintaining a listing of all accounts. His securing the room and meal for the November meeting reflected the organic quality of the society's organization development. Wangler observed that "one of the odd things" that he encountered as "new treasurer was the large number of people with an implied authorization to commit the Society in various financial ways." To regularize the practice, Wangler identified those who had in the past required access to funds, including the president, the convention's executive director, the workshop coordinator, the chairs of the book/essay and president awards, the *Horizons* editor, the publications director, the regional chairs, and the Women's Caucus coordinator.[16] Interestingly, Wangler only produced the lengthy list with no attempt to change it.

Further regularizing in CTS practices came as a result of some confusion surrounding the nomination process for the 1998 presidential election. The reformed procedure included wide consultation and a presentation of a slate for the board's approval at the November meeting at the AAR before publication to the general membership. "Attention should be paid to experience, service, gender, geography when selecting candidates."[17] The minutes contain no specific reference to ensuring diverse theological perspectives or even expertise. The board unanimously approved the change.

At the June 1999 board meeting, CTS president Theresa Moser indicated the need to revise the constitution and the bylaws to align with recently developed practices. One issue that sparked considerable debate concerned the "voting status of *ex officio* deliberative members," such as the chair of the Committee on Research and Publishing. The topic had been a point for discussion several years earlier. One member described the current practice as "a show of respect to allow these members to vote." Others observed that these members, though not directly elected, "do have a long standing membership, and they are approved by the membership upon the recommendations of the board." The decision to maintain the inclusive voting practice reflects again the society's preference for organic organizational development and its general reluctance to sever its current mode of operation from its past one.[18]

The CTS office of vice president provides another example of reluctance to change. A lengthy discussion reviewed a now familiar proposal—making the vice president virtually the president elect. Correspondence via e-mail indicated the change would occur. A couple of members argued against the change, however, by highlighting certain advantages in the current arrangement. One observed that the vice president's lack of extensive duties allowed a certain freedom to respond to situations such as the extensive time required to respond to *Ex corde Ecclesiae* (*EcE*). One other person strongly urged maintaining the current practice noting no clear evidence of "a strong need for a change" existed. In fact, the current two-year term for president supported the cycle of alternating presidential award and president's address. Finally, the same board member asserted that the "CTS had its own practices and traditions. I am reluctant to make the CTS over again in the image of other societies."[19] Evidently others agreed, since the vice president's term of office remained unchanged in 2004. Other changes in the constitution and bylaws did what Moser requested: align the constitution and bylaws with current practices. Observations about the ebb and flow of organizational structures contribute to an understanding of how the Society developed its persona, relatively small, almost familial—substantive with very little increase in pretension.

WELCOMING THE BAPTISTS

A significant change did occur in the annual meeting's programming. Beginning in 1996, the National Association of Baptist Professors of Religion (NABPR) held a conference concurrently with the CTS. Terry Tilley, first as convention director, and then as CTS president, was instrumental in forging the relationship with NABPR. In announcing the 1998 convention, Terry Tilley noted that "we are again meeting with the National Association of Baptist Professors of Religion. There will be joint sessions and a joint worship service." He encouraged CTS and NABPR members to submit papers to each other's sessions.[20] A joint prayer service occurred on Friday evening, a time formerly used by the Women's Caucus for an evening prayer.[21]

The exact nature of the collaboration proved less clear to subsequent CTS presidents and board members. The November 1998 minutes reported a discussion with Beth Newman, then president of NABPR. In responding to an inquiry that balked at joint meetings, Newman accepted the description of the NABPR meeting as "concurrent" even though "before this . . . the meetings were truly joint and ecumenical." Newman indicated her desire to have "more than just a place, and more than a few joint meetings." The CTS board minutes suggest some concern over a lack of coordination between NABPR and CTS. Evidently someone concluded that the society was "subsidizing them, doing more than our share." Noting that the societies had not "merged," some board members considered the two societies distinct identities. "A potential hazard is not distinguishing carefully between the logistics and vision of the two societies and their conventions." NABPR, someone concluded, had its primary identity with AAR/SBL. "We want a joint meeting with preserved identities. . . . On identities: ours was not primarily Catholic when we started; we happen still to be largely Catholic. It was called the College Theology Society because our colleges have non-catholics and they were to be included."[22] A practical measure to maintain distinctiveness was separate registrations and programs for the 1999 convention. Some NABPR members, although not those who actually attended, also questioned the affiliation since, according to them, the CTS primarily focused on teaching rather than scholarship. So, impressions about CTS's identity extended beyond the Catholic circles. Interestingly, no mention was made of its Catholic identity as a reason for not affiliating.

The Baptists provided new dialogue partners for those willing to attend their sessions or participate in joint sessions. Their discussions of intra-Baptist debates about "re-envisioning Baptist identity" shared certain commonalities with the CTS's ongoing discussions of Catholic identity. Some of the intra-Baptist issues appeared in a controversial statement, bearing the title, "A Manifesto for Baptist Communities in North America." Its six authors, Mikael Broadway, Curtis Freeman, Barry Harvey, James Wm. McClendon Jr., Elizabeth Newman, and Philip Thompson, have been regular participants in the CTS/NABPR meetings.

The authors understood the manifesto as an invitation to dialogue, though its reception generated as much conflict as dialogue. Its introductory section warned the Baptist community against "two mistaken paths" in the Baptist witness to God's "gift of freedom in Jesus Christ." "Down one path go those who would shackle God's freedom to a narrow biblical interpretation and a coercive hierarchy of authority. Down the other path walk those who would sever freedom from our membership in the body of Christ and the community's legitimate authority, confusing the gift of God with notions of autonomy or libertarian theories." The alternative, discussed in five sections, called Baptists to reclaim the deeply communal and public dimensions of their origins as distinct from individualized and privatized notions of religious commitment. They offered five specific suggestions: engaging in "Bible Study in reading communities"; committing to a "shared discipleship rather than invoking a theory of soul competency"; participating in "a free common life in Christ, in gathered reforming communities rather than withdrawn, self-chosen, or authoritarian ones"; embracing "baptism, preaching and the Lord's table as powerful signs that seal God's faithfulness in Christ"; and claiming to be "a distinct people under God rather than relying on political theories, powers, or authorities."[23]

NABPR members who come to the annual meetings have participated as dialogue partners and theological collaborators in examining a variety of neuralgic theological considerations on church, its relationship to the world, tradition and history, U.S. Christians and politics in the American empire, and sacraments, to list only a few. They offer opportunities for those who travel in predominantly Roman Catholic circles to engage in conversations about figures and issues influential among those who travel in predominantly Baptist ones.

Despite debates about the exact nature of the relationship between the NABPR and the CTS, the board continued to foster collaborative efforts. Developments in that relationship reflect a reconfiguration of relationships in other locales in the academy. The November 2004 minutes included a proposal from the "Region at Large of the National Association of Baptist Professors of Religion," the principal participants at the CTS. Given the imminent separation of the AAR and SBL in 2008, "the National Association of Baptist Professors of Religion will no longer be able [to] meet during a joint AAR/SBL annual meeting. They have approached CTS to inquire about the possibility of meeting during the CTS annual convention." The logistics include increasing "attendance by another 100 attendees." The only decision made was to "discuss the implications for such an arrangement including the need for more lodging and meeting space."[24]

OLD BUSINESS—NOT AS USUAL

The difficult relationship between the CTS and the CSSR finally resolved itself. At the November 2003 meeting, the board considered the CSSR's financial difficulties and the CTS's need to secure reliable means to maintain member dues, mailing lists, and so on.[25] The following year, the CTS board authorized finding an alternative to the CSSR. An addendum to the minutes stated, "that CTS/Horizons withdraw from CSSR and establish an alternative mechanism for maintaining membership lists, collecting dues, and fulfilling subscriptions."[26] So ended a nearly forty-year relationship that had begun in those heady days after the council when cooperation among fledgling learned societies helped each to flourish.

Challenges related to publication were almost nil in the society's fifth decade. Thanks to the diligence of Dennis Doyle, the board heard in May 1996 that with the soon-to-be published Sloyan volume, all past annual volumes had appeared. He also established a publishing relationship with Orbis Press and Twenty-Third Publications. Getting society members to edit volumes remained a challenge. Difficulties ranged from soliciting suitable essays, getting the completed essays in a timely manner, and preparing them in a camera-ready format. Despite the use of computers, the work on the volume continued to be a labor of love and dedication to the field and to the society.[27] By 2001, Orbis Press had become the sole publisher of the annual volume, in what Dennis Doyle described as a "very good arrangement—we are getting a polished book for a good price."[28] The Society owed a debt of gratitude to Twenty-Third Publications and Orbis whose support allowed maintenance of its publishing tradition. Dennis Doyle's care in this matter extended well beyond his three-year pledge of service for a total of eleven years.

Of course, the print medium was only one of a growing list of publishing alternatives. Walter Conn announced at the 18 November 2000 board meeting that *Horizons* was to be incorporated into "ATLA (American Theological Library Association) for their online serials project ATLAS (American Theological Library Association Serials Project)."[29] The CTS determined at the May 1996 board meeting to revisit the possibility of "establishing a web page for the Society."[30] Through the efforts of Theresa Moser and Jonas Barciauskas, the CTS eventually had that web page in 1998.[31] At the same meeting, Shannon Schrein, executive director of the conventions, introduced the possibility of online registration. An established procedure by 2004 was securing registration information via the web page.[32]

Terry Tilley's "Valentine" 1998 presidential newsletter announced "modifications to the CTS listserv" with gratitude to John Apczynski, who had established it in 1994. Tilley assured those who had unsubscribed from the list that "spamming and the technical glitches" no longer threatened.[33] Since its establishment, the listserv offered an instant means of communication. As the twenty-first century began, members received all relevant information on the society's work through the listserv rather than the biannual presidential letter, faithfully delivered for almost fifty years through the U.S. postal service. Members also can more easily extend the conversations begun at the annual meetings or announce a job at their home institution or inform their colleagues of their views on current ecclesial events and controversies and even offer sage advice on textbooks and teaching techniques useful in undergraduate teaching. Such instant, global communication will surely impact the society's self-understanding in ways yet to be understood.

THE SOCIETY IN THE EYES OF ITS MEMBERS

A membership survey completed in 1995 indicated that people's attachments to the Society emerged from personal relationships developed over time in a collegial atmosphere. "Repeatedly, phrases like 'good friends,' 'caring people,' 'networking,' 'sound scholarship,' 'mutual support,' 'accent on teaching,' 'a sense of community,' show up in the survey." Only about a third of respondents attend the annual meeting regularly, and among those a significant number use their own funds to attend. The survey also revealed that "a considerable number of our members experience discrimination, whether it be for reasons of gender, race, religious affiliation, clerical status, or disability." CTS president Brennan Hill proposed a discussion of this matter to identify possible avenues for "more assistance to our members who are dealt with unjustly." He also mentioned members' desire for "advocacy on the part of CTS on a wide range of issues. Perhaps we need clearer policies and procedures in this area."[34] As will become clear in the subsequent section, advocacy became a major preoccupation of the board.

What remained constant among members was gratitude for companions in scholarship and teaching. In a letter dated 13 May 1996, Loretta Devoy, in writing to her colleagues about the upcoming meeting details, concluded with a retrospective on the society. "We at the College Theology Society are blessed in many ways: friendship, understanding, curiosity, interest in each other's work." She then emphasized how most members "teach students whose last formal contact with the systematic study of religion is with us. Thus, we address questions coming from a group of people who are 'the modern world,' groping their way into Post-Modernity." This engagement with undergraduates makes for "questions . . . different from some other Societies, and, as a community of scholars, we are free to pursue them. This we will do again, in Dayton. Such a blessing! I look forward to seeing you there."[35]

In a letter dated 29 September 1996, longtime member Mike Barnes addressed "the future of the CTS" with a view toward improvement. His major points came via comparison with the CTSA. He commended the Society's diverse membership—diverse in so far as the different locales that members do their work—from research institutions to small colleges with demanding teaching responsibilities. "The CTS should not lose that diversity. It enriches us. But I think that it is time the CTS notched its status upward, partly just to compensate more for what is missing at the CTSA, and partly to increase the CTS's own overall effectiveness." The paying off of the debt to *Horizons* made such discussion possible. He suggested "having one of the plenary sessions" feature "a person or two whose names have high public visibility," to create "extra excitement." Other suggestions included having a plenary on Saturday morning and a "*quaestio disputata* session" on Saturday afternoon. He did not want to duplicate the "semi-seminary atmosphere of the CTSA" but only intensify certain aspects of the CTS's established practices. "So spend some more money on the annual meeting, and find ways to let the CTS shine more clearly."[36] Barnes's suggestions reflect the deep loyalty of active members as well as a certain ambivalence about its "status" in the academy. This ambivalence has appeared throughout the CTS history, often among those whose commitments to the CTS run deep and wide.

In a note of appreciation to Dr. Stanley D. Nel, dean of the University of San Francisco's College of Arts and Sciences, for some financial support, Terry Tilley noted his own fifteen year commitment that "will continue . . . as long as I have strength"; the society "embodies both collegiality and responsible scholarship." To demonstrate the latter, Tilley noted that one of the sections in which he participates could boast 50% of papers from the past three years "had been placed in refereed journals or volumes after presentation." He continued, noting the "recent annual volume, *American Catholic Traditions*, surprised the publisher and the society by going into a second printing within a year of publication. The CTS doesn't have the *cachet* of some other societies, but it produces good scholarship in the context of real fellowship."[37] Though any one of these benefits might explain the Society's endurance, the combination again highlights the CTS's distinctive persona.

THE ECCLESIAL CONNECTION

Aside from the normal business of determining annual meeting themes and sites and considering budget matters, the single topic that garnered the most attention and concern of the board and no doubt captured the minds and hearts of many CTS members was the implementation of John Paul's *Ex corde Ecclesiae*, particularly its juridical elements. Most notable among these was canon 812, requiring a teacher in theological studies to receive *mandatum* from his or her local bishop. As preceding chapters indicate, concern over some variation of the issue emerged in the mid-1970s.

The U.S. bishops had attempted to maintain clear communications with those directly affected by *EcE*'s implementation. In a memo dated 23 February 1996, Bishop John J. Leibrecht, chair of the *EcE* Implementation Committee in the U.S., provided a copy of the revised draft of the 25 August 1995 draft. The bishop's cover letter strongly encouraged continued dialogue given the positive results evident in the "proposed revisions" of the 25 August 1995 draft.[38]

The letter had a conciliatory tone. The introductory comments recognized Catholic colleges and universities' relationships with both the church and "the higher education enterprise of the United States." To foster a dialogue that "clarified" those relationships required inclusion of "faculty *of all disciplines*" as well as "students, staff, academic officers, trustees, and sponsoring religious communities." The "original draft" selected the phrase "*mutual trust, close and consistent cooperation and continuing dialogue*" as the "framework" to consider "the pastoral relationship of bishops with Catholic colleges and universities." The "mutual trust" was rooted in "shared baptismal belief" and "the spirit of *communio.*" Out of such mutual trust, the college or university could provide "public acknowledgment of its Catholic identity in official documentation," and the bishops would recognize and support this identity when "*unjustifiably challenged.*" Mutual responsibilities followed with colleges expected to hire Catholics or those "aware and respectful of that tradition," and bishops expected to use "*established procedures*" as found in *Doctrinal Responsibilities: Approaches to Promoting Cooperation and Resolving Misunderstandings Between Bishops and Theologians.*[39]

The application document itself concludes with a section on "continuing dialogue." That final section begins with a reference to the previous dialogue generated by *EcE* as "graced moments" and encouraged continuation of the "far-reaching implications—curricular, staffing, programming—of major themes within *Ex corde Ecclesiae*. These include Catholic identity, *communio*, relating faith and culture, pastoral outreach, the new evangelization, and relationship to the Church." Implementation included "mutual commitment to regular dialogues" locally and with the Association of Catholic Colleges and Universities (ACCU) as well as "internal" to Catholic colleges and universities, a periodic "review of the congruence of its *mission statement*, its courses of instruction, its service activity, and its research programs with the ideals and principles expressed in *Ex corde Ecclesiae.*"[40]

In reviewing the U.S. bishops' third draft of the "ordinances" that would implement *EcE*, the board passed a motion to write a letter to Father Toland in basic support "*while voicing reservations about the lack of clear due process as well as a lack of a procedure for dealing with bishops who do not follow the Guidelines.*" The board then determined to send the letter to Bishop Leibrecht.[41] So, in a June 1996 letter to Bishop Leibrecht, Brennan Hill, past CTS president, affirmed "the pastoral tone and careful nuancing" and praised the inclusion of "all disciplines" and the focus on dialogue as well as "'communio.'" The "several concerns" centered on ensuring that each bishop "adhere to this pastoral approach"[rather than juridical] and "a clear procedure" be established to ensure "a fair and just 'due process'" to address any "problem" that might occur.[42]

The same month that Brennan Hill sent his letter of cautious encouragement to Leibrecht, the newly elected CTS president, Terrence Tilley, wrote to Archbishop Daniel E. Pilarczyk, chair of the Committee on Doctrines. Tilley communicated the Society's less favorable response to the process utilized in the U.S. Bishops' Committee on Doctrine in their public criticism of Richard McBrien's newly revised *Catholicism*. Tilley's letter communicated the content and tenor of discussion during the May board meeting and the convention's open forum. The discussion's catalyst was "a document submitted by twenty-eight members of the Department of Theology at the University of Notre Dame" intended originally for the CTSA. The Notre Dame document challenged the committee's "refusal 'to grant formal doctrinal dialogue' to Richard P. McBrien" as outlined in the NCCB's *Doctrinal Responsibilities*.

Tilley's letter made clear that the CTS had decided not to authorize a "public statement" at this time, but had questions concerning how "the recent actions of the Committee on Doctrine" related to the *EcE*'s second draft's "call for '*communio* and dialogue'" and why the committee had not followed "the due process guidelines of 'Doctrinal Responsibilities.'" Finally, Tilley questioned the wording of a press release that led to the erroneous conclusion that the "book was 'condemned'" rather than that the bishops had "scholarly and pastoral issues involved in the *use* of the book." Tilley expressed "respect [for] the work of the Committee" and observed that some board and other society members "have voiced concerns similar to . . . [those] in the general review." Regardless of some members' reservations about the content, "the Board is seriously concerned with due process, the role of the Committee, and the use of the media and what these augur for the future."[43]

Archbishop Pilarczyk responded in a letter dated 24 June 1996. His response addressed the particulars of the McBrien case as well as the general anxiety surrounding the implementation of *EcE*. The archbishop thanked Tilley and the CTS board for directly addressing the Committee on Doctrine rather than using the public media to convey the message. The archbishop placed the current discussion in the context of ongoing discussions of

McBrien's *Catholicism* dating from 1981. The current response "constitutes a follow-up on its 1985 statement." The third edition included in its preface a description of the bishops' 1985 statement "as a 'critical but essentially sympathetic review' of the book." Pilarcyzk observed that the comment insinuated "the Committee's endorsement of the book." Dr. Tilley had permission to quote Pilarcyzk's assertion that this procedure in no way established a "precedent that would contravene the spirit of the current draft of the *Ex Corde Ecclesiae* implementation document." He also ascribed to the committee care in "defining the precise and limited nature of its staff review of *Catholicism*" that "Catholic teaching professionals" ought to be able to communicate to counter the "public reception and interpretation" of the report. The archbishop attached to his letter an account that the recent process had upheld "the spirit of *Doctrinal Responsibilities.*"[44]

A Society member, in a letter dated 12 July 1996, reflected the general anxiety concerning *EcE* and a certain puckishness concerning the CTS's contribution to the dialogue. The individual praised both the board and those who participated in the open forum for "having shifted the focus of the discussion away from the CTS becoming the sounding-board for the outrage of Notre Dame faculty and on to the more general principles that affect all practicing theologians in their relations with the hierarchy. The issue here is more wide-ranging than simply a celebrity theologian feeling the heat from the episcopal kitchen." Later in the same letter, the correspondent expressed his skepticism concerning Pilarcyzk's response to Tilley's letter with its "hair-splitting" in the information released to the media. Finally, the member advised the newly elected president to encourage "some official" study of *EcE* given the Society members' "experiences with undergraduates and their families"—a unique contributor to a discussion where "theologians in seminaries and high-visibility graduate programs" appear to dominate.

In the September 1996 president's newsletter, Tilley reported the reception of a "cordial" response from Archbishop Pilarczyk. Cincinnati's ordinary observed that the process "protracted over years" had "followed the spirit of 'Doctrinal Responsibilities.'" Tilley added that McBrien might not share that view. Pilarcyzk also explained that "the circumstances in this case were unique" and should not by interpreted as a precedent. Having the archbishop's permission to quote from the letter, Tilley cited the prelate's observation that "'the Doctrine Committee is confident that Catholic teaching professionals will be able to draw attention to the precisely defined scope of its staff review of *Catholicism* and thus to dispel the mistaken impression that the review constitutes *de facto* warning or ban on the book.'"[45]

The year 1996 proved to be busy for CTS engagement in potentially contentious ecclesial matters. A CTS committee, composed of Maureen

Tilley, Dennis Doyle, and Virginia Ratigan, provided a critical review of "the Canon Law Society of America Report 'The Canonical Implications of Ordaining Women to the Diaconate.'" The report favorably assessed the CLSA's consideration noting that the society had not collapsed ordination to the diaconate with that to the priesthood. The CTS reviewers raised questions about whether "the ministry of deaconesses necessarily has to be patterned on that of deacons." The final comment recommended that besides drawing upon "historical materials to establish the possibility of the ordination of women to the diaconate," the committee ought to examine "current gifts and experiences of women independent of office of deacon." The contemporary focus could help "develop and strengthen a single model for both men and women." An "Appendix to the Report, Specific Comments on the Use of Historical Sources" provided a detailed seven-page commentary focusing on specific paragraphs and lines on certain technical historical issues. These points ranged from readings of references to deaconesses at Council of Nicea to considering why the practice had developed that prohibited deaconesses from marrying after ordination either in a first marriage or after widowhood.[46]

ALL *MANDATUM*—ALL THE TIME

These efforts served more as distractions to the main concerns of the day—implementation of *EcE*. In his presidential letter, dated 10 September 1997, Terry Tilley reported "no real news on any developments" except that the NCCB/USCC implementation committee had begun "negotiations" with church officials in Rome about the implementation document. The ACCU continued to recommend "keeping a low profile." This advice seems to be given in light of the united support among most "academics, academic administrators and the bishops" on the "pastoral approach" taken. "Until more definite developments occur, quiet vigilance seems to me the appropriate stance."[47]

In a letter dated 11 October 1996, Reverend Terrence Toland, S.J, project director of the *EcE* Implementation Committee, wrote Dr. Tilley in his capacity as CTS president. In retrospect, the letter forewarned that any implementation of *EcE* would inevitably include implementing *mandatum*. In the letter, Toland informed Tilley that "interventions from the floor at the Portland bishops' meeting, 20 June 1996" as well as other communication had made clear that some bishops found "unacceptable" the implementation document's "failure even to mention the mandate of canon 812." To avoid an amendment from the floor at the November bishops' meeting, the committee decided to include a footnote: "'the mandate of canon 812 will receive further study by the NCCB.'" Toland assured Tilley that "the amendment leaves unchanged" the committee's choice to propose "a pastoral application of the goal and values of canon 812."[48] Tilley's response indicated the board being "lukewarm about the inclusion of the footnote" continuing with the observation of a "real and palpable fear that the directions such talk might take might well prove disastrous for American Catholic Higher Education."[49]

A memo from Bishop Leibrecht, dated 23 May 1997, recalled the NCCB's passing the implementation document at the previous November's meeting. What followed informed all bishops, college/university presidents, learned societies, and religious community college sponsors of the "Congregation for Catholic Education" request for more attention to "several canonical issues." In response, Bishop Pilla, as NCCB president, directed the subcommittee to address the concerns and resolve them "as soon as possible." Leibrecht expressed appreciation for all "who have helped build positive and trusting relationships between the various representatives of Catholic higher education and bishops." He hoped to maintain the "contacts and the dialogues" around *EcE* and specifically mentioned the Association of Catholic Colleges and Universities. He concluded, "Many thanks for your understanding and cooperation—past and future."[50]

As in 1996, "contacts and dialogues" between the CTS and the bishops exceeded those surrounding *mandatum*. Conflicts between the U.S. bishops and the Vatican Congregation for Divine Worship and the Discipline of the Sacraments arose over the use of inclusive language in the new English-version lectionary. In a letter from the "Office of the President" of the NCCB, Anthony M. Pilla, Bishop of Cleveland, acknowledged a letter from Terry Tilley concerning the implementation and "the resolutions of language questions in our lectionary." He expressed how he "warmly appreciat[ed]" Tilley and other CTS members' "strong expression of support. . . . You should be aware that I have been alerted a number of times in the recent past to the valued encouragement of yourself and other members of the College Theology Society."[51] Ultimately, no assistance was requested.

The many challenges from Vatican officials to practices accepted by U.S. bishops plus other conflicts that Vatican action generated led the CTS president, Terry Tilley, to anticipate a bleak future. In an "editorial opinion," Terry Tilley conjectures on the "next theological locus for *major* friction between the Roman magisterium and Catholic theologians." He identifies the "locus" to be "religious diversity—both internal diversity (inculturation) and the diversity of religious traditions." He cited the case of Sri Lankan, Father Balasuriya, Cardinal Ratzinger's "reductionist speech" on "religious pluralists in Guadalajara," and a "dreadful document on the world religions" for the International Theological Commission. He notes that responding to the various issues related to this topic "theologically" and "practically" remain "open questions in our postmodern, polycentric world." His conclusion evokes the tenuous mood of the time—"a time of prayerful waiting."[52]

One did not have to turn to Sri Lanka to become embroiled in controversies involving theologians. The 29 May 1997 board of directors' meeting minutes (University of San Diego) reported a lengthy discussion concerning the nonrenewal of Aaron Milavec's faculty contract at the Cincinnati seminary, the Athenaeum. The board determined that the pending lawsuit made it impossible for the board to act. If and when the lawsuit was settled, then a resolution might be possible. The refusal to put forward the resolution was done "reluctantly." Tilley, as president, communicated to Aaron Milavec the board's decision.[53]

Such conflicts did not spill over into militant action against *EcE*. An update in the February 1998 president's newsletter offered the advice of ACCU's executive director, Monika Hellwig, to maintain "a low profile on this matter." Tilley once again recommended "quiet vigilance" as Bishop Leibrecht worked with his committee and some college and university presidents to craft the first draft of the implementation.[54] In some e-mail exchanges among board members during early September 1998, however, the discussion focused on anticipated bad news. "The Vatican is insisting on legal or juridical norms and the implementation of canons 810 and 812." The news was, for the moment, to be kept confidential but produced speculation on the dire consequences of the Vatican's bid for control "over all Catholic Colleges and Universities with regard to hiring and dismissal of personnel." Those who teach theology "would have to have a 'mandate' from the local bishop to teach (canon 812)." Canon 810 could empower the bishop "to require the dismissal of other faculty members, administrators, etc., whose lives are deemed not to be in accord with Catholic teaching."

Only a month after the disappointing news concerning *mandatum*, in March 1998, another member of the Athenaeum's faculty, Sister Barbara Fiand, S.N.D., was informed of her reassignment that relegated her teaching only in the lay pastoral ministry program, not the seminary. No clear reason for the change is found in the documents. The board produced a resolution protesting the process used to reassign Fiand. It reads as follows: "Whereas, Sister Barbara Fiand, SND, Professor of Philosophical and Spiritual Theology, has been removed from the seminary program of the Athenaeum of Ohio, and whereas, this has been done without recourse to the Grievance Procedures described in the faculty handbook as we understand them, be it resolved that the College Theology Society protests this failure of due process and the resulting violation of Sister Barbara Fiand's human dignity." The minutes also note a concern to communicate "the impact of this on theologians in general." "Press releases" are noted as the means for disseminating that message. The resolution was approved unanimously.[55] A response came on 3 June 1998 from the rector, Gerald R. Haemmerle. He strongly objected to the resolution's charge of failure to respect due process, given that Sister Fiand resigned her position rather than accept the reassignment.[56]

Tilley's response to a conversation with Haemmerle, prior to Haemmerle's letter, defended the resolution noting "that the *process* looked rather flawed" especially since Fiand had no opportunity "to be confronted with specific complaints from specific complainants." He also asserted that the "whole situation" appears as "a chilling pattern for faithful Catholic women, especially those of moderate and progressive theological views, working in seminaries and some other church-owned institutions. In addition to a desire to stand in solidarity with Barbara Fiand, a concern over this pattern may be a significant motivating factor in the members' support of this protest."[57]

A 20 January 1999 letter from Society president Theresa Moser to her colleagues provided an update on the U.S. bishops' draft of the implementation document. "You are strongly encouraged to participate in the discussion of the sub-committee's proposal with your colleagues, the president of your institution and/or local bishop(s)." She explained that the "legal issues" are not new and "present a strong case for non-juridical norms in the U.S." Moser reported a conversation with the CTSA's president, Robert Schreiter, about a "joint response" from the Catholic learned societies emphasizing "the damage to our institutions if juridical norms are implemented." She concluded, "In the current winter of disappointed expectations," Archbishop Quinn's proposal for a "decentralized and collegial model for the exercise of the papal primacy" functions like "new springtime buds, offering hope."

A one-page letter, dated 23 April 1999, came as a joint response, since it bore the signatures of Michael L. Barre, S.S., president of CBA, Robert Schreiter, C.PP.S., president of CTSA, and Theresa Moser, R.S.C.J., president of CTS. It praised the efforts of the committee in producing the 1996 draft that the NCCB had passed so overwhelmingly. It warned that the "1998 subcommittee draft" with its implementation of norms "would militate against that level of trust and respect" that previous dialogue had established. Dire consequences for Catholic higher education are outlined. The predictions include "probable loss of the level of state funding necessary for their continued existence," the departure of "Catholic scholars" from Catholic institutions because they judge these "norms to be unnecessarily onerous and their academic credibility doubted," and the loss of "gifted Catholic doctoral students." They recommended keeping "the previously approved 1996 document," appending that document "to ensure the practical realization of the goals of *Ex Corde Ecclesiae* in Catholic institutions in the United States," and following "exactly the order and content of the general norms of *Ex Corde Ecclesiae* without adding further rules or regulations from other sources."[58]

In a memorandum dated 21 September 1999, Bishop Leibrecht provided the college presidents, the sponsoring religious communities, and the learned societies the last draft of the implementation document. Consistent with his letter three years earlier, Leibrecht emphasized the positive dimensions of the difficult process noting how several "bishops speak of the new relationship they experience with representatives of Catholic colleges and universities." The portion of the draft of special concern was "Part Two: Particular Norms," with its discussion of "the nature of a Catholic university" and the composition of the university community. The document, focusing on "particular norms," described "education" as the Catholic university's "purpose" and acknowledged "academic freedom" as "an essential component." It used "lawful" to modify "freedom of inquiry"—a choice indicative of the bishops' efforts to respond to the various parties demanding a hearing.

Of greatest interest to the Society's membership was the discussion of *mandatum*. The draft proclaimed *mandatum* as "an acknowledgment by church authority that a Catholic professor of a theological discipline teaches within the full communion of the Catholic church." It is neither an episcopal "appointment" nor "an approbation." Careful wording described *mandatum*. "The *mandatum* recognizes the professor's commitment and responsibility to teach authentic Catholic doctrine and to refrain from putting forth as Catholic teaching anything contrary to the church's magisterium." The local bishop in whose diocese the university/college is located grants *mandatum* in writing. It "remains in effect" unless "withdrawn by a competent ecclesiastical authority." Under "The Local Church," the document identifies "Doctrinal Responsibilities" as a "guide" "to promote informal cooperation and collaboration in the church's teaching mission." It can also serve as guide for "formal doctrinal dialogue" when the informal proves ineffective. The conclusion included a ten-year timeline for reviewing the application of the particular norms with "a mutually agreeable process" involving the NCCB and "representatives of Catholic universities."[59]

Responses to the new implementation proposal came quickly. Strategies to dissuade the bishops ranged from familiar predictions of lost academic credibility to warnings about legal conundrums. In a letter dated 20 October 1999, to the Most Reverend Joseph A. Fiorenza, president, National Conference of Catholic Bishops (NCCB), Margaret A. Farley, R.S.M., CTSA president, Father Robert Schreiter, C.PP.S., CTSA past president, and Kenneth R. Himes, CTSA president elect indicated their concern for clarity relative to the process for handling disputes coupled with a remaining lack of clarity in *mandatum*'s "'very meaning.'" They appealed for "greater dialogue between ourselves and our bishops" and assured Fiorenza of theologians' "deep sense of responsibility to the church and a deep sense of vocation within the church." To prevent compromise of "this vocation and responsibility," they offered a familiar proposal—"rigorous procedures of scholarly peer review and overview at many levels of a college or university." Effective implementation of such procedures could "serve the bishops' concerns while avoiding new juridical ecclesiastical structures."[60]

The CTS Board of Directors, in a letter dated 25 October 1999, was "pleased to support and endorse the enclosed letter from the Board of Directors of the Catholic Theological Society of America" on the newly proposed juridical norms. It was signed by the president, Theresa Moser, R.S.C.J., past president, Terrence Tilley, and vice president, Anne Clifford, C.S.J.[61] Leibrecht acknowledged reception of the CTSA letter on 3 November 1999 in a letter addressed to Margaret Farley and another to Theresa Moser. The letter to Farley emphasized the importance of continuing the dialogue. Moser's letter limited its response to informing her that the implementation committee would consider the CTSA letter.[62]

Theresa Moser presented a document to the board at their fall meeting, entitled "EX CORDE: LEGAL ASPECTS CTS BOARD NOVEMBER, 1999." It outlined twelve potential problems identified by "a lawyer familiar with issues affecting higher education." The items listed involved litigation arising from *mandatum*, financial losses from lawsuits, loss of insurance coverage, loss of federal and state funding, and loss of academic credibility with accrediting agencies.

The January 2000 newsletter to "colleagues" from CTS president, Theresa Moser, reported the CTS and CTSA boards being "very disappointed ('sick at heart') at the vote (223 to 31) to send the document immediately to Rome." Both governing bodies had hoped for more discussion. Moser then noted that the "lack of enthusiasm" among university players "largely because it includes provisions for the implementation of canons 812 and 833." Their lack is "not disloyalty to the Holy See" but concern about how the provisions align with "U.S. constitutional law, as well as with university customs, culture, accreditation requirements and policies." She likened the situation to "the unfortunate experience of U.S. academics with 'loyalty oaths' during the anti-communist scare" and predicted a response "typical of academia. . . . Expect committees, committees, committees" from local to national. Identifying "the perceived breakdown of trust between bishops and theologians" as the "most worrisome" development, Moser encouraged "CTS members . . . [to] take the lead in rebuilding these bonds. Take a bishop to lunch! (And charge it to the president, of course)." Her concluding remarks appealed to common knowledge—"there are laws that are on the books and laws that are enforced. Wise leaders, academic and pastoral, know the difference."

A letter from Bishop Leibrecht, dated 25 January 2000, acknowledged his reception of a copy of that newsletter. He thanked her and explained how "a detailed procedure" for "requesting and granting (or withdrawing) the mandatum" was to be developed. "That procedure will be developed in consultation with representatives of Catholic higher education and theologians."[63] In responding to Leibrecht's willingness to correspond, the CTS president followed her own advice—not so much taking the bishop to lunch, but inviting Bishop Leibrecht to participate in an "Open Forum" on 3 June 2000 at the annual meeting in Philadelphia. The bishop agreed, noting that he needed to return to his diocese that evening for an ordination on June 4th.[64]

Moser maintained a high profile on behalf of the CTS in the *mandatum* debate. In the 4 March 2000 issue of *America*, she responded to Richard McBrien's article, "Why I Will Not Seek a Mandate" (*America*, February 12) to express disappointment in McBrien's failure "to note the active involvement of the College Theology Society in the *Ex Corde Ecclesiae* discussions." She appealed to its members' focus from its 1950s founding to its "900 at last count, and growing" to be "teaching and researching in Catholic colleges and universities." So in mentioning the CTSA, McBrien should have also included the CTS, especially in their collaborative efforts in particular in concern for *mandatum*.[65]

The 2000 CTS convention fully engaged in *mandatum* debate. The Philadelphia convention featured not only the open forum with Bishop Leibrecht but also the president's address, entitled "Between a Rock and a Hard Place: Theologians and the Mandatum." As Moser explained, "The imagery refers to the rock of Peter, the hard place to the problems the *mandatum* raises for ourselves and our Catholic colleges and universities." The paper began with a brief history that focused on how *mandatum* "is inevitably linked to the question of academic freedom." A familiar recent history unfolded with mention of John Tracy Ellis's sharp criticism of the state of "American Catholics and the Intellectual Life" and the impact of the "Declaration on Religious Freedom." Also noted is Catholic faculty's appeal to the AAUP in matters related to academic freedom, citing several cases in the 1960s including St. John's University and the University of Dayton. In the latter case, the archbishop of Cincinnati asked the Marianist president, Reverend Raymond Roesch, to investigate certain faculty's teaching content. The incident culminated in the board of trustees affirming "genuine and responsible academic freedom supported by proper respect for the church's magisterium." Moser also recalled the Catholic University of America's conflict with Charles Curran in the 1960s, the Land O' Lakes Statement, other documents generated by the International Federation of Catholic Universities (IFCU), and important Supreme Court decisions allowing for federal funding at religiously affiliated colleges and universities.

Moser interpreted the significance of the court rulings in terms of episcopal oversight of Catholic higher education. "As understood in the United States, and in line with U.S. law, academic freedom meant that church authority could not directly intervene in the affairs of the academy and specifically in the hiring, promoting, tenuring and dismissing of faculty members." The difficulty originated not from U.S. bishops since "the Vatican was not willing to accept this [freedom], and trouble loomed on the horizon."

The next section examined the Vatican bureaucracy. Moser utilized social science in her analysis to keep with the convention's theme, "Theology and the Social Sciences." Relying upon Thomas Reese, S.J, *Inside the Vatican: The Politics and Organization of the Catholic Church* (Cambridge, 1996), she observed that few who head the congregations, the curia's principal organizing structure, actually have expertise in the areas to which they are assigned. The head of the Congregation of Education at the time of the speech and critical in the *EcE* discussions was a Pole, Archbishop Grocholevski, whose "unique qualification seems to be membership in what has been termed the 'Polish Mafia' in the Curia because of their back-door access to the Pope." The concern is that those making the decision have little understanding of the U.S. situation.

She then summarized the documentary history that eventually led to the *mandatum* beginning with the 1975 proposed norms from the Congregation for Education for "ecclesiastical universities and faculties." A request for "feedback from all Catholic universities" brought a response from the "College and University Department of NCEA (later called the ACCU)." The department was "so alarmed that it responded with a position paper." *Sapientia Christiana* (15 April 1979) required a "canonical mission from ecclesiastical authority" of "all teachers of faith and morals" at institutions like Catholic University and Weston. *Mandatum* first appeared in the 1977 draft of the revised canon law and "was vigorously fought by presidents and members of ACCU," who obviously failed in obtaining its removal.

Looking over the events from the 1960s to the 1980s, Moser saw the movement to assert juridical control over Catholic colleges and universities in the U.S. to be the work of Roman curia staff. Using the work of John Coleman, S.J., she also described "a certain ethos within a bureaucracy" that here is a kind of "Catholic (or Papal) fundamentalism" or "integralism." Its ecclesiology assumes that "the Holy Spirit operates downward, from the Pope through the Curia to the Bishops and then the rest of us. So, to put it concretely, in the light of recent curial statements on the matter of the ordination of women, it seems pretty clear the Holy Spirit doesn't want to hear another word about it!" Citing John Courtney Murray's understanding of the "first amendment of the U.S. Constitution" as "an article of peace, not a theological statement," she identified "academic freedom in the college or university" as "ordered to the common good in a pluralistic society. It is not a theological statement, but a practical *modus operandi*, which, in line with U.S. law, meant that the academy and the people in it are immune from direct intervention by outside authorities of any kind, including the hierarchy of the Church."

Given that the implementation document did not require *mandatum* to be part of a Catholic university's hiring requirement, Moser concluded with the following advice from "a wise and experienced person" in "deal[ing] with a bureaucracy: 'Never neglect your option to do nothing.'" She found the advice to be "prudent counsel" since "we are between a rock and a hard place." *Mandatum* need have no influence on a university's decision on a theologian's "hiring, promoting, and tenuring according to the usual expectations for scholarship, teaching and service. The presence or absence of *mandatum* is not a factor in these decisions. Regarding *mandatum*, both the university and the theologian exercise the option 'to do nothing.'" Her final words at the CTS banquet "acknowledge and appreciate our membership in the church, our love of its genuine tradition, and our relationship in Christ with the Pope and the College of Bishops. Locally, regionally, and nationally we should continue to work in a spirit of collegial cooperation for the good of society and the people of God."[66]

Bishop Leibrecht evidently found her talk less than congenial. In a letter responding to Bishop Leibrecht, Moser assures the prelate that her "concluding advice . . . is not an official position of the College Theology Society." She identifies her "real concern" as avoiding making *mandatum* "a factor in matters of appointment, rank and tenure, matters internal to the university." She explains how it "threatens the livelihood of lay theologians and their families and the vitality of theology as an academic discipline." Because of such threats, "I think the universities should 'do nothing' about the mandatum, while implementing *EcE* in other ways 'to the extent possible.'" She did maintain that "what is desirable is a cooperative and collegial relationship between bishops and theologians."[67]

At the November 2000 board meeting, Terry Tilley, who served as a consultant to the bishops, provided an update on "the guidelines" for implementing *mandatum*. Tilley reported that "the text is geared to be interpreted narrowly and allows for the simple application of proper professional responsibility." Both the CTS and CTSA sought to limit its application "only to full time tenured professors" and avoid making it "an institutional requirement except by the institution." In the discussion, Theresa Moser reiterated the possibility of invoking "the principle of 'non reception of law'" especially given how "canon law and civil law here are in serious tension."[68]

Terry Tilley also shared his "Report on Recommended Clarifications in *mandatum* Procedures," that he had submitted to the bishops' committee. He emphasizes the negative implications "if the *mandatum* is construed as a '*bona fide occupational qualification*.'" Compelling *mandatum* as an employment requirement would necessarily involve the bishops in a variety of hiring and retention issues that could draw them into litigation. Tilley suggests applying *mandatum* "only to 'full-time, permanent faculty.'" He then offers six other additional points of comment from questioning the inclusion of church history as a theological discipline to definitions of "in communion" and "in full communion."[69]

Terry Tilley also wrote a brief essay for CSSR Bulletin (September 2001) on "The Misunderstood *Mandatum*." He provides a history, an explanation of *mandatum* that "means that a professor should neither present as Catholic teaching what the magisterium does not now teach nor directly *advocate* that a student *should* not accept magisterial teaching." Tilley warns that this benign reading does not account for theologians' concerns given other ways in which it might be used already cited elsewhere in this account. Besides the already mentioned legal concerns for the universities and the bishops, Tilley mentions the fear among qualified candidates of coming to Catholic institutions and the threat of the rogue bishop. He agrees with the "wag" who "said that *mandatum* is 'a bad idea whose time has come.'" If *mandatum* had been in place in 1994, he would have refused "the offer from the University of Dayton to leave my tenured position as full professor of religion at Florida State University to chair this department and midwife its Ph.D. program in theology."

About six months later, "Guidelines Concerning the Academic *Mandatum* in Catholic Universities (Canon 812)" were approved by the United States Conference of Catholic Bishops (USCCB). After reiterating the definition of the nature of *mandatum* found in the *Application of Ex Corde Ecclesiae for the United States*, the guidelines indicate that the "request for a *mandatum* by a professor of a Catholic theological discipline should be in writing and should include a declaration that the teacher will teach in full communion with the Church" (4a). It also acknowledged that an "ecclesiastical authority has the right to offer the *mandatum* on his own initiative (which requires an acceptance), provided that the commitment to teach in full communion with the Church is clear" (4c). A deadline was given of 1 June 2002 for those already hired (3 May 2001) and six months after hiring for others. "If the professor does not obtain the *mandatum* within the time period . . . competent ecclesiastical authority should notify the appropriate authority in the college or university" (4d). Sections 5 and 6 concerned "grounds and process for withholding or withdrawing the *mandatum*," and "appeals and resolution of disputes." In the former, withholding or withdrawing *mandatum* has to have "reasons in writing" with specific reference to the "conditions of the *mandatum*" (5c). Judgments on a person's work must include some review of the proportion in the "overall theological contribution," "its relationship to the larger Catholic tradition" and "its implications for the life of the Church." In section 6, "the general principles of canon law should be adhered to in seeking recourse and in the process of appeal."

The sample included an expression of *mandatum*. The first had the person "declare my role and responsibility as a professor of a Catholic theological discipline within the full communion of the Church." The second offered a kind of commentary on the first sentence. "As a professor of a Catholic theological discipline, therefore, I am committed to teach authentic Catholic doctrine and to refrain from putting forth as Catholic teaching anything contrary to the Church's magisterium." As this fifty-year history nears completion, the five-year review of the implementation has begun to be discussed.[70]

THE CTS AT FIFTY

Black balloons, crepe paper, and "over-the-hill" decorations need not be purchased to celebrate the College Theology Society's fiftieth year. The CTS website describes the society as "founded in 1953 as a Roman Catholic organization of lay and religious teachers of undergraduate theology, the CTS today has a membership of over 900 college and university professors throughout the United States, Canada, and Europe."[71] Dues are $50 for full membership, $25 for students, $50 for associates, and $60 for joint membership by a vote of 14 to 1.[72] As of June 2004, the accepted membership count was 895.

The website narrative cites the CTS's "roots in the Roman Catholic tradition" and claims to be "increasingly ecumenical in its membership and concerns." It "provides opportunities to: keep abreast of current activities in the academic study of religion, investigate the relationship of theology/religious studies to other academic disciplines and the place of religion in the total college curriculum, discuss and evaluate ways of teaching theology/religious studies effectively, promote the development of programs which are genuinely intellectual, value oriented, and realistically designed to meet the students needs." Members receive *Horizons* and the annual volume that "contains exceptional scholarly articles on the theme of the Annual Convention."[73]

The fiftieth anniversary brought the society to the site of its origins, Catholic University of America. Special recognition was given to one of its founding and most enduring members, the Reverend Gerard Sloyan, who once again served as celebrant, delivering another of his memorable homilies. The 2005 annual convention would be held at Spring Hill College in Mobile, Alabama, with the theme "Vatican II, Forty Years Later: Envisioning the Church of the Future." The 2006 meeting at Regis University, Denver, found inspiration once again from Father Hopkins, "God's Grandeur: Imagination & the Arts in Theology." Three venues were possibilities for 2007: Creighton University, a return visit to University of Dayton, and, for something totally different, University of Alaska–Pacific with preliminary plans for a theme like "Theology and the Laity" or "Theology and the Laity in the Americas."[74] So the work continues.

This part of the story ends with a handwritten note of thanks (dated 6 June 1999) to the "President," Theresa Moser, from Pat Kleupfel. She, along with her husband Neil, had just received the 1999 President's Award for their dedicated work as editors of Twenty-Third Publications. The stationery bears in bold italicized script at the top, "Join the Revolution!"and at the bottom, "Support Vatican II!" Therein lies the tale of the first fifty years of the College Theology Society whose founders instigated a revolution in theological education long before John XXIII had announced a new Pentecost with the calling of an ecumenical council. Members of the College Theology Society continue to honor those founders every time they walk into a classroom full of undergraduates to introduce them to the wonders of theological studies.

NOTES

1. Brennan R. Hill, Xavier University, Cincinnati, Ohio, to friends, "[College Theology Society] Newsletter February 1996," Binder 1995–, Box 1, CTS Collection 00-8, ACUA.

2. Spring Hill College in Mobile, Alabama, will host the 2005 annual meeting.

3. "Uncorrected Minutes, Board of Directors' Meeting, University of Dayton," May 30, 1996, nonarchived materials.

4. "College Theology Society, Board of Directors' Meeting, Minutes," June 4, 2004, nonarchived materials.

5. "Minutes, Board of Directors' Meeting, Marriott Hotel, Philadelphia," November 18, 1995, nonarchived materials.

6. Thomas E. Wangler, Boston College, Chestnut Hill, Massachusetts, to Brennan Hill, Xavier University, Cincinnati, Ohio, May 13, 1996, nonarchived materials.

7. Terrence W. Tilley, the University of Dayton, Dayton, Ohio, to colleagues, "[College Theology Society Newsletter] September, 1996," nonarchived materials.

8. "Minutes, Board of Directors' Meeting, Marriott Hotel, New Orleans," November 23, 1996, nonarchived file.

9. "Report of the Vice-President, College Theology Society," New Orleans, Louisiana, November 23, 1996, nonarchived file.

10. "Minutes, Board of Directors' Meeting," November 18, 1995.

11. Terrence W. Tilley, the University of Dayton, Dayton, Ohio, to Walter Conn, Villanova University, Villanova, Pennsylvania, June 10, 1997, nonarchived materials.

12. "Raw Minutes, Board of Directors' Meeting, University of San Diego," May 29, 1997, nonarchived materials.

13. "Uncorrected Minutes, CTS Board of Directors' Meeting, St. Norbert College," June 3, 1999, nonarchived materials.

14. "Board of Directors, College Theology Society, November 20, 1999, Report of the President," nonarchived materials.

15. Terrence W. Tilley to members of the board of directors, College Theology Society, "RE: Our Meeting at the AAR," November 5, 1996, nonarchived materials.

16. [Thomas Wangler] "Wangler-TH" to [Terrence Tilley] "tilley," e-mail message with subject: "Re: Job Descriptions," December 2, 1996, nonarchived materials.

17. "Uncorrected Minutes, CTS Board of Directors' Meeting, Saint Louis University," May 28, 1998, nonarchived materials.

18. "Minutes, CTS Board of Directors' Meeting, AAR Meeting, Nashville, Tennessee," November 18, 2000, nonarchived materials.

19. College Theology Society Board Members, the movement toward changing the term is reflected in a series of e-mails, October 1–9, 2001 Jill Raitt to Theresa Moser, a final e-mail, subject "Re: [CTS_Discussion] By Laws Discussion Wrap-up," indicates almost "consensus" on the vice president assuming the office of president, October 29, 2001.

20. Terrence W. Tilley, the University of Dayton, Dayton, Ohio, to colleagues, "[College Theology Society Newsletter] September 10, 1997," nonarchived materials.

21. "Minutes, Board of Directors' Meeting," November 23, 1996.

22. "Minutes, Board of Directors' Meeting, November 21, 1998, Orlando, Florida," nonarchived materials.

23. Mikael Broadway, Curtis Freeman, Barry Harvey, James Wm. McClendon Jr., Elizabeth Newman, and Philip Thompson, "Re-Envisioning Baptist Identity: A Manifesto for Baptist Communities in North America," May 1997, nonarchived materials.

24. "College Theology Society, Board of Directors Meeting, DRAFT Minutes," San Antonio, Texas, November 20, 2004, nonarchived materials.

25. "College Theology Society, Board of Directors Meeting, Minutes (Approved with corrections 6/3/04)," Atlanta, Georgia, November 22, 2003, nonarchived materials.

26. "College Theology Society, Board of Directors Meeting, Minutes," "Addendum to the Minutes (See 7.a.iii above)," Washington, D.C., June 4, 2004, nonarchived materials.

27. "Uncorrected Minutes, Board of Directors' Meeting," May 30, 1996.

28. "Minutes, CTS Board of Directors' Meeting, CTS Meeting—Portland, Oregon," May 31, 2001, nonarchived materials.

29. "Minutes, CTS Board of Directors' Meeting," November 18, 2000.

30. "Uncorrected Minutes, Board of Directors' Meeting," May 30, 1996.

31. Terrence W. Tilley, the University of Dayton, Dayton, Ohio, to colleague, "[College Theology Society Newsletter] February 14, 1998," nonarchived materials.

32. Shannon Schrein to CTS Board of Directors, "RE: Recommendations for CTS Convention," May 25, 2001, nonarchived materials.

33. Terrence W. Tilley, "14 February 1998."

34. Brennan R. Hill, "Newsletter February 1996."

35. Loretta Devoy to CTS colleague, no title, document header reads "St. John's University, Department of Theology and Religious Studies, Jamaica, NY 11439," May 13, 1996, nonarchived materials.

36. Mike Barnes, University of Dayton, to the president, officers, and board of directors of the CTS, "Concerning the Future of the CTS," September 29, 1996, nonarchived materials.

37. Terrence W. Tilley, the University of Dayton, Dayton, Ohio, to Dr. Stanley D. Nels, University of San Francisco, San Francisco, California, March 26, 1998, nonarchived materials.

38. Bishop John J. Leibrecht, chair, *EcE* Implementation Committee, Washington, D.C., to bishops, college/university presidents, learned societies, religious community sponsors, "ON: revised draft, '*Ex corde Ecclesiae,* an Application to the United States,'" February 23, 1996, nonarchived materials.

39. National Conference of Catholic Bishops, *Doctrinal Responsibilities: Approaches to Promoting Cooperation and Resolving Misunderstandings Between Bishops and Theologians,* June 17, 1989.

40. "(NOTE: 8/25/95—original draft; 2/23/96—first revision; changes approved by Implementation Committee are italicized.), (**D-R-A-F-T F-O-R D-I-S-C-U-S-S-I-O-N**), *Ex corde Ecclesiae*: An Application to the United States," attached to John J. Leibrecht's February 23, 1996, letter to bishops, college/university presidents, learned societies, religious community sponsors, nonarchived materials.

41. "Uncorrected Minutes, Board of Directors' Meeting," May 30, 1996.

42. Brennan R. Hill, (CTS past president), Xavier University, Cincinnati, Ohio, to Bishop John J. Leibrecht, chair, *EcE* Implementation Comm., Washington, D.C., June 13, 1996, nonarchived materials.

43. Terrence W. Tilley, president [CTS], the University of Dayton, Dayton, Ohio, to Most Reverend Daniel E. Pilarczyk, S.T.D., Ph.D., Cincinnati, Ohio, June 14, 1996, nonarchived materials.

44. Most Reverend Daniel E. Pilarczyk, archbishop of Cincinnati, chairman, Committee on Doctrine, Washington, D.C., to Professor Terrence W. Tilley, president, College Theology Society, University of Dayton, Dayton, Ohio, June 24, 1998.

45. Terrence W. Tilley, "September, 1996."

46. Maureen A. Tilley, Dennis Doyle, and Virginia K. Ratigan, "Statement from the Ad Hoc Committee of the College Theology Society on the Canon Law Society of America Report 'The Canonical Implications of Ordaining Women to the Diaconate,'" November 3, 1996, nonarchived materials.

47. Terrence W. Tilley, "10 September 1997."

48. Reverend Terrence Toland, S.J., project director, *EcE* Implementation Committee, to Dr. Terrence Tilley, president, College Theology Society, October 11, 1996, nonarchived materials.

49. Terrence W. Tilley to Fr. Terrence Toland, S.J., *EcE* Implementation Committee, October 30, 1996, nonarchived materials.

50. Most Reverend John J. Leibrecht, chair, *EcE* Implementation Committee, to bishops, college/university presidents, learned societies, religious community sponsors, May 23, 1997, nonarchived materials.

51. Most Reverend Anthony M. Pilla, bishop of Cleveland, president, NCCB/USCC, to Terrence W. Tilley, Ph.D., June 20, 1997, nonarchived materials.

52. Terrence W. Tilley, "10 September 1997."

53. Terrence W. Tilley, "Report of the CTS President," November 7, 1997, nonarchived materials.

54. Terrence W. Tilley, "14 February 1998."

55. "Uncorrected Minutes, CTS Board of Directors' Meeting," May 28, 1998.

56. Reverend Gerald R. Haemmerle, president/rector [Athenaeum of Ohio], to Dr. Terrence W. Tilley, June 3, 1998, nonarchived materials.

57. Terrence W. Tilley to Fr. Gerald Haemmerle, rector, Athenaeum of Ohio, June 1, 1998, nonarchived materials.

58. Michael L. Barre, S.S., president, CBA, Robert J. Schreiter, C.PP.S., president, CTSA, and Theresa Moser, R.S.C.J., president, CTS, to Most Reverend John J. Leibrecht, D.D., Ph.D., chairman, Ad Hoc Committee for the Implementation of *EcE*, April 23, 1999, nonarchived materials.

59. Elizabeth Fisher for Dr. Hellwig to Teresa Moser, document, "*Ex corde Ecclesiae*: An Application to the United States," contained in a fax labeled "Re: New Ex corde ecclesiae draft," September 21, 1999, nonarchived materials.

60. Margaret A. Farley, R.S.M., president [CTSA], Robert J. Schreiter, C.PP.S., past president [CTSA], and Kenneth R. Himes, O.F.M., president elect [CTSA], to Most Reverend Joseph A. Fiorenza, bishop of Houston, president, National Conference of Catholic Bishops, October 20, 1999, nonarchived materials.

61. Theresa Moser, R.S.C.J., president [CTS], Terrence W. Tilley, past president [CTS], and Anne M. Clifford, C.S.J., vice president [CTS], to Most Reverend Joseph A. Fiorenza, bishop of Houston, president, National Conference of Catholic Bishops, October 25, 1999, nonarchived materials.

62. Most Reverend John J. Leibrecht, bishop of Springfield–Cape Girardeau, to Sister Margaret A. Farley, R.S.M., president, CTSA, November 3, 1999, nonarchived materials, and Most Reverend John J. Leibrecht, bishop of Springfield–Cape Girardeau, to Sister M. Theresa Moser, R.S.C.J., president, College Theology Society, November 3, 1999, nonarchived materials. Both letters appear on "The Diocese of Springfield–Cape Girardeau, Office of the Bishop" letterhead—personal file.

63. Most Reverend John J. Leibrecht, bishop of Springfield–Cape Girardeau to Mary Theresa Moser, R.S.C.J., president, College Theology Society, January 25, 2000, nonarchived materials.

64. Most Reverend John J. Leibrecht, bishop of Springfield–Cape Girardeau to Mary Theresa Moser, R.S.C.J., president, College Theology Society, February 15, 2000, nonarchived materials.

65. Mary Theresa Moser, R.S.C.J., president, College Theology Society, "letters: **Active Partners**," *America*, March 2000, 30.

66. M. Theresa Moser, "Between a Rock and a Hard Place: Theologians and the Mandatum" (presidential address presented at the Forty-Sixth Annual Convention of the College Theology Society at Villanova University, Villanova, Pennsylvania, on 3 June 3, 2000), nonarchived materials, 8, 10, 12, 13, 14, 15, 17, 18, 19.

67. M. Theresa Moser, R.S.C.J., Ph.D., to Most Reverend John J. Leibrecht, bishop of Springfield–Cape Girardeau, June 6, 2000, nonarchived materials.

68. "Minutes, CTS Board of Directors' Meeting," November 18, 2000.

69. Terrence W. Tilley, "Report on Recommended Clarifications in *mandatum* Procedures respectfully submitted to Most Reverend Daniel E. Pilarczyk, Archbishop of Cincinnati, Chair, Ad Hoc Committee on the *Mandatum*," September 15 2000, nonarchived materials.

70. United States Conference of Catholic Bishops, "Guidelines Concerning the Academic *Mandatum* in Catholic Universities (Canon 1812)"; available from www.nccbuscc.org/bishops/mandatumguidelines.htm, accessed August 8, 2001.

71. "About the Society," available from www2.bc.edu/%7Ebarciaus/about.html, accessed August 8, 2001.

72. "Minutes, CTS Board of Directors' Meeting," May 31, 2001.

73. "About the Society" and "Publications," available from www2.bc.edu/~barciaus/pubs .html, accessed August 8, 2001.

74. "College Theology Society, Board of Directors Meeting," November 20, 2004.

Nos Quedamos (1995–2004)

$\mathcal{F}$orty years plus passed since Sister Mary Rose Eileen Masterman, C.S.C., voiced her desire to found a society to serve the professional interests of that exotic creature, the Catholic college teacher of sacred doctrine. In 1953 she envisioned an organization open to exploring the latest in theological trends especially as they might be translated for the college classroom. Little could she have imagined just how trendy theology would become in the next decade—the results not only of the Second Vatican Council but also of the emerging field of religious studies in the rapidly expanding knowledge industry situated in burgeoning college and university campuses. Given that this is the final chapter in CTS's half century of theological exploration, it seems fitting to view the ten volumes considered in this chapter in light of major themes from the past forty years. The chapter begins with an overview of the volumes. The remainder organizes the essays around key topics and persons that have been the repeated focus of discussion in earlier chapters.

REVIEWING THEOLOGICAL TRENDS

One might review the theological topics recorded in the first decade's *Proceedings* with everything from amusement to bewilderment, or with a kind of nostalgia born out of a realization that the last four decades of the twentieth century brought about change, in all its complexity, that few in 1954 or even 1964 could have predicted. In reviewing the Society's fifth decade of annual volumes, it is as if the board, with the support of the rank-and-file members, determined to review theological trends most critical to the previous forty years of Christian theologians' explorations. The annual volume themes illustrate the point.

In *Religion, Ethics, and the Common Good*, James Donahue, S.J., coeditor with M. Theresa Moser, R.S.C.J., introduces the volume with the assertion that "tensions and conflicts between individuals and community" have resided at the heart of "discourse about social and public life." He identifies the "common good as a mediating construct for understanding some of the most fundamental divisions of our society today" as found "in the life of the church, in the world of business and education, and in the very discourse that permeates contemporary theology and religious practice."[1] In 1996, Sandra Yocum Mize and William Portier edited the forty-second volume, *American Catholic Traditions: Resources for Renewal*. Portier observes in the introduction the "veritable *ressourcement* in American Catholic studies." This retrieval "has happened in an interdisciplinary flurry on the back roads and the borders between history and theology and cultural studies."[2] The following year's volume promoted further explorations of borderlands in *Theology: Expanding the Borders*. As editors Roberto S. Goizueta and María Pilar Aquino explain, "theologians are reconceptualizing the border." "Border" here can "both demarcate identity, and, too often, preclude dialogue and interaction. These include not only territorial or national borders but also epistemological, ethnic, racial, gender, disciplinary, ecclesial, and religious borders." The volume's borderlands' focus is theological.[3]

The next four volumes are a veritable tour through the most salient methodological shifts within theology, beginning with *Theology and the New Histories*. Earlier flirtations with postmodernity now became central to framing the essays found in the forty-fourth volume, *Theology and the New Histories*. Gary Macy, the volume's editor, observes the impact of various "new histories," including "Women's history, ethnic history and different forms of deconstructionism." Such approaches call into question "the idea that history is the simple process of recording 'what happened in the past.'" History is "much more about how historians explain and justify the present cultural location of their own society or group." Given the multiplicity of social locations, "many 'histories'" exist. "Each of these histories, moreover, is not only a narrative, but a narrative which must make moral choices in its very valuing of some evidence and some topics over others." Macy then asks about the implications for theology, especially Roman Catholic theology, centered on "the relation of this new way of writing history to theology, to faith, and to magisterial teaching." The answers, Macy notes, are less numerous than the questions, but this new understanding of history means that "what the past will become" is not determined and "can be an ally in freeing us to choose from any number of possible Christian futures."[4]

The forty-fifth volume (1999) examines the obstacles to the theologian's comprehension of "the meanings and values communicated in the lived experience of Christianity." David Hammond, the volume editor, concurs with Victor Turner's observation about the challenge facing "a modern academic inquirer" in an attempt "to grasp the mentality of those in a pre-modern culture." He calls on his peers to "be as critical of the attitudes toward traditional culture taken for granted by contemporary academic culture as they are of harmful aspects of popular religion." He also offers some gentle criticism of "educated Christians" whose "sympathy and understanding toward 'the others'" was far less when popular practices appear "within their own Church" and not in another religious tradition.[5]

The final volume of the second millennium turns to explorations of *Theology and the Social Sciences*. Michael H. Barnes distinguishes between two approaches to the use of social sciences in theological inquiry. "The first invites the social sciences inside the theological tent to work alongside philosophy in a serving role. The second treats the social sciences less as a servant than as an animal to be domesticated, like goats worth milking once in a while but to be tethered outside the tent where their gamey odor will not disturb the finer air of theology." He associates the first with a "Rahnerian" approach and the latter with a "Balthasarian" framework. He wonders whether these two groups that he identified might be able to heed Rodney King's query, "'Can't we all just get along?'" His own response points to the volume since it "provides specific illustrations of the power of good anthropology, sociology, psychology, and historical methods to advance theological understanding."[6] Recognizing their value as illustrated in the essays might just serve as starting point for more amicable relations between the two groups.

In introducing the volume on *Theology and Sacred Scripture* (2001), the editors, Carol J. Dempsey, O.P., and William Loewe, note the major shifts in the study of the biblical text—from existing as "part of a larger discipline, theology" serving the "much larger agenda of theological studies." As with so many of the other introductions framing the annual volumes from this fifth decade, Dempsey and Loewe emphasize how biblical studies, now a discipline in its own right, was "a multi-dimensional and interdisciplinary field that focused on and was informed by history, archaeology, the social sciences, and, most recently, literary, multi-cultural, and cross-gender studies, to name a few." The "rich dialogue" between "Jewish and Christian scholars" received special mention since, for both religious traditions, the text remains "a living text, a living tradition." The choice of essays reflects this array of approaches to scriptures.[7]

The choice to explore the current research in those areas located at the very heart of Christian theology continued in 2002 and 2003, with volumes dedicated to Christology and the Holy Spirit respectively. Anne M. Clifford and Anthony J. Godzieba edited the volume *Christology: Memory, Inquiry, Practice*. These editors characterize the volume as joining in "a multifaceted conversation" exploring "two fundamental questions (which are really two sides of a single issue), namely, 'Who is Jesus Christ?' and 'Why is he significant?'" They situate this conversation among conversations that had developed "in earnest for at least a half-century, especially since 1951, the fifteen-hundredth anniversary of the Council of Chalcedon." The editors make clear that choosing "Christology" continues the CTS commitment "to enrich the disciplines of our members and to benefit the faith life of the next generation of adults whom we all have the privilege to teach."[8]

The Holy Spirit serves as the focus of theological reflection in the 2003 volume, *The Spirit in the World and the Church*. Its editor, Bradford E. Hinze, observes Western Christianity's relatively "limited attention to this doctrine." Along with renewed scholarly interest was "the new attentiveness and receptivity to experiences of the Spirit among the faithful." Hinze identifies the volume's distinctiveness as its emphasis on "the practical implications of the doctrine of the Spirit for the church and the world," especially "in the promotion of justice and liberation, in the work of forgiveness and reconciliation in a world rife with conflict and division." The context for such comments included the U.S.–led wars in Afghanistan and Iraq, the crisis in the Roman Catholic Church precipitated by clergy sexual abuse, the ongoing plight of the poor, and the degradation of the earth.[9]

Terrence W. Tilley, editor of the fiftieth volume, *New Horizons in Theology*, begins his introduction considering "the changes in *who* is doing theology (layfolk more than clerics and religious) and *where* academic theology is centered (more in the university and colleges than the seminaries)." Yet, as evident in the CTS's fifty years, "much remains the same: we still teach (mostly) undergraduates, we still teach (mostly) in colleges and universities, and we still are committed to excellence in teaching and research as a service to the church, the society, and the academy." While not able to explore every "new horizon," this collection of essays at least offers "perspectives on how we got here, and where we're going as theological and ecclesial communities."[10] Of course, those who have read the last nine chapters may be able to provide their own perspectives on the CTS's past and current location.

THE OLD MADE NEW

The influence of Karl Rahner and Bernard Lonergan remains prominent in U.S. Catholic theology even with the growing prominence of nonfoundational theological perspectives. In "Rahner and the 'New Histories': Everything Old Is New Again," Ann Riggs explored whether Rahner's theological framework remained usable given the "shift within theology from a methodological paradigm taken from philosophy to one taken from the social sciences," a shift evident in the thematic focus on the "new histories." She challenges Fergus Kerr, George Lindbeck, and John Milbank, who attribute to Rahner a strong Cartesian dualism. Against that charge, Riggs argues that his "philosophical anthropology" is "physically embodied, socially embedded, and interpersonally constructed" to highlight the "historical particularity" of "transcendental experience." These historically situated experiences serve as the epistemological challenge to Cartesian dualism. Riggs names this approach "a uniquely non-foundational apologetic."[11] In *Theology and the Social Sciences* (2000), Jeannine Hill Fletcher examines "Karl Rahner's Principles of Ecumenism and Contemporary Religious Pluralism." After acknowledging Rahner's controversial concept, "anonymous Christian," she explores his other writings "on the experience of religious pluralism." Here she finds a more amenable Rahner who recognized positive dimensions of "religious diversity" as a manifestation of "human participation in the God who surpasses all that we can understand." Fletcher's argument turns to Rahner's primary theological conviction in God as Absolute Mystery as the basis for a positive response to religious diversity and pluralism.[12]

Lonergan also received his due in the "new histories," thanks to Donna Teevan's "Meaning and Praxis in History: Lonerganian Perspectives." Drawing from Lonergan's view of "meaning and praxis," Teevan explores how "historical change—be it progress, decline, or redemption—may be understood as a transformation of the meanings that constitute personal and social self-understanding and action." She accepts Lonergan's understanding of history as "an expression of meaning that is open to growth in authentic living or to decline into inauthenticity." For Teevan, "history" becomes a theological "praxis" that "contribute[s] to the building up of the Reign of God in history." Teevan was hardly the only theologian to describe herself as "Lonerganian." Lonergan's careful articulation of theological method drew many late twentieth century theologians to identify themselves as Teevan had.[13]

The 2000 volume includes an essay that reflects a resurgence of interest in the theology of Hans Urs von Balthasar, a contemporary of Karl Rahner and Bernard Lonergan. In "Social Sciences in Ecclesial Reflection," James K. Voiss, S.J., analyzed Balthasar's "disaffection with the efforts of his contemporaries to use the social sciences in their theology." His negative assessment emerged from his commitment to "theological aesthetics" that takes "Christ as the norm for ecclesial life, structure, and mission. Theological aesthetics preserves and intensifies the church's presentation of that form because it privileges revelation and faith over analysis and critical reason, thereby avoiding the pitfalls Balthasar perceived in the Kantian epistemological heritage." With its focus solely on the "observable," social science proves incapable of examining "the divine, revelatory, iconic nature of the church." Voiss offers a critique of Balthasar's position, challenging his theological assumptions that privilege revelation, rather than grace, as his "starting point." To start with revelation, especially as Balthasar defined it, lends itself to excluding the use of social science in theological reflection. This exclusion, Voiss finds unfortunate, since social science might actually further Balthasar's own theological project. It could help identify "non-theological agendas beneath theological formulation" and "cultural assumptions" that obscure the essential Christian message—concerns central to Balthasar's theological project.[14]

Given Voiss's explanation of Balthasar's choice of "revelation" as his theological starting point, it hardly seems surprising that *Theology and Sacred Scripture* includes a Jason Bourgeois essay on Balthasar's "theodramatic hermeneutics" that utilizes interpretive approaches "much broader than that of the historical-critical methods." His hermeneutics assumes that "the interpreter of divine revelation is participating in the drama of divine revelation itself, through her place in its history."[15] Balthasar's insistence upon the interpreter's situatedness in faith provides a challenge to "the project of demythologization," especially when the project results in "conflict between a contemporary mindset and some of the traditional doctrines of faith." Bourgeois concludes that Balthasar's insistence on situatedness in faith clarifies the critical importance of the church's teaching office when a conflict does occur. The magisterium's role is to determine "which doctrines themselves are essential to the faith" and not to be abandoned or minimized for the sake of a contemporary interpretive practice.

Appeals to Balthasar's work even in Voiss's less favorable appraisal reflect some larger shifts in theological concerns and perspectives especially among the generation of theologians who have little or no memory of a preconciliar church. Many of their theological concerns emerged from the chaos frequently found in the midst of the exciting explorations and experimentation catalyzed in the reception of the Second Vatican Council. Yet, the theological worlds of Rahner, Lonergan, and Balthasar, like so many others from the period, are not easily reduced to binary categories like conservative/liberal. Younger scholars' ability to find theological inspiration and guidance from any one of these three theologians should come as no surprise to those who have dedicated themselves to understanding their work in its complexity.

THE CHURCH, THE WORLD, THE STATE

Just as most Catholic theologians recognized Rahner and Lonergan to be the architects of the postconciliar theological systems, they awarded John Courtney Murray the role of Vatican II's champion of religious liberty, key to the church's entrance into "the modern world." In David Hollenbach's query: "The Common Good in the Postmodern Epoch: What Role for Theology?" he credits Murray with anticipating the postmodern era. Like Riggs, Fletcher, and Teevan, Hollenbach welcomed another mid-twentieth century Catholic theologian into the contemporary scene. Murray receives credit for identifying two "'Basic Issues'": "the sacredness of the human person" and its relationship to "the many secular dimensions of social, economic, political existence."[16]

Theresa Moser also calls upon Murray for guidance in her essay "Higher Education and the Common Good: Reflections of John Courtney Murray, S.J." Murray's work made significant contributions to the wider discourse concerning "the American civic tradition" that captured "the imagination of a whole generation of religious and political leaders in the mid-twentieth century." Moser turns to his recognition of "the critical importance of education in the formation of good citizens." The contemporary "educator needs above all . . . Murray's skill in holding in creative tension the accumulated wisdom of the past, on the one hand, and the realities of contemporary American life on the other." Moser finds in this "creative tension" a suitable descriptor for the current demands on Catholic higher education and the church's role in educating the laity as citizen and Christian. Despite Catholic colleges' and universities' struggles over identity, Moser affirms that "the church, with its tradition of reflection on the common good, is singularly equipped." Like Murray, Moser finds in this tradition a counter to the society's rampant individualism and a way to communicate the obligation to ensure human rights for every person within the community.[17]

Selecting the "common good" as the organizing concept for the 1995 volume brought back into focus the highly charged debates about what exactly is the appropriate relationship between church and world, where both terms take on multiple meanings. If John Courtney Murray serves as hero in the quest for the common good, others serve not exactly as villains but at least as skeptics, even about the quest. Hollenbach, for example, located these others in a "closed-tradition communitarianism," which "abandons the Enlightenment hope for a universal rationality and replaces it with tribalism." The more prominent tribal members include Stanley Hauerwas as well as George Lindbeck. Richard Rorty served as representative of another "unfruitful at best and dangerous at worst" response to the common good in the postmodern context. His is a "suspicion-is-all agnosticism."[18]

The "closed-tradition communitarian[s]," under different guises, appeared in other essays in the 1995 volume as well as in other volumes. Michael H. Barnes warned against the "dangers in sectarian separateness" fostered in the "postliberal theology" of "Lindbeck, McClendon, Hauerwas, Baxter, and Milbank." What is notable about that particular lineup is the inclusion of a Roman Catholic, Michael Baxter, who studied with Stanley Hauerwas and eventually taught at the University of Notre Dame. He appeared as part of a new generation of Catholic theologians whose perspectives were not entirely anticipated in the theological movements grounded in Rahnerian and Lonerganian transcendental Thomism with their co-relational thrust.[19]

To note the generational distinction is not to reduce the difference to the chronological. Real differences in theological perspectives also exist within generations. The differences and their effects remain for other historians in subsequent decades to sort out. One tenuous observation comes in returning to Bernard Cooke's 1962 presidential address, in which he called upon theologians to "translate the vision of faith into society and culture,"[20] where the contemporary culture provides the language. Many in the CTS committed themselves to that challenge. Michael Baxter and others of his theological generation have another conviction—the necessity of ensuring that society and culture translate into a vision of faith, with Christian theology serving as the official language.

Michael Barnes, as editor of the volume *Theology and the Social Sciences*, provides an opportunity for Michael Baxter to speak for himself concerning the relationship between sociology and theology. Baxter responds to John Coleman's essay, "Every Theology Implies a Sociology and Vice Versa." Coleman's work, taken from his convention plenary address, focuses upon "methodological presuppositions and implications for a correlation of theology and sociology." The Jesuit argues that sociology is "integral" to engaging in "practical theology and theological ethics." Coleman names "Gregory Baum, Robin Gill, Don Browning" as exemplars of that small number of theologians who use sociology. Theologically informed sociologists included "Bellah, David Martin, Kieran Flanagan, Andrew Greeley." He also names the "opposing camp" of John Milbank and Stanley Hauerwas, with special attention given to Milbank because of his *Theology and Social Theory: Beyond Secular Reason*, a generally unpopular text among social scientists and correlational theologians.

After explaining three "presuppositions" about the testy but mutually beneficial relationship between theology and sociology, Coleman favorably describes Robin Gill's *Churchgoing and Christian Ethics*. The study examines the church's effectiveness in its "socializing in Christian virtue," which, Coleman observes, directly addresses those "Christian ethicists who turn to virtue ethics, principally Hauerwas." In contrast to Hauerwas's "ambivalence about the moral communities necessary to socialize people in virtue and to anchor character," Gill's work demonstrates that "actual churches, in sociological fact, do serve as moral communities."[21]

Baxter's response drew upon Milbank's critique of sociology to highlight how the discipline relegates "theology to an interior realm of religious 'belief' or to a historical sphere of religious 'meaning'" and relies upon efficient causality as "the only causes that meet scientific standards of empirical demonstrations and verification," eliminating, "in Aristotelian-Thomistic terms," final and formal causality. Baxter describes Coleman and Gill as adhering to an understanding of theology that involves consideration of "beliefs, doctrines, ideals, moral norms" or the "'ought,'" with sociology measuring the "'is'"—what Christians actually do. "Ethics mediates between the two"—the "'ought'" and the "'is.'" Baxter notes that Gill's extensive discussion of "moral conflict in the Anglican Church" concerning "polygamy, homosexuality, and divorce" never mentions "theological reasons" and suggests that the omission stems from his assumption of "the validity of a post-Kantian, Troeltschian conception of Christian ethics without considering the merits of, say, an Aristotelian-Thomistic conception." Reminiscent of Balthasar's position described above, Baxter furthered his argument of the primacy of the theological context as "the one that can best account for the extraordinary events surrounding the life, death, and resurrection of Jesus Christ, events that no standard sociological analysis can comprehend, events that are 'inexplicable' except in reference to our nature and purpose as given by God."[22]

Four years earlier, in *American Catholic Traditions,* Michael Baxter had briefly described his own project of developing a "Counter-Tradition of Catholic Social Ethics" identified with "Catholic Radicalism" rather than a "Catholic Americanism." Baxter framed his argument historically, noting the isolation of Catholic theology from all other academic inquiry. This separation allowed the "disciplines of politics and economics" to develop in the twentieth century without being "shaped by substantive theological terms and categories." Theological references were those translated "into the much more general tenets of natural theology" that allowed Catholic political and economic theorists to "posit a harmony between Catholicism and the United States." Baxter noted the major advantage of this harmonizing was "currency in national discourse" in so far as the discourse "conformed to the protocols of the modern liberal state, which preclude the substantive grounding in the beliefs and practices of any specific ecclesial body." Another extant but usually ignored tradition is "that of the Catholic radicalists" whose "more theologically charged vision of politics and economics delivers a general critique of the modern state, and a particular one concerning the political and economic order prevalent in the United States." Baxter's project remains to "historicize what appears to be the only normative Catholic social ethics appropriate for the United States' situation" as a critical "first step in presenting a genuine counter-tradition of Catholic social ethics."[23]

Baxter was not the only "theological upstart," though perhaps the most explicit in his strategy of drawing upon resources and frameworks notably different from those that had preceded him. Vincent J. Miller proposed to use Hans-Georg Gadamer, a familiar, theologically friendly philosopher, and, more controversially, Michel Foucault, in outlining "theologies of Tradition." In explaining his work, Miller cites three major "problems which face contemporary theological reflection on tradition." One concerns "development of Christianity and doctrine"; another is "the question of contemporary innovation in the tradition." Both arise from "historical-critical research" and the concomitant "theological reflection on tradition in the past thirty years." The third concerns "the relationship between diversity and inculturation."

Miller first commends the helpfulness of Gadamer's "utterances" that "become 'traditional' because they bear meaning which transcends their originating horizon (that is they are 'classics')." The limits of Gadamer's approach are then made clear in Foucault's genealogical analysis which illuminates the role of "institutions, technologies, and power" in theologies of tradition. Miller's concluding remarks focus on the traditional marks of the church, finding in Gadamer's approach an ability to consider "the question of apostolicity" and in Foucault an affinity with "the mark of catholicity in its ability to value the particular liberative potential of diverse forms of Christianity." Miller's deft intertwining of the late modern Gadamer, the postmodern Foucault, and the traditional marks of the church displays the kind of bricolage associated with postmodern approaches to theological studies.[24]

RESSOURCEMENT ON THE BACK ROADS

Reviewing these volumes, one also discovers the recovery of figures from the past whose names are less familiar than Rahner, Lonergan, or even Newman and Moeller but whose work provides alternative perspectives to those assumed as normative. Certainly Michael Baxter's recovery of a U.S. Catholic radical tradition of Dorothy Day, Paul Hanley Furfey, and Virgil Michel is one example. The volume in which his essay appears explores possible *American Catholic Traditions: Resources for Renewal*. The opening essay, "On the

Back Roads: Searching for American Catholic Intellectual Traditions," examines the distinctiveness of Catholic intellectual culture, at least historically. Unlike those intellectual traditions that valorize the individual who continuously breaks with the past, Catholic intellectuals clearly express their responsibility to the tradition, their ability to mine "the intellectual riches of the Catholic tradition." In traveling the "back roads," Sandra Yocum Mize identifies five possible sites of American Catholic intellectual traditions in need of further exploration. These include Catholic discourse on its relationship to "America," literature on the Americanizing and Catholicizing of immigrants and the emergence of a middle-class Catholic culture, engagement in various intellectual movements including Catholic women's production of fiction like that of their Protestant counterparts, African American Catholic discourse on being members of a transnational church, and Hispanic theological anthropology embedded in liturgical and devotional practices.[25]

The remainder of the volume presents a variety of American Catholics whose works offer resources for contemporary theological reflections. Already mentioned is Michael Baxter's exploration of Catholic radicalism as an alternative resource for social ethics. Frederick Christian Bauerschmidt considers "The Politics of the Little Way" in his exploration of Dorothy Day's reading of Thérèse de Lisieux as a resource for a "political-mystical theology," along the lines of David Tracy and Edward Schillebeeckx. According to Bauerschmidt, such a reading of a reading provides alternative conceptions of both terms—mystical and political. Thérèse's Little Way centers "resolutely on the mundane, the quotidian, the small. Her 'spirituality' does not occupy a space apart from the details of everyday life" where everyday life too often presents "the modern world of nihilistic doubt and despair." The Little Way serves as "response to the eclipse of God in modernity" in which "*each one of those small sacrifices* is a point of contact with the infinite love of Christ"—made possible "through the sufferings of Christ on the Cross." This contact becomes in Dorothy Day's reading "an alternative conception of politics, the politics of the Little Way in which the weak find their strength. Rather than the art of control, this politics is the art of surrender, the art of precariousness, the art of suffering in a world from which God seems so often eclipsed." Dorothy Day practiced these politics daily in and through the Catholic Worker movement—"the politics of the Cross."[26]

James T. Fisher's brief essay "Dorothy Day, an Ordinary American" stands between Baxter's and Bauerschmidt's essays on Day's alternative vision. He cautions against forgetting the complexity of Day's contexts, including "the ideological assumptions that pervaded Dorothy Day's middle-class, middle-brow, middle-American upbringing" including her "Protestant Midwestern background." Fisher notes that "the deepest roots of Catholic Worker radicalism were much more 'American' than those of the 'Americanist' theorists." Aside from highlighting the contested nature of Dorothy Day's legacy among scholars of American Catholicism, Baxter's and Fisher's essays provide evidence for the contested nature of those terms so casually employed, "American" and "Catholic."[27]

"Aesthetics" serves as title of the second section in *American Catholic Traditions* and features the highly imaginative work of the Jesuit William F. Lynch. The intent here is to bring before a wider audience Lynch's careful and complex analysis of imagination, analogy, and its relation to faith—an additional resource in a theology whose principal framework is ethical.[28] Catholic aesthetics receives additional and extensive attention in Paul Giles's *American Catholic Arts and Fiction: Culture, Ideology, Aesthetics*, a work that in turn received careful scrutiny by Una Cadegan and Peter Huff. Both note Giles's apparent unwillingness, in Cadegan's words, "to pay more attention to the devotion of others [Catholic artists] insofar as it is part of his data."[29] In other words, Giles fails to consider the influence of Catholic beliefs and practices on Catholic believers and practitioners. Again ambiguities surround the descriptor, "American Catholic." Both Cadegan and Huff praise Giles's efforts even as they note, perhaps with a scholar's glee, that much remains to be done in this area.[30]

Of course, the 1996 volume is not the only one to insert these alternative sources for theological work. Several volumes feature essays that do similar work. *Theology and Lived Christianity* features as its opening essay, "A *Ressourcement* from the Margins: U.S. Latino Popular Catholicism as Lived Religion." Here Roberto S. Goizueta considers the ways in which "the contemporary, professional (or academic) theological enterprise is itself challenged by the lived religion of the poor, especially the lived religion of U.S. Hispanic and Latin American Catholics." Goizueta's explorations lead him to raise deeply challenging questions about contemporary forms of "the theological enterprise" with its methodological preoccupations. He finds in "the postmodern assertion that there is, in fact, nothing at all 'behind' the appearances" to be "the logical conclusion of the modern separation of the appearance and the real." The theologian preoccupied with methodology is free from "ever having to commit him or herself to a particular truth, or any truth at all."

This preoccupation stands in contrast to the "lived religion" of the poor with its focus on "Jesus Christ, Guadalupe, San Martin, etc., as the sources of their identity, their own praxis, their own experience, their own justice, their own liberation." Goizueta illustrates his point in the popular outcry against Abbot Guillermo Schulemburg of Mexico City's Basilica of Our Lady of Guadalupe. He eventually resigned after suggesting that Juan Diego "was 'not a reality.'" Goizeuta then relates, as a contrast, his conversation with a Mexican *abuelita* in which she responds to his query of Guadalupe's significance for her "with two words: 'Se quedó.' ('She stayed.')" Guided by the *abuelita* and Gustavo Gutiérrez, Goizueta reflects upon their shared conviction that "the fullness of . . . divine love . . . becomes visible, or tangible in history in a particular form." Theologians in their privileged places can afford "the luxury of avoiding the question of truth" but the poor do not. "Christ on the Cross does not have the luxury of avoiding the truth question until all the evidence is in." Goizueta concludes that only when "our own praxis is conformed to God's cruciform praxis in history, we can become participants in the historical struggle for liberation."[31]

Anthony J. Godzieba turned to an earlier era and the religious art of Caravaggio (Michelangelo Merisi) to offer his corrective to the "fundamental working narrative of theological history" that ignores or dismisses baroque Catholicism. A volume, for the first time, actually includes black and white reproductions of the paintings discussed. In answering the question, "What does Caravaggio the theologian have that we need?" Godzieba focuses upon his "sacramentally voluptuous canvases dripping with flesh and light." Caravaggio's paintings "offer an important testimony to the vitality of Baroque Catholicism, to the earthy, affective, and praxical nature of its spiritualities, and to the fundamental sacramental commitments which characterize the Catholic construal of reality, particularly its optimistic evaluation of materiality." Godzieba's analysis illustrates his desire for "a more general retrieval" that will affirm that "God's communion with humanity is every place and every time" including the recently maligned "modernity." This "positive retrieval of the Baroque" can contribute to retrieving "a multi-layered 'modernity' far more complex than some theological commentators allow, one composed of a variety of cultural and religious histories."[32]

If paintings served as theological medium for the sixteenth century, then clearly movies serve as theological medium for the twentieth. Anthony Smith certainly showed how even a John Ford western can display Catholic sensibilities embedded in a story line as well as cinematography.[33] James Fisher offers a close, contextual reading of *On the Waterfront* as a potent resource for historical theology. Fisher, in his signature style, deftly moves back and forth between the highly acclaimed *On the Waterfront* and the Jesuit, John Corridan, whose work on the waterfront inspired Budd Schulberg's screenplay. Fisher's research on the film's history and the history of Corridan's work on the waterfront made clear that Corridan's "own tenuous stature within the Catholic metropolis was far too complex an issue to be captured on celluloid." Corridan's own commitment to Catholic social teaching placed him at odds with many of the longshoremen he attempted to assist. The gap between the movie and the ministry does not make the film any less valuable a resource.

"Approaching certain films and the products of other relevant cultural forms not as mere artifacts but—as in the case of *On the Waterfront*—embodiments of theological desire, we might help open paths to collective remembering."[34]

Many other examples of theological *ressourcement* exist throughout these volumes. Keith Egan turns to Theresa of Avila's *The Book of Her Foundations* for a practical ecclesiology in terms of "what it means to be a more contemplative church."[35] Peter Bernardi examines a controversy involving Maurice Blondel, whose own work is cited in Gustavo Gutiérrez's *A Theology of Liberation*. Bernardi finds that examining "the dispute between Blondel and [Pedro] Descoqs serves to illuminate several contemporary disputes concerning the church's role in society." He mentions specifically the neoconservatives' championing "liberal free market" and the leftists joining faith with "Marxist social theory."[36] Ann Coble provides an overview of Clarence Jordan's "Cotton Patch" version of scripture and his living out the Sermon on the Mount on Koinonia Farm. His life's work influenced Dorothy Day and the Catholic worker movement and facilitated the conversion of Millard Fuller, who eventually founded Habitat for Humanity.[37] All of these examples highlight the amazing variety of sources, from radical activist to *abuelita*, from movie director to mystic, that inspire and inform theology at the turn of the third millennium.

THEOLOGY'S GEOGRAPHY

Traversing centuries and continents from twentieth-century Hollywood to the New York port to sixteenth century Spain and twentieth century France and Latin America to rural Georgia made contemporary theologians self-conscious of time and place. Geographical metaphors abound throughout these volumes. One might recall Yocum Mize's search of the "back roads" for American Catholic intellectual traditions or Vincent Miller's essay that asks "History or Geography? Gadamer, Foucault, and Theologies of Tradition." Miller is not alone in noting the geographical significance of history. The eminent church historian Justo González titled his essay, "The Changing Geography of Church History." Based upon his plenary address, the essay describes the "polycentric" reality of Christianity with the "vitality, missionary and evangelistic zeal, and even theological creativity" situated now in the South. Church history's "topography" requires the study of more than the "mountains and mountain chains," i.e., figures like Thomas Aquinas or Innocent III. González writes of "descending into the valleys" to examine women's roles, the lives of the poor, or "everyday Christian devotion and practice."[38]

The 1997 annual volume relies upon a more contentious geographical image to describe its overall task. The title, *Theology: Expanding the Borders*, proved especially evocative when one recalls that the convention took place in San Diego, which borders Mexico. In certain places along the major highways of San Diego one can see yellow signs that in the Midwest might bear the silhouetted images of children playing or deer crossing. On San Diego freeways, the images are of two adults and a child, like some rendition of the Holy Family, warning drivers to watch out for illegal immigrants crossing the freeway. Yet, the volume does not espouse eliminating borders but expanding them because the borderlands are also those places rich in the interchange between different cultures, perspectives, commitments.

Two of the plenary speakers' essays highlight the multivalent meanings of "borders." Anne Patrick notes how "borders" can serve as "markers" that can facilitate respect among theologians for difference, as "barriers" that too often "stand in the way of justice and solidarity among peoples, . . . nature and the earth itself," and as frontiers that suggest "hope for a better life."[39] Virgilio Elizondo asks, "Is the transgression of borders destruction of life or the birth of new life?" Elizondo responds with "Our Lady of Guadalupe" who joined "the Iberian soul . . . with the ancient Mexican soul to give rise to the mestizo soul of Mexico. This was the ongoing miracle of Guadalupe, this is what made her the Mother of the Americas, because she had given birth and continues to give birth to the new people of the Americas." Herein lies the future to which theologians are called to respond, finding in Jesus's table fellowship the origins of Christians' "most cherished and sacred rite . . . the festive family meal—sacred because it dared to exclude no one!"[40]

Both Elizondo's and Patrick's essays appear in a section titled "The Border as Epistemology." Among the other six essays in this section, one stands out for its overcoming the barrier of language to expand the borders of what is an acceptable volume submission. For the first time ever, an essay written in Spanish appears. Ruy G. Suárez Rivero, systematic theology professor from Universidad Iberoamericana–Noroeste writes on "Teología en la Frontera: Límite y Encuentro de Dos Mundos," in which he explores the particularities of the borderlands of Tijuana–San Diego, where Mexico and the United States encounter each other. He explores this "*frontera*" as a theological locus of God's self-communication in the "*cotidianeidad*" or the daily life—the here and now—especially among the poor and displaced.[41]

The volume drew attention to other kinds of borders. J. Matthew Ashley considers "A Post-Einsteinian Settlement? On Spirituality as a Possible Border-Crossing Between Religion and the New Science." Ashley's response to the settlement question sounds a warning against too quickly correlating statements from the mystical tradition with claims of the new science.[42] Both

Bradford E. Hinze and Dennis Doyle explore borderlands within ecclesiology. Hinze considers the church's catholicity in light of its past and present response to ethnic and racial diversity.[43] Dennis Doyle examines the theological works of Elizabeth Johnson and Roberto Goizueta through the lens of communion ecclesiology, mindful of their "identifying themselves as operating on the margins."[44]

Whether appealing to specific geographical locales or geography in general, the metaphors of place locate theology within the emerging discourse identified with that wondrously vague term, postmodern. Being a good postmodern term, "postmodernity" is multivalent with meanings dependent on the location of the discourse and its speaker. The postmodern pose might take on a jaunty air of the ironic where claims of truth and commitment bemuse or might acquire a somber tone, evoking near despair. In its less extreme forms, it looks a bit like the virtue of humility as one acknowledges the limits of one's perspective and the partiality of one's response. Method as much as subject matter becomes for most a self-conscious choice.

THE LURE OF METHOD

Theological methods continue to receive a great deal of notice with new variations and combinations evident in these ten volumes. Three approaches that remain deeply embedded in contemporary theological discourse are those of feminist, liberationist, and cross-cultural approaches. Feminist analysis, now with a focus on gendered constructions of reality, appears as a standard tool in theological work displayed in these ten volumes. Anne E. Patrick, in her previously discussed "Markers, Barriers, and Frontiers: Theology in the Borderlands," mentions matter-of-factly her own identity as "a U.S. Anglo feminist theologian."[45] Elizabeth Clark, in similar fashion, notes her identity as a "feminist historian" in "Rewriting Early Christian History." Neither display an apologetic tone. Clark examines "some of the problems that literary theory has posed for feminist historians" and then turns to an analysis of "Augustine's representation of his mother Monica in the *Confessions* and the Cassiciacum *Dialogues*."[46] Feminism fits seamlessly into both scholars' analyses.

Lisa Sowle Cahill made use of feminist analysis to consider family as the mediating structure to connect sex and gender to the common good. After examining the biological and moral dimensions of family, Cahill draws upon the "domestic church image" which has the potential of making "the family itself the social educator of its members for solidarity and service outside the family."[47] In response, Thomas A. Shannon questions her appeal to sociobiology, especially its effect on intentionality and to the "domestic church," given that "the family is no longer the fundamental unit of society." He also observes that the "domestic church" image may "import the concept of hierarchy into the family."[48] Surely Shannon's response as much as Cahill's essay indicates how controverted the issues around gender and family are—not even to mention the theological import of changing views regarding both.

Other examples highlight how feminist theology reshapes questions in every field. Kathleen M. O'Connor's essay, "Surviving the Storm in a Multi-Cultural World," serves as the opening essay in *Theology and Sacred Scripture*. The biblical scholar introduces as one of her fundamental questions: "Can we relinquish Euro-centered male theologies that too often encode and support our present world, either by leaving too much out or by implicitly affirming violence, individualism, and arrogance?" Her ability to pose such a question assumes feminists' trenchant criticisms of "Euro-centered male theologies."[49]

As significant are those instances of constructive feminist critiques of earlier feminist theological perspectives. Two examples appear in the Christology volume. Gloria L. Schaab offers a "*Shekhinah* christology" through "the feminist methodological process of critique, retrieval, and reconstruction." *Shekhinah*, a biblically based feminine personification of God's presence, takes into account Jesus's Jewishness, mitigates his maleness, and avoids valorizing "suffering and victimization as salvific."[50] Linda S. Harrington reads with sympathy the christologies of Rosemary Radford Ruether, Rita Nakashima Brock, Jacquelyn Grant, and Elizabeth Johnson. Drawing on her "own prayerful reflection," however, she pinpoints the need for "a personal Christ, anchored in time and space by a strong connection with Jesus of Nazareth." For her, "continuing dialogue" is the response required to developing feminist Christology.[51]

Other alluring methods, already discussed in this chapter, are from the social sciences. Less freighted discussions of theology's use of the social scientific method than the Baxter-Coleman debates appear in *Theology and the Social Sciences*. Sociologists James Davidson and Patricia Wittberg, S.C., present a two-part essay entitled "Religion and Society—Two Sides of the Same Coin." In his introduction, James Davidson states his and Wittberg's shared assumption of "a close relationship between religion and society" and that both sociologists and theologians benefit from understanding the dynamics of that relationship.[52]

Discussions of sociology's influence are not limited to the volume on social science. In the one on scripture, Victor H. Matthews examines the benefits in his "Traversing the Social Landscape: The Value of the Social Scientific Approach to the Bible." To explore scripture's "social landscape," the biblical scholar uses "a variety of sociological and anthropological methods in conjunction with the emerging field of ethnoarcheology" to examine the cultural and social contexts of the biblical texts.[53] Carol J. Dempsey, the respondent, takes exception to Matthews's claim that these methods enable a scholar "to establish 'the meaning of the text,' because, in my opinion, one can never establish the meaning of the text once and for all." What she seeks to protect is the text as "a living tradition . . . [that] takes on a life of its own in relation to the various communities that hear it, read it, and re-read it." In considering the merits of the social scientific method, she heralds "the visions and values" which are "embedded in the biblical text." Her reasons are reminiscent of Alice Laffey's approach to biblical studies. These "visions and values" are worth "retrieving for the ongoing liberation, redemption, and restoration of all creation." She challenges the audience to consider embracing this "new vision . . . in our midst and within our grasp."[54]

Another social science that appears as an aid to theological analysis is psychology, particularly in relationship to spirituality. Felicidad Oberholzer employed psychology to interpret the dreams of Perpetua as found in the account of her martyrdom. Oberholzer pinpoints that "key to understanding [Perpetua's] dreams and her struggles" is "her relationship with her father." Such "insight into the personal journey" of a great saint and martyr allows one to appreciate "in the deeper layers of her unconscious how she transcended the struggles and conflicts of her journey by her faith, prayer, and God's transforming grace."[55] Mary Frohlich, H.M., provides a "psychological perspective on Thérèse of Lisieux's devotion to the Holy Face." In a manner similar to Oberholzer, Frohlich turned to Thérèse's childhood especially "the initial failure to find libidinal satisfaction in her Mother." Not reducing devotion to neurosis, Frohlich shows how in Thérèse's "mature spirituality, the core focus is clearly shifted from desire for suffering to desire for participation in divine love" that comes about in response to and as transforming of "an immature position of desperate and destructive neediness."[56]

In the provocatively titled essay, "Tribal Encounters: Catholic Approaches to Cultural Anthropology," Elizabeth McKeown explores the uneasy relationship between theology and cultural studies. First, she traces the history of Catholic scholars' engagement in the social sciences, with a special focus on John Montgomery Cooper, who founded CUA's religion and anthropology departments. She concludes with a consideration of "Clifford Geertz's insistence on the priority of 'local knowledge' in human studies." In so far as theology still focused on universal claims, "cultural particularism remind[s] us that cultural anthropology continues to pose challenges for Catholic theology, in what Terrence Tilley calls this '*post*-age.'"[57] Embracing method's lure still has its pleasures and perils.

INCULTURATION, PLURALISM IN A GLOBAL CHURCH

Christianity's universal claims in light of cultural and religious plurality have been the subject of much debate at CTS meetings. In *Theology and Lived Christianity*, Ronald Modras and Peter Phan look at the missionary work of Matteo Ricci in China and Alexandre de Rhodes in Vietnam respectively. In each case, they describe Jesuits who had a sensitivity to the culture of those evangelized. De Rhodes analyzes the necessity of making cultural changes on the basis of "whether it was required by Jesus himself and whether it was opposed to the gospel."[58] Ronald Modras sheds light on de Rhodes's as well as Ricci's practice with his comment: "Accommodating to circumstances was a cardinal principle of Renaissance rhetoric." In other words, Ricci, though exceptional in his brilliance, reflected what other Jesuit confreres attempted to do in their missionary efforts in China and Japan.[59] Like Godzieba's retrieval of Caravaggio, Modras's and Phan's examinations of the mission create a more complex picture of that period's Catholicism.

Francis X. Clooney, S.J., who contributed an essay to *Theology and Sacred Scripture*, shows one possible way of doing comparative theology. The comparative theologian can "gain an overview of how 'sacred scripture' and 'theology' are understood and problematized in a tradition other than our own Catholic tradition." Clooney examines a specific Hindu sacred text, carefully reading back and forth between Hinduism and Christianity to "begin drawing our own Christian theological conclusions." To engage this process offers opportunities to become "educated theologically in a new and richly complicated sense."[60]

Attention to Jewish-Christian relations is evident in several annual volumes. Amy-Jill Levine explores "A Particular Problem: Jewish Perspectives on Christian Bible Study" in *Theology and Sacred Scripture*. For her, maintaining difference is critical. She advises Christians to use "Tanach" when referring to "the Bible of Judaism" but to use "'Old Testament'" when reflecting theologically for the church. Christians and Jews ought to "celebrate our differences" even as we continue "an attempt to determine how we can, each on our own territory and with our own idiom, be good neighbors."[61] In *Christology: Memory, Inquiry, Practice*, Paula Fredriksen contributes an essay that answers the title's questions: "What Does Jesus Have to Do with Christ? What Does Knowledge Have to Do with Faith? What Does History Have to Do with Theology?" Fredriksen provides an overview of various historical developments in the early church's Christology, culminating in an exploration of "Christian constructions of Christian identity" that depends on "the idea of

Judaism as Christianity's opposite." She then looks with hope at the contemporary "Third Quest, the hallmark of which has been the recovery of Jesus' Judaism." She finds in this recovery challenges to those earlier constructions of "Christian identity" and the possibility of an "invigorated modern christology."[62]

THEOLOGY'S CHALLENGES, CHALLENGES TO THEOLOGY

Questions concerning the relationship between history and theology appear throughout these volumes. Terrence Tilley's presidential address examines the relationship in "Practicing History, Practicing Theology." It introduces *Theology and the New Histories*. Tilley argues that previous "construals" of the relationship between theology (or faith) and history depend upon essentializing each term that "obscure[s] the variety" within the various fields of history and in religion and the differences between them. He concludes that conflict often arose from those who "fail to distinguish the descriptive accounts of the historian from the normative recommendations of the theologian." Resolving conflicts, Tilley argues, calls for participants "to rely on that shared practical wisdom, that virtue Aristotle identified as *phronesis* and Aquinas as *prudentia*" to recognize the variations and differences. He concludes by describing "a sacramental universe" in which all "can be signs of God for each other." It is with that conviction in God's presence as sacramental that theologians and historians are called to engage in their disciplinary practices.[63]

Tilley exemplified this kind of work in subsequent volumes. In *Theology and the Social Sciences*, he examines "The Historical Fact of the Resurrection" in which he argues against "a specific view of the relationship between history and theology that is unsustainable" that "makes the Resurrection just the opposite of a fact." Tilley examines the assumptions of those who "accept the relationship of the social science of history and theology" without an adequate assessment of "the 'background beliefs' they hold," most notably the incarnation. To accept the New Testament's witness to the "historical fact of the Resurrection" must be understood in the wider context of beliefs about Jesus and "God acting 'immanently.'"[64] Another essay, "'O Caesarea Philippi': On Starting Christology in the Right Place," in *Theology and Sacred Scripture*, focuses upon "the disciples' imagination" as "(proximate) source of christology." Using the Markan passage depicting Peter's response at Caesarea Philippi and Jesus's subsequent correction, Tilley probes how the disciples' imagination is "disciplined by the very word of God." According to Tilley, this approach "reconceives the place of christology in the life of faith."[65] In *Christology: Memory, Inquiry, Practice*, he puts his reconception in service of "The Practice of Teaching Christology: History and Horizons," where "christology means to develop our students' imaginations through the discipline of understanding biblical and traditional forms developed by the christological imaginations."[66]

Tilley's essay is one of three on "The Practice of Teaching Christology." In "The Evolution of an Undergraduate Christology Course," Patricia Plovanich explores how she developed the course in a series of stages. First she adapted graduate level investigations of Christology for undergraduates. Then she drew from her graduate studies to fashion a course "oriented to the life and faith experience of the students." She finally included the effects of their "geographical and cultural locations" in San Diego.[67]

Elena G. Procario-Foley considers "Christology as Introduction" in light of directing a "cross-disciplinary program in Jewish-Catholic studies." After teaching a course, "Jesus and Judaism," Procario-Foley determined that the course in Christology had to deal with "the christological roots of anti-Semitism." Fully cognizant of "the difficulties inherent in historical Jesus research and in incorporating it into undergraduate christology courses," Procario Foley encouraged her colleagues to "make the effort to integrate story, theology, and praxis in order to excite students about the christological question." Such a course must also make clear Jesus is Jewish as well as critically assess Christianity's long history of anti-Semitism from the Gospels to the present.[68] One ought to pause for a moment to recollect the discussions from almost fifty years earlier regarding teaching undergraduates. The shifts in content and concerns is worth noting even as all three, like their predecessors, continue to be concerned for the students as potential believers and practitioners in faith.

Christology proved to be among the most controversial topics taken up in this decade. Christianity has a long and noble heritage of debating what it means to identify Jesus as the Christ. At the beginning of the third Christian millennium, Roger Haight created a minor controversy with his work *Jesus, Symbol of God*. The Congregation for the Doctrine of the Faith in fact prevented him from teaching at Weston Jesuit School of Theology. The CTS invited him to provide a plenary address on "The Future of Christology: Expanding Horizons, Religious Pluralism, and the Divinity of Jesus" (the topic of Haight's new book project). Haight began and ended his talk with the disclaimer that no one can know the future. What he did, instead, was to consider how changes in "*spatial contexts,*" "*temporal contexts,*" and "*experiential and mental horizons*" affect "development in people's thinking," and then he applied each to understanding of Jesus in light of other religions and to views of Jesus's divinity. The key theological conclusion affirms "both that God is at work in Jesus in a distinctive and historically unique way, and that God can also be present and at work in other historical symbols of God that are unique."[69]

Haight's christological views received further attention at the 2002 convention in Robert Masson's critique of *Jesus Symbol of God*. Masson's critique focuses upon Haight's conceptualizing of "symbol." Masson wanted to appeal to metaphoric analogy, which allows "conceptual room to say what could not have otherwise been said by forcing language and logic to a new use." Haight's concept of "symbol" led him to conclude that such an appeal to "Logos" makes it ontologically impossible to maintain Jesus's humanity.[70] Haight's response ended with "the question on the table in the increasingly globalized and postmodern culture of today, . . . whether we should accept the challenge of a new metaphoric or symbolic understanding of Jesus that breaks open the present Christian field of meaning, allowing it realistically to address this new world."[71]

M. Shawn Copeland's Christological reflections in the same volume offer a very different approach. She opens with a quote from Catherine of Siena about Jesus Christ's body as a "stairway, so as to raise us up from the way of suffering and set us at rest," which she pairs with a portion of the African American spiritual, "We are climbing Jacob's ladder. Every round goes higher, higher, Soldiers of the Cross." She then relates her observations of observing from her apartment laundry a black woman carefully examining the contents of Copeland's building's dumpster for food. The quote, song, and story together serve as a starting point for her reflection on "mystical-political discipleship as Christological locus." Copeland understood being "Jesus' disciple means to live at the disposal of the cross—exposed, vulnerable, open to the wisdom and power and love of God." She brought to this understanding reflections on Jesus's ministry, the true scandal of crucifixion in the first century, and "the cross as a condition of discipleship." The essay's final section offers a meditation inspired by "the mystical experiences of Catherine of Siena and of enslaved Africans in the United States. . . . They capture what it means to understand that the power of God in the cross is the power to live and to love—even in the teeth of violence and death."[72] Two respondents, Mary Ann Hinsdale and Anthony Godzieba, adopted Copeland's reflective tone to consider what it means to be a disciple of Jesus who loves "at the disposal of the cross." The differences between Copeland's and Haight's approaches to Christology highlight in varied and fascinating ways just how disparate theological loci had become even when considering a central tenet of Christian faith.

VATICAN II—AN UPDATE

The ebb and flow of Vatican II's legacy had so shaped CTS's theological discourse that it seemed to be the ancient language of the people. Of course, it resonated with the language of Christians from every generation, but it used that language to consider the work of the Spirit in the church and the world—in its care for all that is human and in its desire, especially through the Eucharistic liturgy, to activate the laity to care for the world. A sampling of essays on church and liturgy from 1995 through 2004 provides a glimpse of Vatican II as part of the stream of the living tradition.

The CTS took the Holy Spirit as its principal focus in 2003. In his introduction, Hinze let his readers know that the volume concentrates on the "practical implications of the doctrine of the Spirit for the church and the world." The pneumatological explorations are framed in "three theological operations: naming the Spirit of God, narrating the action of the Spirit in a divided world and wounded church, and advancing the Spirit's work of communion and justice."[73] Bernd Jochen Hilberath named the Spirit as "sender, receiver, and message."[74] Jane E. Linahan named the Spirit as "Grieving" and in that grief the "Bearer of the Suffering of the World." She relied on Jürgen Moltmann's theology, but takes her primary inspiration from the scripture passage warning against grieving the Holy Spirit. In her conclusion, she worries that some might find her reliance on biblical imagery too literal, but she argues that scriptures' "exhortation not to grieve the Holy Spirit of God is one of profound seriousness: any assault upon any part of creation impinges upon the One who holds it in life and loves it dearly."[75]

Robert Schreiter's essay is a masterful example of "narrating the action of the Spirit in a divided world and wounded church" in "Mediating Repentance, Forgiveness, and Reconciliation: What Is the Church's Role?" The topic had a particular urgency in light of the crisis caused by revelations of priests' sexually abusing minors. Shreiter makes clear that reconciliation requires "creating a new, long-term relationship" rather than a brief utterance of sorrow. Repentance and reparation require "symbolic communicative action" that recognizes "history has been irrevocably changed." One must "communicate about what has been done in the past" and "engage in some restorative rebuilding." The third dimension, "forgiveness is an essential element in the reconstruction of society, in creating a different kind of future." It is also "hard work" and complex, for it also has to do with the "quality of memory . . . a shift in perspective toward the past" but not forgetting it in order to forgive. The church can play an important role in reconciliation if it can provide "safe and hospitable spaces," a possibility deeply compromised in the sexual abuse scandal. Schreiter suggests a purification of church spaces to restore some measure of trust and lifted up "the treasure trove of rituals and symbols" that the church can offer in service to reconciliation.[76]

"Advancing the Spirit's work of communion and justice" through the church is Jamie Phelps's focus in her essay "Liberation for Communion: The Church's Justice Mission in an Unjust Society." She leads her readers through an extensive tour of the "dominative power dynamics" that perpetuate social injustice. The church, by way of contrast, is "the communion of Christian believers and disciples of Christ." To be in "communion" requires the "integration within the church of all those elements 'of positive value' from each culture" coupled with the commitment to "proclaiming to the world the good news of God's call to salvation and the possibility of the full realization of the kingdom through the power of the Spirit."[77] Phelps, as well as Schreiter, offers hope-filled visions of the church's positive impact in the world in and through the workings of the Spirit.

Liturgy served as focus of a few essays scattered throughout the volumes. The presence of the essay "Practicing the Freedom of God: Formation in Early Baptist Life" by NABPR member Philip E. Thompson may be deemed a part of the Vatican II legacy. At least from a Catholic perspective, his piece in the CTS volume is emblematic of the Society's ecumenical commitment. His work examines "a juxtaposition of a certain theological conviction to the ordo of worship, and indeed to the whole of ecclesial life" that was part of Baptists' "spiritual history." He reviewed this early history to provide Baptists with "an entry point" for "sustained dialogue with our own tradition." Such a dialogue may assist in "formation that may properly be called both ecclesial and liturgical."[78]

Michael F. Steltenkamp, S.J., examines the less than successful legacy of liturgical reform in his "New Age, Environmentalism, and Liturgical Inculturation." After asserting that the current liturgy "could be just as uninspiring or lifeless as the old ones they replaced," Steltenkamp describes a positive response he experienced when he served at a Lakota reservation. He adapted the Eucharistic rite "by composing prayers that reflected the reservation milieu." He suggests using a similar approach in other contexts to stop the exodus from uninspiring liturgy to New Age rituals. What Steltenkamp sought is the formation of "'ritual Christians' who are drawn to the prayerfully articulate enactment of human longing."[79]

M. Therese Lysaught also looked to the "Eucharist as Basic Training: The Body as Nexus of Liturgy and Ethics." She observed the role that physical discipline plays in the formation of soldiers and athletes, and in the early Christian church, martyrs who trained their bodies through ascetical practices to withstand the torture of martyrdom. A Christian life requires formation "through a consistent regimen of bodily practices," most notably the Eucharist as "the summit toward which the activity of the Church is directed and the fount from which all her power flows." Lysaught calls for the "production of 'Eucharistic' bodies . . . the bodies of Christians and the Body of Christ." She emphasizes that this is "a gradual process of 'incubation' or habituation over time dependent upon an arduous, complex, and lengthy regimen of physically mediated practices."[80]

The ebb and flow in these volumes, like that in the council itself, seems to be between the local and the global, the particular and the universal. Michael Barnes in both *Religion, Ethics, and the Common Good* and *Theology and the New Histories* upholds not only the possibility but also the importance of defending "a path available which leads away from sectarian separateness towards a more common good." His aspirations are strikingly like those in *Gaudium et Spes*. Drawing from Karl Rahner's theology of creation, Barnes warns against "separatist Christian communities [that] may cut the self off from larger—and graced—social and cosmic reality."[81] In "Universalist Pluralism and the New Histories," he suggests that those with a "universalist bent" might view "the new histories . . . as way stations towards an eventual new single all-embracing history of human activities." After reviewing and critiquing "anthropological and postmodern relativisms," Barnes offers a three-page list of "'human commonalities'" and "commonalities in modes of thought." He concludes that "Western rationality is not really Western; it is human." Acknowledging the importance of "new historics" that express concerns, especially of previously marginalized communities, Barnes remained hopeful that eventually "these histories will also contribute to a larger sense of human solidarity, with trust in the common human capacity for both mutual sympathy and rational reflection."[82]

This turn to the universal may also be a turn to the particular, at least according to Alex García Rivera, who introduces the reader to "the 'little stories' told about San Martín" de Porres within the context of a discussion of the "semiotics of culture." The "'little story' of the dog, cat, and mouse drinking from the same bowl of soup at the feet of Saint Martin [a "mulatto"] represents a view of the common good as this 'imaginal existence.'" The "little story" depicts "a New World understanding of grace" as "healing in the cosmic sense." As portrayed in Saint Martin de Porres's "little stories," the "common good" supports "not . . . the narrow 'rational' beings of the *encomenderos* which live in a tiny universe created through forced human relationships, but as *criaturas de Dios* which live in the expansive universe of cosmic fellowship."[83] So in gazing on the particularities of the "little story," one also recognizes the "Big Story" of God's redemptive love. Whether in the appeal to the universal or the particular, each representation of humans in church and world resonated with Vatican II's emphasis on participation in the life of the world and the liturgy that gives life.

DEFINING COLLEGE THEOLOGY AGAIN

So what of the "theology" of the College Theology Society? The fiftieth anniversary appears under the title, *New Horizons in Theology*. Terrence Tilley, editor of the volume, invited plenary speakers, who turned their attention to various points on that horizon. Elizabeth A. Johnson considered "Horizons of Theology: New Voices in a Living Tradition." She selected "an American voice, a global voice, and the voice of the earth." The American exhibits complexity drawn from "the experience of the church in this country" that has precipitated "something new" in theology—in terms of who is engaged in theological studies and where and what they study and teach. Drawing from "American philosophical and cultural resources" accompanied by criticism of the culture's "consumerist, selfishly narrow, violent, and amnesiac streams," theologians "will bear fruit in ways yet to be envisioned that will benefit the world church." Turning to global voices, Johnson singled out four—the poor; women; black, Hispanic, and Asian peoples; and world religious traditions. "Watered by these global theological flows, the work of trying to 'name the grace' of God's presence in *this* global era and not some other moves theology beyond parochial horizons and narrow interests." Listening to their voices will "demand of us a new mode of working and relating to them." Listening to "the voice of the earth" means putting into practice the principle put forth by Pope John Paul II in 1990, "'respect for life and for the dignity of the human person extends also to the rest of creation.'" Elizabeth Johnson exhorted her audience with "a passionate urgency about the need for theology to engage the real questions of our day." Unless it does, "Christianity will fade away." Johnson, however, placed her "wager" on theologians, including CTS members, responding with the passion and urgency required.[84]

In "The Future of Theology in the Church," Joseph Komonchak refuses to provide predictions and so turns to "the recent past" to explore the expanding "horizon of theology" for "clues as to how to prepare for expansions of our horizons in the future." He begins with the theology that operated when the "Society of Catholic College Teachers of Sacred Doctrine" began with debates between the "scholastic" and an "existential appropriation of the faith and its application to life." Komonchak describes his own scholastic education at the Gregorian University in Rome as "comprehensive"doctrinally, but not in examining "the social, political and economic realms of contemporary life or in the idea that the church might have a role within them or in their regard." Gradual shifts in such engagement were evident in the papally sanctioned Catholic Action, but it was the Second Vatican Council that "transformed the theological scene" including precipitating the "rapid collapse of the neo-scholastic paradigm."

Komonchak identifies "two orientations of post-conciliar Catholic theology"—"a *ressourcement*-approach" identified with the "more biblical, patristic, and liturgical emphases" associated with Henri de Lubac, and "an *aggiornamento*-approach" inspired by *Gaudium et spes* and *Dignitatis humanae* and associated with the Thomist-inspired theology of Karl Rahner and Edward Schillebeeckx. In considering the "church in her relation to the world," Komonchak observes that "there is no church except in the world," and it is "the church [that] is the difference Jesus of Nazareth has made and makes in human history." Theologians serve that church—"a church that is faithful to its own originating center [Jesus Christ], proclaimed, interpreted, and appropriated as the word of life for all circumstances and challenges. To be, by one's research and teaching, of service to that event is a worthwhile way of living one's life."[85]

Two other essays appear in the fiftieth volume's first section, "*Tour D'Horizon*," to illuminate the new horizons in theology. Norbert Rigali offers perspectives on "New Horizons in Moral Theology." He traces the radical changes in moral theology as it transformed from guidance for confessors to Bernard Häring's "'Christocentric turn'" to attempts at a revisionist form of norms-based moral theology. Rigali then cites the various sources of influence including Vatican II's affirmation of the "lay person's vocation" and ecumenism, the emergence of liberation theology and feminism, the "return to virtue ethics," and the church's "globalization." From that confluence of movements, what emerged is no longer "moral theology" but "the foundations for a transformed theological discipline solidly established and in place, and with a new theology of the Christian life rising promisingly on those foundations into the church's third millennium."[86]

J. Matthew Ashley examines "New Horizons for Mysticism and Politics: How the Agenda Has Shifted." After tracing the linking of mysticism and politics to Latin American liberation theology's confronting "dehumanizing poverty and injustice" and Johannes Metz's political theology addressing European secularization, Ashley considers the future challenges with a special eye to his own U.S. context. Ashley identifies the challenges of "radical pluralism and environmental degradation" as well as "the privatization and depoliticization of Christian spirituality." These challenges are critical items on the agenda of those who wish to convey "the hope that is still present and lifegiving in so many Christian communities that, on the surface, would seem to have no reason to hope." He identifies the task as "fundamental theology" that "seek[s] to understand this faith and this hope in order to encourage and nurture them into the next generation." To which he adds, "I can think of no more exciting or fulfilling work."[87]

TEACHING COLLEGE THEOLOGY

The final topic in the fiftieth volume is "New Horizons in Teaching Theology." It would be difficult to imagine a more appropriate way to complete the first fifty years of annual volumes than where it began, with a focus on the latest thinking on undergraduate theological education. The fiftieth annual meeting's final plenary featured a panel: Sandra Yocum Mize, Miguel Díaz, Mary Ann Hinsdale, and James A. Donahue. All were instructed to read an essay from the 1996 volume in which Patrick Carey provides a review of "College Theology in Historical Perspective."

In his introductory remarks, Carey notes that "defining the discipline became a major problem during the twentieth century." The first school of thought he traces historically is that at Catholic University of America, where men like Thomas E. Shields, John Montgomery Cooper, and William H. Russell "had a progressive-era confidence in empirical science and scientific method and [were] very much in dialogue with modern psychology and progressive education." Carey briefly compares the Catholic University approach with that of the manual tradition at his own institution, Marquette, highlighting the uniqueness of the CUA program at that time. Still, criticism of the CUA approach came from a variety of sources, and most concerned its intellectual caliber. Other alternatives appeared, most notably the Le Moyne plan, a frequent topic of the SCCTSD.

The subsequent developments in "the academic study of religion, whether in its religious studies or theological incarnations, [were] attempt[s] to solve some real problems." Addressing these problems constituted a significant portion of CTS's history, including responding to "the needs of a new generation of students of the 1960s and 1970s, the need to justify a universal course requirement, and the desire for respectability within the academy." Carey then identifies other problems including the separation of "theology from spirituality," an exaggerated optimism about "the possibilities of . . . objectivity," the use of "electives" that prevented any kind of intellectual "integration in the discipline," and the challenges for current Catholic students understanding their own identity.[88] All of these problems remain into the Society's fiftieth year.

Sandra Yocum Mize, presupposing Carey's detailed account of curriculum, provides a brief historical perspective on undergraduate theological education organized around the broader categories: "the content, the site, the demographics, and the purpose." She acknowledges the abundance of methodological approaches in considering content but focuses upon the deeper changes affecting content, liturgical practices, and integration of biblical language and narrative into parish and classroom. Her examples include "the stories Catholics tell themselves about who they are when the dominant biblical images become 'Kingdom of God' or 'Jesus-as-the-one-who-defies-all-authorities-on-behalf-of-the-marginalized.'" Under the heading "site," she considers the shift of theology from the seminary to the college or university that also helps to explain the changing demographics from ordained to lay professors. The purpose generated in this new site amidst students who are very different from seminarians remains key. Recalling Sister Mary Rose Eileen Masterman's purpose for founding a professional society, a concern for the academic and formative quality of college students' theological education, Yocum Mize suggests a continuity in purpose. "Most faculty members today still aspire to helping students to integrate theological perspectives within various modes of critical thinking. Many others want to form students theologically so that they might be transformed for an active life dedicated to works of mercy and justice. Of course some professors simply want to do it all in their work as theological educators."[89]

Miguel Díaz, in "Reading the Signs of the Times: A U.S. Hispanic Perspective on the Future of Theological Education," begins with general observations about most undergraduates who lack foundational background "in religious and theological studies." He quickly turns to U.S. Hispanic theologians who "offer a basis from which to begin to re-vision their [U.S. Hispanic] contributions to theological education." Díaz describes a model based upon Gary Riebe-Estrella's conception of "theological education as *convivencia*, a concept that can be loosely translated as 'life-lived communally.'" The model reflects the "U.S. Hispanic theological anthropology" in its embrace of "a communal, praxis-oriented, liberative, and integral approach to human reality"—one that surely offers undergraduates a theology reconnected to spirituality.[90]

Mary Ann Hinsdale, in her reflections on "New Horizons in Theological Education," reiterates Díaz's concern about students and recapitulates issues Patrick Carey had explored. She seeks "to clarify our present understanding of theological education," examined "changing demographics, both of our students and of ourselves as theological educators," and acknowledges "the need to share 'best practices' with regard to undergraduate curricula and graduate student teacher preparation." Hinsdale frames her clarification of undergraduate theological education in terms of whether it ought to "be primarily academic or pastoral—or both?" and challenges the CTS to take up "a task that is *critical*, not only to our profession, but to the future of the local church itself." Under demographics, Mary Ann focuses upon "NBIASCs: 'never-been-in-any-seminary-or-convent,'" with particular attention to younger women. She wanted to consider "from the standpoint of spirituality" how "women theologians integrate their vocations as theologians with their vocations as committed life-partners." Finally, Hinsdale calls upon the Society to begin "a study of 'best practices' that exist in our Catholic colleges and universities." Her conclusion identifies some "emerging issues," like the "'commodification of theology,'" the uncertain survival of "feminist/womanist/*mujerista* theology," and finally questions around "how spiritual formation can be integrated with the academic study of undergraduate and graduate theology." She welcomes the challenge and had "confidence, drawn from these last fifty years, that we are up to it."[91]

In "Teaching Theology for the Future," James A. Donahue offers his perspective, based upon fifteen years as an undergraduate teacher and student affairs administrator at Georgetown University, and five years as Graduate Theological Union president. He asserts that now "is a most decisive moment for theology" and points to four major factors that "necessitate a new kind of religious leadership for the academy, the churches, and the world." The first is personal fragmentation that fosters a "kind of religious orthodoxy" manifest in an "inexcusably simplistic and reductionistic" piety. The other three are *"globalization," "religious pluralism,"* and *"spiritual hunger."* Donahue accepts the plurality in students' religious background that creates a need "to clarify the landscape of theology" through a well-structured undergraduate curriculum. After considering "the role that theological questions play" in everyday campus life, Donahue turns to graduate education, listing seven "skills and habits of thought and practice"—"dialogue"; "bridg[ing] differences"; especially in interreligious and ecumenical contexts, "community-building"; the obvious acquiring of "knowledge of history and traditions" as well as "knowledge of practices"; a "commitment to inclusiveness"; and "adaptive leadership." Donahue, like others, encourages the CTS to continue "fulfilling its mission" by attentiveness to the present, its use of "insights and resources from the past," and its desire "to provide resources for thinking theologically about our future."[92]

Or perhaps college theology teachers should aspire to a Caravaggio artistry that Tony Godzieba described—an aspiration to express the "incarnational impulse in its sacramental manifestation." The theologian might hone the artistry of teaching that *"actively* discloses or reveals," like Caravaggio's paintings, "works of *poiesis* . . . authentic *performances* in the full Baroque understanding of the term . . . too over the top, too fleshy, too outrageous, too colorful, too 'lacking in decorum' . . . in short, a perfect model of the Catholic theologian."[93] Or perhaps some who teach prefer to turn with the *abuelita* to Guadalupe, who in her own embrace of mestizo reveals God's work in the flesh—outrageous, colorful, and for some 'lacking in decorum.'[94] May others say of all who teach college theology amidst challenges and promises that in the company of Guadalupe and all her companions—living and dead—*nos quedamos!*

NOTES

1. James Donahue, "Introduction: Situating the Common Good in Contemporary Moral Discourse," in *Religion, Ethics, and the Common Good: The Annual Publication of the College The-*

ology Society, vol. 41, eds. James Donahue and M. Theresa Moser, R.S.C.J., (Mystic, CT: Twenty-Third Publications, 1996), ix, xviii.

2. William Portier, "Introduction," in *American Catholic Traditions: Resources for Renewal: The Annual Publication of the College Theology Society*, vol. 42, eds. Sandra Yocum Mize and William Portier, (Maryknoll, NY: Orbis Books, 1997), xi.

3. María Pilar Aquino and Roberto S. Goizueta, "Introduction," in *Theology: Expanding the Borders: The Annual Publication of the College Theology Society*, vol. 43, eds. María Pilar Aquino and Roberto S. Goizueta, (Mystic, CT: Twenty-Third Publications, 1998), x.

4. Gary Macy, "Editor's Preface," in *Theology and the New Histories: The Annual Publication of the College Theology Society*, vol. 44, ed. Gary Macy, (Maryknoll, NY: Orbis Books, 1999), vii, viii, ix, xi.

5. David M. Hammond, "Introduction," in *Theology and Lived Christianity: The Annual Publication of the College Theology Society*, vol. 45, ed. David M. Hammond, (Mystic, CT: Twenty-Third Publications, 2000), ix, x, xi.

6. Michael Horace Barnes, "Introduction," in *Theology and the Social Sciences: The Annual Publication of the College Theology Society*, vol. 46, ed. Michael Horace Barnes, (Maryknoll, NY: Orbis Books, 2001), xi, xvii–xviii.

7. Carol J. Dempsey and William Loewe, "Introduction," in *Theology and Sacred Scripture: The Annual Publication of the College Theology Society*, vol. 47, eds. Carol J. Dempsey and William P. Loewe, (Maryknoll, NY: Orbis Books, 2002), xl,

8. Anne M. Clifford and Anthony J. Godzieba, "Introduction," in *Christology: Memory, Inquiry, Practice: The Annual Publication of the College Theology Society*, vol. 48, eds. Anne M. Clifford and Anthony J. Godzieba, (Maryknoll, NY: Orbis Books, 2003), xi.

9. Bradford E. Hinze, "Introduction," in *The Spirit in the Church and the World: The Annual Publication of the College Theology Society*, vol. 49, ed. Bradford E. Hinze, (Maryknoll, NY: Orbis Books, 2004), xi, xiii, xiv.

10. Terrence W. Tilley, "Introduction," in *New Horizons in Theology: The Annual Publication of the College Theology Society*, vol. 50, ed. Terrence W. Tilley, (Maryknoll, NY: Orbis Books, 2005), xiii.

11. Ann R. Riggs, "Rahner and the 'New Histories': Everything Old Is New Again," in *Theology and the New Histories*, 133, 139, 140.

12. Jeannine Hill Fletcher, "Karl Rahner's Principles of Ecumenism and Contemporary Religious Pluralism," in *Theology and the Social Sciences*, 181, 191–92.

13. Donna Teevan, "Meaning and Praxis in History: Lonerganian Perspectives," in *Theology in the New Histories*, 150, 161.

14. James K. Voiss, S.J., "Hans Urs von Balthasar on the Use of Social Sciences in Ecclesial Reflection: Exposition, Analysis, and Critique," in *Theology and the Social Sciences*, 112, 113, 119, 124, 125.

15. Jason Bourgeois, "Balthasar's Theodramatic Hermeneutics: Trinitarian and Ecclesial Dimensions of Scriptural Interpretation," in *Theology and Sacred Scripture*, 128, 132, 133.

16. David Hollenbach, S.J., "The Common Good in the Postmodern Epoch: What Role for Theology?" in *Religion, Ethics, and the Common Good*, 7.

17. Mary Theresa Moser, R.S.C.J., "Higher Education and the Common Good: Reflections of John Courtney Murray, S.J.," in *Religion, Ethics, and the Common Good*, 237, 249, 250.

18. Hollenbach, "The Common Good in the Postmodern Epoch," 8, 9.

19. Michael H. Barnes, "Community, Clannishness, and the Common Good," in *Religion, Ethics, and the Common Good*, 27, 29, 30.

20. Bernard Cooke, S.J., "Presidential Address," in *Proceedings of the Society of Catholic College Teachers of Sacred Doctrine: Eighth Annual Convention, Detroit, Michigan, April 23–24, 1962*:

The Annual Publication of the College Theology Society, vol. 8, (Weston, MA: Regis College, published by the Society, 1962), 7–10 passim, 8.

21. John A. Coleman, S.J., "Every Theology Implies a Sociology and Vice Versa," in *Theology and the Social Sciences*, 13, 28, 29, 30.

22. Michael J. Baxter, C.S.C., "Whose Theology? Which Sociology?: A Response to John Coleman," in *Theology and the Social Sciences*, 35, 39, 40.

23. Michael J. Baxter, "Notes on Catholic Americanism and Catholic Radicalism: Toward a Counter-Tradition of Catholic Social Ethics," in *American Catholic Traditions: Resources for Renewal*, 53, 54, 54–55, 60, 61, 68.

24. Vincent J. Miller, "History or Geography? Gadamer, Foucault, and Theologies of Tradition," in *Theology and the New Histories*, 57, 62, 66, 69, 71, 79.

25. Sandra Yocum Mize, "On the Back Roads: Searching for American Catholic Intellectual Traditions," in *American Catholic Traditions: Resources for Renewal*, 12, 12–20 passim.

26. Frederick Christian Bauerschmidt, "The Politics of the Little Way: Dorothy Day Reads Thérèse of Lisieux," in *American Catholic Traditions: Resources for Renewal*, 77, 81, 86, 91–92.

27. James T. Fisher, "Dorothy Day, an Ordinary American," in *American Catholic Traditions: Resources for Renewal*, 73, 75.

28. Gerald J. Bednar, "The Contours of the Valley: William F. Lynch, S.J., and Theology," in *American Catholic Traditions: Resources for Renewal*, 141.

29. Una Cadegan, "The Limits of Parody: An Analysis of *American Catholic Arts and Fictions: Culture, Ideology, Aesthetics* by Paul Giles," in *American Catholic Traditions: Resources for Renewal*, 163.

30. Peter A. Huff, "Paul Giles and the Tar-Baby," in *American Catholic Traditions: Resources for Renewal*.

31. Roberto S. Goizueta, "A *Ressourcement* from the Margins: U.S. Latino Popular Catholicism as Lived Religion," in *Theology and Lived Christianity*, 3, 4, 7, 10, 15, 28, 29, 35.

32. Anthony J. Godzieba, "Caravaggio, Theologian: Baroque Piety and Poiesis in a Forgotten Chapter of the History of Catholic Theology," in *Theology and Lived Christianity*, 207, 224, 225, 226.

33. Anthony B. Smith, "Sinners, Judges, and Cavalrymen: John Ford and Popular American Catholicism," in *American Catholic Traditions: Resources for Renewal*.

34. James T. Fisher, "The Priest in the Movie: *On the Waterfront* as Historical Theology," in *Theology and the New Histories*, 182, 183.

35. Keith J. Egan, "The Ecclesiology of Teresa of Avila: Women as Church Especially in *The Book of Her Foundations*," in *Theology: Expanding the Borders*, 146.

36. Peter Bernardi, "Liberation Theology: Looking Back to Blondel and Social Catholicism," in *Theology: Expanding the Borders*, 294, 295.

37. Ann Coble, "Cotton Patch Justice, Cotton Patch Peace: The Sermon on the Mount in the Teachings and Practices of Clarence Jordan," in *Theology and the New Histories*, 202.

38. Justo L. Gonzalez, "The Changing Geography of Church History," in *Theology and the New Histories*, 26, 29, 30, 31.

39. Anne E. Patrick, "Markers, Barriers, and Frontiers: Theology in the Borderlands," in *Theology: Expanding the Borders*, 8, 10, 15, 16.

40. Virgilio P. Elizondo, "Transformation of Borders: Border Separation or New Identity," in *Theology: Expanding the Borders*, 24, 26, 30.

41. Ruy G. Suárez Rivero, "Teología en la Frontera: Límite y Encuentro de Dos Mundos," in *Theology: Expanding the Borders*, 52.

42. J. Matthew Ashley, "A Post-Einsteinian Settlement? On Spirituality as a Possible Border-Crossing between Religion and the New Science," in *Theology: Expanding the Borders*, 99.

43. Bradford E. Hinze, "Ethnic and Racial Diversity and the Catholicity of the Church," in *Theology: Expanding the Borders*.

44. Dennis M. Doyle, "Communion Ecclesiology on the Borders: Elizabeth Johnson and Roberto S. Goizueta," in *Theology: Expanding the Borders*, 200.

45. Patrick, "Markers, Barriers, and Frontiers," 4.

46. Elizabeth A. Clark, "Rewriting Early Christian History," in *Theology and the New Histories*, 96.

47. Lisa Sowle Cahill, "Sex, Gender, and the Common Good: Family," in *Religion, Ethics, and the Common Good*, 162, 171.

48. Thomas A. Shannon, "Response to Lisa Sowle Cahill's 'Sex, Gender, and the Common Good: Family,'" in *Religion, Ethics and the Common Good*, 171.

49. Kathleen M. O'Connor, "Surviving the Storm in a Multi-Cultural World," in *Theology and Sacred Scripture*, 9.

50. Gloria L. Schaab, "The Power of Divine Presence: Toward a *Shekhinah* Christology," in *Christology: Memory, Inquiry, Practice*, 92.

51. Linda S. Harrington, "Feminists' Christs and Christian Spirituality," in *Christology: Memory, Inquiry, Practice*, 230.

52. James D. Davidson, "Religion and Society—Two Sides of the Same Coin, Part 1," in *Theology and the Social Sciences*, 197.

53. Victor H. Matthews, "Traversing the Social Landscape: The Value of the Social Scientific Approach to the Bible," in *Theology and the Social Sciences*, 217, 229.

54. Carol J. Dempsey, O.P., "The Value of the Social Scientific Approach to the Bible: A Response to Victor H. Matthews," in *Theology in the Social Sciences*, 237, 240.

55. Felicidad Oberholzer, "Interpreting the Dreams of Perpetua: Psychology in the Service of Theology," in *Theology in the Social Sciences*, 310, 311.

56. Mary Frohlich, H.M., "'Your Face Is My Only Homeland': A Psychological Perspective on Thérèse of Lisieux and Devotion to the Holy Face," in *Theology and Lived Christianity*, 200, 201.

57. Elizabeth McKeown, "Crafts of Place: A Response to Jon Roberts," in *American Catholic Traditions: Resources for Renewal*, 217–218.

58. Peter C. Phan, "Alexandre de Rhodes' Mission in Vietnam: Evangelization and Inculturation," in *Theology and Lived Christianity*, 104.

59. Ronald Modras, "The Inculturation of Christianity in Asia: From Francis Xavier to Matteo Ricci," in *Theology and Lived Christianity*, 83.

60. Francis X. Clooney, "Theology and Sacred Scripture Reconsidered in the Light of a Hindu Text," in *Theology and Sacred Scripture*, 211, 230.

61. Amy-Jill Levine, "A Particular Problem: Jewish Perspectives on Christian Bible Study," in *Theology and Sacred Scripture*, 17, 22.

62. Paula Fredriksen, "What Does Jesus Have to Do with Christ? What Does Knowledge Have to Do with Faith? What Does History Have to Do with Theology?" in *Christology: Memory, Inquiry, Practice*, 13, 14.

63. Terrence W. Tilley, "Introduction: Practicing History, Practicing Theology," in *Theology and the New Histories*, 3, 8, 12, 13, 14.

64. Terrence W. Tilley, "The Historical Fact of the Resurrection," in *Theology and the Social Sciences*, 89, 100, 103.

65. Terrence W. Tilley, "'O Caesarea Philippi': On Starting Christology in the Right Place," in *Theology and Sacred Scripture*, 147, 150, 151.

66. Terrence W. Tilley, "Teaching Christology: History and Horizons," in *Christology: Memory, Inquiry, Practice*, 273.

67. Patricia A. Plovanich, "The Evolution of an Undergraduate Christology Course," in *Christology: Memory, Inquiry, Practice*, 238.

68. Elena G. Procario-Foley, "Christology as Introduction," in *Christology: Memory, Inquiry, Practice*, 257–258, 258, 259, 261.

69. Roger Haight, "The Future of Christology: Expanding Horizons, Religious Pluralism, and the Divinity of Jesus," in *Christology: Memory, Inquiry, Practice*, 48, 59.

70. Robert Masson, "The Clash of Christological Symbols: A Case for Metaphoric Realism," in *Christology: Memory, Inquiry, Practice*, 81, 82.

71. Roger Haight, "Response to Robert Masson: The Clash of Christological Symbols," 91.

72. M. Shawn Copeland, "To Live at the Disposal of the Cross: Mystical-Political Discipleship as Christological Locus," in *Christology: Memory, Inquiry, Practice*, 177, 180.

73. Bradford E. Hinze, "Introduction," in *The Spirit in the Church and the World*, xiv.

74. Bernd Jochen Hilberath, "Sender, Receiver, and Message: The Holy Spirit as the Communicator between God and the World," in *The Spirit in the Church and the World*.

75. Jane E. Linahan, "The Grieving Spirit: The Holy Spirit as Bearer of the Suffering of the World in Moltmann's Pneumatology," in *The Spirit in the Church and the World*, 45.

76. Robert J. Schreiter, "Mediating Repentance, Forgiveness, and Reconciliation: What Is the Church's Role?" in *The Spirit in the Church and the World*, 56, 59, 60, 61, 62, 63, 65.

77. Jamie T. Phelps, "Liberation for Communion: The Church's Justice Mission in an Unjust Society," in *The Spirit in the Church and the World*, 128, 141, 142, 146.

78. Philip E. Thompson, "Practicing the Freedom of God: Formation in Early Baptist Life," in *Theology and Lived Christianity*, 120, 133.

79. Michael F. Steltenkamp, S.J., "New Age, Environmentalism, and Liturgical Inculturation," in *Theology and Lived Christianity*, 232, 235, 252.

80. M. Therese Lysaught, "Eucharist as Basic Training: The Body as Nexus of Liturgy and Ethics," in *Theology and Lived Christianity*, 268, 269, 268–277, 277.

81. Michael H. Barnes, "Community, Clannishness, and the Common Good," in *Religion, Ethics, and the Common Good*, 33, 47.

82. Michael Horace Barnes, "Universalist Pluralism and the New Histories," in *Theology and the New Histories*, 33, 35–37, 41–44, 49, 50.

83. Alex García-Rivera, "St. Martin de Porres and the Common Good," in *Religion, Ethics, and the Common Good*, 107, 114, 115.

84. Elizabeth A. Johnson, "Horizons of Theology: New Voices in a Living Tradition," in *New Horizons in Theology*, 3, 4, 6–7, 9–10, 10, 12, 13, 14.

85. Joseph A. Komonchak, "The Future of Theology in the Church," in *New Horizons in Theology*, 16, 17, 19, 26, 28, 29, 30, 37.

86. Norbert Rigali, "New Horizons in Moral Theology," in *New Horizons in Theology*, 42, 40–49, 50–53, 53–54.

87. J. Matthew Ashley, "New Horizons for Mysticism and Politics: How the Agenda Has Shifted," in *New Horizons in Theology*, 56–62 passim, 66.

88. Patrick W. Carey, "College Theology in Historical Perspective," in *American Catholic Traditions: Resources for Renewal*, 243, 244, 266–268.

89. Sandra Yocum Mize, "Changing Contours of Theological Education: A Retrospective," in *New Horizons in Theology*, 219, 222.

90. Miguel H. Díaz, "Reading the Signs of the Times: A U.S. Hispanic Perspective on the Future of Theological Education," in *New Horizons in Theology*, 225, 228.

91. Mary Ann Hinsdale, "New Horizons in Theological Education," in *New Horizons in Theology*, 231, 235, 238–239, 240–241.

92. James A. Donahue, "Teaching Theology for the Future," in *New Horizons in Theology*, 244, 245–246, 247, 249, 251, 251–252, 252, 253.

93. Godzieba, "Caravaggio, Theologian," 226.

94. Goizueta, "A *Ressourcement* from the Margins."

Conclusion

*W*hy do college and university theology and religious studies professors still attend the annual four-day CTS meeting that comes just as the invariably exhausting academic year ends? It is not a particularly glamorous or high-profile gathering. The meetings take place, after all, not in a four-star or even a two-star hotel, but on a college campus where one sleeps in a dorm room and feasts on cafeteria food. The attendees are for the most part professors in small Catholic colleges, and a few come from Catholic universities. Perhaps the more salient question is why should anyone, besides attendees, care about the annual meeting of a learned society whose membership has never exceeded fifteen hundred members?

The key to answering both questions is in the rhythms of the meetings. If Catholic theological studies has any semblance of a grassroots movement, the CTS's annual meeting must surely be one of its most enduring sites. On the first evening, the common dining hall eases renewal of friendships made through these once-a-year meetings. College teachers of theology catch up on the latest news from each other's home institutions, discuss works still in progress, ponder the latest worry on the theological horizon, and simply learn about events in each other's family or community life. A plenary on the convention's theme soon follows with the requisite social to encourage more conversation. People slowly drift off to their nearby dorm rooms to rest after a long day, and so ends the first evening with that lovely mix of intellectual engagement, conversation with colleagues, and food and drink. Here is the academic endeavor at its most pleasurable and most elusive. Such conversations among friends animate and influence the participants' intellectual life in ways nearly impossible to capture in any historical account.

The first full day of the meeting resembles most professional conferences though collegiality remains in the foreground. The morning begins for the vast majority with breakfast, again in a common space. One has the opportunity to continue conversations from yesterday or commence new ones with those who happen to sit at the same table. Then people scatter to different sessions, perhaps to convene, give a paper, respond, or simply hear a colleague's work in progress on a topic of interest. One's affiliation with a specific section may have endured for a decade or more, with intellectual exchanges deepening over the years. A graduate student may be presenting for the first time at a professional meeting. She or he usually finds seasoned members attentive and constructively critical. After a coffee break, attendees have an opportunity to participate in another session. Perhaps this time, one chooses a joint session with the NABPR (National Association of Baptist Professors of Religion) or discusses strategies for teaching undergraduates. Lunch in the dining hall is followed by one more slot of multiple sessions and the second plenary focusing on the convention theme. The day concludes for those who so desire with evening prayer, a joint venture of the CTS and NABPR. Hymns are sung, scripture proclaimed, and prayers lifted up to God revealed in Jesus Christ. Then smaller groups of friends disperse to enjoy the area's local cuisine and sights.

The next day follows the same pattern with common meals at breakfast and lunch, multiple sessions, and a plenary presentation. The business meeting, featured regularly in this history, occurs in the afternoon. What follows is the celebration of the Eucharistic liturgy, a sign that most CTS members remain committed to Roman Catholic sacramental practices. The presence of Baptists at Mass reminds all in attendance that life together as Christians still awaits reunification. After partaking in the Lord's banquet, almost everyone joins for a social and then the CTS banquet. Toward the end of the meal, members honor one of their own with an award for best book or article and recognize a graduate student's promise with the Best Essay Award. In alternate years, members hear a presidential address or a citation for the winner of the Presidential Award. After one of these activities, the president announces the evening's end.

That announcement is usually followed by another—the location of the postbanquet party. For those who have never had the good fortune of attending the gathering, its full effect eludes description. Soft drinks, beer, and wine, accompanied by the usual chips and pretzels, are available. Small groups gather for informal conversation, most anticipating the main event. The evening really begins when Mary Ann Hinsdale, I.H.M., or a qualified substitute, organizes the rowdy crowd to sing in rounds, "*Jubilate Deo.*" Then the group continues with some Catholic standards, including but certainly not limited to "*Tantum Ergo*," "Long Live the Pope," and the Catholic Action anthem. Then there is the not so standard, "Vatican Rag," written by Tom Lehrer and usually sung by Michael Barnes, sometimes solo, sometimes in a group. The Baptists sing some of their favorites, including "How Firm a Foundation," "I'll Fly Away," and one that everyone sings with gusto, "Amazing Grace." On occasion, younger participants have led the group in a Saint Louis Jesuit song or summer camp favorite.

Sometime during the evening, William Portier and Terry Tilley sing a remarkable rendition of "House of the Rising Sun"—a prelude to songs by Bob Dylan; John Denver; the Beatles; Van Morrison; John Prine; Crosby, Stills, Nash and Young; Simon and Garfunkel; and the Band. The evening hardly seems complete without a rousing version of "Gloria," "The Weight," "Leaving on a Jet Plane," "Knocking on Heaven's Door," "Teach Your Children," "Spanish Pipe Dream," and the list goes on. It is, to borrow a phrase from the Baptists, a night of fellowship—an act of remembering the past which has formed this Society and its members. Most arise, a little bleary-eyed, the next morning to attend one more session if possible, and then to depart with plans, at least for many, of a return next year.

To include these details in a history of the College Theology Society may seem too in house, of little importance except to those members who attend annual meetings. Yet, such details disclose something crucial about how Catholic theological studies have developed in the last fifty years. The meeting's rhythms display the academic, ecclesial, devotional, social, and cultural elements that have informed U.S. Catholic theology during a remarkable fifty-year period of extraordinary change. Perhaps nowhere in the Society's meetings is the rapidity of generational change among Catholics in the latter half of the twentieth century more evident than in the songfest. Those only a few years younger must learn songs that their only slightly older peers know as Catholic standards.

This history of the College Theology Society provides an entrée into the manifold changes that occurred in theological education, decade by decade, from 1954 to 2004. To teach theology to Catholic undergraduates in 1954 was a relatively novel idea. So novel, those who did thought it wise to form a distinct society to discuss how to improve their craft. None could have foreseen what unfolded in the subsequent decades. Over the next fifty years, certain basic questions continued to be asked about teaching theology, especially to undergraduates. What are the pastoral dimensions of an academic theology course? What obligation, if any, does the college theology professor at a Catholic institution have to grant official Catholic teachings privileged treatment in courses? What ought to be included in a Catholic college's curriculum to ensure that a graduate has a solid grasp of basic Christian theology and a knowledge of other religious traditions? Shouldn't desired outcomes include deepening a student's faith commitment? The questions remain the source of debate and experimentation among those who spend the better part of their lives before students in the classroom.

Answers to these questions have changed over time especially as theologians debate Christianity's uniqueness relative to other religious traditions. Some seek to identify certain principles drawn from Christianity but with a universal appeal. This approach appears, for example, among those trying to translate Catholic social teaching into the common parlance of U.S. culture. Others seek to locate Christianity as one among the many religious traditions seeking the same end. A third approach, frequently the recipient of CTS members' criticism, claims the importance of maintaining Christianity's distinctive identity, especially over against the modern nation-state. This position is frequently labeled sectarian, with Stanley Hauerwas serving as a primary exemplar. All the positions above are responses to the pervasive experience of religious and cultural pluralism in the late twentieth century consumer capitalist democracy.

Method provides another preoccupation among theologians. Concerns about method are found in the preconciliar discussions of neo-scholasticism as much as in Rahner's and Lonergan's thought and in postmodern ruminations. The "turn-to-the-subject" and the concomitant questions concerning hermeneutics clear the path for new approaches to theology. Among the most influential are various liberation theologies with preferential options for the marginalized—the poor, women, gays and lesbians, African Americans, Latinos and Latinas, and others. The postmodern dissolution of the "subject" has, in turn, created new challenges especially for those who have appealed to personal experience as the primary theological locus.

Privileging those previously marginalized contributed to the rethinking of other fields, especially biblical studies and history. Biblical scholars reviewed here moved from introducing historical-critical approaches to championing the text's liberationist elements. Historians eventually began including the previously ignored. Julian of Norwich provides an alternative to Anselm's soteriology, and the "little stories" of St. Martin de Porres inform epistemology. In rereading the past, historical accounts become more complex and variegated than earlier ones. Not only do theologians expand the kinds of written works examined but also turn to alternative resources. The artist, Caravaggio, becomes theologian. The movie director John Ford exemplifies a Catholic sacramental imagination. *Ressourcement* takes on a depth and breadth hardly imagined in 1954.

If some rediscovered a forgotten past through *ressourcement*, others turned resolutely, as Joseph Komanchak has already suggested, to a future viewed through the lens of aggiornamento—a hope-filled openness to the world. "Solidarity" frequently served as aggiornamento's principal virtue, expressed in praxis that turns one's attention once more to the marginalized. So many essays invoked the breaking of God's kingdom through a praxis-defined justice. Theologians challenged systemic evil in the guise of racism, sexism, and other forms of prejudice. Some focused on ecological justice, with an attempt to raise consciousness about humans' place in the cosmos. Still others sought dialogue—ecumenical, interreligious, intercultural, and certainly interdisciplinary. Aggiornamento even led in some cases to breaking with past Catholic practices and even beliefs.

On this ever-expanding theological landscape, a theologian's location relative to church and academy became a most vexing question. Of course, many in the Society clearly saw themselves located in both. Yet, in reviewing resolutions, debates concerning *mandatum*, and specific instances in which church officials sought to remove or silence a theologian, the Society usually appealed to academic freedom, placing the theologian squarely in the academy. Such responses failed to resolve questions concerning what, if any, teaching authority theologians ought to claim in their service to the church—whether broadly conceived as the people of God, or more focused on formal hierarchical structures. To return to an earlier question, what are the pastoral obligations, if any, of the Catholic theologian teaching in a Catholic college? One's answer to the question often reflects how one understands which identity is most threatened—academic or Catholic. Many Catholic theologians have tried to maintain both.

To consider theological conversations from 1954 to 2004 is to witness generational shifts signified most dramatically in memories, displayed to some extent at the annual meeting's songfest. The College Theology Society was founded and formed by those who remembered with varying degrees of fondness and abhorrence a Catholic Church "before the council." These memories often attach themselves to formulaic Tridentine liturgies, memorization of catechism questions as well as answers, and an unrelenting, and seemingly unchanging, enforced uniformity in every aspect of Catholic life. That past is remembered in stark contrast to the three years of the Second Vatican Council and the innumerable changes and diversity that the council precipitated, even if the actual historical developments were far more complex than memories can sustain.

Many of the first and second generation CTS members, like most of their Catholic theological colleagues, were formed in seminaries and religious communities. Some of these theologians remained as ordained and vowed religious; others chose to leave their religious communities or, in the case of priests, seek laicization while remaining active theologians, often teaching in

Catholic colleges and universities. Those demographics are more than likely unrepeatable. The third generation of CTS members is shaped by very different memories. Their recollections of the Catholic Church also vary in degrees of fondness and abhorrence, but their memories often attach themselves to liturgies that vary widely in style and delivery, catechetical chaos, and an uncertain Catholic identity. They have no direct memory of the church prior to the council. They live in a world no longer enamored by modernity's projects; theirs is the postmodern world of multivalent meanings, situatedness, limits, hybridity, and uncertainty. Developments in Catholic theology under their leadership are for a future fifty-year retrospective.

These differing perspectives often are manifest in the recurring debates between the "universalists" and the "particularists," a.k.a., sectarians. The differences reflect, at least in part, those deepest felt concerns attached to generational memories situated in conjunction with the academic currents in which various scholars swam as graduate students. Such observations are not intended as reductive explanations because, in fact, the concerns articulated in all the essays here surveyed address important and enduring theological questions. The Christian faith in the scandal of its particularity, faith in Christ Jesus, claims a universality, a catholicity that endures through every time and speaks in every place. May the faith seeking understanding of God's revolution in Christ continue for years to come. *Jubilate Deo!*

Index

About the Author

Sandra Yocum Mize is the chair of the Religious Studies Department at the University of Dayton. She received her doctorate in historical theology at Marquette University. Her research and publications have focused on a variety of areas in U.S. Catholic life and thought from the nineteenth century to the present. She is married to Bryan J. Mize and has two grown sons, Matthew and Christopher.